The Cryptopians

The Cryptopians

Idealism, Greed, Lies,
and the Making of the First Big
Cryptocurrency Craze

Laura Shin

PUBLICAFFAIRS

NEW YORK

PublicAffairs
Hachette Book Group
1290 Avenue of the Americas, New York, NY 10104
www.publicaffairsbooks.com
@Public_Affairs

Printed in the United States of America

First Edition: February 2022

Published by PublicAffairs, an imprint of Perseus Books, LLC, a subsidiary of Hachette Book Group, Inc. The PublicAffairs name and logo is a trademark of the Hachette Book Group.

The Hachette Speakers Bureau provides a wide range of authors for speaking events. To find out more, go to www.hachettespeakersbureau.com or call (866) 376-6591.

The publisher is not responsible for websites (or their content) that are not owned by the publisher.

Library of Congress Cataloging-in-Publication Data

Names: Shin, Laura, author.
Title: The cryptopians : idealism, greed, lies, and the making of the first big cryptocurrency craze / Laura Shin.
Description: First edition. | New York : PublicAffairs, [2021] | Includes bibliographical references and index.
Identifiers: LCCN 2021035607 | ISBN 9781541763012 (hardcover) | ISBN 9781541763005 (epub)
Subjects: LCSH: Cryptocurrencies—History. | Money—History— 21st century. | Finance—History—21st century.
Classification: LCC HG1710.3 .S55 2021 | DDC 332.4—dc23
LC record available at https://lccn.loc.gov/2021035607

ISBNs: 978-1-5417-6301-2 (hardcover), 978-1-5417-6300-5 (ebook)

LSC-C

Printing 1, 2021

To my parents

Contents

Notes on Reporting

THIS BOOK IS the culmination of more than three years of reporting and writing. It is based on more than two hundred interviews conducted on background, meaning that, for the most part, I promised not to attribute information to any particular source. Not everyone in the book chose to speak to me, but I was able to interview nearly all the main players, including all eight Ethereum cofounders, as well as many additional people whose names do not grace these pages.

To depict events, I combed through archived internet pages, social media postings, block explorers, forums, and other online materials, as well as documents, emails, screenshots, photos, recordings, videos, and other files my sources generously shared with me. In many cases, I was able to re-create dialogue from text chats, and for spoken conversations, I sometimes obtained recordings; when I did not have the language verbatim, I did my best using multiple sources' memories. I'm especially grateful to the technical people who gave me their time and energy and to blockchain and crypto data and analytics providers Chainalysis, Coinfirm, CoinMarketCap, CryptoCompare, Etherscan, ShapeShift, Smith + Crown, TokenData, and YCharts, who helped me parse blockchain data and track people's movements on-chain and/or gave me other data, charts, and analytics to paint a fuller picture. For prices, I generally used CoinMarketCap; for earlier crypto history, I used Bitcoincharts and either Mt. Gox or Bitstamp prices, depending on the time frame.

For the infrequent cases in which I wasn't able to verify specific details around what happened when, I used my best judgment, letting stronger, more specific memories take precedence (unless they could be cross-checked in other ways and disproven) and/ or going with the most likely or logical version of events based on other known facts.

In recounting these events, many of which occurred online, I've chosen to leave in all typos, mispunctuations, miscapitalizations, and other grammatical and spelling errors without a *sic*. There were so many that it became more distracting to note them than to let them live on in all their internet-y glory.

To make it easier to follow this unwieldy, "decentralized" story about a subculture with a sprawling set of actors and its own jargon, I've included a list of characters up front, as well as a timeline and glossary in the back. However, for those of you who don't care about spoilers, you'll miss much of the story if you only skim the timeline.

Disclosure: Some companies in this book have been sponsors of my podcasts and/or videos. They are *CoinDesk* (owned by Digital Currency Group), ConsenSys, Cosmos, Kraken, Microsoft, ShapeShift, and Tezos. Also, in September 2021, I began writing a Facebook Bulletin newsletter.

List of Characters

Ethereum Cofounders

Vitalik Buterin, creator of Ethereum
Mihai Alisie, founder of *Bitcoin Magazine*
Anthony Di Iorio, founder and chief executive officer of Decentral, funded Ethereum pre-crowdsale
Gavin Wood, started C++ client, chief technology officer (CTO)
Jeffrey Wilcke, started Go client (Geth)
Charles Hoskinson, CEO
Joe Lubin, chief operating officer (COO), founder of ConsenSys
Amir Chetrit, cofounder of Colored Coins, a Bitcoin-based project

Ethereum Leadership Group

Taylor Gerring, director of technology
Stephan Tual, community/communications, chief communications officer

Staff in Zug, in the Spaceship

Roxana Sureanu, executive assistant
Mathias Grønnebæk, operational manager
Ian Meikle, graphic designer
Richard Stott, graphic designer
Jeremy Wood, Charles Hoskinson's assistant
Lorenzo Patuzzo, carpenter

ETH Dev in Berlin

Aeron Buchanan, Gavin Wood's friend and business partner
Jutta Steiner, chief of security
Christoph Jentzsch, lead tester
Christian Reitwießner, C++ team/Solidity
Péter Szilágyi, Geth team
Lefteris Karapetsas, C++ team
Alex van de Sande (aka Avsa), user experience (UX)
    designer
Bob Summerwill, software engineer, C++ team
Kelley Becker, COO
Frithjof Weinert, chief financial officer
Christian Vömel, office manager

Ethereum Foundation

Ming Chan, executive director
Lars Klawitter, board member from Rolls-Royce
Wayne Hennessy-Barrett, board member from Kenyan
    fintech start-up
Vadim Levitin, board member; physician and technologist
    with United Nations Development Programme
    background
Patrick Storchenegger, board member, Swiss lawyer

Hudson Jameson, Ming Chan's assistant, DevOps (development and operations), helped with DevCons
Jamie Pitts, assisted with DevCons
Toya Budunggud, Ming Chan's assistant

The DAO/Slock.it

Christoph Jentzsch, cofounder, CTO of Slock.it
Simon Jentzsch, cofounder, CEO of Slock.it
Stephan Tual, cofounder, COO of Slock.it
Lefteris Karapetsas, lead technical engineer at Slock.it
Griff Green, community organizer at Slock.it

Robin Hood Group

Jordi Baylina, programmer in Barcelona who took the DAO ninja course
Griff Green
Lefteris Karapetsas
Alex van de Sande (aka Avsa)
Fabian Vogelsteller, Ethereum Foundation front-end developer eventually credited as the "father" of the ERC-20 token standard

White Hat Group (Known Members)

Jordi Baylina
Griff Green
Lefteris Karapetsas

Bity

Gian Bochsler, one of four cofounders
Alexis Roussel, one of four cofounders, CEO, and chairman of the board

MyEtherWallet

Taylor Van Orden/Monahan, cofounder and CEO
Kosala Hemachandra, cofounder and CTO

Poloniex (aka Polo)

Tristan D'Agosta, founder and co-CEO
Jules Kim, COO and co-CEO
Mike Demopoulos, co-CEO and chief experience officer
Ruby Hsu, management consultant
Johnny Garcia, head of customer support
Tyler Frederick, senior compliance specialist

Preface

IN THE END, it took only seven weeks to trigger the slow-motion toppling of global finance and, though no one saw it then, begin upending the centuries-old method for establishing societal trust.

On September 15, 2008, the 158-year-old investment bank Lehman Brothers filed for the largest bankruptcy in history. Television and computer screens worldwide broadcast images of its twenty-five thousand employees streaming out of the firm's global offices, carrying their belongings in bankers' boxes.[1] The same week, the sixty-thousand-strong "herd" of Merrill Lynch, the world's largest brokerage, whose bull logo also symbolized Wall Street, suddenly found itself reporting to a group of what some employees saw as "hillbillies" at North Carolina–based Bank of America.[2] In mid-October, the S&P 500 suffered its worst week since the Great Depression, while the Dow's loss broke its Depression-era record.[3] But the damage wasn't contained to one week: year to year, as much as $8.4 trillion in investor wealth had vanished. And then, although it generated no news at the time, on October 31, a person or group named Satoshi Nakamoto published a white paper that described how people could bypass banks and use the internet to send each other money.[4]

Over the next nine years, during which a seven-year stretch of 0 to 0.25 percent interest rates managed to produce only the slowest

1

economic recovery in history, this strange new network attracted a peculiar pastiche of supporters.[5] Geeks were seduced by its magical fusion of cryptography, game theory, and the age-old ledger. Drug users loved it because, instead of having to meet strangers on street corners, they could have their postal carrier deliver illicit substances with a few mouse clicks. Libertarians adored its potential for enabling people to transact outside the thousand-year-old system of government fiat currencies. Silicon Valley entrepreneurs dreamed it could form the foundation of a faster, cheaper financial system. And the 1 percent, investing either on their own or through hedge funds and family offices, grew a taste for returns of not just 10 percent but 100,000 percent from this futuristic asset: bitcoin.

What was so revolutionary about it was simple, really. Previously, whenever someone sent something on the internet, he or she was always sending a copy. So, if Alice sent Bob a PDF, photo, or text message, she always had a copy of that PDF, photo, or text message. With bitcoin, for the first time, she could send him something online, and everyone in the world could be certain that she no longer had the item (in this case, a bitcoin), that Bob now had it and therefore Alice could not spend a copy of it elsewhere. Better still, even if Alice were in Afghanistan and Bob in Zimbabwe, he could have the money in ten minutes, and Alice would have paid a fee of just a fraction of a cent rather than exorbitant fees of $30, $50, or more for an international wire transfer that could take a week. Making all this possible was a blend of technologies called a blockchain.

Technologists quickly understood that a blockchain could be applied beyond Bitcoin. In the aftermath of credit default swaps and banks' confusion over which balance books held bad mortgages, even stodgy, marble-halled incumbents, perhaps mindful of the Occupy Wall Street protesters who had once camped out a stone's throw from the former headquarters of Merrill Lynch and Lehman Brothers, could see how novel a blockchain was.

Soon financial institutions as powerful as JPMorgan Chase, Nasdaq, Visa, HSBC, State Street, UBS, Santander, and many others worldwide began exploring the technology. In late 2015, "Blockchain, not bitcoin" became the mantra on Wall Street, and from January 2014 into February 2017, more than fifty financial services firms invested in the space.[6] Throughout 2016, firms raced to be the first to adopt "permissioned" (or private) blockchains akin to private intranets. Having seen what the open, permissionless internet had done to the media and music industries, they knew what happened to those who didn't at least attempt to innovate: disruption.

But before any of those private blockchains could be implemented in any meaningful way, a new idea got the attention of investors large and small: initial coin offerings (ICOs). A cross between a Kickstarter campaign, an IPO, and bitcoin, ICOs enabled projects to raise funds in cryptocurrency by giving people a new token, and they took off, showing how quickly a tsunami of economically incentivized developers could raise money to shake up financial services. In 2017, everyday people from Argentina to Zimbabwe disbursed $5.6 billion worth of digital coins into decentralized projects aiming to disrupt titans such as Amazon, Facebook, and Apple, dwarfing the paltry $558 million of venture capital investment in the space, and making these hot but speculative, and even scammy, investments more democratic than those owned by a small number of big-money firms.[7] By the end of the year, an asset class that had started 2017 worth $18 billion had ballooned thirty-four times to $613 billion. Two massive commodities exchanges—including the storied CME, which had been founded in 1898 as the Chicago Butter and Egg Board and, the year prior, had cleared more than $1 quadrillion worth of contracts—began trading rival bitcoin futures contracts within a week of each other.[8] The price of bitcoin, which had started the year around $1,000, flirted with $20,000. Another asset, ether, from a newer blockchain, Ethereum, created by Vitalik Buterin, saw an even steeper rise from $8 to $757, a return of ninety-five times in less than a year. Early adopters who were now millionaires (or just a lot wealthier than they'd been a year ago) glutted Reddit with "Lambo" memes—or actually bought the Italian sports car. Bitcoin's every price jump was recorded for posterity and hashtagged #tothemoon on Twitter, where discussion of Bitcoin grew at unprecedented rates.[9] And to think—it had all begun nine years earlier as a quiet white paper proposing a "peer-to-peer electronic cash system." That obscure submission to the cypherpunk mailing list for encryption enthusiasts had now snowballed into the phenomenon that every cable news channel, website, magazine, newspaper, podcast, and video was breathlessly covering: "crypto."

To understand how we got here, let's go back to a mid-November day in 2013, to where the roaring blue Pacific meets San Francisco's green northwest tip, the Presidio. There, amid the forested hills, eucalyptus-scented air, and remnants of the Spanish Empire and the Gold Rush, walks a lanky nineteen-year-old.[10] A few years ago, he was earning $4 per hour writing about a breakthrough technology; now, he is noodling on a new computer science problem. In less than five years, the solution will be worth more than $135 billion.

1

1994 to January 20, 2014

VITALIK BUTERIN WAS like a seed that had been blown far out of its habitat and struggled to take root in its new environment but was about to find the right soil in which to grow tall and flourish. Commonly described as "alien" by all manner of people—both strangers online and close collaborators, by those who meant it affectionately as well as those who didn't—Vitalik exuded an awkwardness that practically manifested physically. His father was tall and muscular with a round face and a soft smile. His mother was blue-eyed and petite, with curly red hair and full cheeks. But with Vitalik, it seemed as though, before birth, his whole body had passed through a fun house mirror. His build was tall and slight, his gait gawky and stretchy. His nose was pointy, his ears craned forward to hear, and his chin jutted into the future. His deep-set, blue eyes were burrowed in so far, they didn't seem to be windows to the soul so much as the soul itself, peering out, and the top of his head stretched up and out, as if to make a statement about the intellect housed within.

It was the fall of 2013, and he had been ruminating on an idea he was calling "cryptocurrency 2.0." In February 2011, when he was seventeen, his father had told him about Bitcoin, a new currency not controlled by the government or banks. Vitalik had at first ignored it, thinking it was a weird digital token with no intrinsic value, though it was trading at roughly eighty cents. But after seeing another reference to it a couple months later (in April the price surpassed $1, then $2), he figured he should research it more.

Since then, he'd written extensively about Bitcoin, had paused college to travel and hang out with the global Bitcoin community, had become an owner of *Bitcoin Magazine*, and had worked as a freelance cryptocurrency developer. After several months in Europe and Israel, plus a pit stop in Los Angeles, he was in San Francisco, working out of the office of a cryptocurrency exchange called Kraken and staying in the cofounder and CEO Jesse Powell's apartment. But the problems he saw with blockchain technology, which make cryptocurrencies like Bitcoin possible, gnawed at him.

Bitcoin was built for payments. The Bitcoin white paper was subtitled "A Peer-to-Peer Electronic Cash System."[1] Developers were now realizing Bitcoin's underlying technology could also be used to create things like a decentralized domain name system or to underpin more complex contracts like bets.

The problem, Vitalik felt, was that each project was building a blockchain for one function, like a calculator performing basic arithmetic. A few blockchains were trying to be more like Swiss Army knives with multiple functions. But still, each of those would lose out the second a blockchain came along offering a new function. Vitalik wondered why they couldn't be more like smartphones, able to support any application created by any developer, who could then upload it App Store style to be used by anyone.

Finally, Vitalik, long an avid rambler, spent a few hours wandering the Presidio. In the hilly, wooded former army base, an expanse of green with incredible views of the Golden Gate Bridge, he worked out how to create one blockchain on which people could perform all these functions, forming a decentralized computer that could support many kinds of applications. He wrote up his idea in a white paper. On November 27, 2013, the same day

Bitcoin crossed $1,000 for the first time, he emailed it to thirteen friends.

Though he thought his idea was the next logical step with blockchains, he wasn't sure why something so obvious—a blockchain that wouldn't quickly be rendered obsolete—hadn't been done before. Perhaps the design had a fatal flaw. He could imagine accomplished cryptographers reading his white paper and putting him, a nineteen-year-old with two terms of college, in his place. His fears weren't unfounded. Although he was unaware of it, when he went to Bitcoin conferences to staff the *Bitcoin Magazine* booth, sometimes technical people—even if he said he was interested in technical matters—would think, *Yeah, right*, and peg him as "a magazine person" who couldn't "possibly be interested in the *really* cool stuff." Nevertheless, he clicked send.

VITALIK WAS BORN in 1994 in Kolomna, Russia, a town of more than 150,000 people seventy miles southeast of Moscow whose major landmarks lent it a Disney-like air. His parents, Dmitry and Natalia, two computer science students, finished their college degrees in Moscow with the help of their parents, who looked after him as a baby; when he was three, they separated. Both his parents ended up working for American companies—his father at Arthur Andersen before starting his own ventures, his mother at Heinz, where she switched from programming to finance and accounting, before jumping to other multinationals. Later, Natalia moved to Canada to get a business degree in Edmonton, and a year and a half later, by which point the couple had divorced, Dmitry followed with six-year-old Vitalik, settling in Toronto.

From the beginning, it was apparent that Vitalik was smart. Natalia's father taught him the times tables when he was three or four years old. On a doctor's visit, where five-year-old Vitalik ran around the waiting area multiplying three-digit numbers, other patients widened their eyes in disbelief. Like his father, he began reading at around age three, and because Dmitry had dreamed of getting a computer when he was young but hadn't been able to, he excitedly gave Vitalik a computer at age four. The boy loved playing with Excel and eventually produced the seven-year-old's equivalent of an Excel masterpiece, "The Encyclopedia of Bunnies," a treatise on the lives, culture, and economy of the long-eared, short-tailed creatures. The table of contents contained sections such as

Bunnies Ships
How long does it take to eat one ship?
When did the bunnies pass the weight 100 tons?
Holidays
When will they die?
When did they start fighting with bombs?
Bunnies Money
How do they use a bunny card?
How do they earn money?
At what temperatures can bunnies live?
How can bunnies pass the speed of light?
Bunnies computers
What number system do bunnies computers use?

The text read,

How much do the bunnies weigh? Tons. They weigh about 614.3 tons by the year 2000…What do they drink? A bunny drink. How to make that drink. Step 1: put ships in the blender and grind it. 2: mix it with water. 3: take the ships out…How many man and women bunnies are there? There are: 8 men. There is only 1 woman. That is the cat…How do bunnies use their credit card? They put their card in the machine and hold A. They put their card in the machine and hold B. How much money you want to take? Then wait two seconds, and they take their card out. They take the card that's paying.

There was even a bunny periodic table.

Despite how precocious Vitalik seemed on the computer—he also played and developed video games—talking to him gave a different impression. For almost his first decade, he barely spoke. He would start to express himself, then find it difficult, get frustrated, and give up. Dmitry would see other six-year-old children speak in long, complicated sentences, but Vitalik would talk in random little bursts. His stepmother, Maia, Dmitry's second wife, thought Vitalik did not always connect the vast thoughts in his internal world to life on earth. She and Dmitry would tell Vitalik, "If you need something, stop, formulate it." Although Dmitry worried about Vitalik's delayed speech, he didn't take Vitalik to a therapist, thinking psychological labels would be unhelpful.

Finally, when Vitalik was nine, his speech began to blossom, but his newfound communication abilities didn't translate into social success. Loneliness marked his early years in Toronto. He and Dmitry settled in on the fifth floor of a thirteen-story building in North York in an area with many Korean shops and restaurants. Vitalik attended public elementary and middle schools with mostly Asian kids. But his isolation didn't come from having a different heritage. In junior high, he suddenly realized his classmates were hanging out after school—they'd go to each other's houses and have parties and get-togethers. Not only was he not a part of that, but he had no idea *how* to be part of that. His sense of solitude cemented. He just wished he could be normal.

Then came a turning point. For high school, he enrolled in the Abelard School, a private academy with a total student body of fifty across all four grades. Founded in 1997 by a group of teachers, Abelard boasted a student-teacher ratio of 5:1 and an average class size of ten.[2] It had a preschool's atmosphere of trust and informality but a graduate school seminar's structure and intellectual rigor. (Also, Abelard's student body was mostly white, a shift he found jarring.)

Vitalik excelled academically. He took twelfth grade calculus in ninth grade, won a bronze medal at the International

Olympiad in Informatics in Italy, and competed in National Model United Nations in New York City.

Finally, he found his tribe. Vice principal Brian Blair, who was also Vitalik's Latin, ancient Greek, and philosophy teacher, had seen brilliant students before, but often they were arrogant and less popular with their peers. In contrast, Vitalik was well-liked. An older boy indoctrinated him in Linux (an open-source operating system preferred by coders for its customizability) and hacker spaces where people would do things like 3-D-print charts of math equations. During this period, he also attended, with his father, some Tony Robbins seminars that got him interested in health and a pescatarian diet and helped him understand better what drives other people and how to communicate his needs and wants to them.

Perhaps that is why, despite the loneliness Vitalik had experienced during childhood, in his senior year he displayed a highly attuned sense of social relationships in a short story he wrote for Abelard's literary journal. Titled "On Christmas Presents and Friendship," the story recounts a Secret Santa gift exchange among friends. In it, one boy, Ulrich, judges his friend Yasmin for her happiness over a mall gift card, while their friend Xavier looks down on the gift card as inferior to the cash that he has, in his eyes generously, bequeathed to Wesley, who is drowning in debt. But Wesley resents the cash, feeling that Xavier has done the equivalent of giving someone "slightly plump" a weight loss package. And so on—with each gift sparking different internal reactions in each person.

The story also describes the unconventional lifestyle Vitalik himself would someday attain. Ulrich, as he disdainfully observes Yasmin's joy over the gift card, begins musing how, while she will someday save enough for retirement, she can never hope to reach what he is working toward, financial independence, which is "mathematically" different. "Retirement meant that you were spending the money you had saved up, independence meant that all you were spending was just the interest on your money," Vitalik wrote. "It was as if your contribution to society were complete, and you had fulfilled your debt to this world and could now peacefully live off the proceeds of your work until the end of time."

But at that time, Vitalik himself had not only not achieved financial independence but had never held a job. He got his first one the summer after graduation. Although Vitalik hadn't taken computer science classes in school, he did take a couple "MOOCs," or massive open online courses, on machine learning and artificial intelligence. In those, he created a game that got mentioned in a *Wired* article, which landed him an internship at an Oklahoma-based education company, NextThought.[3] After graduation, he went to Norman, Oklahoma, one of the state's few liberal enclaves, where he found hip Indian restaurants and diners with veggie burgers and okra, which he liked more than the state's more typical hamburgers. His crowning achievement that summer was making the NextThought web app compatible with Internet Explorer 9.

Then it was off to the computer science powerhouse University of Waterloo.

ON A PARALLEL track to his schooling was Vitalik's life in Bitcoin. Once he decided to research it in the late winter of 2011, he started poking around a forum called BitcoinTalk, where he viewed a video encouraging people to use the asset. He trolled the boards looking for someone to hire and pay him in the digital currency. Someone who went by the handle kiba offered to pay him five bitcoins (BTC) ($4) to write an article for *Bitcoin Weekly*.[4] After earning 20 bitcoins, he spent 8.5 of them on a Bitcoin T-shirt. Completing a full loop of Bitcoin commerce felt good; plus he liked researching and writing, so he kept penning articles until kiba, despite the fact that he was paying Vitalik less than minimum wage and had slashed remuneration to 2.5 BTC, began running out of money.

Vitalik had an idea: he and kiba could keep *Bitcoin Weekly* going by writing two articles a week, publishing the first paragraph and then hiding the rest of each article until the community had sent a requested amount in bitcoin to a specified address.[5] Shortly before then, on June 1, 2011, *Gawker* published an article titled "The Underground Website Where You Can Buy Any Drug Imaginable."[6] It was about Silk Road, an Amazon for drugs where sellers from all over the globe purveyed everything from weed to heroin. Even though it was 2011, more than a decade after the web became popular, nothing like it had ever existed before because, prior to Bitcoin, drug dealers could not take payments online since that required using the normal banking system. They always had to use cash, which required face-to-face contact. But the advent of Bitcoin had now made it possible for them to send their Molly, blow, or acid right to people's mailboxes, rain or shine, in exchange for the equivalent of digital cash. And unlike electronic payment via a credit or debit card, Bitcoin was decentralized, meaning there was no company to shut down or CEO to put in jail for facilitating illegal transactions or for creating this new nongovernmental currency. The network was maintained by people all over the globe running the Bitcoin software on their computers or other computer-like equipment specifically made to run the Bitcoin software. (These so-called miners were incentivized to participate because adding their computer to the network gave them a chance roughly every ten minutes to earn new bitcoins.) Shutting down Bitcoin would require tracking down and switching off the devices of every single person running the software—and *that* would require the coordinated action of every government in the world. But even shutting off all existing computers on the network wouldn't stop anyone else from spinning up the Bitcoin software. The inadvertent publicity from the *Gawker* article helped send the price shooting up from under $9 to $32 a week later. Although it ultimately leveled off in the teens, from his Bitcoin articles, Vitalik was now earning about $6 an hour.

Although he didn't have particular goals around Bitcoin, it combined his interests in social and political theory, math and science, open-source software and programming. Plus, his father had been listening to Doug Casey, an anarcho-capitalist who subscribed to Austrian economics and had a theory that government-issued fiat currencies would collapse, causing a massive depression. Vitalik thought if that happened, he'd have to work hard to survive. Bitcoin seemed like a good hedge against disaster because of its monetary policy. It had a fixed supply of twenty-one million bitcoins, and new ones would be minted by the software, on average, every ten minutes until the cap was reached, making it deflationary. It was like a digital version of gold.

Vitalik became known for his straightforward, comprehensible writing on Bitcoin, which typically is written with a capital *B* to describe the network and a lowercase *b* to refer to the coin. Here is how he explained some of its oft-misunderstood basics:

> The value of a currency does not depend on its value as a good, it depends only on its value as a currency itself, in a circular loop… This is where arguments such as the idea that Bitcoin's value is zero since "it is just bits on a computer" fall apart: these bits have value because people are willing to pay for them. The "supply" part of the demand and supply equation is also important: Bitcoins maintain their value due to scarcity; no person or organization has the power to print bitcoins at will.[7]

He further explained in another article, "One of the unique features of Bitcoin is that it enforces certain features of social organization in code—the inflation rate is precisely controlled in code, and it is impossible for anyone to force a different inflation rate into existence."[8]

His writing on this complex topic was so easy to follow that in August 2011 someone named Mihai Alisie emailed, asking him to become the first writer for a new publication: *Bitcoin Magazine*.

Vitalik, with all the nonchalance of the Swedish chef, switched over, and soon after *Bitcoin Weekly* shut down.[9]

MIHAI WAS A tall, pale, lanky, brown-haired Romanian who liked to talk with his hands. Garrulous and affable, he would often, when telling stories, play both sides in a conversation, his lean frame swiveling from one side to the other as he switched between roles. The previous year, he'd finished undergrad, but instead of working, he played a lot of online poker.[10] He was fascinated by the levels of game theory at which one could play. At level 0—the game itself—the player asks, *What is the best combination I can play with my cards?* Once a player understands level 0, he or she moves up to thinking, *What hand does my opponent have?* The next stage is asking not just what hand do I have and what hand does the other player have, but also *What hand does the other player think I have?* And beyond that, *What hand does the other player think that I think he or she has?*

For Mihai, online poker was a godsend. Romania's monthly minimum wage was about $200, and he was often gambling double that in one session. The first time he earned some winnings, he watched people taking the bus to work and was amazed by his life.

In the winter of 2011, he heard about Bitcoin and, like Vitalik, spent a lot of time reading BitcoinTalk.org. He noticed many of the highest-quality articles were by Vitalik and saw that mainstream media about Bitcoin tended to focus on Silk Road. Mihai saw a need for a coherent information source that was more Bitcoin-centric. He hired Vitalik and brought on other cofounders by soliciting them on BitcoinTalk.

Mihai's initial idea for the magazine was a PDF with a pay-what-you-wish model; after some success, they could eventually publish an ad-supported print edition. But one night in December 2011, when the first PDF started coming together, a business partner, Matthew N. Wright, suggested they "do it big or go home"—meaning, print the magazine. Mihai resisted, pointing out that they had no money. But the next day, after he'd been uncharacteristically offline for several hours, he found around six hundred unread Skype messages waiting for him. Matthew had announced on BitcoinTalk .org that *Bitcoin Magazine*'s first edition would be printed.[11]

After the post–*Gawker* article price jump in the summer, BTC had dwindled to $3 or $4 that December, so Bitcoin companies weren't exactly flush. Mihai and the others hustled, and eventually, between subscription pre-orders and ads, they obtained enough money for physical copies. The problem was shipping them to their subscribers around the world. Mailing from the United Kingdom, where they had staff, was expensive. Matthew, a US citizen, was living in South Korea, but the subscribers were mostly in the West. From Romania, the price to send a magazine was €1 to €2 within Europe and €3 to €4 to the United States, though delivery could take a month. Mihai volunteered.

Soon, five thousand issues of *Bitcoin Magazine*'s inaugural issue were shipped from the United States to the United Kingdom and then put on a twenty-ton transport truck to Romania, eventually arriving at Mihai's parents' place. As they were dropped in the front yard, Mihai thought, *Maybe I should have told my parents.* The fifty boxes filled the living room. Mihai, his girlfriend Roxana, and her brother put each copy in an envelope and handwrote each recipient's name and address. Finally, they took them to the local post office, which didn't have enough stamps. (Over time, the local post office embraced the new business brought in by the fledgling magazine, and Roxana, a college senior, took over the logistics. Each day after school, she'd go to Mihai's parents' house, managing subscriptions, handling advertisements, and labeling and shipping each copy. Eventually, *Bitcoin Magazine* got a label printer.) Despite the stress, Mihai felt it was worth it, that the magazine made him part of the community.

When the May 2012 issue went out, it was the spring of Vitalik's high school senior year. Since starting at *Bitcoin Magazine*, he'd continued writing his clear prose about the cryptocurrency online:

> The **Bitcoin network** is the network of computers through which Bitcoin transactions are broadcasted and which maintains the public blockchain. Sometimes, the term is used to refer to just miners... The **blockchain** is a public list of all transactions that have ever been sent, ensuring that everyone knows which bitcoins belong to whom... A **miner** is someone who tries to create blocks to add to the blockchain (the term also refers to a piece of software that does this). Miners are rewarded for their work by the Bitcoin protocol, which automatically assigns 50 new bitcoins to the miner who creates a valid block. This is how all bitcoins come into existence.[12]

He also wrote an article, for journalists, on misconceptions about Bitcoin, explaining, **"Bitcoin does not have a central organization or authority**... Rather than thinking of Bitcoin as a product released by a traditional corporation, it is more appropriate to think of it as a self-sustaining digital commodity, similar to gold. It has a healthy satellite industry that provides products and services based around it, and it has its own business and advocacy organizations, but there is no central Gold Corporation."[13]

When the first printed edition arrived, he saw it featured twelve articles on topics such as the personality of anonymous Bitcoin creator Satoshi Nakamoto, the history of previous attempts at cryptocurrency, and the Bitcoin bubble of 2011. (The price had barely budged from Christmastime and was now about $5.) Scanning the magazine's sixty-nine pages, Vitalik realized that nine of the twelve articles were by him. Concluding they must have had a hard time finding other writers, he was grateful for the opportunity.

BITCOIN MAGAZINE'S DRAMA continued. On BitcoinTalk, Matthew contended something called Pirate was *not* a scam, betting anyone who believed that it would not pay out within three weeks twice as much as they were betting. Less than a month later, he resigned from *Bitcoin Magazine* when, according to Matthew, what he owed from the bet "reached into amounts that are impossible to pay in this lifetime."[14] Additionally, another business partner was caught gouging the company, charging what Mihai says was $8,000 for eight months of WordPress hosting and $3,000 for software for "digital publications"—an idea they'd had for a downloadable "digital rights management" version of the print magazine, a souped-up PDF with built-in protections so it could not be changed—even though there was no digital publication.

During this turmoil, Vitalik was in his first term at the University of Waterloo, taking four and then five advanced courses, plus doing an undergrad research assistantship and writing for *Bitcoin Magazine*. He was living alone in a prison-cell-like room, eating in the cafeteria, and occasionally stopping at the supermarket for fruit. The routine was wake, work for two hours, eat, work for four hours, move to another location, eat, work for four more hours, and so on. His life was a grind, and he was lonely.

He wanted to branch out from just writing about Bitcoin. He solved problems for a programmer who rewarded him in bitcoins and, due to various *Bitcoin Magazine* transitions, started receiving a salary. Finally, after two terms, between his freelance gigs and the fact that BTC had appreciated from $6.50 in summer 2012 to as high as $266 at one moment in April (though it more typically hovered around $100), he had about $10,000 worth of Bitcoin.

Waterloo offered a co-op program that allowed students to alternate terms of study and terms of work as long as they could find companies willing to collaborate. Vitalik wanted to do a co-op at Ripple, a San Francisco–based cryptocurrency company aiming to be "an open source person to person payment network."[15] He got an immediate yes from the founder, Jed McCaleb. But due to a visa rule requiring the company to have existed for a year, the co-op at the then nine-month-old firm fell through.

Instead, Vitalik decided to travel the world to see the Bitcoin community, finding himself in New Hampshire, Spain, and Italy, sleeping on futons (including one in an "ecoindustrial post-capitalist" colony) and spending long days jogging and thinking and working on the puzzles that appealed to him. But it wasn't until a monthlong trip to Israel that his understanding reached a new level. There, he spent time with people working on Colored Coins, a new concept to enable people to trade real-world assets using the indelible ledger of the Bitcoin blockchain by attaching metadata to a transaction of one satoshi, or 0.00000001 BTC, the smallest unit, equivalent to a tiny fraction of a penny. For instance, one could send a transaction whose metadata said a share in a company had been transferred from Alice to Bob. Because it was nearly impossible to tamper with a universally agreed-upon ledger of transactions, the Bitcoin blockchain could serve as a golden historical record for other assets or transactions attached to these negligible amounts of bitcoin. Vitalik's mind was opened to the possibility of "layer 2" functionalities. At Waterloo, he'd studied data structures and programming languages. The people creating layer 2 were building features specific to each application. *Why*, he wondered, *couldn't they devise a general-purpose programming language that would enable anyone to build any application he or she wanted to build?*

Vitalik tried to nudge another project, Mastercoin (a "Swiss Army knife" of blockchains, in that it contained multiple features), in this direction. At first, he proposed something called "contracts for difference" on Mastercoin via a BitcoinTalk post.[16] Then he wrote up something he named Ultimate Scripting (asking Mastercoin for a $250 fee), a proposal for how to upgrade Mastercoin to make two-party financial contracts possible with whatever rules one wanted. The first paragraph stated that the key advantage of Mastercoin over Bitcoin was the potential for more advanced transaction types. Mastercoin didn't have to stop at merely one person paying another; it could handle a binding exchange (one that, if you made an order for something, would force you to pay if someone fulfilled your request) or bets and gambling. He concluded,

> However, up until this point Mastercoin has been a relatively un-structured process in developing these ideas, essentially treating each [transaction type] as a separate "feature" with its own transaction code and rules. This document outlines an alternative way of specifying Mastercoin contracts which follows an open-ended philosophy, specifying only the basic data and arithmetic building blocks and allowing anyone to craft arbitrarily complex Mastercoin contracts to suit their own needs, including needs which we may not even anticipate.

On November 13, he sent it to the Mastercoin team, expecting them to jump all over it. Instead, Mastercoin's J. R. Willett emailed back that, while it could someday be an advanced feature, "doing it now could result in our developers getting bogged down in the details, and slowing our progress a lot. The number of corner cases would (I expect) multiply exponentially, and I'd rather see Mastercoin doing its core functions before we start experimenting with scripting."[17]

Vitalik decided he'd do it himself. He finished his travels in San Francisco around the time the Bitcoin price was going haywire. After starting October 2013 in the low $100s, by early November it was in the low $200s, and when he was in San Francisco, it was in the $400s, then broke through $800. Amid the mania, Vitalik proposed his idea as a Mastercoin-style layer on top of a blockchain called Primecoin, the way Mastercoin was built on Bitcoin. Since it would probably just be him and a couple other coders, this method would be a good way to just get something out. After the long walk in the Presidio where he figured out how to technically accomplish his vision, he reworked his white paper and scrolled through a list of elements from science fiction for inspiration. The word "Ethereum" caught his eye. It sounded nice; plus it referenced the nineteenth-century scientific theory of ether as a substrate of the universe, the medium through which light waves travel. Vitalik hoped his network would be the substrate of a lot of things—a platform that enabled any kind of transaction, just like he'd proposed to Mastercoin. And so he christened it Ethereum. He sent his proposal to friends on November 27, the day Bitcoin passed $1,000 for the first time—on its way, a few days later, to reaching a new all-time high of $1,242.

One recipient was a slight, dark-haired Bitcoin entrepreneur in Toronto named Anthony Di Iorio, whom Vitalik had recently featured in a two-part *Bitcoin Magazine* Q&A.[18] Anthony had started the Toronto Bitcoin Meetup in 2012, created and sold a Bitcoin gambling site called Satoshi Circle, and founded the Bitcoin Alliance of Canada.[19] Before that, he'd worked in his family's sliding door manufacturing business and started a geothermal drilling company. Because of his early Bitcoin purchases, the Satoshi Circle sale (for twenty-four hundred bitcoins, of which about two thousand went to him when the price was below $150), and the skyrocketing price of bitcoin, Anthony now found himself with more than $2 million worth of bitcoin. He had become what the community called a "Bitcoin millionaire"—someone who had obtained a lot of bitcoins very early and whose net worth was now in the millions of dollars.

Anthony was a marketing and business person, not a technical person, so he asked his friend Charles Hoskinson, a Colorado-based mathematician and PhD dropout who had created an online course called the Bitcoin Education Project and had recently left another project called BitShares, to look over the white paper.[20] Charles, a bearded twenty-something with the demeanor of a middle-aged man, thought it contained a couple novel ideas: first, the notion of a world computer in the cloud whose computation was metered so that each step had to be paid for, and second, the idea of putting a programming language on a blockchain. With

Charles's thumbs-up, Anthony offered Vitalik an initial $150,000, in bitcoin, to develop Ethereum.

In December 2013, Vitalik and Anthony attended a Bitcoin conference in Las Vegas.[21] It was a heady time. With the BTC price quintupling in the last few weeks, Vitalik found more people receptive to his idea. With Anthony's investment, he could make Ethereum a full-fledged cryptocurrency with its own blockchain rather than building it atop Primecoin. In a hot tub at the MGM Grand, with Anthony and Anthony's business partner, Steve Dakh, Vitalik talked about how he'd decided against a "pre-mine," in which the creators of a new coin mine it for themselves before the public release so as to compensate themselves with their own coins.

By not pre-mining any ether (the name given to Ethereum's coin), the cofounders would give everyone, including themselves, an equal chance to mine it. It was the most selfless way to launch a new coin, akin to self-funding a start-up without granting oneself equity. He announced this decentralized plan to a wider group of interested people and then solicited developers to create the software clients, like desktop apps, that people could download to run the network.

As for the idea itself, one of Ethereum's more novel aspects was that *two* types of entities could send and receive transactions: first, as one would expect, people, but second, and more intriguingly, contracts. Similarly to how one can exchange messages with a person or a chatbot, Ethereum would enable financial transactions between (1) two people, (2) a person and a "smart contract," a sort of software-based financial vending machine, or (3) between two smart contracts. A contract would be a little bit of code on Ethereum with an address and balance, and it, like a person, would be able to send and receive transactions. If someone sent a transaction to a contract, that would activate the contract's code, changing the record of the contract or possibly causing the contract to send transactions.

For instance, imagine you wanted to create a decentralized ride-sharing network—an Uber-like network of cars without the company Uber. You mint a new cryptocurrency—let's call it CabCoin—and create CabCoin's fund-raising contract on the Ethereum network. The contract could be programmed to send out the new token to anyone who sent it ether, at some predetermined ratio, such as ten thousand CabCoins per ether. Holders of CabCoin could then use it to pay for rides or vote on changes to the network, such as the pricing, drivers' wages, and the network's marketing budget. No need for phone calls or any human interaction—just anyone who wanted to invest in and use CabCoin could transact directly with the contract, or they could program a contract of their own to do it, eliminating the need for people entirely.

Everything on Ethereum—a trading exchange, a betting site, a decentralized domain name system, a corporation of shareholders, insurance, a decentralized marketplace—would be a contract. And the language used would be "Turing complete," meaning it would be able to express any concept a developer might want. Vitalik ended this new version of the white paper as follows:

> The Ethereum protocol's design philosophy is in many ways the opposite from that taken by many other cryptocurrencies today. Other cryptocurrencies aim to add complexity and increase the number of "features"; Ethereum, on the other hand, takes features away. The protocol does not "support" multisignature transactions, multiple inputs and outputs, hash codes, lock times or many other features that even Bitcoin provides. Instead, all complexity comes from an all-powerful, Turing-complete assembly language, which can be used to build up literally any feature that is mathematically describable. The language itself follows an Orwellian Newspeak principle; any instruction which can be replaced by a sequence of less than four other instructions has been removed. As a result, we have a cryptocurrency protocol whose

codebase is very small, and yet which can do anything that any cryptocurrency will ever be able to do.

Welcome to the financial singularity :)

Four days later, on December 19 at 11:53 a.m., Vitalik received an email from a prospective worker named Gav Wood. It said, "Johnny gave me the heads up—I can do C++ (e.g. github/gavofyork). How far are you with ethereum?"

Vitalik welcomed more help. He and two other developers were already coding away. He figured they could get it up and running in a few months, and afterward he would return to *Bitcoin Magazine* and university.

Vitalik responded to i@gavwood.com twice—the second time seeming not to realize he'd written fifteen minutes before. Both emails started with Vitalik expressing that he would be happy to have Gav on the team and asking what he'd like to build for the C++ client. He ended both emails noting there would be "generous bounties."

GAVIN WOOD, THIRTY-THREE, an Englishman with dark brown eyes, an intense, direct gaze, and mop-like gray hair that went straight down his high forehead, was a peripatetic coder with a PhD in computer science who had been hacking on open-source projects, including one called KDE. His PhD project had been software that would turn music into "vaguely pretty" pictures. At one point he and his high school buddy Aeron Buchanan had gone into business together, turning his PhD project into a device that could turn audio into light shows, which they sold to a few London nightclubs. He'd dabbled in various start-ups, made little money, but finally had a funding offer for a business contracts software firm called OxLegal that looked promising.

However, earlier in 2013, he'd also started looking into Bitcoin, which had piqued his curiosity after he'd read a *Guardian* article about Silk Road.[22] Featuring Vitalik's friends Amir Taaki and Mihai, who were squatting in a London office building that spanned a city block, the story showed them roaming the erstwhile conference rooms and quoted Mihai criticizing anti-Bitcoin politicians, saying banning Bitcoin was "like burning an entire village to roast a pig. It's like shutting down the internet because someone's posting pornography." An accompanying video showed a wooden door on which someone had written in green marker, "Bitcoin Magazine Global Headquarters." At the end of the article, on the roof of the squat, Amir faces London's skyscrapers in the distance and raises his middle finger.

Gavin wanted to meet this establishment-disdaining Bitcoin revolutionist. Gavin sent Amir an email from his KDE.org account, hoping he would recognize it. The anarchist invited him to the massive seven-story building, which featured smashed walls, broken toilets, and destroyed electrical transformers. For Gavin, who had spent most of his life in York and Cambridge and had never been in a squat, it was a sight to behold. At one point Amir opened a door to an office that was empty save for a mattress on the floor—and Mihai and Roxy lying under the blankets. (After a wave hello, they quickly shut the door.) It was on this visit that he met Jonathan James Harrison, who went by the nickname Jonny Bitcoin.

That December, they met again, and Jonny suggested he code Ethereum—a challenge Gavin took up to prove himself. Gavin got the white paper, which appealed to him because, for the last few months, working on the business contracts start-up OxLegal, he had to deal a lot with Microsoft Office software, including Word, which was difficult to use and needed to be backward compatible—ugh. With Ethereum, on the other hand, he could build from scratch. It looked like a fun project to work on for a few weeks after Christmas.

For the holiday, he went to his friend's dairy farm near Lancaster. There, near the ocean, on a muddy, windswept plain, among big and small barns, broken tractors strewn about, bales of hay piled up, and one hundred or so cows roaming the fields, his friends cozied up to a fire in a Victorian-era house. They ate Christmas dinner, played games, and occasionally emptied the fireplace of ash. Gavin, meanwhile, sat on the couch, coding Ethereum. The next week, he returned to Oxford, where he worked on OxLegal for eight hours by day and Ethereum for eight hours by night. As a cofounder of OxLegal, he wasn't being paid, and funding was only tentative. On top of that, Gavin had not had a proper income for the past two years. He was broke. Jonny Bitcoin, who had gotten into the cryptocurrency early, paid Gavin's rent for December and January so he could work on Ethereum. Gavin's financial situation forced him to set a deadline to get either a proper job or funding for OxLegal. But this Ethereum thing was intriguing. His deadline to make a decision: February 1.

AROUND THE TIME Gavin heard about Ethereum, so did a Dutch coder named Jeffrey Wilcke. On Christmas Day, he also began coding an Ethereum client, this one in the language Go. Short, bald, and fit but soft bodied, Jeff, thirty, had an egg-shaped head, a cleft in his chin, and a laid-back demeanor that put other people at ease. A college dropout who had been on his way to a computer science degree, he had worked at a kids' math-learning platform, which was how he'd taken notice of Bitcoin.

He explored cryptocurrencies and even worked on Mastercoin briefly. Then a friend from Mastercoin sent him the Ethereum white paper, since Jeff enjoyed writing computer languages. He found the paper technically interesting. In addition to writing languages, Jeff liked building virtual machines, or a software version of a computer within a hardware version of a computer. For Christmas, he was at his parents' place in a child-friendly, pedestrian-only Amsterdam suburb called a *woonerf*, and between festivities, he would whip out his laptop. He chose the Go language because he wasn't good at it and wanted to improve. Plus, it was fast, simple, and didn't have many quirks—potentially advantageous qualities for a project like Ethereum.

He and Gavin got in touch, and on Christmas Day, while Gavin was on the couch at the farm and Jeff was at his parents' house in the *woonerf*, they Skype-chatted about the white paper's intricacies.

BY THIS POINT, various Ethereum Skype channels were sprouting up. Gav, Jeff, Charles Hoskinson of the Bitcoin Education Project, Anthony Di Iorio of the Bitcoin Alliance of Canada, Mihai, and others began piling in, including Vitalik's Colored Coins friend Amir Chetrit, whom Vitalik had nicknamed "capitalist Amir," whereas Amir Taaki was "anarchist Amir." Capitalist Amir had previously hit it off with Anthony Di Iorio.

Another Skype participant was Taylor Gerring, a compact, outgoing Chicago-based developer with an easy, boyish smile and laugh lines around his eyes, as well as a tattoo of the word "love" with a row of hearts under it on his arm. Mihai had met Taylor at a conference in Milan in December and had enlisted him to keep the Ethereum website up because it kept crashing due to unforeseen interest. The many others also included a round-faced programmer-turned-cannabis-edibles-entrepreneur with a beard and mustache named Anthony D'Onofrio, whose online handle was Texture (and who eventually went by that in real life).

Meanwhile, Anthony Di Iorio, who was enjoying the Toronto Bitcoin Meetups he had founded, was inspired to create a Bitcoin hub downtown. He rented an old, brick, three-story, 5,550-square-foot house that he named Bitcoin Decentral.

Back home in Toronto after his globe-trotting, Vitalik was coding up a client using the language Python for Ethereum, while Gavin and Jeffrey worked on the C++ and Go clients, respectively. (Vitalik wanted Ethereum to work on different software clients so that a bug in one wouldn't take the whole blockchain down; the entities on the network could run another one while the buggy one was fixed.) On January 1, 2014, when it was five degrees Fahrenheit outside, Vitalik attended the opening for Decentral, which featured Canada's second Bitcoin ATM.[23] A lively crowd—nearly all men—packed into the narrow space. Vitalik was dressed in a black sweater with thin blue, purple, and white stripes; others kept their fur-hooded coats on. The most interesting person Anthony talked to all night was Joseph Lubin, a bald, soft-spoken Toronto native who had a habit of standing with one arm crossed, grasping the other. A Princeton alum nearing fifty, he had retired from Wall Street, where he'd done a stint at Goldman Sachs, and was now living in Jamaica. Anthony invited Joe into the Skype groups.

A community around Ethereum was forming. A solidly built Frenchman living in London, Stephan Tual, who had slicked-back black hair, a mustache, and a thick beard that almost ran down his neck, came on board in mid-January to do communications and community building—a particularly important role for the upcoming crowdsale.

Anthony suggested that everyone meet in Miami at the North American Bitcoin Conference from January 25 to 26, where Vitalik was slated to speak. Feeling flush due to his new Bitcoin millionaire status, Anthony offered to rent a house in Miami for everyone as long as they paid their own airfare. If they liked each other, they would keep working together.

The weekend before, Gavin had been staying at Jonny Bitcoin's room in a London commune. Because he hoped to have something on Ethereum ready before Miami, he spent the entire weekend in, coding and ordering takeout. But he was broke, so he was also Skyping with Vitalik, trying to figure out a way to get to the conference.

Finally, on Sunday, Charles picked up Anthony Di Iorio at Miami airport. By funding Ethereum's development so far and offering to pay for the house, Anthony had established himself as the money man. Charles asked if Anthony would cover Gavin's flight, and Anthony said yes. Gavin, who had only been to the United States three times before, was now flying out the very next day for a week.

In early January, Gavin had met up with Jonny Bitcoin and his Bitcoin-millionaire friend for a dinner. The Bitcoin millionaire gave Gavin some advice: if you're making Ethereum, don't let them shaft you.

Gavin carried the advice with him as he boarded the flight to Miami.

2

January 20, 2014, to June 3, 2014

COMING FROM THE United Kingdom in January, Gavin arrived in Miami and thought, *Wow.* The weather, a perfect seventy-two degrees, set the scene.[1] Walking into the 1,550-square-foot waterfront home Anthony had rented on Bay Harbor Islands on Biscayne Bay, he could feel, under his feet, large, cool, cream-colored tiles. The living area featured a pool table, sumptuous brown leather couches, and a bar. Outside the back sliding glass doors was a deck, lounge chairs, an industrial-sized grill, and the shimmering, turquoise bay, across which lay a golf course and more palm trees. The chirping of birds sweetened the breeze, which smelled of summer. Those who jumped in the water could swim with dolphins.

The Ethereum crew arrived several days before the conference in order to work. With a few exceptions, most of them were meeting for the first time. About a dozen or so people were staying in the house at any given time: Vitalik, Anthony, Charles, and Joe; Vitalik's Colored Coins friend, "capitalist Amir" Chetrit; Taylor Gerring, who was keeping the website up; Texture, who had been working in cannabis edibles; and some people Anthony had brought along, like a videographer, his business partner Steve, and several others. (Mihai hadn't even attempted to come; Romanian citizens traveling to the United States had to release a ton

of information, including in his case, he says, the names of all of
Bitcoin Magazine's customers.) Whereas on the first night about
ten people slept at the house, the number grew as the week went
on. People also visited, including a number of female conference
attendees. (A few of the almost entirely male house crew were
happy to invite some of these guests into a bedroom.) In free-
wheeling conversations, the newly acquainted group realized the
vast majority of them had tried psychedelics, an unusual situation
given the drugs' illegal status. Every particle of air was charged,
with the Bitcoin price hovering tantalizingly close to $1,000. They
were jazzed about announcing Bitcoin 2.0.

Or, at least, most of them were. The nineteen-year-old Vitalik
was nowhere to be seen for the first few hours. When he finally
emerged, Texture said, "It's nice to meet you." Vitalik, a sprin-
kling of pimples on his cheeks and forehead and peach fuzz on
his chin, said hi and then, with his slight lisp, added, "I'm prac-
ticing Chinese on my phone." He stared at the device a fair bit in
Miami, whipping out the language app during car rides. At one
point, Anthony's business partner Steve nearly convinced Vitalik,
who was still underage for alcohol, to smoke weed, but Steve got
momentarily called away, and when he returned, Vitalik's interest
had waned. In general, the group had to take care of their boy
genius, who was often engrossed in thought, oblivious. At restaurants, he would be looking lost, and they'd have to call, "Come
this way!"

Gavin had been told there would be a hackathon, but aside from
the wallet programmer, he was pretty much the only developer, as
Jeff Wilcke, the coder in Amsterdam building the Go client, who
was an admitted homebody, had decided not to come. No matter. Charles, who had put himself forth as Ethereum's CEO, had
given Gavin a goal of getting Ethereum working before Charles's
live demonstration onstage that weekend, so he stationed himself
at the dining table to work. The others sat around in one of the
couch areas, making the big decisions about Ethereum.

At one such meeting, Vitalik came in all idealistic: no hierarchy, no special founders group, no pre-mine, just release the client, make it an open community project, be noble like Satoshi, and not guarantee anyone "equity" in the form of coins.

Anthony sprang into action: "No, we talked about this, Vitalik, we talked about this. There should be founders. There needs to be people with fiduciary responsibility."

At this point, Anthony had put in nearly all the funds for the project—$150,000 in development costs, plus what he was paying for the house and transportation for people like Gavin. And, he thought, to pay back those who invested money, time, and energy into the launch, a pre-mine would be necessary. To that end, the team needed to have a fund-raiser. As for the no-hierarchy bit, although Satoshi hadn't wanted to be visible, Anthony said Ethereum would be different: it would be about openness and trustworthiness, revealing the people responsible for the project.

With a pad of paper on an easel, they began drawing up who the founders would be. Hearing this, Gavin, who was still working at the dining table, kitty-corner to the conversation on the couches, perked up. At this point, the Brit still didn't know everyone was meeting for the first time. They all had American-ish accents, gave each other hugs as greetings, and acted bro-ish. He'd assumed they'd been working on Ethereum for a while, that everything was stitched up. *Why are they discussing this? If Ethereum hasn't been founded yet, then damnit, I want to be a founder!*

One issue was "capitalist Amir." He was involved with Colored Coins, which could compete with Ethereum. Although no one forced an ultimatum, the question of whether he was in or out hung in the air.

Meanwhile, Gavin, with Jonny Bitcoin's friend's advice to get his fair share ringing in his ears, decided to make a case for himself as a founder. Having been in school until he was twenty-five and having worked on pet projects since then, Gavin had almost no negotiating skills. But he walked over and made his best pitch—after all, while they were *talking* about what to do, he was actually building the thing. Charles, the self-appointed CEO, and Joe were supportive since Gavin had start-up experience and technical expertise.

But Anthony, the man who had so far paid for most everything, including Gavin's ticket there, and the person who felt most closely aligned with "capitalist Amir," said, "It's not going to happen Gav, it's not going to happen." Anthony told Gavin he'd joined the project too late. To Anthony, Gavin was "just some guy like the other 50 people there at that time—he was just working on code the whole time…[He was] somebody nobody on the founding team really knew but Vitalik." He saw Gavin as not involved in anything structurally when it came to Ethereum. "You got developers and you don't necessarily have the core people involved in the decision making that was happening," he would later say. To Anthony, just because someone like Gavin was coding didn't mean he would be a cofounder. Gavin looked pissed off. He pointed out he was actually *building* Ethereum. After five minutes of an increasingly heated back-and-forth, Anthony's business partner, Steve, says he invited Anthony outside for a smoke.

They went out on the back porch. Feet away, the sun glistened on the wavelets, and on the other side of the bay lay the placid golf course, pinned down by palm trees. Steve said, "Bro, you have to at least *tell* Gavin he's a founder. Just tell him he's a founder. You don't have to give him as big a share, but you can't tell him he's not a founder. He's the only one who's building the C++ client. Vitalik isn't even working on it—he's just working on a Python client." (Python is a slower programming language.)

Anthony, who later wouldn't recall this incident, took a drag on his cigarette and exhaled. Finally, Steve says he admitted, "You're right, you're right," and they went back in.

Whether there was ever one single final agreement on the cofounder/leadership structure is unclear, but there were various compromises that messily befit a "decentralized" project as opposed to a traditional company with a clear hierarchy. To this day, no one disputes the five original cofounders were Vitalik, Anthony, Charles, Mihai, and Amir. (Gavin sensed, however, that Anthony would have liked to restrict the founder group to himself and Vitalik—that he tolerated his friends Charles and Amir as cofounders but wasn't keen on including Vitalik's friend Mihai. Anthony disputes this since he says—and Vitalik recollects this as well—the five cofounders were already settled before Miami.) It seems there was also a group of four fiduciary members—the same group minus Amir—who would be responsible financially; they were the ones listed on the website. (Amir would later say his personal privacy mattered more to him than feeding his ego, but others believed he didn't want to be responsible if anything went wrong with the Securities and Exchange Commission [SEC]. Gav thought he didn't because he was working on Colored Coins.) Finally, at least Gavin also recalls a decision to anoint three lower-tier founders: Gavin, Jeff, and Amir. The latter group would sit in on the founder meetings, help break impasses, and get half as much ether (ETH) as the fiduciary group members. Gavin thought this was a final decision; Amir did not. Later, Gavin would feel shafted as a lower-tier founder when he says he eventually found out that Charles had gotten into the Skype group only a day before he had.

Later that day, Anthony, the main obstacle to Gavin's being named a cofounder, came up to the Brit, bearing a gift bag. (Years on, Anthony wouldn't remember this moment but would surmise that he had been buying supplies for the house.) Although unaware of Steve's conversation with Anthony, Gavin got the impression that someone had pointed out to Anthony that he would have to keep working with Gavin, so he should make nice. Gavin took a look. Inside was a bottle of Johnnie Walker Red Label. *The cheapest Scotch*, he thought. Five years later, he would still have the bottle as a reminder that no matter how determined someone might be to stop him, doing so wasn't in their control.

THAT SUNDAY, JANUARY 26, at 9:30 a.m., Vitalik gave his talk.[2] It wasn't a prime slot, and parties had raged all night, but conference attendees still dragged themselves to Vitalik's presentation. The room filled until it was standing-room only, four people deep; the organizer estimated there were more than six hundred people total. Vitalik, stuttering, talked for less than thirty minutes. But he made his pitch—that Ethereum was taking a different strategy from other cryptocurrencies, not building specific features but instead creating a programming language. "Out of this one building block, this one single Lego brick of cryptocurrency, you can make pretty much anything," he said. Not only that, but these applications could potentially be, like Bitcoin, decentralized—meaning, they could, if structured correctly, be impossible for anyone or any government to shut down. Although many Bitcoin knockoffs existed, at least one audience member sensed this was the first time a cryptocurrency idea wasn't just a variation on Bitcoin and was instead something significant in its own right. At the end, arms shot up, but time for questions was short, so after Vitalik's standing ovation, a throng of people followed him outside.

As Ethereum's promise became apparent, people jockeyed for position. Charles, who had lobbied to be CEO, had casually asked Gavin, over a game of chess, to be his chief technology officer (CTO). Gavin, who, on Wednesday, sent the first ether transaction from his laptop to Charles's, asked Vitalik if that was cool. Vitalik, being less interested in a title or in ordering people around than in conducting research (or learning Chinese), said sure and gave himself the title C3PO.

Aside from the Ethereum business, the weekend showcased the glitz and glam of the Bitcoin bubble. One of the earliest "whales"—someone with such a large number of coins, they can influence the price—threw a roof party with ice sculptures and female dancers dressed only in gold paint. To Gavin, it was like something out of James Bond. The party shouted, *How can we demonstrate we have more money than anyone else?* He wondered, *Is this what life is going to be like now?*

Upon arriving in Heathrow, he called his business partner: "I'm not going to do OxLegal. I'm going to see how Ethereum pans out."

THE CROWDSALE, IN which the Ethereum team would accept bitcoins from anywhere in the world and return a wallet with which the purchaser could receive ether when the network launched, was scheduled to begin February 1.[3] But during the conference, concern began brewing about that date. People like Joe, Charles, and Amir ("the business guys") thought it prudent to postpone the crowdsale until they could be sure it would not run afoul of SEC regulations regarding the sale of securities. After all, the crowdsale was legally questionable. They were essentially holding what looked like an initial public offering, and in the United States, all IPOs must be registered with the SEC unless they qualify for an SEC-approved exemption. The Ethereum crew not only didn't *want* to register the IPO but also weren't typical candidates for one since they didn't have a working product, or revenue, or the money needed to hold an IPO. Ethereum would not qualify for any of the exemptions either. They were essentially doing what many would call an initial public offering without following the law. Joe, who was older and had a trading background, knew the penalties for this could include jail time, and through Amir's connections to interested investors, they realized they could raise a crazy sum, like $20 million. Charles claimed he had left BitShares over arguments about the regulatory implications of doing a token sale, among other reasons. Besides, on a technical level, they weren't ready to do one. So after the conference's last day, January 26, they postponed the crowdsale.

Meanwhile, Gavin went to Amsterdam to meet Jeff, where, in a Hogwarts-style Red Light District pub, the two created an early

Ethereum network between the Go and C++ clients, along the lines of an email network that functions even though one friend uses Gmail and the other Yahoo! The number of people Gavin interacted with shot up from four to five in a week to fifty in a day. He would often be toggling within a checkerboard of thirty tiled Skype windows. From Christmas to mid-February, for their respective Ethereum clients, Gavin and Jeff wrote more than seventy thousand lines of code.[4] (Eventually, Vitalik's Python client would mostly be used for research.)

As CEO, Charles looked into jurisdictions suitable for Ethereum to establish itself and hold the crowdsale. Switzerland's Zug, a small canton hugging the northeastern corner of Lake Zug and ringed by verdant hills and mostly low-slung mountains, had, by offering corporations favorable tax conditions, transformed itself from a canton of dairy farms and cherry trees into one of Switzerland's wealthiest areas. Mihai held a series of meetings with the relevant tax authorities and regulators to get them comfortable with the idea, and cutting-edge Swiss consulting and law firm MME agreed to do its best to get the authorities to bless a token sale from Switzerland.

When Charles told Anthony of the momentum toward establishing an Ethereum business entity in Switzerland, he felt Anthony was pissed—and Charles thought this was because Anthony, who was funding much of the project, was losing control. (Three days before Charles had gone to Switzerland, Anthony had founded Ethereum Canada in part so the fiduciary members could "do background/criminal checks on the founders," and he would later proclaim that Decentral, where Ethereum Canada registered, was Ethereum's first headquarters.) Joe, on the other hand, because of his Wall Street experience—in addition to managing a hedge fund, he'd also worked briefly at Goldman Sachs—thought Switzerland was perfect.

Meanwhile, as the developers Gavin and Jeff continued to create yet more code, both felt that if they, along with Vitalik, were building Ethereum, then they deserved to be full-fledged founders. They made their case to the five upper-tier founders.

Around this time, Charles complained to Mihai that only five people cast votes. Mihai, who had watched him tussle with Anthony in the founder calls, perceived that CEO Charles wanted more power to counter "venture capitalist" Anthony. So when the question of adding additional members came up, Charles told the developers Gavin and Jeff that if the others wouldn't accept them as cofounders, he was going to leave because he loved them so much. Mihai, who overheard this conversation, thought that, in reality, Charles wanted to butter up Gavin and Jeff so they would side with him against Anthony. When the original five founders discussed adding new ones, Anthony was the only person opposed. Charles called Gavin and Jeff to break the news that they were now cofounders, in addition to Joe, who could continue funding development, especially now that the crowdsale had been postponed. Although years later Jeff would say the way Charles became CEO was "like someone stepping in, saying, 'Hey, I'm the CEO of Apple right now,'" at the time Jeff was quite happy and grateful to CEO Charles, and Gavin felt vindicated that the others recognized that he and Jeff were important.[5]

Each founder would get the same endowment and vote, except Vitalik would get double the amount of ether as well as a second vote, essentially to break ties among the eight cofounders.

THE CREW WORKING on Ethereum's legal and administrative structure first stayed in an Airbnb at Meierskappel, a municipality across the lake from Zug. Mihai was a big proponent of holons, live-work spaces, to complement the decentralized Ethereum network. They worked, cooked, and filmed each other in the small space. Charles would be on the phone with a reporter. A twenty-three-year-old Dane named Mathias Grønnebæk, whose experience watching his grandfather lose millions in the financial crisis had sparked his path to Ethereum, would be coding the website.

Another member of the tribe would be cooking. It felt like a kib-butz. Stephan Tual, who was focused on communications, would later call this early period his best Ethereum memory. When the Airbnb ended, Herbert Sterchi, their Swiss liaison to the Zug authorities, offered his Lucerne apartment. One IKEA trip later, at least eleven people crowded into his now-mattress-strewn two-bedroom flat.

Roxana found what became Ethereum's home, a modern, three-story, taupe-colored bulwark they nicknamed the Spaceship. Set amid the bucolic Swiss hills in Baar, the neighborhood behind Zug, away from the water, the Spaceship had three floors and a basement; the top level, which featured two balconies, had space for a long worktable for everyone. They felt it wasn't *that* expensive, at least for Switzerland, especially with roughly ten people living and working there at any time.

The sleek, light-filled, minimalist-style home, which featured an elevator, was perfect for them, but the landlord didn't feel the same about renting to this brand-new legal entity, Ethereum GmbH (a GmbH is the Swiss equivalent of an American limited liability company), with no track record. At this point, Mihai went all in, exchanging his remaining bitcoins to pay a year's rent upfront: 55,000 Swiss francs (CHF), while Joe covered the deposit of 16,500 CHF. (The CHF-USD exchange rate is roughly 1:1.) They didn't have a bank account but converted their bitcoins into Swiss francs through Bitcoin Suisse, a company that facilitated large bitcoin trades and was founded by pirate look-alike Niklas Nikolajsen, a Danish former Credit Suisse banker who sported a long gray ponytail, bushy mustache, and goatee and dressed in leather necklaces and silver chains sporting skull pendants.

The Zug live-work holon got under way. Despite having pushed for holons, Mihai found living in one intense. From the time one woke up, one would bump into coworkers, and since the kitchen and work areas were the same, those working would be annoyed by others cooking. To lighten things up, they got bikes, and on the middle floor, Mihai and Roxy's friend Lorenzo Patuzzo, the carpenter, built a wall to create an extra bedroom that, during the day, functioned as a family room where they would watch *Game of Thrones.* They also had weekly barbecues that were sometimes drunken affairs but not extravagant. Since most of them were broke and no one was being paid, on the door they put a Bitcoin QR code at which they could receive coins for beer money. Once, when a Bitcoin Suisse employee brought a whole case of beer, they were so happy, they gave him a promissory note for four thousand ether.

But soon, tensions in the house began to rise past the normal annoyances of living and working together. Although Charles could be charming—even in a bright blue Oxford, pens in his pocket, the CEO could wow the troupe with his performance in promo videos—he could be discourteous, like the time he left his nail clippings on the Meierskappel Airbnb staircase. There were red flags too. One day in Meierskappel, when Charles was alone with Roxy, he told her he was Satoshi. He said he'd created Bitcoin in an attempt to distract himself after a woman had left him. Satoshi Nakamoto's identity is the ultimate mystery in cryptocurrency, and he, she, or they are now, for all intents and purposes, a god in the crypto community for performing the ultimate cypherpunk act: creating a decentralized currency that no government can control and walking away for seemingly zero personal gain.

When Roxy told the others about Charles's claim, it turned out he had told a similar story to two other nontech people: the designers, one of whom had believed Charles. Another time, while the Zug group was hanging out in the gabled-ceiling TV room at the Airbnb, Charles showed them an email account on his phone that looked related to Satoshi. In hindsight, one person thought he'd registered some email address and imported a bunch of emails by Satoshi. Later on, in the Spaceship, he tried a similar move with a forum account named Satoshi Nakamoto, registered in 2009; a witness speculated he had just changed the name on an account created in 2009 shortly before showing it to the group. With others, Charles was more oblique. To Mihai, he would say things like "Ah yes, 2008, 2009—those were nice years. I was working on something interesting." When Mihai asked what it was, Charles would say something like "Oh nothing." Later, he'd say he'd gone through a breakup in 2008, drowned himself in work, and then months later, *boom*—Bitcoin came out. Mihai, the *Bitcoin Magazine* founder who idolized Satoshi, eventually asked Vitalik, "Could Charles be Satoshi?" When Vitalik told Mihai he didn't think Charles had the necessary understanding of the mathematics and "cryptoeconomics," Mihai breathed a sigh of relief.[6] The real Satoshi could easily prove his/her/their identity by moving a coin in the first block of the Bitcoin blockchain. There was no need for all of Charles's hocus-pocus. Ultimately, most of the Zug group decided Charles was not Satoshi.

Charles would sometimes drag his leg while walking around the Spaceship, and when asked if he was okay, he would talk about having injured himself doing HALO jumps (high-altitude military parachuting) out of an Apache helicopter in Afghanistan. Similarly, he advertised himself as a CIA asset, one day casually promising Stephan to take him to "the farm." When Stephan googled it, he learned it was a covert CIA training ground called Camp Peary, but the idea that Charles could just bring Stephan along struck the Frenchman as implausible. Charles also claimed to have met a female spy when falling from an Apache attack helicopter and falling in love with her after going from building to building and bumping into her gun to gun. Not only did the story sound unbelievable, but also, given what was publicly known about him, they thought it did not work out mathematically for him to have been in the army. He also hinted to Mihai he'd worked with the renowned Defense Advanced Research Projects Agency (DARPA), doing cryptography, and had told Mathias he'd started college young but had gone crazy trying to solve Goldbach's conjecture. Mihai, with his poker background, couldn't help but wonder, *Why is Charles saying X? Is it because he actually believes that or it is true or because he is trying to get me to do something?*

On top of all this, his handling of relationships—from innocuous-seeming things to serious ones—bothered several of the people in the Spaceship. The way Charles spoke about his girlfriend struck a number of them as strange. He was constantly telling Roxy, apropos of nothing, when they weren't even discussing anything personal, "I miss Marlene so much." Roxy got the impression he was trying to pose as the perfect boyfriend, another part of his fake persona. When Marlene actually came, Taylor says he and his then girlfriend, who was visiting, thought their interactions were "fucking weird." To them, Marlene, who was in fact older than Charles, acted more like his mother.

More sinister was the way he tried to manipulate others. They felt he had a strategy of taking people out on walks to find out their aspirations and then later using that information to sow discord or control them. "Like a cult leader is the best way I can describe it," one Zug staffer said.

Even more chilling, in the first Airbnb, Charles had projected his laptop onto a shared screen where they normally showed code they were working on. One person recalls he displayed what he claimed was a restraining order against himself by someone who had interviewed for a job at BitShares. Charles said something about how he was so smart and powerful that she was trying to crush him. (There is no restraining order by her against him. After one interview, Charles did not respond to further queries.) Someone with whom Charles worked closely suddenly realized, *This guy could be a fucking sociopath.*

While they didn't know it then, many other people not in Zug had also had off-putting or creepy experiences with Charles. Someone staying in the Miami house noticed that while Gavin and Vitalik worked most of the week, Charles spent his time in the mansion lighting up big, fat cigars and talking about how someday Ethereum would make them yacht-owning billionaires. People felt

Charles purposely tried to imitate Steve Jobs and was insincere—a fake. In Miami, at one point, Charles showed Texture a text message from a girl saying, "I want to suck your dick." Texture said, "I don't know why you're showing me this." Charles talked about how he had worked at DARPA on the front lines in Afghanistan and met a female military officer there, and she now texted him. A college student who had worked for Charles found him to be "patronizing as fuck," pretending to be forty-five, as he constantly called the four-years-younger college student "a good kid."

In the Spaceship, as people were diligently working on things like the crowdsale website or legal and administrative work, Charles, who had commandeered the basement bedroom for himself—a prime spot since it was the only private area; plus he'd had the carpenter build a desk there—would come upstairs and talk about Lamborghinis and sports cars. Taylor felt that though Charles was technically the CEO, he didn't work shoulder to shoulder with them. If there were two types of leaders, Charles was the boss from on high shouting down, "Go that way!" rather than a leader in the trenches, directing while working alongside them. He also would call his assistant, Jeremy Wood, "Boy"—as in "Wake me in the morning, Boy." The others found this behavior appalling and his superiority farcical, considering Charles was CEO simply because he had requested the title.

THE NEXT TIME all the Ethereum cofounders (again, except Mihai) met was from April 11 to 13 for the Bitcoin Expo in Toronto. Anthony got his organization, the Bitcoin Alliance of Canada, to hold the Bitcoin Expo. A big reason was to showcase Ethereum, which, with Anthony's funds, became the title sponsor for $30,000. When people walked into the sponsor area of this Bitcoin conference, front and center was Ethereum. The booth featured flat-screen TVs displaying a rotating version of Ethereum's logo—a double tetrahedron, or two stacked pyramids, the top one pointing up, the other down—as well as black leather armchairs and a couple high tables featuring Ethereum business cards, buttons, round stickers, and half-pagers on thick card stock.[7] They gave away one thousand T-shirts. Vitalik's talk was the most popular, with three hundred attendees. Taylor thought, *Wow, so this is how marketing works. Throw an event so you have something to sponsor.*

Most of the cofounders stayed at Anthony's Decentral, sleeping on mattresses in the slope-ceilinged attic. Amir ticked some people off by showing up wearing another crypto project's T-shirt. (Amir says he was wearing a Bitcoin T-shirt at a Bitcoin conference and Bitcoin center.) In tense talks, they addressed his conflict of interest with Colored Coins again. Gavin tried to force him to commit solely to Ethereum so that if he received a founder's reward, it would be after he'd dedicated himself to Ethereum, not because he'd secured a title early but hadn't pitched in. To make his argument, Gav called Colored Coins a competing project. Amir retorted that Vitalik and Mihai were working on *Bitcoin Magazine*, and Anthony was working on Decentral.

(Outside the cofounder discussions, Amir went about doing whatever he wanted. When Anthony organized an Ethereum group photo onstage, one attendee recalled Amir was busy eating and responded to Anthony's invitation, "Nah, fuck that," though Amir says he politely declined. He was known for often saying, "I only care about money." Amir notes that the team was building a money platform and says this anecdote is an attempt to discredit him by those who hid behind a veil of selflessness but only cared about lining their own pockets.)

But the main power struggle was basically between the business guys and the developers over profits for themselves versus tools to help others, greed versus altruism. This played out as a debate over whether to structure Ethereum as a traditional for-profit start-up or a decentralized network. One low-stakes version of this argument concerned titles. Since half the group cared about traditional hierarchies (the more business-minded folks) and the other half didn't (most of the techies), anyone could willy-nilly claim a title.

Charles was officially voted in as CEO though the only actual supporters were Charles himself and Anthony. (Gavin says, "It became clear he largely viewed himself as Ethereum's CEO," while Vitalik describes it as "the thing about him insisting on being CEO," then describes the process of him obtaining that title as "Charles convinced us all to make him CEO with a title.") Gavin was named chief technology officer and Joe chief operating officer (COO). Gavin remembered Jeff being named chief software officer, but maybe since Jeff didn't care about a title, he never knew.

However, the main debate, begun in Miami, concerned how Ethereum would pursue its vision as a platform for decentralized applications. Some cofounders, such as Charles, Anthony, and Joe ("the business guys"), wanted a for-profit Crypto Google that would take customer data, profit off it, and keep all the gains of the network for itself. This was the model that internet giants like Google, Facebook, and Twitter followed, which the libertarian and cypherpunk Bitcoin and cryptocurrency crowd eschewed. Anthony, a believer in capitalism and incentives, even wanted its software to be closed-source, with the company itself the only entity that could access the code. (Anthony, who, years later, would say he sees the benefits of both approaches, doesn't remember what he supported at this time.) This made Mihai think, *No! No! If there's anything we can agree on, it should be open-source!* Open-source code would put the users first, ahead of any corporation profiting from them; plus the code would be more resilient since any developer anywhere in the world could contribute to it. Those in favor of a nonprofit organization envisioned it building open-source software, not exploiting customers, and instead shepherding a new, decentralized network that no one could own or stop, run, like Bitcoin, by computers anywhere in the world—even if the nonprofit ostensibly in charge of it disappeared. Even though Vitalik very much wanted Ethereum to be stewarded by a nonprofit, the others said creating a Swiss foundation was more time-consuming and bureaucratic than establishing a company, so he grudgingly went along with a for-profit.

With the arguments around the optimal organization for Ethereum percolating in Gavin's head, a few days after the Bitcoin Expo, he published a blog post whose title referenced "decentralized apps," "ĐApps: What Web 3.0 Looks Like," which began by calling out what was by then the dominant business model on the web, used by Google, Facebook, Twitter, and countless other companies: consumers handing over their data in exchange for free ad-supported services.[8] In a revised, "less-techy" version posted a few days later, he began,

> Even prior to Edward Snowden's revelations, we had realised that entrusting our information to arbitrary entities on the internet was fraught with danger... [E]ntrusting our information to organisations in general is a fundamentally broken model... Given they tend to have an income model that requires they know as much about people as possible the realist will realise that the potential for convert misuse is difficult to overestimate.[9]

He then proposed reconceiving the web so that big corporations didn't provide products for content publishing, messaging, or financial transactions; rather those services would be remade as public goods in the form of decentralized software, the way the internet itself is a public good, not run by any one profit-making corporation. This vision would eventually seize the imagination of many.

ANTHONY HAD ALSO prevailed over Vitalik on the pre-mine issue. But how should the 10 percent of it set aside for founders and early contributors (defined as people who worked on the project before the crowdsale) be allocated? After the crowdsale, once they were building the network, another 10 percent would go to the long-term endowment, as well as those employees allowed to purchase via an employee buy-in scheme. Because getting into Bitcoin early had turned so many everyday people like Anthony into Bitcoin millionaires, everyone understood that getting coins early, when the price was low, put them on the train to becoming Ethereum millionaires.

Gavin, who had been advised before boarding the plane to Miami to make sure he didn't get shafted, felt they should factor in someone's value to the project when divvying up the 10 percent among the early contributors. Someone who took a few meetings or a personal assistant shouldn't get the same percentage of ether as someone who wrote Ethereum (like Gavin). In his view, making high-level connections was the role of an advisor or angel investor, whereas building the technology, as Gavin was, was more of a founder position. He suggested they use market salary to determine allocations, but his proposal didn't go over well with many of the others, since they were the people making introductions. He lost.

Instead, they decided the 10 percent pre-mine would be apportioned equally among every month since November 2013, when Vitalik had written the white paper, until the crowdsale. They disbursed each month's allocation equally among all the people who worked on Ethereum that month, with distinctions made for full-, half-, or quarter-time. For November, Vitalik, being the only contributor, got the entire allocation. In December, Jeff, Gav, Mihai, Charles, and Anthony joined, so they split that month's allocation with Vitalik. In February, when Lorenzo worked full-time on building the wall in the Spaceship, he got the same allocation of ether as Gavin. To Gavin, the fact that he, one of Ethereum's main coders, was paid the same monthly rate as the carpenter would still rankle years later.

The next topic of conversation was their salaries. Gavin figured if he'd lost the allocation argument, he could at least gun for a high income. Using standard salaries gleaned from sites like Payscale, they awarded Gav and Jeff $190,000 annually, while Vitalik was given $185,000. But Vitalik found Gavin's push distasteful—he later described this process as "people just deciding to give money to themselves"—and in the end Vitalik took $152,000 a year.

THE ARGUMENTS AT the Bitcoin Expo were only a microcosm of tensions that had been bubbling up ever since Bitcoin Miami. For example, Mihai and Anthony were at two ends of one spectrum. The Romanian Mihai, the *Bitcoin Magazine* founder who had lived in anarchist squats, enjoyed drinking, and was sociable, spontaneous, and creative, wanted Ethereum to comprise a series of live-work holons. At the other end was Anthony, the money man who wanted control, saw himself as the "VC" nearly single-handedly funding the project, craved a return on his investment, questioned every decision that hadn't involved him, down to the logo design, and saw a flat structure of holons as anarchy: little hacker nests in former drug dens with no electricity. Unfortunately, these polar opposites both saw themselves as marketing people. There was Gavin, the developer building one of the main clients, who had positioned himself as CTO and saw himself as the real brawn behind the project, one of the people without whom Ethereum wouldn't even get delivered. (That month, he would also publish the Ethereum "yellow paper," a technical version of Vitalik's white paper.) Then there was Amir, the Bitcoin-rich man-about-town from Israel, who was also doing the Colored Coins project on Bitcoin and whose Ethereum duties no one could exactly pinpoint. (He would later claim he came up with the idea for the token sale, road-showed across the world to meet dozens of investors, helped craft the tokenomics, advocated for legal compliance, and was involved with branding, marketing, technology, and logistics.) There was Charles, the erstwhile math PhD candidate in Colorado with no business background who had, at first, proclaimed himself CEO, and there was his opposite, the peripatetic Vitalik, the creator who not only wanted no title for himself but also opposed the idea of titles in general.

A core tension was that, though Charles was CEO and Vitalik rejected titles, Vitalik was the one with the power. And while, at twenty, he wasn't aware of it, many people observed, first, that he was pure, innocent, and naive; second, that others noticed it too; and third, that some would try to manipulate him. In addition, Vitalik was not fixed in his opinions. To Anthony, who had very set ideas about everything, Vitalik's views were like an inflatable dancing air doll flapping about in the wind. On top of all that, everyone realized Vitalik was conflict averse. So those angling to sway him would just hang out with him, get his ear, and—since he couldn't say no—have their way.

Another contributing factor was that the others saw him as different. Many speculated or joked he was "on the spectrum," or autistic. He could be mechanical, not wisecracking or affectionate like many of the others. For instance, at a restaurant, everyone else might browse the menu and remark on dishes and wines, while Vitalik would scan the menu, decide on his dish, and then stare into his phone. People couldn't make small talk with him. With women, he was noticeably awkward and brief. While his parents had been aware of his social issues as a child, even during his period of long-delayed speech, which can be a characteristic of autism, they never took him to a therapist, instead focusing on his actual problems—that he had few friends or got overwhelmed by his emotions. (Vitalik says he has no idea if he is autistic and has never researched the definition or classification of autism.)

Whether or not he actually was on the autism spectrum, everyone saw he couldn't read social cues or body language or between the lines—even when someone was taking advantage of him. Vitalik was more honest and pure than the others. If someone said something to him, it wouldn't occur to him that that person was lying. This gave others an opportunity to push their own agendas forward. Some observers felt Vitalik had no idea what was really happening.

GAVIN WAS STILL brooding over how much more important his job as a developer was compared to other people's, how anyone could build a wall to create a fourth bedroom but only a select group of coders around the world could build Ethereum. On top of that, many early contributors would not be needed after the crowdsale, such as the people getting the legal stamp of approval to launch it. To Gavin, several cofounders would have been better as advisors. The only founders he saw as indispensable and legitimately deserving of the title were the developers: Vitalik, Jeff, and himself. To him, the business guys were more or less replaceable, and in particular he was suspicious of Joe Lubin. This was partially because Joe had worked for Goldman Sachs but mostly because rumors swirled that his former hedge fund partner had gotten into regulatory trouble and that was why Joe had gone to Jamaica. (Joe says his partner's former employer had the regulatory problem, not his partner, and that he went to Jamaica to work with a friend on a music project and because it's nice.)

Gavin became increasingly annoyed because the crowdsale kept being postponed. "Two more weeks" became the running joke. Gavin couldn't understand why it had been "two more weeks" for the past three months. What the hell were they doing?

Gavin, who had moved to Berlin, deeming London too finance focused, also was concerned about the many stories he was hearing about the Switzerland crew partying. While they contained nothing shocking, there was a fair amount of beer drinking and occasional weed smoking. The fact that the Zug group had bought a large drag-along speaker that could instantly produce a thumping beat said everything. Gavin thought, *Vitalik, Jeff, and I are building Ethereum. What are you doing?*

In Amsterdam, Jeff felt the same. When he looked at the eight founders, he saw three doing programming and five others doing who knew what. Were they spreading the word? If so, did they really need five people doing that but only three to do the work?

On the weekly calls, when cofounders talked about what they had done, it just sounded like a bunch of words to Jeff—*I've been going to this conference, that conference, getting people to understand Ethereum.* Jeff thought perhaps they should actually *build* something before attending conferences. As for Joe, Jeff didn't dislike him, but like Gavin, he didn't trust him. Jeff had a gut feeling Joe was someone to be cautious around, that if circumstances called for it, he would backstab you. (Joe believes that, at this time, Jeff was deeply manipulated by Gavin.) But to Jeff, the most egregious cofounder was Amir. If anyone in the group was doing as little as possible, it was Amir.

Gavin and Jeff, the two coders, would have said their grievances were mostly with the business guys (Charles, Anthony, Amir, and Joe), especially since most of them were in favor of a for-profit entity, giving Gavin and Jeff the sense that they didn't understand open-source software. The developers, plus Mihai, were in favor of a Mozilla-style foundation focused on serving people and creating something for the greater good, not maximizing profits for themselves.

Meanwhile, the business guys had their own opinions. As Joe watched the growing split between the devs, Gavin and Jeff, and the business guys, he believed the division was due to a power grab by Gavin. Anthony felt that, now that code was being written, the developers found the funding—*his* money—less important. Anthony, who was then thirty-seven—four years Gav's senior and seven years Jeff's—saw them and also the twenty-six-year-old Mihai as neophytes who didn't understand the real world and were naively ignorant of laws and regulations.

But even if Gavin and Jeff thought they were mostly against the business guys, some nonprogrammers, even the nonbusiness people, like the folks doing administrative work in the Spaceship, felt forced to take sides. It seemed the developers resented them too. In Zug, Taylor, who was a programmer but handled the website, thought Gavin and Jeff lumped him in with the little-value nontechnical people. He felt the devs thought pretty much no one in Zug was necessary. (Although this wasn't exactly true, Gavin and Jeff did question their relevance. For instance, Jeff thought Mihai was nice but that his weird projects, like the live-work holons, had nothing to do with Ethereum.)

The group began to realize these issues were going to come to a head in some fashion. In fact, two high-ranking team members who were not cofounders and not even in Zug were about to force the issue.

IN MAY, MATHIAS, the now twenty-four-year-old Dane who had been working on the website and then later on legal and regulatory issues in Switzerland for the crowdsale, went to Stephan Tual's home in Twickenham, southwest of London, to help set up the London branch. Mathias recalls that when he first arrived, Stephan didn't like Mathias because the Frenchman thought the Dane was aligned with Charles. (Stephan denies this, saying they built a relationship from Day 1 in Zug.) Either way, an all-night conversation lubricated by wine sorted that quickly. Over the next few weeks, they discussed the distrust and split within Ethereum. Eventually, they decided they could not continue the way things were. Not only that, but they were willing to be kicked out of the project in order to salvage it. The main issue, they agreed, was Charles.

It wasn't just Charles's perceived creepy manipulations. (Yes, those were big—it was not possible to have a CEO almost no one trusted.) But as they thought it over, they realized, at the core of the tensions was a divergence of opinion about the project's mission. And an organization with two missions was like a ship heading toward a cliff wall—if one captain wants to steer left and the other right, it will crash. To put it plainly, Charles's vision for Ethereum did not seem compatible with Vitalik's. They didn't have money for both. By Mathias's budget calculations, a minimum viable product would cost more than $15 million to develop. They had no idea how much they would raise, and software projects almost always have cost overruns. The current budget, however, allocated only about 60 percent to development and the other 40 percent to what they felt were Charles's "vanity" projects, like an incubator. As Stephan and Mathias considered this dire situation, they realized the only indispensable cofounders were the developers, Gavin and Jeff; they were even more important than Vitalik, who wasn't going to build Ethereum himself. It was a software project: it could not be built without developers.

Once they realized the stakes, for Mathias, since he didn't have a family, the calculus was easy. Ever since he had learned about Bitcoin, he had imagined that decentralized exchanges not under the supervision of governments were the solution to the 2008 financial crisis that had incinerated his grandfather's millions. So when Ethereum came along, he saw it as the platform that could enable his dream. He was willing to risk everything to save it. Mathias remembers that, for Stephan, the calculus was different but yielded the same outcome: he had a wife and children and had spent almost half a year working without pay; he would be ruined if Ethereum failed. Stephan says that, while that's true, he wanted to save Ethereum because he believed in a fairer, decentralized world and was convinced that Ethereum was the only crypto project that would become an uncensorable planetary computer.

Each cofounder had one vote, except for Vitalik, who had two. They surmised that Joe, Anthony, and Amir would not vote Charles out (and Charles himself would not). That left Stephan and Mathias to try to convince Gavin, Jeff, and Mihai to remove Charles—and if they succeeded, the ultimate decision would rest with Vitalik.

They had to be shrewd because they knew if they made any missteps, Charles would have their heads. They first reached out to Mihai. On a late-night Skype call on May 26 with Mihai, Roxana, Taylor Gerring, and Richard Stott, Stephan and Mathias brought up the issue of Charles. Mihai soon agreed that Charles's behavior represented a real problem.

The call was also significant to at least one person in the Spaceship for a separate reason. Taylor recalls that Stephan and Mathias were somewhat drunk and loose-lipped and that Stephan, who as the head of communications was in both the business and dev Skype groups, mentioned that he saw a big political chess match going on. Taylor says Stephan indicated he was convinced that, once the crowdsale money came in, Switzerland and the business guys would lose power and the devs would hold the purse strings. And since they saw Gavin as the ringleader of the devs, that meant Gav was going to win. (Both Stephan and Mathias say they were not drinking in excess, and Stephan reiterates this call was about Charles, not Gavin.)

At this point, no one had been paid a salary for months. After Anthony and Joe's initial large funding contributions, people like Taylor were loaning Bitcoin to keep things going. So Taylor says that Stephan told the others he was going to go with Gavin since he needed a salary to pay for his wife and kid. (Stephan does not recall saying this but said that because he and Gavin had a mutual friendship and respect for each other, the perception is understandable.)

This alarmed Taylor. *Oh shit, people are now moving into their cliques.*

AFTER THIS FIRST successful call, Mathias and Stephan next rang Gav and Jeff. They outlined the issues they had highlighted with Mihai and the crew, but this time they added a twist. They made Gavin and Jeff aware that the two of them had the power to invoke a nuclear option: they could threaten to leave the project if Charles was not removed. Because Gav and Jeff were the only two people with the ability to build Ethereum, that would force Vitalik's hand.

Jeff was already aware of this—and had been for a while. Knowing everyone was all on the same page, Mathias and Stephan celebrated with some more wine.

A FEW DAYS later, Gavin, Vitalik, Ethereum researcher Vlad Zamfir, and another friend, Yanislav Malahov, showed up in Vienna at the ornately decorated, 198-year-old Vienna University of Technology for a Bitcoin conference, to which Vitalik wore the same purple-, blue-, and white-striped sweater he'd worn at the January Decentral opening.[10] Gavin drank and was out late with Yanislav, while the younger Vitalik and Vlad stayed in the Airbnb on their computers. But during the day, Gavin and Vitalik discussed weightier issues. Both of them had always been in favor of Ethereum being a Crypto Mozilla, a nonprofit to support opensource development, and they finally discussed their misgivings about a for-profit model. According to Vitalik, in a discussion at their giraffe-figurine decorated Airbnb, although Gav would later say he didn't remember it, Gavin expressed that if a for-profit rather than a nonprofit were to be stewarding the technology, he wasn't willing to stay. Gavin recalls saying he would be willing to work as an equal to Vitalik or directly under him but not under Charles.

Vitalik was aware of Gavin's belief that the nontechnical leaders were dead weight, just people who had luckily nabbed positions they didn't deserve, and to some extent Vitalik agreed. He didn't necessarily feel, like Gav, that technical things mattered much more than everything else, but he did acknowledge the nontechnical people were not contributing enough. Amir was working on Colored Coins and so didn't even seem to fully believe in Ethereum; Mihai, whom Vitalik loved as a friend, was not a good match for his marketing position; Stephan had interpersonal issues; Joe was fine but mostly provided value through connections and angel investment; and Anthony was useful but overstated his importance and inserted himself as a businessperson. And then there was Charles, the "mathematician" with no real business experience, who had nabbed the top business executive role.

But even though Vitalik agreed with Gavin to a certain extent, he also felt that if the project suddenly began demoting people, they could quit, and Ethereum would collapse. For instance, a number of these people were figuring out Ethereum's legal strategy so that the cofounders would not run afoul of securities law—an area with which Vitalik and Gavin were unfamiliar. Vitalik felt Gavin perceived those roles to be more replaceable than they really were and that it was more important to get the crowdsale done and the project up and running without perfecting the personnel issues first.

At some point, according to Vitalik, Gavin did float the idea of just the developers—Vitalik, Gavin, and Jeff—continuing without the others. Although Vitalik, concerned that everyone had waited for the sale for so long, wasn't inclined to do that, he saw clearly that something drastic needed to happen.

The same weekend, Stephan and Mathias in Twickenham gave Gavin and Vitalik a foreboding Skype call. They said something like "There are big problems with the team in Zug. Something's going to happen, Ethereum's going to fragment, there's going to be a huge walkout." Stephan and Mathias had just had a call with Mihai and Taylor, who had found out some important stuff about Charles that everyone needed to know. Mathias and Stephan sided with Mihai and Taylor and said these issues needed to be sorted before the project could go forward. This put Gavin and Vitalik on alert. For Vitalik, this was the first he was hearing of any kind of upset within the Zug-based team.

Vitalik was especially surprised because he had always found Charles to be nice and friendly; they would eat together and talk about math. Nevertheless, Vitalik and Gavin agreed to discuss these issues with the others.

Fortuitously, Vitalik and Gavin were scheduled to take a train to Zug in a few hours. A meeting in Switzerland had been previously set for all the cofounders to sign documents and formally become directors of the Ethereum GmbH. It was to take place on June 3, in a couple days.

WHILE THE ZUG group had had misgivings about Charles for a while, Taylor's curiosity about Charles was really piqued on the

May 26 late-night Skype call. At some point during the conversation, Mathias asked the others if they had researched Charles. He had heard rumors; plus, when he searched, he could find no information whatsoever on Charles prior to a certain date. The group became so unsettled once they listed all Charles's fantastical tales that Roxana went to get the copy of his passport that they had for bureaucratic purposes. (It bore the name he used, to their relief.)

After the call, Taylor began digging around the internet, trying to figure out if Charles really had hurt his leg jumping out of army helicopters in Afghanistan; instead he found some companies Charles had established. Taylor carefully followed the online trail, but none of it corroborated Charles's tales. As far as he could tell, Charles's own story about going to college early contradicted his claims about the army, as would the dates on his internet posts.

In his burrowing online, Taylor sussed out some internet pseudonyms that Charles had used on sites like Reddit. One was Ravencrest, which, when cross-referenced on Google, turned up an account under the same name, from Boulder, Colorado, on a forum. There was a post that made them uncomfortable from the period Charles had lived there, written in a tone similar to how he expressed himself.

Taking screenshots, Taylor assembled his findings in a dossier. In his opinion, Charles was misrepresenting who he was and telling tall tales.

A FEW DAYS later, Anthony, Amir, and Joe started flying into Switzerland to sign the documents establishing the directors of Ethereum GmbH, the for-profit entity for Ethereum. The documents had already been drawn up and only required everyone's signatures. According to Swiss law, a physical meeting was necessary. Roxy had spent a couple days getting enough mattresses for what would end up being eighteen people staying at the Spaceship. Mathias and Stephan were not invited but paid their own way to fly in. On the way, they hummed the *Game of Thrones* theme song.

Even someone in New York had gleaned via conversations on the organizational discussion platform Slack that things weren't quite right with Ethereum. A lawyer-turned-technologist named Steven Nerayoff, with whom Joe was working on the legality of the crowdsale in the United States, says he told Joe and Charles as he dropped them off at the airport, "Something's wrong, guys."

Steven believes that Joe, who doesn't recall this conversation, said, "You worry too much."

Charles asked what Steven thought was wrong.

Steven replied, "Did you read *Lord of the Flies*? One of you is Piggy, but I don't know which one."

As everyone came together, there was a weird feeling in the Spaceship. Taylor, Mihai, Roxy, and some of the others knew what was going to be discussed, but because not everyone had arrived yet, there was a weird pent-up energy since they could not open up about it till the next day.

Still, some tension found its release. At one point, when Anthony and Mathias were having a smoke "under" the house (parts of the second floor overhung the first), Anthony turned to Mathias and said, "I don't like you." Mathias responded, "I don't like you either, Anthony."

THE MORNING OF June 3 arrived. The sky was blue, dotted with streaks of thin, diaphanous clouds. The air had a slight chill. Jeff, ever the homebody, was the last to arrive, from Amsterdam, and would be one of the first to leave. Vitalik, wearing that same purple-, blue-, and white-striped sweater, went with Gavin, Mihai, and Taylor to the train station to await Jeff's arrival. Due to a delay in Jeff's transportation, they hung out on the mottled, gray boulders by Lake Zug. Taylor found it ironic that he and Mihai were spending the morning with Gavin, who they thought was against everyone in Zug. But they were united against Charles—that was enough for him, for now.

Once Jeff arrived, on their way back to the house, about a thirty-minute walk from the station, they stopped in a park near the gleaming, mirrored City Garden Hotel and sat on a bench on a small hill. Taylor showed the others his dossier. One finding was that Charles might not have left his previous project, BitShares, because, as he had claimed, of concerns that it would do a token sale that could draw the SEC's ire. Instead, it appeared there had been a sexual-harassment allegation by a job applicant.

Gavin was concerned that, regardless of the particulars, Charles's closest collaborators did not trust him. Taylor had chosen to make a dossier, and he and the other Zug staff were revealing it to everyone before even showing it to Charles. That alone spoke volumes about the level of distrust. Even though Gavin had mostly been a lone coder and had no experience with personnel issues, he could tell at least this much: these people were not meant to be working together. Vitalik was going to have to decide which group to back.

The five of them, along with Stephan, talked about removing Charles and Amir. Some of them also wanted Anthony gone, and maybe Joe as well. Basically, the business guys. But after some discussion, they realized they needed Joe since they couldn't complete the project with only technical people.

When they got to the Spaceship, Joe Lubin, who enjoyed spending time with his twenty-something son, arrived with Kieren, which got a few people like Anthony rolling their eyes. *Why the fuck did he bring his son?* Gavin and Jeff, along with some others, told him and Anthony that they weren't actually there to sign documents. They also gave a recap on the dossier. Gavin saw Joe give his usual wry smile, as if he were above the fray.

On the top floor, in the work area, Stephan, Taylor, and perhaps Mihai met with Joe. Taylor handed him the dossier. As he read it, one observer says, Joe's face went white. His look said, *This absolutely cannot get out. We have to get rid of this guy now.* Then he joked that no one would want to be enemies with Taylor.

Mihai overheard Charles talking to someone on the terrace, saying, "They're going to stab me in the back." He was telling Roxy he thought they were going to fire him. Charles was starting to get a cold, and Roxy, who knew about Taylor's dossier, was uncomfortable. She told him as diplomatically as possible, "Don't be pessimistic. Let's see what happens." When Charles approached Mathias for information, Mathias, even though he felt guilty about it, feigned ignorance.

Charles also proposed to Stephan, "If you vote Anthony out, I will give you Anthony's shares and his founding title."

Stephan's response was essentially *Go fuck yourself.*

FINALLY, IN THE early afternoon, everyone began gathering on the top floor at the long table. It was made of six long and wide bleached-wood kitchen countertops arranged three by two, with thin gray streaks, laid on blond-wood workhorse-style table legs. Some sat in the high-backed, mesh-fabric black swivel office chairs with cervical and lumbar support and wheels that rolled almost too easily on the smooth wood floors. Others stood. Vitalik, who sat at the head of the table, his back to the smaller deck, facing the kitchen at the other end of the room, said a few words and then asked everyone to go around and say their piece.

Jeff thought that he, Gavin, and Vitalik had made a pact to say that they didn't think Charles could lead and therefore had to leave. (Gavin and Vitalik deny this.) So Jeff was surprised when Vitalik didn't mention that. Then it was Gav's turn, and again, Gavin didn't explicitly say Charles needed to go (although others would later claim he did say that if Charles stayed, he would go and do a new project). He did, however, say something along the lines of "Amir is contributing astoundingly little to the project." (Amir says that since he was on the business side and Gavin was a dev,

Gavin was not aware of what work Amir did and that Gavin was saying these things so he could consolidate power under himself.)

But his not mentioning that Charles should be removed took Jeff aback. Jeff looked at him, and Gavin returned his gaze. Jeff felt betrayed by Gavin and Vitalik. *Motherfuckers, why didn't you say anything?*

So, ever the honest Dutchman, Jeff told it like it was: "Charles, we feel you are leading us in the wrong direction. We don't want to be a Google, we want to be a Mozilla, and we'd like to see you leave. I don't want you to be CEO." To at least one person watching, Jeff seemed absolutely livid. He was really letting Charles have it.

Charles looked shocked, but Jeff, who had always found Charles fake, couldn't tell if it was sincere. Then Jeff invoked the nuclear option: he made it clear he would no longer be part of the project if Charles stayed.[11] Charles objected, talking about all the things he'd set up, but Jeff said, "It doesn't matter. I don't believe in becoming a Google. We need to build something for people, not corporations."

Jeff also said, "Amir, I'm sorry I gave you the benefit of the doubt, but I don't think you belong here because I have not seen much contribution from you."

Mihai went next. He said he agreed with Jeff with regard to Charles. Jeff was outraged: *Don't just agree me with me—say what's wrong!* Mihai added he couldn't trust what was real or not—basically it seemed Charles sometimes lied. Joe said he trusted Charles, believed Charles wanted the best for Ethereum, and supported him staying with the project, but he would support any final decision. Someone felt he seemed flabbergasted. (Joe denies this.) At least Stephan also said Charles had to leave, though Stephan, who felt that the dossier's becoming public would be the end of Ethereum, didn't go into details. He just said, "Charles has got to go. The guy is a liability"—and used more colorful language, like the word "sociopath."

Taylor pushed for Amir to go because Amir was technically his boss, but Taylor considered him MIA. Taylor did all the work but was not allowed on decision-making calls. Despite having compiled the dossier, he didn't say much about Charles.

Gavin, who had spoken early, was watching the proceedings, appalled by how Vitalik had invited everyone to point fingers and name names. And everyone who happened to be in the house, including Joe's son, was privy to this sensitive discussion. Sitting through an hour of people proclaiming their enemies was excruciating. He felt Charles didn't deserve a public bashing, even if it was by the people who'd been living with him. Gav felt calling a meeting when Vitalik knew in advance that people were unhappy with Charles was a poor decision. (Vitalik felt that the meeting was spontaneous, rather than organized, and doesn't see any smaller group with which the problems could have been discussed.)

Mathias, one of the main orchestrators of this moment, was conflicted. Even though he knew this was the right thing to do, he'd always struggled with confrontation, and the way everyone was airing their grievances about Charles made him feel awful. So when his time to speak came, he held back and said only a fraction of what he truly felt about Charles.

Roxy was stressing about what to say, but when the moment came, she spoke her truth. She said she didn't trust Anthony because he acted like he was superior to everyone else. Plus, he was pushing for a for-profit structure. Then she looked them dead in the eyes and said, "Charles and Anthony are not trustworthy. You can't trust them."

In one of the most uncomfortable moments of their lives, she made the most directly negative remarks. Charles widened his eyes at her, as if he was surprised she hadn't believed all his stories. She'd never said to his face that she thought he was lying. She thought it absurd that he hadn't realized she had her own thoughts.

Gavin, watching from the other end of the table, knew then that Charles could not recover. To him, until then, it had been all "boys" condemning Charles, so the disagreement had felt like a fight among boys. But for the only "girl" who lived in the house full-time to say she didn't trust Charles felt decisive.

Charles, who would later say that this meeting was an hour of the others "brutalizing" him, defended himself, saying they could make things work, that he promised things would be better, that they could do the nonprofit. He seemed to think the for-profit versus nonprofit issue was the crux of things. No one brought up the dossier.

FINALLY, THE MATTER couldn't be discussed anymore. Everyone agreed Vitalik needed to make a decision. As Mathias and Stephan predicted, the votes fell with four—Joe, Anthony, Amir, and Charles—for keeping Charles and three—Jeff, Gavin, and Mihai—for booting him, leaving Vitalik to decide with his two votes. (However, a few people remember this moment differently: two say there was no vote, and one of them says that Gav and Jeff gave Vitalik an ultimatum that it was either them or Charles and Amir. Vitalik says the only people who stood up for Charles and Amir were themselves.) The eight voted to disband the fiduciary member group, aka the leadership team. The cofounders would remain, but the executives would all leave, so Vitalik could have a think. When he returned, he should rehire whomever he wanted.

Vitalik walked out onto the front deck, the larger of the two on the top floor. It was drizzling outside. Beneath his feet were perfectly straight, cherry-stained wooden slats, and off to the side, a black barbecue grill, four black planters with bushes, and a yellow flower pinwheel. Ahead of him stood another house identical to the Spaceship, apartment buildings with gray and terra-cotta exteriors, then a bit beyond, verdant hills with trees cascading down them, and beyond that, the town of Zug. But all this was somewhat obscured by the mist. As was his habit, he began walking. Compared to the parks where he usually took his winding rambles, it was a constricted space. Still, for the next hour, it was enough.

3

June 3, 2014, to July 30, 2015

VITALIK PACED ON the Spaceship's front deck. He'd just witnessed a damning condemnation of Charles by multiple team members, and yet, each person, including Charles, felt indispensable to him. In fact, Charles had one of the most critical roles. As the CEO, he was charged with keeping all the project's moving parts together. Even while Vitalik knew the other members looked past Charles to Vitalik for a number of decisions, the twenty-year-old wanted to spend as much time as possible on research. Every time he contemplated kicking out the honcho managing the administrative and organizational details he didn't want to deal with, he got nervous.

At the same time, he knew what he had to do. As he thought through what it would mean to remove Charles, he tried to persuade himself the project would survive.

The Amir situation was easier. Vitalik had known all along it would be okay to get rid of him. This meeting simply provided Vitalik the opportunity to do what should have been done earlier.

As Vitalik mulled his options out front, the other cofounders, including Charles, crammed onto the smaller, less scenic back deck, which faced several apartment buildings. Venetian blinds mostly concealed anyone within.

Anthony, who saw the writing on the wall for his friend Charles, kept saying, "Well, Charles is a founder—can't take that away from him." Same with his other buddy Amir.

But Mihai said, "Charles needs to go."

Seeing how strongly people like Mihai, who had been working with Charles in Zug, felt, Gavin thought Ethereum's CEO had to leave.

Jeff was still stunned by how the others had not followed through on what he thought had been a pact. At one point, Gavin and Jeff went downstairs, and Jeff says he asked Gav why he hadn't said that Charles should be removed from the project, as they had agreed. Gavin, who later wouldn't remember this interaction, evaded the question. Jeff also berated Mathias for not having said enough, but Mathias said because he was not part of leadership, it was not his responsibility. He also said that he'd been placed in an awkward position because if Vitalik voted to keep Charles, his employment would be at risk.

Later, they went back up, and Amir, who was tall, confronted the shorter Jeff. "You don't like me," he said.

Jeff responded, "No, I don't."

Jeff recalls that Amir, who would later recall this exchange differently, said, "You don't like me because I'm Jewish."

Jeff was floored. *What the fuck is this?* he thought. "Why do you say that?" he asked Amir.

Amir, who would later say that he never experienced direct racist remarks from the group but in hindsight thinks he may have been stereotyped based on his heritage—for instance, he and others remember jokes that because he was Israeli, he might be co-opted by the Israeli government—responded, "You're a fucking racist." (Amir denies saying this and using the word "fucking," saying it's "simply not how I speak.")

"No, I'm not," Jeff said, an edge in his voice. "I didn't even know you were Jewish, and even then, why would it matter? I don't like you because you don't do anything, and you're being very rude right now, because I'm not a racist."

At that point, Jeff felt a strong hand on his shoulder. It was Gavin, pulling him back. Jeff told Amir, "You're being ridiculous."

VITALIK FINALLY CAME to the back deck and announced he'd made his decision. The cofounders gathered around. The devs, Gavin and Jeff, stood next to each other, and to Jeff's right, at the end of that arc, stood the cofounder who had just accused him of being racist, Amir.

Vitalik began, "Everyone who is a founder will stay a founder. That will not go away. Founders will keep their founder's share of ether."

Gavin saw a look cross Amir's face: *Bingo!* Gavin felt that Amir, having secured what he'd wanted all along, was happy he could continue his normal course of duty. Primarily that duty was to himself, and his friends knew, due to what they considered his endearing honesty, that it mainly consisted of sleeping with women. (Amir says that founders keeping their founder share of ETH had already been decided before this moment, so Vitalik was only reaffirming what he already knew. And as for his romantic life, he says, "I think for a group of highly introverted computer nerds, the normal dating life of a well-adjusted, well-spoken adult male would seem like he were a casanova. I'll take it as a compliment.")

Vitalik continued, according to Mihai's recollection, "After the conversation we had, it's clear that there are two sides at the table, and that's the problem. We should all be on the same side." He said that Charles had lost the respect of the people he was trying to lead. But even as he spoke, he still wasn't totally sure. At one point, maybe from the stress or the sadness of what was happening to his creation, according to at least one cofounder, Vitalik started to cry.

He pulled himself together and invited Gavin, Jeff, Mihai, Anthony, and Joe back into the project. Left uninvited were Charles and Amir.

They went inside, to the big table, where Vitalik announced the new leadership to the wider group. At some point earlier, Mihai and Joe had suggested inviting Taylor Gerring—the IT person who had been doing all the work under Amir but was not included on the founder calls and who had compiled the dossier on Charles—to join the leadership. Joe also nominated Stephan, the Frenchman in London who'd been doing communications and community building. Vitalik brought them both on—Stephan took over the communications and interviews Charles had been doing, and Taylor stepped into Amir's role.

The Zug group didn't clap or celebrate, but they were relieved Charles was gone.

Right at the table, Amir, according to several people, began negotiating his pre-mine share with Vitalik, asking him how much ether he would receive. He did not seem particularly bothered about no longer being a part of the leadership. As one Zug staffer would later recall, "For Amir, he got all the ETH he wanted and didn't have to pretend to be a board member anymore, so it was a win-win." (Amir says the ETH was worthless at the time and meant nothing to him since he had lost money by funding the project, but also that the allocation had already been decided.)

Charles, who was still sick with a cold, didn't take the news as well. At first he went out onto the terrace, where Mathias was sitting in the sun, and tried to chat with him. Mathias was a bit scared because he did not trust Charles. Plus, he felt guilty. Even though he knew he had done the right thing, he felt he had betrayed Charles. Mathias had always pitied Charles, wondering what had happened to him to turn him into a deceitful person—he thought it must have been horrible. Even though Mathias believed that, more than anything, Charles needed help, he also felt he had no choice but to do what he could to save Ethereum; otherwise Charles would have destroyed it.

Charles then went down to his room on the ground floor with his assistant Jeremy, where he is said to have bequeathed to Jeremy his entire founder's share of ETH. Vitalik, at first, was at the table on his computer, as if nothing had happened. Later, he went down for a one-on-one talk with Charles, whose cold had worsened to the point that he was sweating. Charles expressed his disappointment and sadness but accepted the outcome.

That night, Gavin, Vitalik, Mihai, and Roxy all slept in the same room—Gavin and Vitalik on one mattress, Mihai and Roxy on the other. After they'd all gotten into bed but before they'd fallen asleep, Gavin, without saying a word, got up and locked the door.

At 5 a.m. the next morning, Charles, his cold now in full swing, left the Spaceship for the last time, ending up back in Colorado, where he tried to figure out what the hell to do with the rest of his life.

WITH CHARLES (AND Amir) gone, the group felt considerable relief, but it was short-lived. Homebody Jeff went back to Amsterdam, and the others met on the top floor, in the very spot of the previous day's bloodletting, to discuss the way forward. It was then that Vitalik realized that some of the cofounders had misinformed him—that it was actually fairly easy to create Swiss foundations quickly. Vitalik was horrified they'd misled him in hopes of making more money. He thought, *You're in this blockchain/cryptocurrency project that hopes to change the world, and all you care about is making a few extra million dollars off it?*

He put his foot down about creating a nonprofit, Mozilla-like foundation, known as a Swiss Stiftung (pronounced SHTIF-toong), to steer the open-source Ethereum project. Although Anthony had been the loudest for-profit voice, he acquiesced (perhaps relieved that he remained on the project at all after his chums Charles and Amir had been booted).

The next day, June 5, Vitalik was awarded a Thiel Fellowship, which offered college dropouts $100,000 over two years to build something. He'd kind of known it was coming, because the organization had called, urging him to apply, and retroactively put him in the running for it. Since "VC" Anthony's Bitcoin funds were dwindling due to the slumping price—it was now around $640, about half its December value—Joe had had to step in with funds. Vitalik lived on his $4,000 or so a month from the Thiel Fellowship and didn't claim a salary to help keep the project afloat till the crowdsale.

But the group was now fighting about other things, such as how to allocate the crowdsale funds. In a long email to friends and family, after attending the Thiel Fellowship Summit in San Francisco, Vitalik wrote about what Ethereum insiders came to call the Game of Thrones Day or the Red Wedding.

> People were splitting into factions, everyone was at each other's throats, words that I had thought were vicious lies from the CEO of one of our semi-competitors about one of our employees turned out to be essentially true...I just want everyone to work together, and am spending hours every day trying to pull people together and then seeing glimmers of success, but then hear five hours later that they are arguing again...I'm the only person everyone still consistently respects. I was thinking that I would pass off the hard organizational work to a competent team of people so that I could focus on writing code and solving difficult but fun challenges of cryptoeconomics, but now it turns out that I have to be the one to keep the ship even pulled together in the first place. Sigh.

Over the next few weeks, after the non-Zug people departed, and as the Zug group formed Stiftung Ethereum, arguments continued over how much to allocate to various initiatives. Some, again, perceived Gavin as being especially money and power hungry. One afternoon, when those living in Zug were riding their bikes back to the Spaceship and running late for a meeting, they hopped on their phones to join the already-in-progress call. One Zug staffer says that Gavin commented that they needed to resolve budget issues before the crowdsale because the fighting would only worsen once they had the money. Finally, someone had explicitly said what everyone had been feeling: there was a lot of moneygrubbing before even a cent had come in. It became clear just how important it was to establish a Stiftung before the crowdsale. A Swiss Stiftung isn't necessarily a charitable entity; it simply has a purpose unrelated to turning a profit. The foundation ensures the funds are used in accordance with that mission, and a Swiss government agency oversees that. Stiftung Ethereum's aim would be to steward Ethereum's decentralized "world computer," the way various nonprofits manage the internet. Founding the Stiftung in time would prevent potential millions of dollars from going toward something different from what had been promised.

Related was the question of how to hold the presale and reward themselves without triggering the Securities and Exchange Commission's wrath. Earlier that spring, in Switzerland, their lawyers had determined that the instrument they would be issuing in the crowdsale, due to the decentralized nature of the project, would not be considered a security. Not being issued by a central body, it would not be taxed as if it were a product, which would incur VAT, but the money coming in would still be seen as an investment for tax purposes. It also helped that what they were issuing had utility in itself and that its success would rely not on the performance of third parties but on user acceptance of the protocol. For a while, they'd been working on how to pull a similar legal maneuver in the United States, which had large pools of money. The New York Ethereum crew had engaged the law firm Pryor Cashman to write an opinion letter saying Ethereum's crowdsale would not be considered an unregistered securities offering in the United States. The main lawyer there was so excited about Ethereum that he offered a 10 percent discount on the firm's standard rates, "which is more than I ever have offered a client," he wrote when sending the letter of retainer.

This discussion about how to legally hold a crowdsale was unresolved when the Game of Thrones Day occurred. The same day, the SEC charged a Bitcoin entrepreneur, Erik Voorhees (who had connected Anthony to the anonymous buyer of his Bitcoin gambling site), with offering unregistered securities—exactly what the Ethereum crew feared happening to them.[1] The Pryor Cashman lawyer wrote, "My initial view is that the [Voorhees] filing underscores—again—that it is highly likely that the payment of bitcoin in the Ether pre-sale will constitute an 'investment of money' under the first prong of the Howey test."

That was not good. The courts used the Howey test analysis to determine whether an investment contract constituted a security. Based on a 1946 case, *Securities and Exchange Commission v. W. J. Howey*, the test had four prongs, and an investment that met all four was deemed a security. It would have to be (1) an investment of money, (2) in a common enterprise (a venture in which the investor's fortunes were tied with someone else's, such as those of the person offering the investment), (3) with an expectation of profits, (4) dependent on an identifiable party.[2] If the Ethereum presale met the first prong, as the Voorhees case suggested; and if Ethereum could be considered a "common enterprise" (second prong); and if people bought ETH in the crowdsale hoping the price would rise the more people bought ETH and used Ethereum (third prong); and if the Ethereum team was an identifiable party responsible for those profits (fourth prong), then it looked like the presale could be considered an unregistered securities offering.

The legal ideas from the Switzerland team trickled out to New York. Talking with Vitalik at a bar, Steven Nerayoff realized that since ether was necessary to use Ethereum (because people needed to pay for computation), it was like gas needed to drive a car. Thus the presale was selling a product, something that people intended to use, rather than a security. (Similarly, court cases had decided even though a condominium might be purchased with an expectation of profits, a condo was not a security because it was for shelter.)

Pryor Cashman's opinion letter distinguished between the nonprofit foundation and the for-profit GmbH, the latter of which would cease to exist once the network went live and presale participants had received their ether. Theoretically, this meant responsibility for the network's success could not be placed on the same party holding the sale—perhaps making it harder to fill that last prong of the Howey test. The letter tried to refute that the profits from purchasing ether would be dependent on the Ethereum Foundation (EF) by noting that neither the EF nor any of the associated for-profit entities could dictate changes to the system. Additionally, it stated that pre-mined ether would not go to the for-profit company that developed Ethereum but to the people who had been working on Ethereum until then (perhaps a too-obvious sleight of hand since, ultimately, many of the same people would be involved) and that the company would promote ether the way it would a product, not a speculative investment. (That was the "utility" argument, similar to the one characterizing a condo as a nonsecurity.)

Stiftung Ethereum was finally established on July 9.[3] By Friday, July 18, the Ethereum crew had Pryor Cashman's draft opinion letter. On Monday, July 21, they received it signed. On Tuesday, July 22, at midnight Central European Summer Time, they launched the crowdsale.

WITH THE SALE, they let their geek flags fly. As Vitalik wrote in his blog post announcing the crowdsale, "The price of ether is initially set to a discounted price of **2000 ETH per BTC**, and will stay this way for **14 days** before linearly declining to a final rate of **1337 ETH per BTC**. The sale will last **42 days**, concluding at 23:59 Zug time September 2."[4] They'd chosen 1,337 ETH per BTC as the final rate because "1337" is "leetspeak" for the word "elite," signifying prowess or accomplishment. In the internet's early days, people would replace letters with numbers to discuss censored topics on early internet message boards. A word like "elite," which could not be written using numbers, would be changed to "leet," which could be "1337." The "1" resembles an *L*, the "3" a backward *E*, and the "7" a *T*. The sale would last forty-two days because forty-two is the answer to the "ultimate question of life, the universe, and everything" in Douglas Adams's book *The Hitchhiker's Guide to the Galaxy*.

Despite this silliness, Vitalik's blog post clearly had the lawyers' fingerprints on it—as well as his own flair. Two of the thirteen bullet points said,

- Ether is a product, **NOT a security or investment offering.** Ether is simply a token useful for paying transaction fees or building or purchasing decentralized application services on the Ethereum platform; it does not give you voting rights over anything, and we make no guarantees of its future value.
- We are not blocking the US after all. Yay.

He stated that for the pre-mine, they had finally decided on two endowment pools, each sized at 9.9 percent of the initial quantity of ether sold, with one to be allocated to the contributors who worked on the project before the sale and the other to the foundation's long-term endowment.[5]

The terms and conditions began, "The following Terms and Conditions ('Terms') govern the sale of the cryptographic fuel—Ether ('ETH')—that is required to run distributed applications on the Ethereum open source software platform ('Ethereum Platform') to purchasers of ETH ('Purchasers' collectively, and 'Purchaser' individually)."[6] Marketed as a product? Check. Had utility like gasoline? Check. Hopefully regulators would agree this sale was not a securities offering.

IN THE FIRST two days, 5,742 BTC came in. At a price of $620, that was about $3.6 million. By the end of the first fourteen days, before the number of ETH for 1 BTC dropped from 2,000 to 1,337, they had brought in 12,872 BTC, which, at the exchange rate of nearly $590, was worth $7.6 million. There were still twenty-eight days to go.

Before the sale ended, the leadership group wanted to clear some debts, but again, money became a point of tension. They needed to pay the lawyers, early contributors' back salaries, Anthony, Joe, Taylor, and others for loans, and roughly sixty thousand Swiss francs to Herbert Sterchi, the Zug liaison who had made introductions to the right authorities, but the optics of removing bitcoin from the multisig before the crowdsale ended weren't great. (A multisignature Bitcoin wallet, aka a multisig, requires more than one private key to approve a transaction in order to move money from it. Many require two of three possible signers or three of five.) For one, taking money out of the multisig before the sale ended raised the possibility that they were funneling the bitcoin back into the crowdsale, to make it appear as if they were raising more than they were and to create a fear of missing out among buyers. And even if they weren't doing that and were as transparent as possible about these moves, spending early would feed the Bitcoin and other trolls who had been sowing what in crypto parlance was called FUD (fear, uncertainty, and doubt) about Ethereum. For instance, BitShares, the other project that Charles had left on bad terms, had released a video of founder Daniel Larimer interrogating Vitalik after his talk at BTC Miami, criticizing Vitalik for not answering his questions, and saying Ethereum was unsustainable and centralizing.[7] Meanwhile, many Bitcoiners claimed "alt-coins" like Ethereum were unnecessary. For instance, a March blog post titled "The Coming Demise of the Altcoins (and What You Can Do to Hasten It)" said, "When people say, 'But Ethereum can do smart contracts!' this is actually false... Ethereum will therefore soon be forgotten like the rest once it inevitably fails to deliver on its promise."[8] Or, on BitcoinTalk, within two days of the crowdsale start, under the title "[ETH] Ethereum = Scam," Spoetnik posted, "it's an **IPO** and **IPO's in crypto are ALL scams**."[9] TaunSew wrote, "Ether could be laundered Bitcoin or it's them buying their own

volume to make it look like there's actual demand." Seriouscoin
responded, "Anyone has met Antony (the founder of Ether) knows
hes shaddy as fck." TaunSew replied, referring to Joe, "You forgot
about the Goldman Sach's connection."

Meanwhile, Gavin, Jeff, and Stephan were creating Ethereum
entities in their respective cities. Mihai felt that Gavin—still seen
as the most controlling person among the leadership group—was
trying to get the funds siphoned off to his own for-profit entity in
Berlin away from control of the Swiss mothership. (Gavin would
say he was pushing to make sure Ethereum got built.) But Mihai,
Taylor, and Vitalik were on the Swiss foundation board, which the
government was overseeing to ensure it was fulfilling its expressed
purpose. Mihai worried that Gavin's move to send the money to
the Berlin company could put the project—and himself, a foundation director—in jeopardy with the Swiss authorities. Gavin
indeed did want minimal interference from outside—but mainly
from Joe, whom Gav found increasingly obstructionist. Later, Gav
would also rationalize creating a separate for-profit entity in Berlin
by saying Zug had too little technical talent and what was there was
expensive. So in Germany, he'd created a subsidiary of the Swiss
foundation, Ethereum Dev UG (dubbed "ETH Dev"), because a
German business entity was necessary to hire German citizens. Jeff
set up an entity in the Netherlands since only legal Dutch residents
can own Dutch companies. And an English entity, Eth Dev Ltd,
was created in London, with Gavin, Jeff, and Vitalik as directors.

But the biggest financial pressure they faced was the Bitcoin
price, which tumbled during the forty-two days of the crowdsale.
It was around $620 on launch day but closer to $477 when it closed.
That meant, for instance, the Bitcoins raised in the first two days,
worth $3.6 million at the time, were worth $2.7 million by the
end. If they had converted each bitcoin right when it had come in,
the crowdsale would have brought in $18.4 million. But when the
crowdsale was over, the 31,530 bitcoins raised were worth only
about $15 million—more than $3 million in value *gone*.

At the beginning of the sale, Vitalik, Gavin, and Jeff, who were in constant contact about their various Ethereum clients, all urgently wanted to sell at least half the bitcoins as soon as possible because they had promised the platform would launch that winter. There were offices to open; developers, managers, and office staff to hire; tests to write; tooling to create; security audits to commission; and more, so they needed those millions of dollars or euros in the bank *now*. Joe, as COO and because of his hedge fund experience, was in charge of exchanging the bitcoin. But he didn't want to sell. Gavin thought part of it was his trader mentality: never sell when the price is down; only when it's up. Gavin and the other devs thought, *No! We don't have time—we need fiat to run the organization! We need it in fiat!*

The discussions grew heated and desperate. Bitcoin's value continue to falter. A few weeks after the crowdsale ended, it was below $400. And although they didn't know it then, by the end of October, it would drop below $340, and in January it would slip under $300, finally trading at less than $172 in mid-January.

In chats and meetings, Joe said if it were up to him, he would keep it all in bitcoin. (This was a common mind-set of Bitcoiners known as HODL, which was a typo from the BitcoinTalk forum, in which a drunken poster had meant to exhort people to HOLD.[10]) However Joe never directly refused to sell the bitcoins. He would come up with reasons to put off selling until their next meeting—he needed to do more research first, to figure out which fiat currency to convert to, and so forth. Gavin felt that because Joe knew Vitalik always sought consensus, suggesting they look at more options would delay action. Jeff thought Joe's actions amounted to gambling with other people's money. They had told him plenty of times, "Sell the fucking bitcoin." But Joe had held onto it to see if the price would go up, and instead it had fallen. Joe would later claim he did not know Vitalik, Gavin, and Jeff all perceived him to be in charge of converting the bitcoins. He would also deny having any awareness that they wanted him to sell and that they thought he was thwarting their wishes and would say it was odd they were mad at him, considering all of them made their decisions as a group.

From Joe's perspective, Gavin was power grabbing, funneling money to his Berlin-based entity, ETH Dev, which he'd established way back in April, and *that* was why Gavin was so keen to sell the bitcoin. He also felt that since the Swiss foundation had raised the money, immediately sending the majority of it to the German entity would have been inappropriate. Joe instead wanted to release the money in tranches, verifying that milestones were being met along the way. He asked the developers to write progress updates every few weeks. Gavin countered with the condition that the report should be published on the Ethereum blog. He didn't want Joe to have inside information. The reason? Joe was starting his own for-profit in Brooklyn that would foster decentralized applications on Ethereum. He was calling it Consensus Systems, or ConsenSys.

FINALLY, WITH THE German, Dutch, and UK entities set up, Joe began selling the bitcoins via LocalBitcoins, a sort of Craigslist for exchanging Bitcoin, and Bitcoin Suisse and handing over fiat to the developers in intervals.[11] Gavin and Jeff began hiring for their teams. In September, Gavin started with a half table at a coworking space called Rainmaking Loft Berlin, growing to two tables with new hires. One was Christoph Jentzsch, an earnest, bushy-browed PhD candidate in physics who was Mormon and hailed from a conservative area of Germany. He talked a lot with his hands, and his eyes crinkled kindly when he smiled, which was often. As lead tester, he wrote trials that the three clients—Gav's in C++, Jeff's in Go, and Vitalik's in Python—would run to see if any of the clients failed or if one client started creating a separate blockchain instead of syncing with the main chain. These experiments were the equivalent of ensuring that, say, a document (in this case, the Ethereum blockchain) could be read and edited by users of Microsoft Word, Google Docs, and Apple Pages and appeared the same for each person, no matter what changes were made to it. He also closely read the yellow paper, Gavin's technical specification of Vitalik's white paper, to check that the clients were implementing it correctly. His job, basically, was to try to break the chain. He agreed to freelance for Ethereum, planning to take six to eight weeks off from his PhD. Two other hires were directed to focus on Solidity, a language thought up by Gav for implementing smart contracts: Christian Reitwießner, a quiet, reserved, and bespectacled German with a PhD in multiobjective optimization, algorithms, and complexity theory, and Lefteris Karapetsas, a self-deprecatingly funny Greek software developer with dark, wavy hair who had studied at the University of Tokyo and recently worked at Oracle in Berlin.

Jeff's team, which was building the Go client, was mostly remote, with programmers like the skinny, talkative, smiley, and energetic Berlin-based Felix Lange, who had been in the same coworking space as ETH Dev and had found Ethereum to be much cooler than his failing start-up. Despite being in Berlin, he ended up on Jeff's team since he was a Go programmer. There was also Péter Szilágyi, an unassuming, curly-haired, gap-toothed Hungarian-Romanian who had just finished his PhD thesis in distributed and decentralized computing and who really enjoyed the Go language.

Gav put a lot of care into the Berlin office. In contrast to Jeff, who rented a space, put some furniture in it, and called it the Amsterdam office, Gavin took an abandoned space, renovated it to his specification, and hired a designer, who outfitted it with custom-built lights and Edison-style bulbs dangling on black cords from the ceiling, as though it were a restaurant or Scandinavian home design store, and filled it with secondhand items from eBay. The Berlin hub featured turntables, shag throws, a row of ochre theater seats (row D), Dan Flavin–style fluorescent lights, a 1960s-era brown-and-gold *Jetsons*-style credenza with a vinyl record player tucked inside, army-green school lockers that seemed cooler out of their normal context, pre-Hitler maps of "Europa" and "Mittel Europa," and a minimalist wall clock that featured one number, twelve, and chimed every hour.

The differences in their styles weren't limited to how they out-fitted their offices. Gavin felt *all* Ethereum's presentation had to be nice. He applied his marketing attitude toward the employees themselves. Many of these geeky programmers were not exactly eager to work on this new cryptocurrency they'd never heard of. For instance, to Felix, the idea that they could create money from nothing—or write up a table of balances, some of which were worth a lot—was weird. (Though once he began getting paid, he found it cool.) Gavin tried to motivate them by saying the project would be the hallmark of their careers. Others in the Berlin hub noticed Gavin was not shy about announcing things that did not yet exist or aggressively marketing things as being "first" or putting the word "turbo" in a product's name. Felix, being German, sur-mised it was a British thing, whereas Jeff had a more continental European attitude; he believed people would see how cool Ethe-reum was and bragging wasn't necessary. But once the space was done, some Germans felt visitors *were* wowed by the Berlin office.

The first time that happened was Monday, November 24, for DevCon 0, an Ethereum developers conference held at the Berlin hub, which was still so new—they'd only moved in the Friday before—the dishwasher was being installed as the few dozen at-tendees strolled in. Some Berlin employees who were completely new to cryptocurrency, like Felix, found the event way over their heads but magical. Gustav Simonsson, a programmer who'd been watching Ethereum but had thought that its token sale might be a scam, attended and realized that many of the people involved had PhDs, such as Gavin, Christian Reitwießner, and Jutta Steiner, who had a PhD in math and years at McKinsey & Company; she was managing security and audits. Plus, Vitalik had just won the 2014 World Technology Award for IT software, beating out Mark Zuckerberg, among others. Gustav cast aside his doubts to work with Jutta on security.

The developers entered a heavy work period. Every day, Jeff would wake up in his small Amsterdam West apartment, walk his bull terrier Bruce, drink coffee, and then code until bedtime, with a break for dinner. In Germany, Christoph, who mostly worked remotely from his small town, Mittweida (population fifteen thousand), but occasionally went into the Berlin office, initially found a lot of exploits that could break the protocol—usually in Jeffrey's Go client, since Gavin had written the yellow paper.[12] As time went on, there were fewer and fewer bugs. Christoph became so enamored with Ethereum that he abandoned his PhD. The goal was to reach six weeks with no bugs found in either client. After that, they'd launch.

Both the Berlin office under Gav and the more distributed Go team under Jeff would do daily stand-ups in which team members would state what they'd accomplished and what they were now working on. As Gav had kept harping about to Vitalik earlier, many of the "cofounders" and other founding team members, such as Anthony, Joe, Mihai, and nearly all the Zug staff, were not involved in building Ethereum. (However, Jeff did hire Taylor for basic testing.) With Charles and Amir gone, Joe starting ConsenSys in New York, and Anthony working in Toronto on his wallet, Kryptokit, almost no business guys were left. The devs were in control.

Jeff's team in particular found their boss flexible and easygoing. He told them they could work on whatever they wanted, however much they wanted, but if they abused his trust, they would be fired. Jeff was also funny. He played the grumpy guy but was actually a teddy bear. He often teased and screwed around with people, but it was obvious he was joking. He was a boss who didn't want to be a boss. Plus, he was always accessible. He was logged onto Gitter, on a public Go Ethereum channel, all day long, which was nice for his remote team members, such as the black-, curly-haired Péter Szilágyi in Transylvania and Alex van de Sande, aka Avsa, a designer in Rio de Janeiro whose high forehead and disheveled locks gave him a professorial vibe. Everyone felt part of the team.

Those under Gavin had a different experience. If he didn't like something they did, he said so with no sugarcoating. (At least he was just as upfront with compliments.) Although some people took his criticism personally, one worker found that five minutes after Gavin had found fault with his work via chat, Gav would see him and say, "Where are we going for lunch?" Gavin was skilled and productive, but also competitive, so if he and another team member split up tasks, Gavin would finish first and then impatiently ask the other person, "Have you finished it yet, have you finished it yet?" In contrast to Jeff, who hated micromanagers, Gavin had strict ideas about how things should be done. If a few developers came up with an idea, he would sometimes immediately shoot it down. Often he was right, but still, it was frustrating to work with someone who was constantly telling you that you were wrong and, even if maybe you weren't, forcing you to do things his way. He would even berate Vitalik, telling him on Skype, "You said you were going to do x," or "This is what's more important," or "This idea is going to be better." Everyone found him at the very least "intense" and, as one person put it, "always expecting everyone to be as productive as him." Once, when Avsa was in Amsterdam from Rio, working with Jeff, the second Gav heard he was there, he immediately asked Alex to take a train to Zug to work with him. The same thing happened on Avsa's second Amsterdam trip—that time he was called to London.

As time went on, however, his employees found Gavin became more of an "ideas guy" who made his underlings execute his vision, while claiming credit and never praising them. Still, they found him "brilliant" or thought him "a smart guy, but not the best boss." One worker felt Gav was "justified" to be "very full of himself... because...he's very good at what he does." One supporter compared Gav to Steve Jobs. "Can he rub people the wrong way? Yes... but does that make him a bad person? No." Because he was aloof, Gav's C++ team conversed in a private Skype group, which at least one person felt made the C++ client less approachable than Jeff's Go client, whose Gitter was open to the public.

Despite his difficult personality, Gavin was admired for his charisma, language skills, and aesthetic sense. When presenting, he had an appealingly calm voice that would draw in an audience. (In contrast, Jeff preferred not to present at all.) Gav's strong vocabulary combined with his good taste made him particularly good at naming things. For instance, he'd christened the secure messaging protocol he had dreamed up Whisper. When describing "finalizing" a block—the process by which the transactions in a block become irreversible—he coined the term "sealent," a more artistic and visual description (though he may have meant to spell it "sealant"). His style was evident even in the yellow paper (aka "the specification") published in April 2014, which showed how Ethereum worked technically and turned Vitalik's abstract ideas into math and code.[13] First, in the white paper–heavy cryptocurrency world, he'd chosen to make it yellow.[14] Second, it seemed to demand that the reader bend the knee to intellectual superiority, illustrated with unusual fonts and Greek-symbol-laden math equations. (It spawned multiple Reddit threads about how it was "hard to understand," "amazingly complex," etc.[15]) In fact, the paper was so aesthetically impressive it wasn't until a few years later that an Ethereum researcher caught a few small typos and mistakes.[16]

Jeff and Gav were similar in one way: each wanted to build his client his own way, forcing the other to follow. Fabian Vogelsteller, a German developer based in Berlin who joined the Go team in January 2015, realized Gavin and Jeff didn't talk to each other much. He would tell the C++ team things like "You should talk to the Go team, because they're also working on [fill-in-the-blank product or feature]." Whenever he did this, Gavin would seem displeased, as if he wanted to be the one to come up with ideas.

While the purpose of having three implementations of Ethereum was to strengthen the network, Jeffrey perceived that Gavin had turned this multiclient strategy into a contest. Gavin wanted his C++ client to win, but Jeffrey refused to compete. Driven to come out on top, Gavin focused on optimizing everything. Jeff just wanted to create something functional. Gavin called his version "Turbo Ethereum" because it was supposed to be the fastest, and his target users

were developers and miners—the network's "professionals." Since
Jeff didn't care about making his client the best one, its intended
users were everyday consumers without technical knowledge. It had
fewer bells and whistles. In the beginning, Gavin's client indeed
functioned better, and Jeff's was in a pretty bad state.

Every time Jeff's client had a mistake, Gavin would loudly point
it out, making sure everyone saw. In contrast, Jeff says he forbade his
team to ever badmouth the C++ team or call out its missteps, since
the two clients were being developed for the same employer, the
Ethereum Foundation. Jeff and a C++ client developer say Gavin actually instructed his team not to work with the Geth team. (Gavin
says rivalry existed on both sides and Péter was especially partisan
for Geth, but Jeff refused to rein him in. Jeff says Péter lashed out
because of the rivalry Gavin started and that even before Gav talked
with him about Péter, Jeff had already told Péter he should not act
out.) Gavin's competitiveness weighed on the members of Jeff's
team in Berlin. They found the CTO's way of publicizing all their
screwups demoralizing. Because the two teams were not working
well together, a Friday afternoon gaming session was scheduled. The
first time, everybody joined in. For the second, only four showed
up. There were no more games after that. Jeff, dismayed at how his
friendship with Gav had deteriorated, tried to talk to him about it,
but Gavin would deny he'd meant things the way Jeff had taken
them or evade his questions. (In private to Vitalik, however, Gavin
made the case a few times that his team was technically stronger
than Jeff's.) Eventually, Jeff found it impossible to work with Gav.

Even Vitalik chafed at Gavin's style, writing in an email to
friends and family,

> Gavin is quite authoritarian with his team generally and
> prefers decisions to be made by what he believes to be
> small groups of qualified experts, whereas I believe in a
> more open style of decision making where everyone should
> be given a chance to voice their opinions. I prefer increasing

transparency for the foundation toward the public as much as possible, whereas he prefers keeping things closed essentially because he believes people are too ignorant and uninformed to understand the nuances of what is going on.

In this dysfunctional way, the developers chaotically lurched closer to the finish line.

While the plan was always to launch Ethereum and improve on the software in iterations, the launch version also had to be stable enough that they could deal with issues while it was live and running without worrying about those problems bringing the network down. Plus, the blockchain was going to create money, and users would lose trust in Ethereum if it wasn't secure. To that end, Jutta had a $750,000 budget for security audits (for which they chose auditing company Deja vu Security). Additionally, they announced a bounty for developers in the community who found and reported bugs to the team.

As the clients got closer to being ready for launch, the foundation's funds were tight. Having sold their bitcoins at exchange rates close to $480 on September 11 and dropping to $227 in early February 2015, they'd only gotten around $9 million, less than half of what they would have made if they'd cashed out the bitcoins as they were coming in. By early April, only 486 bitcoins remained. Based on the closing price on April 2, they only had less than $123,000 left in bitcoin.

Vitalik was peeved about how high Gav had pushed his and Jeff's salaries, writing to his friends and family, "They point out that the wages are below market-level for their skills (and earned equal or higher amounts in previous jobs), though I think that such a standard is wholly inadequate for nonprofits, for which people are often happy to work for near-subsistence wages"—and all three of them were pissed at Joe for not immediately selling at least half of all the bitcoins raised. But the budget issues also stemmed from the massive burn rate of Gav's entity, ETH Dev, which Vitalik estimates was churning through $200,000 a month. After $2.2 million in legal costs and $1.7 million in backpay, very little was left. One admin person saw the leadership calls often turn acrimonious, with people saying things like "Why is your girlfriend on the payroll? She's not doing anything, you're not doing anything. I think we should kick you out."

Regardless of the cause, there wasn't enough money to audit both the Go and C++ clients. (Vitalik's Python client was for research, so it was less critical to audit.) Along with Gavin, Jeff, and Vitalik, Jutta, who had started dating Gavin, had to determine which client to have audited with her limited budget. Since Gav's C++ was for technical types and Jeff's consumer-facing Go Ethereum, aka Geth, would suffice for them as well, she, Gavin, Jeff, and Vitalik decided to audit Jeff's Go client first. The plan was to audit Gav's C++ client in the fall, after the network launch gave them ether.

IN EARLY MAY, they published the "test net" of the first version of Ethereum. It featured a prize fund of twenty-five thousand ETH for developers who found bugs or created a significant fork, or split in the network, creating two competing blockchains.[17] (They wanted to find this kind of bug before launch so as not to accidentally create a second blockchain once the network was live.) They were on track to finish soon, still undergoing audits on Geth, when, on June 12, an employee in Anthony Di Iorio's Decentral in Toronto emailed Vitalik. Writing "CSD inaccessible" in the subject line, he wrote, "I've received notice that Anthony has taken the CSD home and won't make it available until after he's had a chance to talk to you."

Copied on the email was Michael Perklin, a Bitcoin security consultant who had been hired the year before to create a so-called cold storage solution to store the Ethereum Foundation's crowdsale bitcoins offline. (In addition to the funds being disconnected from the internet, it was set up as a multisig, in which multiple signers were required to move money.) Michael had previously built such systems for cryptocurrency exchanges and gambling sites. He'd developed a thirteen-page cold storage policy and a six-page key compromise protocol, which outlined the procedure to be followed if a hot wallet or cold storage key was "compromised," or in the possession of someone who should not have access to it. The CSD mentioned in the email was the cold storage device in Toronto—the others were in the London and Berlin offices—any two of which were needed to move the crowdsale bitcoins. Not only were two of the three CSDs necessary to execute transactions, but each site needed two of three official signers.

Anthony had taken one of the "footballs," their nickname for the Chromebooks with access to the foundation's bitcoin wallet—a serious security breach. Michael invoked the emergency key compromise protocol, asserting that, if what he was being told was true, Anthony's actions essentially amounted to "holding the keys hostage." After a tense hour or so, Anthony returned the CSD, saying he had removed it from Decentral because renovations had turned the Decentral door to a "piece of plywood," making the location insecure, and he'd forgotten to inform the others. Vitalik sent a group email saying the incident "was eventually resolved and agreed to by all parties that no hostage situation had taken place."

Although not a single Satoshi (the smallest unit in Bitcoin, representing 0.00000001 Bitcoins) was lost, the incident was one in a series that had soured the Ethereum team on Anthony. For a while the other cofounders, particularly the devs, thought he had little to contribute. One saw him as a "failed business guy who wanted to tag along [on Ethereum] and get rich." While the other two didn't consider him a failed business guy, they would agree that one of his primary motivations was "huge personal profit." A team member concluded he was a "twerp," after realizing every person who had worked with Anthony had had a bad experience. One early contributor believed Anthony had no awareness he was "scummy" and a "shitty person" because he thought everyone acted like that. (Anthony says these people are jealous and "don't understand what it is to take risks and put money in." He also reminds the people

who thought he wanted to tag along on Ethereum that he was the
first person to whom Vitalik showed the white paper; Vitalik says
Anthony was one of the first.) One Torontonian who worked with
him noticed he was thin-skinned and got bent out of shape if the
spotlight wasn't on him. When members of the Bitcoin Alliance
of Canada (BAC) presented to the Canadian parliament's banking
committee, Anthony was so upset he hadn't been asked to give the
presentation with them that he was still bringing it up months later.
(Anthony still asserts he, as executive director, should have been
included.) Previously, when Anthony and the BAC had presented
to the Ontario Securities Commission and a regulator asked about
the security of cryptocurrencies, Anthony had said, "Well, you're
at risk *now*"—referring to the traditional financial system. (Anthony says the regulator's question was about quantum computing,
to which the traditional financial system would also be vulnerable.)

Especially galling was his rabidity about reserving the "cofounder"
title to as few people as possible, even though he himself did nothing
but fund Ethereum. Additionally, he gave the Zug team the feeling
he was monitoring them. At one point, they say, he was under the
impression they were doing drugs (there was some weed smoking)
and he'd flown to Zug without telling anyone. (Anthony says he
gave them notice—"you don't just show up"—and that if the Zug
staff smoked weed it was "not a big deal.") The day he and his assistant arrived, the Zug crew had gone camping, so he waited outside
the Spaceship for a long time, fuming in the rain, eventually booking a hotel. Although several members of the Zug crew say they had
no idea he was coming, he says it was a "coordinated," "childish"
effort to not be there and to have their phones turned off.

But the Toronto crew who had worked for Anthony had the
worst stories. Most of them had entered into verbal work arrangements with Anthony, but they say when it came time to document
the agreement, Anthony always seemed to come out ahead. When
Michael Perklin first met Anthony, Michael had just started with
his bitcoin consulting company. Anthony needed staff to answer

questions from walk-ins at Decentral. They made a handshake deal: instead of Anthony hiring him, Michael would handle walk-ins at Decentral in exchange for a free coworking space. A week after Michael invoiced the EF for the cold storage system, Anthony asked him outside for a smoke, and Anthony's lawyer, Addison Cameron-Huff, joined. Michael thought it strange since Addison didn't smoke.

When they got outside, Anthony told Michael he'd only been awarded the contract for the cold storage system because Anthony had campaigned for him. He concluded something along the lines of "So I think fifty percent is fair."

Michael said, "Fifty percent? Fifty percent of what?"

Michael says Anthony replied he meant 50 percent of what Michael made.

Michael responded, "For this invoice?"

According to Michael, Anthony said he wanted 50 percent of all invoices perpetually.

Michael looked at him over the rim of his glasses: "Excuse me?"

Michael says Anthony explained that the only reason Michael was successful was because he was working from Anthony's space and that the Ethereum board had actually wanted to select a different security provider but Anthony had championed Michael. He said that was also the case with the other gigs Michael's consulting company was getting—that they were due to the fact that he was working in Anthony's space, Decentral—and so for that reason, he felt that 50 percent of all invoices going forward would be fair.

Michael said, "Aren't you describing a kickback scheme, and aren't kickbacks illegal?"

Anthony would later remember this conversation as being about "referral agreements," a new program he was implementing at Decentral that would take a commission from the companies offering services from his space—*not* a kickback scheme. However, he wouldn't remember what percentage Decentral took. Michael says Addison jumped in, saying something about how, in the province of Ontario, kickbacks weren't necessarily illegal.

Michael also asked Anthony if, in those board meetings, he had been making decisions on behalf of Ethereum, or if he'd been making decisions knowing he could make money from Michael to pay himself. He finished by saying, "Isn't that a textbook conflict of interest?"

Michael says Addison interjected something to the effect that whether his client Anthony had a conflict of interest or not in a board meeting was immaterial and what was under discussion was Anthony's contention that, going forward, 50 percent of Bitcoinsultants' invoices were due to Decentral as a finder's fee.

Michael refused. After that, the relationship between the two broke down. Michael says Anthony began charging Michael rent to work at Decentral. (Anthony says if that was the case, it wasn't related to this.) Ultimately, Michael moved out.

It wasn't the only story about an aggressive maneuver Anthony made. Back when he and Steve Dakh had created the gambling app Satoshi Circle, Steve says Anthony had had his lawyer advise Steve that it was illegal for Steve to own a gambling company since he was a US citizen. (Anthony remembers it differently: that Steve himself had concerns.) Anthony agreed to pay Steve a fee as if he were an employee rather than a business partner, though he did promise him a cut of any sale if it occurred within 120 days. However, Steve says Anthony had promised he wouldn't sell the app anytime soon. Two days later, Anthony sold the app that Steve had built. (Anthony says there was always an intention to sell it.) That sale led to his becoming a Bitcoin millionaire, which later enabled him to bankroll the Ethereum project and nab the "co-founder" title.

According to employees at Kryptokit, he'd promised the two marketing people 2.5 percent equity verbally, but when it came time to document everything, he withheld their pay until they signed papers saying they would get no equity. (Anthony says, "Pay is never withheld for somebody...In terms of equity, if there wasn't an agreement, it didn't get signed.")

Vitalik heard these stories and others from various Toronto-nians, and though the CSD incident wasn't conclusive, it contrib-uted to a feeling of suspicion about Anthony, so, although it would take several months, the EF began distancing itself from the man who saw himself as Ethereum's main VC.

FINALLY, IN LATE July, launch day arrived. For a few months, it had been clear that Geth, created by Jeff's team, outpaced Gav's C++ client in at least one critical way. It only took a few seconds, or at the most a few minutes, to install (or "build by source," in developers' terms), whereas the C++ client, due to C++ being an older language, could take a half hour or so. Plus, while the C++ implementation had more features, the Go client worked better. And there was the fact it had been audited. The superior usability and reliability of Jeff's Go client must have been a crushing blow to Gavin, the CTO who had seemed to relish every mistake made by Jeff's team and had ambitions for his client to be "Turbo Ethereum."

Gavin didn't feel Geth should be promoted more heavily than the C++ client. He wrote in a June blog post, "please let's be clear: there is nothing magical about the Go client having gone through an auditing process...I see no reason to use the Go client over other clients (C++ or Python)...No clients come with any guarantees. Indeed there's the argument that minority clients"—such as his C++ client—"being a smaller target, are less likely to be attacked."[18]

He may have had a good point, but he did not have goodwill to call on among other team members. By launch, all the main links on Ethereum.org pointed to Geth. Occasionally the site pointed to C++ as another option.[19] Even though he was CTO, Gav could not tell the communications team to randomize the order or put the Go client below the C++ one. Geth—Jeff's baby—became the main client promoted for launch.

Vitalik created a script to scan the bitcoin blockchain to come up with a list of who had purchased ether and how much so that this could be coded into the genesis block and presale participants could receive the ether they had purchased at predetermined Ethereum addresses. Vitalik, Gavin, Jeff, and Aeron then selected a block of the test network, 1028201, chosen because it was a palindromic prime, and told anyone who wanted to run the Ethereum software to put the hash of that block into their genesis file. Once they did that, they could then start their client, which would find the other clients that had created the same block, and thus the chain would come alive. Rather than a person at a crypto company launching the chain, it was a "Look, Ma, no hands!" approach.

Vitalik flew to Berlin from China on July 28. On July 29, the Ethereum crew did some last-minute security checks. On July 30, amid the Berlin office's ambient restaurant-style lighting and retro furniture, they stared at a TV displaying a timer, waiting for the test network to hit block 1028201. Finally, on July 30, 2015, at 3:26:13 p.m. UTC, it did. On the screen popped up a Ron Paul "it's happening" gif of the political figure waving his arms in the air excitedly. Gavin generated a genesis block, shouting, "I got it!"

Finally, the idea Vitalik had dreamed up a little less than two years prior had become a reality.

ON LAUNCH DAY, after the initial blog post about it, the Ethereum Foundation published a second post, titled "Announcing the New Foundation Board and Executive Director."[20] It said there were now four board members and a new executive director, who was "an alumni of Massachusetts Institute of Technology" and had "spent decades leading and completing complex IT and management consulting projects, founding and growing business ventures, and working with top educators, scientists and investors to bring inspiring research innovation to life." Featuring a photo of an Asian woman with bangs and a sweet smile, wearing what looked like a Nordic ski sweater, the email said she was Swiss-born and had been following Ethereum since 2013, which meant when just a few people had the white paper. Her name was Ming Chan.

4

February 2015 to late November 2015

IN LATE FEBRUARY and early March, the leadership group of Gavin, Jeff, Joe, Anthony, Vitalik, Mihai, Stephan, and Taylor met in Zug for a week in the Spaceship. Also present were Aeron Buchanan, Gavin's longtime friend and right hand at the Berlin office, and Jutta Steiner, the Ethereum security audit manager who was also Gavin's girlfriend. Aeron was starting to burn out. In those talks, Gavin and other ETH Dev management suggested Ethereum dissolve the leadership group, which then included foundation board members Mihai and Taylor, plus Vitalik, as well as Jeff, Gav, Anthony, and Joe, and professionalize the foundation board, which would then manage the foundation's long-term strategy. Meanwhile, ETH Dev in Berlin would be the executive branch, making the day-to-day decisions, with Vitalik, Gavin, and Jeffrey in charge, though only Gavin lived in Berlin. Vitalik felt he was being pressured into the situation—Gavin, Jeff, and Aeron made the case to him privately that the rest of leadership was more a burden than a help—but went along with the plan, as did Joe, who was already tapering down his involvement at the Ethereum Foundation and ramping up ConsenSys.

When Taylor signed the minutes from that board meeting, he was not aware he had signed off on his removal; it had not been discussed. He wondered if this was yet another power grab by

Gav—a way he could, by proxy, exert control over the foundation. (Gav says this was Vitalik's decision, and so any deception Taylor felt would be between him and Vitalik; Vitalik says he thought Taylor knew what was going on.)

To replace Aeron, ETH Dev in Berlin hired a chief operating officer for all the entities, a straight-talking American expat named Kelley Becker, who wore her long, dark, wavy hair in a deep side part, as well as a chief financial officer (CFO) named Frithjof Weinert.

Kelley, who had experience at a few nonprofits in finance, operations, and development, at first gave some in the Zug group the impression she was a know-it-all who thought everything they'd done was wrong. At least one tried to hint to her that by carrying out Gavin's orders, she was a pawn in a larger game. (Kelly says that she was sorry they had a negative impression of her but that they were inexperienced with nonprofits and Gavin was her boss, so she was supposed to carry out his orders. Also, she says, these comments show how toxic the situation was.)

Landing as she did in early 2015, nine months after the Game of Thrones Day, Kelley realized she needed to understand what the hell had happened to the Ethereum crew. Her sense was they were a bunch of kids who had opportunistically created business entities in various countries willy-nilly, and so millions of dollars had been wasted. She gleaned they had been traumatized by Charles and felt that Joe could have been the adult in the room but had scared them off with what she felt was his aggressive money-making approach. (Joe, who within a few years would be a billionaire, says he has never cared about money.)

She focused on what Vitalik had tasked her with: building out Stiftung Ethereum into a pure, educational foundation that would protect the technology. She says, unlike with Joe, making money was the last thing on his mind. Vitalik wanted to do an open call for board members. Kelley explained that wasn't the best method, that he should talk to his network, but Vitalik insisted, so on April

10, the EF put a job posting on its blog and published an ad in the *Economist*.

That resulted in some impressive resumes, but with the launch coming up, they hurriedly conducted interviews over Skype. Eventually, they chose a bespectacled Englishman named Lars Klawitter who had an IT background, currently served as a general manager at Rolls-Royce, and had attended London Ethereum meetups and played with Ethereum on his home PCs. He responded to Vitalik's blog post. The other two selections, Wayne Hennessy-Barrett and Dr. Vadim Levitin, had come in via the *Economist*, with Wayne having an extensive background in the British army and management consulting; he was now at an African fintech. Vadim had several years' experience with the UN Development Programme and had been CEO of a global education and training company. Vitalik was the fourth board member.

The foundation also advertised for an executive director (ED) to oversee operations in the subsidiaries.[1] They interviewed three candidates in person at the upscale, sleek, and minimalist B2 Boutique Hotel + Spa in Zurich, which featured cathedral-like windows and towering bookshelves in its wine library, an infinity pool with views of Zurich and the mountains, and access to thermal baths. Of the couple dozen applicants, their final three choices were a local Swiss banker, someone with what Vitalik deemed a "fancy" resume who had extensive UN experience, and a woman named Ming Chan who had recently spent eight years working on a University of Michigan educational website called the China Mirror Project, where she was an assistant. An MIT alum—a credential that impressed Vitalik—she had also spent a few years creating a mobile app called iWrite Wenzi, a Chinese-language educational app with two App Store ratings, and had also dabbled in launching a ski start-up while living for almost a decade in Colorado.[2]

In her interview with Gavin, Jeff, and Vitalik in their hotel room, Ming was chaotic. They started with some chitchat just to get to know her, and she took off in all directions. There was no stopping her. She talked on and on and on in an excited tone, and when they asked her something, she didn't even listen to the question. She kept prattling away. After that, Jeff and Gav preferred the more qualified candidate from the UN. But before that meeting, Ming had called Vitalik one evening, and they had had a three-hour conversation that he had enjoyed. They bonded over being geeks and how they'd both survived the traditional school system. Plus, they talked cryptocurrency.

Since Gavin and Jeff preferred the UN candidate, Vitalik, who wanted Ming, came up with a compromise: if the UN candidate requested a high salary, then they would opt for Ming. When he tried to negotiate a $230,000 salary, plus moving expenses, Vitalik felt free to instead choose Ming at a salary of approximately $150,000.

FROM THE START, Ming seemed full of energy and enthusiasm. One of the first things she told the board was that she saw herself as a prodigy, almost alongside Vitalik. She and the board members worked together from their respective locations—Michigan, London, Las Vegas, and Nairobi—for a little more than a month before the blog post about her appointment.

But interpersonal drama began almost as soon as Ming joined Ethereum. In early August, three days after the announcement, she accused Vadim of having bullied and abused her in a sexual manner during a two-hour Skype call. She implied he was trying to control and sideline her and the other board members.

Although Lars and Wayne were just getting to know Vadim, such behavior seemed out of character for the man they'd been dealing with. He was the oldest member, a retired professor and former executive who had been on a lot of nonprofit boards. Though he had no cryptocurrency background, based on his real-world experience, he gave pointers on how nonprofit organizations work, explaining what boards did in certain situations and how to set up the voting structure or constitution. The idea that he was power grabbing didn't match what they'd seen. Also, Wayne and Lars could not imagine what his motivation would be for attempting a coup. Still, since Lars and Wayne took Ming's statements seriously, they did not alert Vadim to her assertions so they could investigate what had happened first.

Lars emailed Ming, thanking her for sharing her concerns about Vadim's conduct. "Please rest assured that the board are taking this matter very seriously and we will make sure that there is a fair and thorough conflict resolutions process and that the appropriate consequences will be drawn," he wrote. "In order to be able to do that, can I please ask you to document and substantiate the extent of the transgressions, so we have a basis to act upon?"

The next day, Lars got a ping on Skype. It was Ming, who went by the handle "Bumper Chan."

[Bumper Chan: August 4, 2015] Lars sent me an email yesterday with this request

August 3, 2015 at 8:06 am lars.klawitter@ethereum.org

[Here she pasted verbatim the email Lars had sent her the day before]

[Bumper Chan, August 4, 2015, 20:05:15] Wayne is dismissive of everyone, including the other board members. He says he will handle everything. It sounds like Wayne convinced Lars to write this letter. Wayne told me 'You're not going anywhere' and neither is anyone else

[Bumper Chan, August 4, 2015, 20:06:07] He is worse than Vadim.

[Bumper Chan, August 4, 2015, 20:06:59] Thankfully Nora believes I can gain control together with Vitalik, with your help to walk me through it

[Bumper Chan, August 4, 2015 20:08:37] She described a scenario later, where I could, if I wanted, become Pres of the Board, with Vitalik as Chairman. Also she let me know I can choose my own advisory board (not Kelley).

I had so little time with her, but she did say this is not a good situation and sounds like a hostile (board) situation

Lars could barely process what he was seeing. He immediately copy/pasted the messages into Evernote. Suddenly, Ming must have realized her mistake. His Skype chat log with her now read,

[This message has been removed]
[This message has been removed]
[This message has been removed]
[This message has been removed]
[This message has been removed]
[This message has been removed]
[This message has been removed]
[This message has been removed]

Lars was surprised. Ming was unhappy he'd requested details of the incident so they could deal with the situation appropriately. And her scheme to "gain control" seemed Machiavellian.

Still, because they could not be sure they had not misjudged Vadim, whom they barely knew, not only did Wayne and Lars not tell him about Ming's accusations, but they also cut him off from all communication so they could verify what happened. But when asked detailed questions, Ming toned her accusation down from sexual content to verbal abuse. And from Ming's now-deleted Skype messages to Lars, it seemed she was discontent with Wayne and Lars for not just believing her. She began making comments about their own behavior similar to her accusations against Vadim, eventually alleging that Wayne had screamed at her.

When she was questioned more, her charge against Vadim changed so much that some of the ETH Dev group thought Vadim had simply forcefully given Ming his opinion on how to organize the council. One person believed he hadn't really abused her at all, least of all sexually, and that her perspective was skewed. However, this person could not say so since Ming was this staffer's boss. And the accusation against Wayne really struck people as farfetched; they felt he did not have a nasty manner about him at all. One person called him "positive, fun, easygoing," and another described him as a "proper man. Always very polite." Vadim wasn't nasty, but because he was an older, Russian-born American who had served in the Russian army and perhaps a tad paternalistic, Ming might have interpreted his remarks as aggressive, as one other Ethereum developer felt he'd been.

During this time, Vitalik had just flown from Korea to Beijing, where he was teaching about Ethereum at a university. After waking, he'd go teach, eating lunch and dinner with the students; during the breaks, he'd field calls from Ming, who would keep him for up to two hours. He was also trying to do protocol research. Vitalik really did not know whom to believe—Ming or the board.

When Lars showed him Ming's deleted Skype messages, Vitalik said things like "You have to appreciate her side of the story. She feels uncomfortable with you guys." When Lars pointed out that her messages showed a plot to oust people, not discomfort, Vitalik would again take both sides. (Vitalik says Ming's side of the story was that these people were overbearing and aggressive to her in a way that a particular type of older male can be toward women.)

At the same time she was accusing Vadim, during her phone calls with Vitalik, Vitalik says Ming was telling him the most important thing was for him to keep control of the foundation and not let the board reduce his role to just vetoing. The more Vitalik listened, the more he realized she was right. He began to trust Ming more than the board. She also told him she wanted to get rid of the others. Although Vitalik didn't necessarily want power, he also didn't have confidence in these board members they'd barely vetted.

Ming told one friend not involved in Ethereum that she did not trust the board members because they seemed to be in it just for the money. The friend didn't know that the board members were working pro bono.

THE FOLLOWING WEEK, Vitalik faced yet another crisis. The previous October, after the crowdsale, the foundation board, back when it comprised him, Taylor, and Mihai, had met to finalize the early contributor distribution. For the eighty-four people on the list, they confirmed that each person had in fact contributed to Ethereum, what they had done, and how much ether that would merit under Vitalik's formula of full-time, half-time, or part-time work. This was the compensation structure Gavin had fought during the Toronto Bitcoin Expo meeting.

Now that the network was live, they were going to send ETH allocations to the early contributors who had triple-confirmed their ETH address. At this point, Stephan Tual, the chief communications officer, tried to lower some people's allotments, based on his perception of whether those people really deserved that much ether. He was galled by Mihai's and Roxana's shares—nearly half a million between the two of them, amounts dictated by the formula Vitalik had created long ago. Although he didn't mention it on Reddit, Stephan was also upset by Charles's allocation (296,274.826), considering that Stephan felt he had actively hurt Ethereum. And one friend of Stephan's also noted that given how much he had busted his ass growing the Ethereum community, Stephan resented how much the Amir Chetrits of the world were making off with (308,324.368 ETH, in the case of Amir—only a smidge less than Gav, Jeff, Anthony, and Mihai and 64 percent more than Stephan's allocation of 188,139.623).

Vitalik blocked the move to reevaluate the early contributor shares because, by this point, the board had triple-confirmed the distribution amounts; plus, he could not think of how to change them fairly. Additionally, he had personally promised some people their endowments would be honored. He did not want to go back on his word, believing it would hurt the foundation's reputation and create enemies. Beyond that, he fundamentally disagreed with Stephan about the sheer number of people being overpaid.

After consulting with some others, Vitalik decided that because he had the power to block resolutions within the board, he did not even need to bring it up with Lars, Wayne, and Vadim.

That seemed settled until August 16, when a Redditor posted a link to an Ethereum transaction that seemed to be the release of ether from the Ethereum Foundation's multisig to what were likely the project's early contributors.[3] Stephan decided to air his grievances, launching a public feud on Reddit. He responded to the post that what he called "roughly eighty-two" early contributors would receive around five million ether but that "only 12 had anything to do with Ethereum and even less are still with us (disclaimer: I am on that list)."[4]

Vitalik responded on Reddit that he'd used the formula of 1 for full-time, 0.5 for part-time, and 0.25 for minimal work "because I wanted to avoid pissing contests over exactly how valuable everyone's work was."[5] He recounted the arguments from the week before and his decision-making process, saying that, of the recipients, thirty-three were still actively contributing to the ecosystem.

Stephan responded that because Vitalik did not run the suggested revisions by the board, he had not followed due process.[6] He also pointed out that now the matter would not be recorded and was public only because Stephan had responded to this Reddit post. He complained that Vitalik consulted with "multiple people" whom he kept secret from the senior management team, which at that point consisted of Vitalik, Gavin, Jeff, Aeron, and Stephan. (Years later, Vitalik would claim not to remember whom he had consulted.) Stephan then challenged Vitalik to make the list of the early contributors public "**so the community could decide if indeed the reward levels are in proportion to the effort put in the project, community or developmentt.**" He also predicted that the amount disbursed would "negatively affect the valuation of ether going forward"—most likely because if large amounts were to be sold and demand didn't keep up, the price might drop.

Responding at multiple points in the thread, Vitalik conceded, "Arguably, the largest mistake that we made was setting that hard cutoff of 9.9% rewards to people before the sale and 9.9% to the foundation; it would have been quite fair had the project launched in Oct 2014, as we were anticipating, but that ended up not happening; had we known then that we would launch in Jul 2015, I would have made the split closer to 4.9/14.7 and this discussion would be much different."[7] But he rejected Stephan's argument about the potential for these people to dump their tokens, saying, "Also, it's worth noting that 'swamping the market with people dumping en masse' isn't an argument that should be raised here; the Ethereum foundation is not in the business of manipulating cryptographic token prices."[8]

Deep in the threads on the Reddit post, Vitalik did mention that, with ETH at $1.50, the Ethereum Foundation had another year of funding left. He didn't know that, on that day, mere hours after they'd made the first disbursements to the early contributors, the ETH price would close slightly higher, at $1.69—but trade below that, and at times well below that, for the next five months.

THE FIRST IN-PERSON board meeting was scheduled for August 23 and 24 in Zug at the Spaceship. According to one staffer,

Ming, who wanted it to emulate a big company board meeting, got extremely stressed out about making it as professional as possible. She spent ages filling maroon metal-ring binder folders with bank statements, regulatory letters, and other documents. Vitalik landed in Zurich from Beijing; Jeff came from Amsterdam and Gavin from Berlin. And though they worked for ETH Dev run by Gavin, not the EF, with Gav came Kelley the COO, Frithjof the CFO, and Aeron. Additional non–board members came, such as Anthony Di Iorio from Toronto, but the others felt he seemed desperate to maintain relevance—he cooked eggs and prepared sandwiches for everyone. And of course Ming, dressed in a suit, and the board members attended. Wayne had a last-minute family emergency, so he Skyped in from Kenya.

Vadim had finally been looped in about Ming's allegations against him and had vehemently denied having abused her in any fashion. He'd even threatened to sue her, claiming defamation and slander. When this happened, Gavin called Ming, who he thought had previously fan-girled so hard over his work that he found it hard to take her seriously. He says he told her about Vadim, "Since he's now threatening legal action and he probably knows some good lawyers, you need to make sure you're on solid ground." She seemed thankful.

By this point, most everyone was skeptical of Ming's claims. Everyone, that is, except Vitalik. He kept saying they had to see her side, even though, to the board, its merits were never clear. To the board it seemed that despite his brilliance, Vitalik struggled to discern who was helping and who was taking advantage of him. They believed Ming was in the latter camp and, without being too invasive, tried to show him that.

One ETH Dev member witnessed an exchange out on the deck in which Ming appeared to be manipulating Vitalik. He had made some inconsequential decision, and Ming wanted him to do something else. She said something like "I really care about you. I'm here to protect you, and if you do it this way, it will be easier for us." Because the matter was unimportant, it looked to this person like Ming was testing whether she could exert power over Vitalik, "like a toxic girlfriend."

On the second day of the board meeting, held at the long tables where Ethereum's Game of Thrones Day had occurred, the three board members insisted on an executive session between them and Vitalik—without Ming. They tried to be as casual about it as they could: "OK, next agenda item. Can we have the room please?" Everyone else filed out of the area (which, being next to the kitchen, was a sort of commons), including Anthony, Jeff, Gavin, Aeron, Kelley, Frithjof, and any others who did not have official foundation roles.

Once they were alone on the Spaceship's top floor, they asked Vitalik, "Do we all agree that Ming's accusations were not acceptable behavior?" By this point, the directors were frustrated. The facts about Ming's seemingly Machiavellian behavior had been known for weeks, but nothing had changed. They were exasperated at having to spell it out. Vitalik was emotional and extremely uncomfortable. The board members talked about how they'd made the wrong decision and needed to rectify it by letting her go. They felt having Ming as ED was a toxic and dangerous situation that would hurt the foundation.

Eventually, Vitalik agreed. Because of the friction between her and the board members, he said he would talk with her.

AFTERWARD VADIM, LARS, and Vitalik were scheduled to meet with Ethereum's Swiss lawyers from MME.

On his way out of the Spaceship, Vitalik told Ming the board had decided not to keep her on as executive director. Vitalik says she followed him on the twenty-minute walk to the MME offices near the Zug train station and cried the whole way.

He went inside and met with the board members and the foundation's main counsel, Luka Müller-Studer, to discuss legal, bureaucratic, and financial issues. Then the new board members asked Luka what a foundation director's personal liability was under Swiss law.

Each board member had one vote. But Vitalik had three votes plus the tiebreaker. This meant Vitalik was entirely in control. The board had first noticed this odd setup back in June. When questioned about it, Vitalik had said, "That's a holdover from before you arrived, as I needed to make sure I couldn't be outvoted by the others. But now we're going to change that. Don't worry." It was late August now, and the situation was the same.

Though the board members couldn't be sure, they suspected Ming was trying to sow in Vitalik seeds of mistrust of the board, telling him something like, *You need to be careful—these people are after control of the board and will rob you of your life's work.*

One board member recalls that Luka responded to their question about their liability that it was full and personal. When they pointed out that the voting structure actually gave them no control, he said it didn't matter—they were legally responsible for what the board did or didn't do. (Luka, who could not speak specifically about the Ethereum Foundation, said, "A general full and personal liability of a board member of foundation for action and non-action of the foundation does not exist. In certain cases, a foundation could hold its board members liable for damages caused to the foundation if such board members had acted against the law and the foundation deed.")

As they shuffled out of MME, Lars and Vadim ran to Zurich to catch their flights home. But the risk-reward calculus of their pro bono board positions, which came with no salary, no ether allocation, *nada*, except for paid transportation to and from Zurich for this board meeting, made no sense. As they boarded, little did they know that this trip would be the first and last "compensation" they would receive.

AFTER LEAVING ZUG, the board members heard nothing for a week and a half. They emailed Vitalik, asking him how Ming had taken the news and what the next steps would be. While they didn't immediately get a response, they did receive emails from Ming requesting their signatures on documents.

They wrote Vitalik again, asking why they were getting business correspondence from this person they thought had been fired. On September 2, Vitalik wrote saying he was delaying substantive decisions until September 10, since he had previously been too hasty. They sent him more queries, and finally on September 26 he wrote that the "universal advice" he had received was that he should retain all control over the foundation, that he understood it was unfair for them to have personal liability with no actual power, and that he wanted to restart the board selection process.

At that point, one person close to the matter says their legal jeopardy became clear: they were liable for the actions of the foundation, but their votes were meaningless, while a Machiavellian executive director was handling all the day-to-day decisions. They decided remaining board members a moment longer was not worth the risk to their lives, careers, and reputations.

On September 28, 2015, they emailed Vitalik and mailed physical letters to the Spaceship and MME resigning, effective immediately. Beginning "Dear President Buterin," they wrote, "Promises and warranties made by you, Vitalik, in your role as the Stiftung Board president have never materialized. Rather you have chosen to claim three board votes for yourself, effectively rendering us irrelevant. For all intents and purposes, it appears that our sole function as directors would be to rubber stamp any and all decisions made by you." They wished him the best.

THE BOARD NEVER found out that, after he'd fired Ming, Vitalik had had a change of heart when he, Lars, and Vadim met with MME. The whole reason for hiring the board members was, as Gav had said, to have highly professional people who would take care of the foundation. When Lars and Vadim asked Luka about their personal liability, Vitalik felt their responses and body language showed they didn't really care about the EF.

In contrast, Ming's actions made him think she really *did* care. After all, even after he'd fired her, she'd kept working on financial audits even though she had no reason to believe she would keep her job. (At the time he'd told her about the board's decision, her contract had been provisional.)

From September 2 to 7, Vitalik, Ming, and Ming's boyfriend, Casey Detrio, a Michigan native more than fifteen years her junior, rented a cabin together for five days in Toronto. They discussed how to restructure the foundation and what its mission and values should be; they also worked on the budget and website, with Casey assisting Ming.

While they were there, the day before an Ethereum event at Decentral, Anthony pinged Ming on Skype.

[9/7/15, 9:52:59 AM] Anthony Di Iorio: Good morning Ming. I'm concerned a bit about your plan to keep V isolated. It does not seem like a balanced approach and a bit controlling, especially since he is working on a decision about your future with Ethereum and he's still on the fence in that regards.

[9/7/15, 11:24:04 AM] Bumper Chan: We are making good progress and we both appreciate your support and concern. Will be looking forward to the Decentral event. Will retweet the event now.

[9/7/15, 11:38:12 AM] Anthony Di Iorio: No offence but "we appreciate?" Are you speaking for V now? If I wanted his opinion, I'd ask him, which I did earlier today. Hence my concerned message to you. Please don't try to brush me off and then try to speak for the both of you when I bring up concerns to you.

Another person in a finance role in Toronto, who had been extremely sympathetic to Ming's experience with the board members and had supported her during the period of her accusations, found that, once Ming seemed to have prevailed over the board, she started treating him poorly. "She went from the extremely sympathetic person that was really awesome to all of a sudden, she was like, 'Oh, I hold all the power. Get lost,'" he recalled. "She changed personality. A completely different person." He warned Vitalik, "I don't think Ming is who we think she is."

None of these entreaties got through to Vitalik—he no longer trusted Anthony or the board members, and though he still trusted this finance person, he accepted his or her opinion and sat on it. But the more he thought about it, the more he felt it made sense to keep Ming. He finalized her contract in September.

AS THE BOARD and Stephan dramas were unfolding, another crisis was playing out: the Ethereum Foundation was running out of funds. Every month through the spring, what looked like three to six years of runway based on the price of bitcoin suddenly had become more like eighteen months, then sixteen, then fourteen. Ethereum's launch had given the foundation some access, at least, to ether—just in time. Despite that, in August, the foundation's finances were precarious. The bitcoins were worth less than half a million dollars, and their fiat holdings were around $200,000. With the foundation's ether—7.75 million ETH ($10.5 million)—they only had a year of runway.

This was the August 23–24 board meeting's main agenda item. Vitalik, Lars, Wayne, and Vadim discussed the finances against the product road map: Would the foundation be able to cover the development of things like the Ethereum browser Mist thought up by Gavin and the messaging protocol Whisper? Already it was paying the Go and C++ teams' salaries.

They created a spreadsheet of possible budget cuts. At the top: the 5,500-Swiss-franc-per-month Spaceship, which housed only

Ming, Casey, and Aeron regularly by this point and served as a crash pad for other founders like Vitalik. Another unreasonable expense: conference travel by the cofounders, for which they expensed everything, with no per diem limit. Still, it became clear the foundation would not have enough to fund both the Go and C++ clients.

At this time, Gavin was starting his own venture, which at least one board member gathered he had been itching to do. The board member believed Gavin realized he wouldn't be able to turn the foundation into a for-profit organization, since Vitalik strongly opposed that, and says he'd even begun talking to VCs. After launching his company, Ethcore, he would be part-time with the foundation, which would free up more funds.

Another line item they scrutinized was DevCon 1. The plan had been to hold it the first week of October in London. But due to the drama with Ming, plus the financial straits, they delayed it until further notice.

These were the budgetary decisions made at that first board meeting. The plan had been to make further cuts—after they'd replaced Ming.

THE STEPHAN TROUBLE also came to its final conclusion right around this time.

In the previous months, Gavin, Jeff, Mihai, and others had become concerned about Stephan's erratic behavior. Some of it was personal. All day long, in the middle of the London coworking space, he smoked a vape—a giant, round, tanklike object that sat on a gigantic double battery and had to be held in his open palm. He kept it connected to his laptop so it would always have a charge. Surrounded by a persistent cloud, he was like a human fog machine. Some of the trouble was work related. For instance, one day, after Mihai had left the foundation to work on his own Ethereum app, Mihai says Stephan deleted all Mihai's posts on the Ethereum blog, as well as his early Ethereum Meetup YouTube videos. When the Ethereum cofounder confronted him, Mihai says Stephan pretended nothing was wrong, saying, "Ha, you don't know a joke!" The blogs were republished. (Stephan recalls he deleted some, not all, of Mihai's blog posts, saying they were "unrelated to the truth" and "the stupidest thing I ever read.") Stephan got to work as early as possible and stayed as late as possible, and he seemed to measure how hard others worked by how stressed out they seemed and how long they were in the office. One day in London, Texture started leaving at 8 p.m.—twelve hours after he'd started. Stephan asked him if he was going home early. Other actions were more sinister. At a certain point, the others realized he kept a detailed dossier on everybody. He had recordings of all the calls. One guest who stayed in his home says he heard him raving about all the dirt he had on all the members of the Ethereum Foundation. (Stephan denies these assertions.)

Between the latest altercation on Reddit and his deletion of Mihai's blog posts and early Ethereum Meetup YouTube videos, Vitalik, Gav, and Aeron had had enough. Before the board meeting, from the Starbucks in Zug, Vitalik says he and Gavin called Stephan by Skype and fired him on August 20. (Gavin does not remember firing Stephan, and Stephan does not remember being fired this way.)

Undeterred, Stephan came to the board meeting. Outside the Spaceship, Ming, with Vitalik standing beside her, demanded he leave. Stephan turned to Vitalik, "Can you speak for yourself, Big Boy?"

Vitalik said, "I agree with Ming."

Stephan spat out, "Fine," and stormed off.

Almost as if to prove his critics right, Stephan demanded a large severance package (according to Mihai, of one hundred thousand ETH) and blackmailed the foundation, threatening to release all the chat logs to regulators. Although no one had done anything illegal, they didn't want regulators to be able to spin up a tale based on their comments. (Stephan denies he did this but agrees he didn't take his firing well and felt strongly he'd been wronged. He says he told Ming it was bullshit.) Vitalik recalls that Ming, yelling at him, put the kibosh on his threat, warning him that doing so would be extremely risky not only for Ethereum but for himself as well. Stephan says he also received a legal letter stating he was under a strict nondisclosure agreement.

On September 3, while Vitalik, Ming, and Casey were at the cabin, Stephan published his final Ethereum Foundation blog post. After waxing poetic about how Ethereum was "both an idea and an ideal," he wrote, "Due to divergence in personal values, Eth/Dev and I have mutually decided to part ways."[9]

A DAY OR two after Anthony's Skype messages, Ming and Vitalik were working at Vitalik's parents' place. She began screaming, her high-pitched howling terrorizing the whole house. She shrieked that Vitalik had not accounted for all Ethereum's transactions and payments to developers. "You're going to go to jail!" she wailed. Vitalik joked, "At least I could do research and exercise in jail." Ming didn't calm down. Vitalik's stepmom, Maia, went down to where they were working. "What are you doing?" she said. "I can no longer stand this." Dmitry, watching his son fight back tears, was astounded. Ming, who was almost fifty, was supposed to help Vitalik, but instead the twenty-one-year-old was playing the adult.

To save money, Vitalik, Ming, and Casey drove to New York for a meeting with ConsenSys because Joe had offered to pay for DevCon 1. Joe had, by this point, gotten a number of people in New York excited about Ethereum. Its earliest offices at a coworking space in Bushwick, Brooklyn, were grungy, with murals lining the walls and hipsters roaming the halls. Everyone shared a massive box of Soylent. Before launch, people began snapping up GPUs (graphics processing units, which would be used to mine ether) to start mining the second the network went live. Once the company got its own offices in a heavily graffitied building nearby, they had a mini putt-putt green, and on Saturdays Joe sometimes played squash against the walls.

There, Vitalik, Casey, Ming, and a C++ dev met with Joe and his deputy, Andrew Keys. Before the meeting started, Andrew recalls Ming stuck her torso out the window to take a phone call with her dad and began screaming at him about a flight he was booking for her. The conversation over this flight became so intense that she began to cry. During the meeting, they agreed on terms that would enable DevCon 1 to happen in London in the second week of November. Perhaps because the foundation's coffers were so depleted or because organizing DevCon was her responsibility, Ming cried again. Some of the ConsenSys employees present found her breakdowns both before and during the meeting so bizarre that months later they would still be telling visitors to the office stories about the incidents. In the middle of her crying jag, she revealed she hadn't eaten anything either that day or the day before, so they went to a restaurant. Once there, Vitalik and Casey tried to feed her because she wasn't eating or taking her medicine. Whether because she was so emotional, or because of an increasing closeness after they had spent five days together in the cabin in Toronto, or because of something else entirely, at one point, on the way to or from the restaurant, Vitalik and Ming held hands.

ON SEPTEMBER 3, the week after the board meeting, Gavin incorporated Ethcore, his new start-up, in the United Kingdom. His plan was to make it like Joe's ConsenSys but focused more on software client development. He didn't see Ethcore as taking him away from Ethereum. He'd be at the foundation part-time, and the work would be the same. But now, he'd be funded by investment.

Another factor in Gav's decision to found Ethcore was that, since launch, Geth had become the most popular client, claiming 99 percent of the network. The C++ team was already behind because it aspired to have more features and also because the C++ client was still unaudited. Plus, with funds so low, there was a feeling that maybe the remaining resources should be allocated to Geth rather than to the C++ client. Gavin felt that even though he was CTO, he would never be able to speak for the Geth team, so a cleaner way forward would be to set up an external company.

Initially, Gav thought the founding members of Ethcore were supposed to include him, Vitalik, and Jeff in an equal partnership, along with Aeron and maybe Jutta. Years later, Jeff would say he didn't remember agreeing to be a founding member, unless Gavin was counting a time when he and Gavin, high on excitement about what they were building, made a brotherhood pact that, if Ethereum failed, they would start a company. When Gavin approached him about Ethcore, Jeff says Gavin had said Jeff would get shares but no decision-making authority, while Ethcore could claim the Go Ethereum creator was involved. Jeff said, "Thanks, but no thanks."

MEANWHILE, THAT FALL, Ming met with Jeff, Gavin, and some of the people who reported to them. Because money was tight, she had to decide (with Vitalik's blessing) between the C++ and Go teams. One of Gavin's employees, Christian Reitwießner, the main Solidity developer, expressed annoyance with Gavin's management style of keeping the team in the dark about higher-level decisions. He was especially miffed Gavin took all the credit as the creator of the smart contract language Solidity when he'd only thought it up. Meanwhile, Christian had done all the work, while Gavin had been jetting around.

At the end of September, Vitalik published a blog post telling the Ethereum community straight up, "the foundation's finances are limited, and a large part of this was the result of our failure to sell nearly as much of our BTC holdings as we were planning to before the price dropped to $220; as a result, we suffered roughly $9m in lost potential capital..."[10]

He explained the project's needs had grown to the point where the foundation and its subsidiaries were no longer sufficient to complete the project. Plus, at that moment, the value of ETH had been dropping so precipitously since mid-August that it had lost two-thirds of its value from the day he'd disbursed the presale allotments to early contributors. The foundation could run out of money in nine months. He said that made a community-driven model necessary and then detailed other entities' efforts to push Ethereum forward. The biggest one was a deal Vitalik brokered with a Chinese blockchain investment firm to purchase 416,666 ETH for $500,000, which was $1.19/ETH—a good deal since ETH had started September at about $1.35 but on the day Vitalik published his blog post closed at $0.58.[11] On October 21, ETH had sunk further—to $0.42. (Soaking up a lot of attention in the blockchain world at this time was the idea of banks using blockchain technology to make their operations more efficient—a trend captured with the slogan "Blockchain, not Bitcoin." A banking consortium called R3 had recently announced it would launch with nine members, including Goldman Sachs, JPMorgan, and Barclays, and on the day of Vitalik's blog post, it announced that thirteen more banks, including HSBC, Citi, and Deutsche Bank, were jumping in.[12] Headlines about R3 adding more and more banks dominated the blockchain world that fall, with stories about new members and early trials coming out that winter and spring.)

After interviewing team members, Ming decided to shrink Gavin's team but maintain Jeff's at the same level of resources. She began telling Vitalik she did not trust Gavin and believed he was swindling money from the foundation. She also found his salary unreasonable. Simultaneously, Ming told Vitalik that his being a board member of Ethcore would create a conflict of interest, although he later wouldn't remember why. Eventually, he relented and told Gavin he wouldn't be involved with Ethcore.

Then DevCon 1 happened between November 9 and 13. Set at Gibson Hall, a neoclassical building not far from Liverpool Station originally commissioned in the 1860s to be a bank, DevCon 1 attracted around four hundred attendees (including many bankers), featured speakers not only from Ethereum but also from UBS and Deloitte, and nabbed Microsoft as a sponsor.[13] Also, the software giant announced it would integrate Ethereum into its cloud computing offering, and Omise, the Thai payments company, made a $100,000 donation to the foundation's grants program. The atmosphere was electric. Developers showcased demos, such as one by Christoph Jentzsch, the C++ team developer who had created the tests trying to split the network and dropped out of his PhD program for Ethereum. He showed how one could use Ethereum to control a lock that would enable people to rent out belongings to people who had paid. While standing at his laptop, he created a transaction that turned on an electric kettle several feet away.[14] For those who'd thought they'd seen the last of Stephan Tual, he was now a cofounder at Christoph's start-up Slock.it. When the water began boiling, Stephan made a cup of tea for himself and an audience guest who requested a sugar cube. (The announcement about his joining Slock.it said Stephan "has an excellent standing within the community."[15])

Still, anxiety about the budget cuts dampened the conference. At least one person remembers some people crying. At one point, Jeff and Joe agreed that if the foundation no longer had money to pay its devs, the two of them would discuss how to continue the development of Go Ethereum. Joe told Jeff not to worry, that he and his team would be covered—if not by Joe/ConsenSys, then by someone else.

Fear of the budget-cutting Ming temporarily reunited Gav and Jeff. At a small coffee shop, they and another dev hung out, half-joking about creating a "Jedi Council"—an alternative Ethereum organization not controlled by Ming.

Vinay Gupta, who worked with Stephan Tual in London, had a party, during which Vitalik and Ming spent two hours alone in a room. Vitalik would later say they were likely working.

Before DevCon 1 was over, Ming went to Zug to help the Berlin office manager look in the Spaceship for receipts, invoices, and contracts that had not been organized. Though someone needed to do it, it wasn't clear why Ming, of all people, should undertake the task, especially during DevCon.

But her presence was still felt. Gavin threw a party during DevCon. Most attendees were his C++ client developers, and during the soiree, he told them the team would be reduced—he'd been told to cut the budget by 70 percent—and even those who stayed would have their salaries slashed. This was a complete surprise to some of his staff—it seemed incongruous that the foundation would hold a conference with only a few months' runway left. Additionally, the week before DevCon, Gavin, Jutta, and members of the communications team had done a tour of Asia; Jutta had gone to Singapore, and Gavin had gone to Tokyo and Seoul. This hardly seemed like the behavior of the CTO of an organization on its last legs. They were told they could be fired in a few months, which would be more beneficial for them than quitting, since they would then be eligible for Germany's unemployment insurance for a longer period.

The same evening, Gav invited each of them to join Ethcore. He even asked Felix Lange, who was on Jeff's team but worked in Berlin. One employee, who had not enjoyed working under him, found it strange that he was essentially firing them from the foundation with one hand and offering to hire them at Ethcore with the other. Another, who hadn't reported to him, was also asked to "join the dark side," as the dev put it. (Gavin says he doesn't remember firing anyone.)

Not realizing how some people viewed his actions, after DevCon, Gavin was eager to launch his start-up. Now that they'd built Ethereum, he thought it was time to get other projects within the ecosystem going and not to rely anymore on the cash-strapped foundation. By this point, Gav's arrangement with the foundation (i.e., Ming) was that he would retain a title, something like "ecosystem architect," but not be paid by the EF.

On Monday, November 23, at 12:12 p.m. Berlin time, Marek Kotewicz, one of Gavin's C++ developers, made the first GitHub commits, or snapshots of the codebase, for a new Ethereum client, one Gavin was planning to build using the Rust language, for Ethcore. Ethcore's website was also up, soliciting four senior and junior developers.[16]

In recent weeks, Ming had tried convincing Vitalik to let Gavin go, but Vitalik—whose whole life revolved around cryptocurrency broadly, if not Ethereum exclusively—was resistant. Even though Gavin berated him and could be dismissive (in the yellow paper, he credited Vitalik with proposing "the kernel" for it), Vitalik was still attached to this person who had, from the earliest days, helped turn his idea into reality. In his talks with Ming, both she and he would cry, as he had when he'd removed Charles and Amir. Armed with what she said was evidence that EF employees on payroll were contributing to Ethcore during working hours, she had enough ammunition to win over Vitalik.

Kelley, ETH Dev's COO, had just given birth in an emergency C-section, and she and her baby had been in the neonatal intensive care unit (NICU) for the previous week. Ming got the Berlin office manager to go to the hospital. There, in the NICU room, he handed Kelley, whose memory of this time is still blurred, papers to sign. One was Gav's termination letter.

5

December 2015 to June 17, 2016

GAVIN WAS CAUGHT off guard by his firing—especially as it had been executed by the "professional" executive director for whom he'd advocated. Feeling overwhelmed, he asked Jutta to help negotiate his exit. Although she would later leave the Ethereum Foundation for his start-up after returning from maternity leave, and although someone in a management position at ETH Dev says she would have been fired when Gavin was, at the time she was pregnant with the first of what would eventually become her and Gavin's two children, and Germany has strict worker protections for pregnant women. Over the next few weeks, as Ming was moving the EF out of the Spaceship into a small apartment in central Zug, she and Jutta emailed back and forth, while Gavin, Jutta, Vitalik, and Ming collaborated over memos announcing Gavin's departure. Even after primary Solidity developer Christian Reitwießner's claims, Gavin and Jutta insisted the memo replace "creator" with "lead developer" for Christian's role, "as it was Gavin who conceived and designed Solidity, and it was Christian who implemented it." Ming ended her emails with statements like "I hope we can all recharge and acclimate for a bright new year." But privately, she told Vitalik she thought Gavin had embezzled up to half a million dollars. (Gavin says he had no role in ETH Dev's finances, which were at that time handled by Aeron. When asked if she had ever presented him with any evidence or if he'd ever looked into it, Vitalik says he trusted Ming.)

Around the same time, Ming made a trip to the Berlin office. Gavin and Jutta were not around. Ming told the employees there the budget cuts were due not to a lack of funds but to misuse.

ON JANUARY 11, 2016, Gavin published what he titled "The last Blog Post" on the Ethereum blog, beginning it with the Pink Floyd quotation "The time is gone, the song is over, Thought I'd something more to say."

A draft that he never published began, "~~Ming fired me so I'm off to Thailand for the year.~~" The actual post began, "It is with no small amount of sadness that I must bid ye farewell. Like The Floyd's work, in the time I've been involved with Ethereum, I've sampled the full gamut of emotion." In a few brief paragraphs, he talked about "so many cool people" he met, naming ten, including Jeff, and saying he would do his best to support the C++ team. At the end, he wrote, "The road ahead is surely bumpy but we know what we have to do and the views, I expect, will be magnificent. Goodbye and thanks for all the fish." (Yet another reference to *The Hitchhiker's Guide to the Galaxy*.) Nowhere in the post did he mention Vitalik.[1]

ONCE GAVIN WAS gone, competition in the Berlin hub evaporated. Even C++ team members under Gavin were now friendly with Geth developers like Péter Szilágyi in Transylvania who, in turn, realized that the C++ crowd were normal people.

The EF's spending also got under control. Back on January 7, Vitalik posted on the Ethereum blog that it had cut its monthly expenses from €400,000 ($435,000) to €175,000 a month ($190,000) by, among other things, moving out of the Spaceship and cutting the C++ team by approximately 75 percent, Geth's budget by roughly 10 percent, communications by about 85 percent, and admin by around 50 percent.[2] At this point, it had 2.25 million

ETH (about $2.1 million), 500 BTC ($230,000), and $100,000 in fiat—roughly $2.4 million total—which, with their current budget, meant about a year of runway. (He did not mention that Lars, Wayne, and Vadim had left, leaving him the sole board member.)

Then, in late January, the Ethereum price finally ticked past the $1.69 it had been on the mid-August day of the disbursements to the early contributors. Shortly after that, it was at $2—almost four times its value of $0.58 in late September, when Vitalik told the community that, at that price, the foundation might have to close in nine months. Not only did the foundation have much more money than before, but $2 ETH made Ethereum the third most valuable blockchain, surpassing Litecoin, known as the silver to Bitcoin's gold.

At this point, some developers who had been let go were offered positions to return to the foundation (though not Gav). A new C++ hire, an Englishman living in Canada named Bob Summerwill, who joined in February, had actually been working for free since launch the previous summer. Back then, he'd noticed that whenever he asked a question of someone on the Go team, he got a response easily. But nobody on the C++ team ever replied. When he officially joined, he heard about the "Fortress Berlin" days when the two teams wouldn't talk, but with "egotistical" Gavin gone, things functioned peacefully.

But that was *within* the foundation. Now with Gavin at an outside company, the competition carried on—in public. On February 2, Ethcore blogged about its new client, Parity: "So with the latest benchmarks (available to see at parity.io), it's clear Parity has head and shoulders the fastest and lightest Ethereum block processing engine amongst the available clients."[3] One of Jeff's top deputies, Péter Szilágyi, examined the post and realized Ethcore had modified Geth to skip optimizations the Go team had put in place.[4] Then Ethcore compared that disadvantaged form of Geth against the new Parity, which he considered a "nasty move." He could accept if Gavin had legitimately built something better—but falsifying the numbers was something he could never forgive. Even Gavin's own employee, Marek Kotewicz, would admit that their tactics made it seem as if Parity were multiple times faster when in reality it was about 20 percent faster. But Gavin, who denied competing with Jeff's Go team while at the foundation, would later say that *this* was the point when competition between the Geth and Parity teams arose—because the Geth team saw Parity as a threat.

While the Go developers wouldn't have described things that way, they did say the Parity client created new problems: while it was a good Ethereum client, it did not follow the same spec, so developers interacted with the clients differently—not enough to cause a fork in the protocol but enough to create difficulties for the people building on top. And Parity refused to talk about how to reconcile those differences. (Gavin says, "Parity is and always was about developing and delivering the best technology, not about playing politics and fighting with other teams over 'standards.'")

All the issues with Gavin were still there. A year later, when Lefteris saw his former boss at a conference in Paris, he tried to talk about Gavin's battle with Christian over who had invented Solidity. Lefteris had seen that, from the beginning, Christian was the Solidity guy. He'd made the entire thing. Lefteris pointed out that Gavin could be credited with the yellow paper, the C++ client, and now the Parity client. Why did he have to also take the title for Solidity? Lefteris, who despite being a nonnative speaker speaks excellent English, recalled that Gavin "started to lecture me because of my not too good English," saying he was the inventor because he'd thought of it, and no matter who came after, he would always be the inventor, and the rest were just developers. Lefteris felt Gavin was looking down his nose at him. It pissed him off so much, he never spoke to Gav again.

But the foundation had more positive things to focus on. By mid-February, the price of ETH had shot up to $6. Ethereum was now the second-biggest blockchain, after Bitcoin, ahead of a bank-transfer coin called Ripple. The EF now had enough funding for a year or more. Then, on March 1, ETH hit $7. By mid-March, it was $15. Suddenly, the foundation had a couple years of runway. Around this time, the Bitcoin Suisse employee who'd brought a case of beer to the Spaceship cashed his four-thousand-ETH promissory note in for more than $10,000 and bought himself a nice watch.

Things were finally looking up for Ethereum. Vitalik felt relieved—he knew he had at least three years of runway. He did not know, however, that they were in for a bumpy ride.

CHRISTOPH JENTZSCH, THE C++ developer from Mittweida, Germany, who had, before launch, created the tests that aimed to fork the network, was now working on a new venture. Slock.it was an internet-of-things company to enable a blockchain-based, decentralized sharing economy. As he had demonstrated at DevCon 1 with the electric kettle, the Slock was a device that could be unlocked with an Ethereum transaction so that, for instance, the door to a decentralized Airbnb could open as soon as the guest paid.

Christoph, his older brother Simon, and Stephan Tual, who were cofounders, and two employees—Lefteris and an American from Seattle named Griff Green—needed funding for Slock.it. They could go the traditional route and look for venture funding. They could do a token sale, as Ethereum had. Or they could do something more interesting: sell a token that conferred voting rights. Even better, they decided, not only would they do that, but Slock.it would not raise the funds itself: the sale would create a decentralized autonomous organization (DAO) whose decisions would be controlled by its token holders, and *that* would pay Slock.it for developing the decentralized sharing economy. If Slock.it alone worked for the DAO, the DAO would function, in effect, like Slock.it's executive board. As Christoph explained at DevCon, "You fund the development, you are able to vote on major decisions, and very importantly, you control the funds... [T]he money will not just go to us." Slock.it, however, would hopefully become one of the first "service providers," or contractors, to the DAO.

Basically, people would send ether to the DAO and receive Slock tokens (later called DAO tokens), which would confer membership and voting rights in the DAO. "It's like buying shares in a company and getting actually dividends," he said. The dividends would come in one of two ways: for instance, if the DAO members did indeed hire Slock.it as a service provider, a Slock owner renting out his or her apartment could decide to automatically give the DAO owners either a certain percentage of or a flat fee for every transaction, with that figure set by the DAO. Those dividends would be paid out automatically on the blockchain.

Some of what inspired Christoph was a Web 3.0 talk Gavin had given in late 2014 on the concept of *alegality*, the state of being neither legal nor illegal. In the remarks, Gav had talked about how the current dominance of SaaS, or "software-as-a-service," products—such as companies using Eventbrite to sell tickets or Gmail for corporate email—would give way to what he called DsaaS, or "*decentralized* software-as-a-service," products. PayPal, for instance, was PayPal, Inc., an entity that employed people who could be sued by regulators, brought to court, or put in prison. He noted that there was no company called Bitcoin—that, as a DsaaS, it was more of a "force of nature."

"When you're creating new decentralized software as a service, you're actually kind of creating a whole new force of nature," Gav said. "In general, if they're properly implemented, these things cannot be shut down. Not by a court, not by a police force, not by nation-state...Forces of nature don't care about us, they don't care about our worries or our qualms or our insistence upon intellectual property laws..."[5] They are *alegal*.

In this new decentralized, alegal era, VC funding was old-fashioned—and centralized. (And legal.) In order to create this alegal force of nature, Slock.it said it would create the code for the

DAO smart contract for free, and once it launched, anyone could make a proposal to the DAO to try to get funding from it, which really meant from its members. Although Christoph said Slock.it would like to work for the DAO, the DAO token holders would decide. Slock.it planned to release version 1.0 of the code and then stop work on the DAO, leaving it to become a force of nature.

After DevCon 1 in November 2015, Christoph and Lefteris began programming the DAO in earnest.[6] They projected it would take them one month; it took them until spring. Christoph, because he'd worked on the C++ team, worked only half time at the EF in December. In order to build the DAO before starting Slock.it, he was living on savings. The company had no backup plan in case DAO token holders decided not to fund Slock.it. Meanwhile, Lefteris was paid €500 a month, a minimum part-time salary for 10 hours of work a week, based on the premise that after Slock.it got DAO funding, *then* the company would give him a normal salary, plus back pay. As a cofounder, Stephan earned nothing. And since Griff only wanted crypto, and Slock.it could not pay its employees that way, he also made no money.

TO GET UP and running, the DAO—which was really *a* DAO, since "DAO" was a generic term for any decentralized autonomous organization—needed human help.[7] As Stephan described it in an April 9 blog post, one group providing it consisted of "contractors," who would submit proposals to develop products or services. A proposal would consist of a smart contract, plus a "plain English description."

Another group of people, "curators," would validate that contractors' smart contracts did what the description said they would.[8] If a contract passed muster, the curators would authorize, or "whitelist," that contractor's Ethereum address to receive ether from the DAO.

DAO token holders might vote on things like whether to approve a contractor's proposal.[9] The minimum quorum required

would be proportional to the proposal's monetary value, ranging from 20 percent for proposals spending no money up to 53.5
percent to spend all the DAO's money. Approval of the proposal
would require a simple majority.

Another kind of proposal was a split, which could be used to
create a new venture fund that could fund different ideas than the
main DAO, but the most important reason to split was to leave
the DAO—to remove one's funds. Splitting required a seven-day
proposal, which would create a new DAO, often called a child
DAO or split DAO, and move into it all the ETH backed by all
the tokens of those who had voted for the split. If the DAO was
the mothership, a split or child DAO was like a lifeboat, and the
seven-day waiting period was like the time it took to lower the
lifeboat into the water. As one could imagine, the one DAO would
eventually splinter into many.

To participate in the DAO, you needed to send ETH to the
DAO smart contract during the DAO creation period. (This
would be like if, to create a new venture capital fund, you could
only participate if you bought shares during a certain window.)
The DAO tokens would give you a right to vote on proposals in
proportion to the number you held, as well as a proportional right
to DAO "rewards" from the revenue brought in by approved contractor proposals. (This would be like your VC fund shares also
giving you influence over what the fund invested in and the number of shares you had representing your voting power, as well as
your cut of the profits.)

Discussing the way it worked in the Slack channel, one member
commented it was "crazy" that Slock.it's proposal would come *after*
the token sale. "That's like saying to a VC 'Give me some cash and
we'll give you a business plan after, maybe.'"

THOUGH THE RULES of the DAO, as complicated as they were,
were spelled out, what the DAO actually was remained unclear.
Christoph would later describe it as "a joint bank account" owned

by thousands of people or founders of a company that could not do any work itself and could simply commission other entities to do work for it. He would say Slock.it's legal point of view was that creating the DAO was the same as gathering thousands of founders to create a company that didn't need to register with the Securities and Exchange Commission. Slock.it's other cofounders had slightly different conceptions, with self-described "crazy anarchist" Griff thinking of it more as a nonprofit governing body for the universal sharing economy that he was obsessed with—one that would allow him to be a nomad who lived out of a backpack and to rent things he needed on occasion. Lefteris and Stephan described it as a traditional company, except with token holders operating a smart contract at the center, which would return profits to them.

Regardless, many people in the community and would-be investors/participants viewed it as a "decentralized venture fund"—for which a buyer did not need to be an "accredited investor," defined in the United States as someone who makes more than $200,000 a year ($300,000 for joint income) or has a net worth of more than $1 million (individually or jointly). As such, the DAO was the first global, decentralized venture fund open to anyone, from any country, rich or poor, young or old, experienced or naive, who had access to the internet.

EXCITEMENT ABOUT THE DAO was building. Back in February, the DAO Slack had started seven foreign-language channels. (The Polish one was the most active.) By late March, the DAO's general Slack channel had nearly three thousand members. Some active Slack members took it upon themselves to create a forum, launching daohub.org, by April 3.[10] Around this time, other token sales were bringing in respectable sums of money, with both blockchain platform Lisk and DigixDAO, a decentralized autonomous organization for tokenizing physical assets, raising more than $5 million.

But Slock.it was experiencing a few hiccups. First, its lawyers said what it was doing—mostly the selling of tokens—was not legal. One US lawyer, who got the impression Slock.it wanted to launch the DAO before the biggest US blockchain conference, Consensus, began on May 2—Christoph denies this because Consensus isn't considered an important conference for the Ethereum community—said if they allowed US investors to participate, they would need a securities lawyer, an engagement that would take six months. At that point Slock.it stopped responding to that attorney's communications—because, Christoph says, it had all the information it needed. But Christoph felt the idea the DAO tokens were securities did not make sense, since Slock.it was not selling the tokens. The DAO was a different organization, and it would pay Slock.it. The company was not selling shares of itself. After a discussion with lawyers in Germany and Switzerland, Christoph came away with a different understanding: people could buy DAO tokens without a problem, but if they later wanted to sell them, the tokens would become, in effect, securities—which meant they needed to comply with a whole suite of regulations, the very thing he had been trying to avoid.

With the legal implications of the presale unclear, Stephan took to starting blog posts with disclaimers like "It is important to remember that anyone who uses DAO code will do so at their own risk. We can't speculate about the legal status of DAOs worldwide."[11] On Slack, Griff wrote, in reference to the DAO crowdsale, "We stopped calling it a presale months ago because the DAO is going to be made live on the blockchain, no one is preselling anything…When someone fuels a DAO by sending it ETH during its Creation Phase, new DAO tokens are created **in that moment**… This is hardly a sale, it is truly an act of DAO Creation!"

Regardless, in Slack, people kept asking when the presale would happen. Two interested DAO investors in Neuchatel, Switzerland, Gian Bochsler and Alexis Roussel, noticed that Slock.it kept demurring. Alexis finally called Stephan to ask why. Speaking in their native French, Stephan explained that the German tax authority told Slock.it a company could not receive funding from an organization that had no legal standing. Alexis was the cofounder of Bity, a place to buy, sell, and trade bitcoin, ether, and DAO tokens. Alexis—who had a law degree, was previously president of the Pirate Party Switzerland, a political party focused on digital rights and privacy, and had worked at the United Nations for nearly five years—interpreted the German tax authority's problem as, if Slock.it got funded by the DAO, there would be "nothing to put in the VAT field."

The day after their phone call, Simon, Christoph's brother and the CEO of Slock.it, came to Neuchatel to work out a solution. Alexis determined that, under Swiss law, the structure of the entity with whom you are transacting is immaterial; if he, she, or it has the ability to pay you, you two can enter into commerce. They decided to make a Swiss proxy called DAO.link, whose VAT number could be put on German tax documents. If Slock.it's proposal to the DAO was approved, then the DAO could pay the funds to DAO.link, which would in turn pay Slock.it.

ON APRIL 21, the DAO's website, at daohub.org, launched.[12] The homepage read, "THE DAO IS," followed by an electric-tangerine cursor. Moved by an invisible hand, it finished the thought:

THE DAO IS REVOLUTIONARY.
THE DAO IS AUTONOMOUS.
THE DAO IS REWARDING.
THE DAO IS CODE.

Underneath sat a line graph showing an overall trend: up and to the right.

The homepage said, "The DAO's Mission: To blaze a new path in business organization for the betterment of its members, existing simultaneously nowhere and everywhere and operating solely with the steadfast iron will of **unstoppable code**."[13]

By the time of launch, the fine print at the bottom would read, "This website is owned by the DAO community, it is managed by the DAOhub team and hosting is generously offered by dao.link Sarl, Switzerland." (Read: *SEC, it's not owned by Slock.it, so don't come after us!*[14])

In the blog post about the website launching, Stephan noted the Slack group now had almost four thousand members; he pointed to one of the first proposals that would likely be submitted to the DAO—to build self-renting electric urban vehicles—and encouraged readers to submit their own on the daohub.org forum.

Stephan also mentioned the DAO's code had been audited by "one of the most prestigious security companies in the world, Deja Vu." The blog also noted, "Vitalik presented a couple of days ago at the London Ethereum Meetup. Most of his engaging presentation...focused on DAOs, warning against the dangers of badly written smart contracts, careless crypto-entrepreneurs and DAOs that are...well, not really DAOs at all."[15]

ONE SECTION OF the website, still unfinished at launch, was the curator section. Stephan and Christoph had invited well-known names—mostly Ethereum Foundation developers—to be curators, saying their duty was to check people's identities and make sure that if an entity, say, Slock.it, submitted a payment request, the account requesting it was indeed Slock.it's. In cryptocurrency parlance, they would serve as "oracles"—agents that verify non-blockchain-based information for use by a smart contract.

One curator, Fabian Vogelsteller, the full-stack designer who had worked with both Jeff's and Gav's teams, felt that since curators only whitelisted the correct addresses, his role was simply "doorman, not DJ." Gavin found the main responsibility to be like "maths," in that the correct answer could be proven.

Four days after announcing the website, Slock.it named the curators, with Stephan calling them "the Who's Who of crypto" in a blog post. The site's curator page featured large black-and-white headshots of all eleven,[16] causing Gavin to do a double take: *If I'm just here to make sure that an utterly simple assertion is correct, why is my photo being used, and why am I called a curator? A curator selects and chooses things, they don't just do basic oracle work.*

One invited curator had held out: Jeff. He'd considered accepting but felt if he took responsibility for anything, he could also be accused of something. Plus, the DAO made him nervous because there was no limit on how much money it could raise. He told Stephan, "Cap it, please. Because if you fuck up, you're going to fuck up good, and there's so much interest in it. Please cap it." Stephan reassured Jeff it would be fine. Before the Ethereum crowdsale, Stephan had advocated for a cap but been overruled. He later felt he had been wrong and so was now against one for the DAO. But Jeff responded, "If it's not going to be fine, you're going to lose so much money, and it's going to look very bad for Ethereum."

But the Slock.it team was against a cap. Griff, for instance, felt that capped token sales, such as those for MaidSafe, which focused on securing data, or Digix, finished quickly, leading them to be less decentralized and to exclude people who weren't the most rabid crypto enthusiasts. In Slack, he pointed out that, for the Digix crowdsale, he had been on the West Coast and so it was over before he'd woken up. He also worried that if a whale maxed out the cap, then the whale could split from the DAO (take all the money into a lifeboat), and leave them with nothing. Then he added, "I think people forget that this is a very different set up than a normal presale or crowdsale. All the DAO Token Holders have control of their share of the assets at all times, because of the split possibility"; he was referring to DAO token holders' ability to leave the DAO at any time by splitting or creating a child DAO.

In the end, the eleven curators were nine people from the Ethereum Foundation, including Vitalik, the Brazilian designer Alex van de Sande (Avsa), Christian Reitwießner, who had written

Solidity and been central to Gavin's firing, Taylor Gerring from the Spaceship, and others; the only two nonfoundation people were Gav and his buddy and business partner Aeron Buchanan of Ethcore, both of whom had just left the EF.

WHILE CHRISTOPH AND Lefteris were coding, a passionate community was forming—ranging from skilled devs to complete crypto newbs. Not only did the Slack have several thousand extremely chatty members, but Griff, the community lead, had gotten engineers on board by paying people who completed a DAO ninja test to learn how to submit proposals to the DAO.

Additionally, Slock.it went around to the exchanges and convinced Kraken, Gatecoin, Bity, ShapeShift, and Bittrex to use code that enabled people to buy DAO tokens with many fiat currencies, such as US dollars, euros, Swiss francs, and Hong Kong dollars, not just digital currencies.[17] This opened the door to complete crypto newbs.

Similarly, MyEtherWallet, a website that enabled people to directly interact with the Ethereum blockchain with simple buttons but did not require them to turn over control of their coins to a company, set up an option on the site that would enable people to participate in the DAO without having an exchange hold their tokens.[18] It was the digital equivalent of having a wallet, paying with cash, and putting the DAO tokens right back in your billfold—all with a web page.

ON APRIL 26, the day after announcing the curators, Slock.it made public the establishment of DAO.link, the company Slock.it had set up with Bity. The DAO's smart contract had been audited, eighteen people whom Christoph highly respected, including Vitalik, had looked at the code, and Christoph himself had tested it several times for worst-case scenarios. At this point, Christoph felt, they had done all they could do. But, he felt, if something went wrong, people could split. As long as that function worked, people could get their money out, and the whole thing could be undone.

It was time to launch the DAO, which, in order to follow the principle of decentralization (and not trip all four prongs of the Howey test, which could bring the SEC's wrath), meant getting community members to deploy instances of the DAO smart contract code they'd written and then having the community decide which one of those would be labeled *the* DAO. To "create" the DAO, someone would just need to initiate the first transaction to it—that is, send in ether, which would trigger a return to that person of DAO tokens. That way, the DAO's creation could not be pinpointed back to any one individual or group—it would be a digital immaculate conception.

On April 29, Taylor Van Orden, one of the creators of MyEther-Wallet, posted in Slack, "Hey everyone. If you want to deploy the DAO, check out this thread. We're going to pick a random one from this thread to be **the official DAO** very soon. Get yourself some untraceable / no history coins (ShapeShift, btc mixer, etc) and deploy." Then, in the private Slack channel where Slock.it and other high-ranking community members discussed management-type issues, they assessed the eight deployed instances of the DAO. It took them two hours, but they finally got it down to two optimal DAOs—both deployed fairly anonymously. One had gotten its money from the crypto-to-crypto exchange ShapeShift, which did not take account information, and the other had been funded from the San Francisco–based exchange Kraken, which had identifying information about its customers but would never reveal it without a court order.

What they liked about the ShapeShift one was that its "blockie," or identicon, was a rounded, turquoise square containing a brown heart that had come untied at its base, like a bag with a hole in the bottom.

On Slack, Taylor and her companions decided to leave the final decision up to chance. In their downtown Los Angeles loft, Taylor got her fiancé, Kevin, to do a coin toss while she took a video. In

Slack, she wrote, "heads = 011, tails – BB," referring to the hashes for each instance of the DAO, which began 0x011 and 0xbb, respectively. Kevin, in a red, long-sleeved sweater, his nails painted dark red and two fingers sporting silver rings, flicked a dime into the air. It hit the counter, once, twice, three times, and then circled briefly before stopping: tails.

The "BB" instance of the DAO was the ShapeShift-funded one, the one with the blockie that, as a blog post put it, "looks like a mix between an open heart and a space invader."[19] Now that they knew where to point people, they could launch. That particular DAO had been instantiated at block number 1428757 on the Ethereum blockchain at 3:42 a.m. Berlin time on April 30.[20]

AT 12:04 P.M. Berlin time, ch405 posted in the Slack channel, "IT IS ON!" and then sent a link to daohub.org, which now pointed to the instance of the chosen DAO and featured a world map in the middle and, on either side, counters for stats such as DAO tokens created, total ETH, USD equivalent, the current rate of one ETH per one hundred DAO tokens, days until next price change, and days left until the presale ended on May 28 at 9:00 GMT. Then it gave instructions on how to receive DAO tokens.

Within fifteen minutes, seven transactions from five different accounts had come in, for 2 ETH, 3.1415926 ETH, 5 ETH, 5 ETH, 42 ETH, 83 ETH, and 500 ETH. Later, on the community Slack, something bigger happened:

Erik Voorhees 12:37 PM
Someone just deposited 9k ETH
Taylor 12:38 PM
Just saw my balance SHOOT up.
12:38
Wow!
Africanos23 12:38 PM
this is going to be HUGE

It was huge. In fact, on the first day alone, the DAO received 564,858 ETH, or $4.2 million. On the second day, it received $4.9 million. One person alone put in $2 million worth of ETH on May 1, first sending 1 ETH, then 50,000, then 75,000, then 135,000, and finally 5.5555—plus another 54,000 a couple weeks later.[21] The next day, the DAO's Twitter account posted a meme of an aggressive-looking Shia LaBeouf with the phrase "JUST DAO IT"—but the encouragement wasn't necessary.[22] According to a May 6 blog post by Stephan Tual, the birth of the DAO led to the highest number of new accounts on Ethereum and the highest number of Ethereum transactions ever.[23]

Back when he and Lefteris had been coding it up, Christoph had thought the DAO might raise $5 million. Since Ethereum had garnered $18 million, he thought it would never receive more than that. Another anticipated crowdsale from the previous fall, for Augur, had taken in $5 million, and some other recent ones had also picked up $5 million apiece. Christoph figured, with five thousand members on Slack, if each person gave $1,000, that would generate $5 million. But when the raise hit nearly that on the first day, he realized it could get quite a bit bigger.

By this point, Christoph was on a two-week break. After having worked on the DAO since DevCon 1 in November, he needed to unwind. But when the DAO hit $5 million on the second day and continued to climb, he could not relax. He realized, now, things were serious.

On May 6, the seventh day of the sale, it surpassed the amount the Ethereum crowdsale had raised.[24] Even Vitalik had thrown coins in. The next day, The DAO Project's official Twitter account tweeted, "The #DAO now has 3% of ALL #ETH in existence!!"[25] The day after that, the @DAOhubORG account, which belonged to the community members who had created the DAO forum, tweeted a screenshot of the homepage featuring the stats "2.87 M total ETH, 27.15 M USD equivalent" and commented, "This is going to be the most epic crowdfunding project in history."[26]

To incentivize early participation, the price of DAO tokens had been set to slowly increase over time. Midway through, it rose by 0.05 ETH per one hundred DAO tokens per day until it reached a price of 1.5 ETH per one hundred DAO tokens for the final five days of the sale.

After the first two days of more than $4 million in ETH each, the money coming in tapered off slightly. For several days, amounts ranging from $1.8 million to over $3.4 million came in, but before the price hike, the amount coming in jumped up, surpassing $26.8 million on the fourteenth day, which was supposed to be the last chance to get one hundred DAO tokens for one ETH.

But the price didn't increase after the fourteenth day as Slock.it had advertised. It increased after the fifteenth—*another day at the cheapest price!*—which allowed them to rake in $21.2 million in twenty-four hours. They had counted wrong, though at least one commenter jumped to a conspiracy theory: "And we're supposed to believe this was an honest mistake?...You f#@kers are even greedier than I thought."[27] A Redditor wrote, "This is the first evidence of a bug in the contract. Are you sure the contract was scrutinized enough?"[28]

On May 6, Stephan published a blog post titled "The Inexorable Rise of The DAO." It began,

> As I write this article, "The DAO" has become the second largest holder of ether on the planet (overtaking the Ethereum Foundation in the process) with 2,289,016 ETH.
>
> Fun fact: that's over 38% of all ETH in all Ethereum contracts combined. And just a few hours ago, it zoomed past Pebble, Prison Architect and even Ethereum, landing at a mind-boggling third position in the list of the world's highest funded crowdfunding projects in history with an historical **USD 21.96M** equivalent.

By the end of May 14, the last day at the one hundred DAO per ETH price, the DAO had raised $98.8 million. It also may have pushed up the ETH price, which at the DAO's launch was around $7.50. It was just under $12 when the DAO closed on May 28—a jump of 60 percent.

AS THE DAO hoovered up ETH, the Slock.it team felt mixed emotions. Christoph distanced himself. His mental state was "leave me alone." Lefteris, who had put just $500 in the DAO (he felt weird putting his savings into the vehicle that was supposed to fund his salary), at first thought it was funny how big the DAO was getting. But he also felt good since some of it would hopefully go to Slock.it. Stephan agreed it was great Slock.it could potentially have a lot more money, but he was less impressed because he'd been through this with Ethereum. Griff was excited about what he considered the first real DAO and thought Slock.it was killing it.

Like Christoph, Gavin, watching the ballooning DAO, felt queasy. On May 13, he published a blog post titled "Why I've Resigned as a Curator of the DAO." He began with an intro that explained that the DAO was decentralized and autonomous, and because the "curator" role required no judgment, the title should instead be "identity oracle." He said that service as a curator should not be seen as an endorsement and that he'd agreed to the role precisely because it was limited in scope. In fact, he said, confusion over the role's purpose had caused him "unnecessary faff." Then he wrote,

> To make it as clear as possible that I, and indeed any, individual is irrelevant to the DAO's operation, I have rescinded my position as "curator". I urge all those who have placed Ether under the DAO to look beyond the faces and research the structure of the contract and understand properly what agreement your funds are tied to. Obviously,

you should seek professional advice before acting. Don't
forget: In this case, it is the code which rules; the faces
don't matter a jot.[29]

CHRISTOPH WAS PREOCCUPIED by the fact that the DAO
could never be stopped. Like Bitcoin and Ethereum, it started and
was supposed to exist forever. He realized the project would hang
over his whole life and might one day become something he hated.
He thought of a poem, "The Sorcerer's Apprentice," by Goethe,
about starting something small that gets bigger and bigger until
you no longer have control over it. One of the last lines is "Spirits
I have conjured, no longer pay me heed."[30] After his break, he just
responded to emails, ignoring many messages from people saying
they had lost tokens or money, often because they had mistyped
and sent money to an address with nothing behind it. But receiving
these notes made him realize that the DAO participants weren't
ETH insiders. Many were mainstream people who had no clue
what to do with a technology that didn't have an easy user interface but instead required them to deal with things like JavaScript
Object Notation (JSON) files and interact directly with a contract
on the Ethereum blockchain.

Many of them may not have understood what the DAO was.
When Avsa gave talks about the DAO, the audience would not
even know the difference between the DAO and Ethereum. After
he'd explain it, they'd respond, "Soooo…you're working for a big
company that gives money to people." He would have to go over it
again: it was decentralized, with no CEO and no employees—just
a smart contract operating by a set of coded bylaws. He loved to
show his laptop screen, deploy a DAO, and show how one could
use it to vote and move money from one place to another transparently. He would joke that in one hundred lines of code he was
building a democracy, but one better than just any democracy, because everyone could see the rules.

GIVEN THE CLUNKY user interface, what the crowdsale accomplished was incredible: upon closing on May 28, the DAO had more than 11.7 million ETH—14.6 percent of all ETH in existence.[31] That totaled $139.4 million. It was the largest crowdfunding event in history.[32]

A huge amount of money came in from the crypto exchanges—871,000 ETH from Poloniex alone via 10,269 transactions. But the whales sent from their own wallets—one whale who withdrew 2 million ETH from Poloniex to his or her own wallet sent 315,000 ETH into the DAO.[33] (That one person contributed as much as 36 percent of all Polo's customers.)

So much more money poured into the DAO than any previous crowdsale had raised in part because, by this point, the crypto space not only had Bitcoin millionaires but, with ETH at $12, also many Ethereum millionaires. They were hungry for more returns, and because the split DAO (lifeboat) function would enable them to withdraw their money at any time, many of them thought, as one user tweeted, "#theDAO is a risk-free investment."[34]

On May 25, a few days before the crowdsale ended, Stephan Tual published a blog post called "DAO.Security, a Proposal to guarantee the integrity of The DAO."[35] Since, by this point, such a large percentage of all ETH resided in the DAO smart contract, Slock.it proposed a DAO Security group. It wanted to establish a monitoring unit of two to three "expert security analysts resources," including Christoph, to "continuously monitor, preempt and avert any potential attack vectors the DAO may face, including social, technical and economic attacks." The total cost was about $1.6 million, based on that day's ETH price.

The community was outraged. As one Redditor put it, "Slock is trying to loot the DAO. If the DAO 'only' had $10 million they would've made a proposal for $100K. But they're want $1.5 million for a part-time job!"[36]

Other Redditors criticized the penny-pinchers, saying that those making $45,000 a year "FINALLY have a shot to compete with the big boys [VCs], and you guys want to get all cheap and shit." Slock.it ultimately went back to the drawing board and the next day published another proposal: to have one full-time expert covering DAO security for eight thousand ETH (around $99,000) for one year.

THE NEXT DAY, a day before the crowdsale ended, a Cornell professor prominent in the cryptocurrency space, Emin Gün Sirer, along with Ethereum Foundation researcher Vlad Zamfir and Dino Mark, an entrepreneur who also collaborated with ConsenSys's Joe Lubin, published a blog post titled "A Call for a Temporary Moratorium on The DAO."[37] In it, they wrote about seven game theoretical ways in which the DAO might be attacked strategically so that "honest DAO investors [would] have their investments hijacked or committed to proposals against their interest and intent." Essentially, due to the DAO's rules, they asserted people were more inclined to vote yes on proposals even if they weren't in favor. The paper's findings were chronicled on May 27 in the *New York Times*.[38]

Worried that the DAO's structure would not lead to informed decisions, the Slock.it team looked into making an upgrade for free but realized passing it would require a 53.3 percent minimum quorum.[39] With the tooling then available, and because so many DAO token holders were complete crypto novices, this would be nearly impossible. They thought, *Oh, we built a bank vault, got a bunch of people to put money in it, and now the door is closed.* In a *CoinDesk* article, Stephan was quoted as saying, "You don't want a bad story about Ethereum. If [the DAO] were to crash, people would compare it to Mt. Gox," the exchange that had suffered the largest crypto hack ever.[40]

DAO token holders began submitting proposals anyway. Those that did not spend money had a lower threshold for voting—only a 20 percent quorum was needed. But even that appeared unreachable. Unlike the DAO itself, which saw a lot of activity from day one, the first proposal had 0.01 percent of the necessary votes on the first day of voting. The moratorium on the DAO until the contract was upgraded also needed just a 20 percent minimum quorum, but on the first day it had only 0.02 percent of the needed votes.

Another issue with the DAO's structure came up: taking one's money out was too hard. It required creating a split child DAO, which took technical knowledge, and waiting different periods of time for various deadlines to pass. Lefteris had proposed an instant withdrawal function, in which the user's DAO tokens would be burned and his or her ETH would be promptly returned.[41] Griff protested such a move would only help day traders. Lefteris suggested that those who wished to withdraw immediately could pay a fee; others could withdraw for free by choosing a delayed withdrawal. A community member wrote back, "Changing the rules to the detriment of investors is a very bad idea that would invite legal action."[42]

Behind the scenes, curator Vlad Zamfir says (and two curators affirm, though another says this wasn't a formal arrangement), he got a majority of the curators to agree not to whitelist any proposals for the time being—effectively instituting a moratorium. However, the curators did not want to announce it publicly. This decentralized project was not supposed to have a centralized control point.

And so, in this way, arguments over what to do about the flawed DAO sprawled across Slack, Reddit, GitHub, the DAOhub forum, and Twitter.

IN THE EARLY morning of Friday, June 17, among the wildflowers and grassy meadows of the small German town of Mittweida, in Christoph's parents' three-story house, in a top-floor bedroom, lay a sleeping Griff Green.

Six-foot-three, with long brown hair punctuated with a flat widow's peak at one end and a man bun at the other, a sloping forehead, a prominent brow, and a beard, Griff was an unusual person to be working in an industry centered around money. During the financial crisis, Griff had experienced his own disaster: the sale of the Seattle SuperSonics basketball team and its transformation into the Oklahoma City Thunder. Back then, he was a chemical engineer for a biopharmaceutical company, where he genetically engineered hamster cells, and a rabid SuperSonics fan. His bleached hair was shaved into a mohawk, and the roots were the team's signature color, green. He sported Hulk gloves and green- and gold-colored plastic jewels and only wore Sonics Gear. If they ever lost, he would be in mourning the next day. The team's impending move spurred him to help found an organization, Save Our Sonics, to keep them in Seattle. When that failed, since he was already interested in libertarianism and Austrian economics, he decided to exit the economy. His company was undergoing layoffs, so he volunteered. He was twenty-four.

He was on unemployment for a while, but even when he'd been a chemical engineer, he had transacted in gold and silver. He would take his paycheck to the Northwest Territorial Mint, turn it into gold and silver nuggets, and get dollars by selling to friends from the Seattle Austrian Economics Reading Group. He went full-on hippie, eating raw vegan and losing one hundred pounds. Eventually, in 2011, after his unemployment ended, he closed his bank account, sold everything he owned, bought a van, and checked out Burning Man. Then he exchanged the van for money and said good-bye to the United States (coming back only for his brothers' birthdays and Burning Man). He traveled to South America, spent a lot of time in Ecuador, and then went to Thailand, where he bought Bitcoin for the first time.

From the start, because of his fascination with money, Griff liked alt-coins. They embodied his philosophy that the story of money could be rewritten to have other meanings. He was fascinated by how Namecoin was a coin for censorship-resistant domain registration, and Primecoin was a system for discovering prime numbers. He began buying alt-coins like Litecoin, Namecoin, Peercoin, Feathercoin, Terracoin, and so forth, but lived off his savings from the appreciation of gold, his chemical engineering earnings, and his unemployment checks.

At one point, when he was in Los Angeles doing Thai massage, Litecoin went from $2 to $40, netting him $17,000. *That was a year of living expenses!* During a short-lived stint trying to become "the Bitcoin guy for Ecuador," he completed a master's in digital currency from the University of Nicosia and wrote his thesis on a bike-sharing economy that functioned via decentralized autonomous corporations. The motivation? He wanted to contribute to a world in which he could backpack around but wear nice shoes to a wedding without owning a pair.

After hearing about Slock.it, he emailed the company multiple times with his paper, a video of himself, and an offer to work for free. He became Slock.it's first employee.

Now, here he was nine months later, having helped create the largest crowdfunding campaign in history. The day before, ether had seen its highest-volume trading.[43] And because ETH, on the morning of June 17, was reaching a new high of $21.52 while he slept, the current value of the DAO was $249.6 million.

AT 7 OR 8 a.m. Berlin time, Griff woke up and checked his phone. He had a message from a Slack community member named Mo who said something weird was happening with the DAO—it looked like funds were being drained. Griff checked: there was a stream of 258-ETH ($5,600) transactions leaving the DAO. *Oh shit.*

He called the other Slock.it members. Mo got ahold of Christoph's brother, Simon, and Griff implored him to tell Christoph asap. "I don't care what you have to do—you might have to drive to his house," he said.

Christoph had, as usual, been up late since he often worked with people in the United States. He was woken by his wife. Simon was calling. Christoph got on the phone. Simon said, "Something strange is happening with the DAO. Please have a look," and sent him a link to Etherscan, a website that provides data on the Ethereum blockchain. Christoph got his laptop and went downstairs. Although he could not immediately figure out what was happening, he knew someone had split from the main DAO, and something was very wrong. Thousands of people around the world who had invested in the DAO were losing money—258 ETH at a time. His gut said, *Game over.* In a way, he felt relieved.

For a moment, in an open carpeted area in his small office, he laid down, hands folded behind his head. Around him, the walls were white. One small window let in light.

6

June 17, 2016, to June 21, 2016

CHRISTOPH DECIDED THAT with God and his wife, he could handle anything. He got up from his office floor to notify the Ethereum Foundation and corral Stephan and Griff, the megaphones to the world. He, Simon, and Lefteris tried to figure out how the attack worked and what could be done.

In Shanghai, Vitalik got a Skype message from an Ethereum community member about the attack at around 3 p.m. local time, about an hour after Griff woke up. The community member asked if this could be a hack. Vitalik thought, *Ninety-nine percent chance it's totally fine.* But then he saw the balance was 9 million ETH and change, down from 11.7 million.

Meanwhile, at 8:15 a.m. Berlin time, Griff posted in the DAOhub forum, "@channel EMERGENCY ALERT! IF YOU HAVE A SPLIT OPEN PLEASE DM A SLOCK.IT MEMBER ASAP!!!" He posted a similar message in the Slack channel.

The responses were not promising:

uh oh
What is going on?
Oh shit
Plop
What does it mean to have a split open? A proposal for a split?

Eventually, Taylor Van Orden explained, "Shhhh. If you have initiated a split and it's currently open, message @griff. If you don't know what a split is then don't worry."

Meanwhile, Christoph, Simon, Vitalik, and the others hopped on Skype calls and created a few Skype groups with all the old faces—Lefteris, Vitalik, Gav, Jeff, Aeron Buchanan, Péter Szilágyi, Christian Reitwießner, Avsa, Taylor Gerring, Fabian Vogelsteller, and so on. They tried to discern the method of attack to be able to counterattack and recover the coins.

Several of them jumped into a Skype group with exchange operators, where Vitalik wrote,

possible mitigation strategies are:

1. seizing any stolen either that goes through exchanges
2. there is one person who will split within 2 hours

if we can contact him
then we may be able to copy the attack and recover a large portion of it

Vitalik was referring to the fact that the DAO attacker had used a split DAO to perform the attack. It was as if, had the DAO been a ship, the attacker had launched his or her attack from a lifeboat in the water. If developers trying to fight the attacker could find another lifeboat to enter, they could perform a similar attack so as to drain the funds themselves and keep them away from the attacker. Since it took a week from initiating a split DAO to being able to put tokens in one, they were looking for one either already open or about to open.

An Ethereum communications team member, George Hallam, wrote, "ALL EXCHANGES: please pause ether trading as soon as possible."

This was a serious measure. It would stop the attacker from being able to cash out his or her stolen ETH but punish ETH traders who wanted to sell, costing them the ability to take profits before the ETH price dropped based on the news. But Dino Mark, an Ethereum insider, posted, "The ethereum foundation can reimburse exchange losses. Without a hard fork and rollback this damage will be permanent and the ecosystem will die."

The mention of a rollback put the exchange operators on alert. A rollback was like an undo—reneging on the inviolable blockchain principle of immutability. This principle made a blockchain different from any old database. Bitcoin, the blockchain with which many people were most familiar, was a time-stamped ledger chained to earlier versions of itself by cryptography. It was impossible to change a past transaction without breaking the mathematical link between older versions of the ledger and more recent ones.

But Dino defended himself: "This happened with Bitcoin in 2013. Exchanges rolled back trades." (He was referring to an incident in 2013, when an upgraded version of the Bitcoin software was incompatible with the previous version, causing the chain to fork in two. To resolve the issue, developers decided to support the older version, the path of least resistance; they had to contact exchanges, mining operators, merchants, and other large Bitcoin operators to resolve it.[1])

Dino had also mentioned another term, "hard fork," that could be innocuous or controversial, depending on the circumstances. A hard fork was an upgrade to the software that was not backward compatible. This meant that if a significant portion of the miners and other nodes on the network chose not to upgrade to it, the Ethereum chain would split in two, creating a new chain that shared a history up to a point before it branched off, creating a second ether currency. Although Ethereum used hard forks to add features to the network, these were system-wide upgrades that faced no opposition from the community and were as carefully planned and publicized as space launches. However, a hard fork to bail out only the DAO token holders would likely not have the support of the entire Ethereum community, such as, among others, the exchanges that sold ETH—and that could create a competing

Ethereum blockchain with its own currency. And the attack was on the DAO, not on Ethereum. If Ethereum hard-forked because of the DAO attack, it would be like Apple doing something potentially harmful to itself because of an attack on its most popular app. In that scenario, some portion of the other apps and users would likely refuse to go along. But with Ethereum, there was no CEO who would decide; the community, as a group, would have to.

Someone else cautioned everyone,

> keep the big picture in mind: What we are facing is a crappy smart contract, and careless investors. This is their risk of investing without proper due diligence. Don't risk the reputation of Ethereum as an independent, decentralized platform because of it by taking hasty measures like hard forks or roll backs . Doing so will create a highly dangerous precedent, giving political authorities an entry whenever required in the future!

As another executive, Philip G. Potter, at the exchange Bitfinex put it,

> this is problem with DAO not ETH

Dino insisted Bitcoin's 2013 rollback was precedent. Phil asked, "if you screw exchanges, will ETH survive"? Dino said yes and asked the exchanges yet again to freeze trading.

Phil wrote, "fuck this coin"

Dino insisted Ethereum would not recover if the DAO theft was allowed to happen and the hacker sold millions of ETH on exchanges. "The price will be $0.50," he wrote. "Think logically. Irrecoverable PR disaster."

But as Tristan D'Agosta of Poloniex pointed out, "It is much more likely to cause market panic if the blockchain is considered unreliable."

In addition, as Phil wrote, "if any government entity realizes that they can potentially pressure a 'leaderless' DAO (or ETH for that matter) into a rollback, the consequences will be far reaching, I promise you."[2]

MEANWHILE, THE SLOCK.IT team and other developers, in Skype groups, quickly figured out how the attack worked. Back on June 5, Christian Reitwießner, the developer whom Gavin refused to credit as the creator of Solidity, had emailed key devs about a bug that exploited how smart contracts work differently from real-life financial transactions.[3] In real life, if you withdraw from a bank teller or an ATM, the teller or ATM updates your balance after you get your money. But a smart contract needed to change the balance first. Otherwise, a malicious smart contract could interact with it and force it to restart the process back at the withdrawal before the balance was updated. That was what the DAO attacker had done. It was like going to an amnesiac bank teller when you have $259 in the bank, withdrawing $258, interrupting the teller before he or she can update the balance in your account to $1, and withdrawing $258 again and again and again and again (except, in this case, the DAO attacker was getting 258 ETH each time).

On June 9, Peter Vessenes, a Bitcoin Foundation cofounder, had published a blog post, calling it "a terrible, terrible attack," and the next day, Christian himself had written about the attack vector.[4]

Slock.it found the vulnerability in the DAO in the function that enabled people to execute proposals. For this, they created a fix; the majority of DAO token holders just needed to vote on it. A DAOhub forum member also found the bug in an area of the DAO called the Reward Contract. However, since there was no money in that contract, Stephan published a blog post on June 12 titled "No DAO funds at risk following the Ethereum smart contract 're-cursive call' bug discovery."[5] He wrote, "**The important takeaway from this is: as there is no ether whatsoever in the DAO's rewards account—this is NOT an issue that is putting any DAO funds at**

risk today." Even Vitalik seemed unworried. The day before, he had tweeted, "I have been buying DAO tokens since the security news."[6]

The Reward Contract was a potential weak spot in the DAO, because that was the point at which it could interact with a smart contract written by someone unknown. Basically, if the DAO invested in something profitable, the earnings from that investment would go into the Reward Contract to be paid proportionally to every DAO token holder who had invested, much like a dividend. If someone were to leave the DAO by splitting into a child DAO, Christoph decided he or she would have rights to the future rewards associated with his or her contribution(s). In order to keep that promise, the DAO would ask the person leaving to specify an outside address or contract where the reward should be sent. (Accounts in Ethereum can be owned by people or contracts, and if you send a transaction to an account that is a contract, then that triggers the execution of the code of that contract, like making a selection in a vending machine that spits out a product.) Since Christoph didn't have to grant those leaving the DAO the dividends from the future rewards and was choosing to do so, benevolently, Christoph had written a comment: "be nice, and get his rewards." (Depending on how a developer counted the lines in the contract, the vulnerability was on line 667—or 666.)

But though Christoph was being nice, the attacker wasn't. He or she knew that the splitDAO function consisted of four steps (that occurred all in one go): (1) the person leaving the DAO creates a child DAO and sends in their DAO tokens, which get burned, (2) the main DAO sends the requester's ETH into the new DAO, (3) the main DAO releases the reward (to the account the DAO token holder has specified), and (4) the contract updates the balance of the person exiting. The attacker had a regular address and had created the malicious contract. With that address, the attacker signaled to the DAO, *Hey, I want to take my tokens out of the DAO*, and then sent in the 25,805 DAO tokens he or she had to initiate the withdrawal of 258 ETH.

For step 2, when asked where to send the money, the attacker had just the spot. Back on June 8, at 7:38 a.m. Berlin time, someone (later determined to be a DAO token holder in China) had created a child DAO (#59), which he named

lonely
so lonely[7]

On June 14, that Chinese DAO token holder deposited 305,000 DAO tokens with Kraken and all the remaining DAO tokens, which totaled 306,914, with Poloniex.[8] Child DAO 59 was now empty.

At 5:34 a.m. Berlin time on Friday, June 17, 2016, the attacker began the recursive call, sending his or her withdrawal to child DAO 59.[9] In step 3, the moment the DAO asked, "where do I send the Reward?" the hacker provided the Ethereum account for his or her malicious contract. The Reward Contract would ping that malicious contract, which was designed, each time it received a ping, to start the process again at step 2, the step where the DAO sends the money to the child DAO. And it did that over and over and over again, sending ether into child DAO 59 each time. It never let the DAO reach step 4, the point at which the balance would be updated, making it impossible to withdraw more ETH. In this case, the hacker had been doing this for a few hours, 258.056565 ETH at a time. (Based on the gyrating exchange rate that day, that was anywhere from $3,500 to $5,550). The recursive call (also called a re-entrancy attack) was so fast, in fact, that the attacker was taking that amount roughly every second—for, based on the high and low of that day's exchange rate, $210,000 to $330,000 per minute, or anywhere from $12.6 million to $19.8 million per hour.

However, the robber could not just take the money and run. The rules of the DAO had trapped the attacker's money too. On calling that function to take his or her ETH out of the DAO, the attacker could only move the money into a child DAO (lifeboat). (Since there were no funds in the Reward Contract, nothing was actually being sent when the attacker was asking for the reward.) Those tokens would be locked in child DAO 59 for twenty-eight days—or twenty-seven and change, since the clock had started ticking. (Since splits were used both to create new DAOs and to withdraw money from the system, if the purpose of this split DAO had been to create a new DAO with a different agenda, then the twenty-eight days would have served as a DAO creation period, during which others who agreed with the vision of this DAO could have joined by sending in funds.) After the twenty-eight days, the attacker could make another proposal, which would have a voting period of seven days, to split off into a second child DAO, or grandchild DAO. Once there, he or she could make a proposal to have the members of *that* child DAO vote on the new curator or make him- or herself the new curator so the attacker could have the necessary control to move funds to an exchange. (And if the exchange let the attacker, he or she could cash out.) (Creating this additional child DAO in order to cash out wouldn't have been necessary if the attacker had created child DAO 59 him- or herself.) Regardless, for the next thirty-five days, the hacker could do nothing about the money in this child DAO. This created an opening for those who wanted to try to rescue the funds—a window that would close on July 22.

Since it wasn't clear if Slock.it and the other developers would ever be able to stop the attacker, they decided to spam the Ethereum network to slow down the siphoning of the funds. It was like flooding the highway with cars to try to stop an automotive conga line of robbers in getaway vehicles.

However, this was only a stopgap for two reasons. First, it made Ethereum unusable for *all* applications. Second, since the Slock.it and Ethereum developers had been able to re-create the attack, others could too. Now, *anyone* could steal funds from the DAO.

THE ATTACK HAD been in the works for days. On Tuesday, June 14, two days after Stephan's blog post explaining the Reward Contract vulnerability but stating that funds were safe, at 1:42 p.m. Berlin time and then again later at 11:05 p.m., the attacker used ShapeShift to exchange bitcoins for DAO tokens—2 BTC for 7,910 DAO tokens ($1,321) at first, and then that night 2 BTC again for 8,307 DAO tokens (worth $1,387), another 2 BTC for 8,306 DAO tokens, plus another 1.4 BTC for 52.02 ETH ($950). He or she transferred all the DAO tokens and ETH to an address that began 0x969.[10]

On Wednesday, June 15, at 6:26 a.m. Berlin time, the attacker, using two different contracts, voted yes on child DAO 59 (the one owned by a Chinese DAO token holder, but which was currently empty).[11] A little over an hour later, the seven-day voting period on child DAO 59 closed, meaning no one else could enter it. Since the Chinese DAO token holder had never voted yes on his own proposal, the DAO attacker was the only person who could split from that DAO.

On Thursday, at 11:58 a.m., the attacker attempted to do an exchange of about $500 worth of Bitcoin (0.677 BTC) on Shape-Shift, but it was returned. Two types of transactions were possible on ShapeShift: quick or precise. The attacker had selected precise, which meant that he or she would have to send the money for the order within ten minutes or the order would be canceled. Sometimes users, like the attacker, would not do it in time, particularly if they were unfamiliar with the process.

At 12:46 p.m., as if uncertain what had happened, the attacker filled in a customer service request to ShapeShift, giving a return address from a Mailinator account.[12] (Mailinator is a "receive-only" email system in which one can create an email address to fill in a required box on, say, a customer ticket request, and then the response is public and can be read by anyone and is deleted a few hours later. It enables email senders to obscure their identities.) The hacker created the email address Dephisicru@mailinator.com. After filling in the transaction ID number, he or she wrote a simple note in the ShapeShift customer service request form, in what is, to this day, one of the only communications to have provably come from the attacker: "check order please."

The customer service person explained, "Your deposit timer expired, so the transaction could not complete. However we did return the BTC funds as you can see here: http://blockr.io/tx/info /afd6fc9cb2910445b126cbfd8a8dd58b4d5359356688f416635c12b 15fcab7bf."

The attacker, despite what he or she was about to do, seemed unfamiliar with the crypto exchange that was known for not taking customers' identifying information. At 1:11 p.m. Berlin time, he or she sent another customer service request: "please check order"

By the time "Megan Mempool" (Mempool was a fictional last name based on blockchain jargon) wrote back five hours later, the attacker had already received the funds from turning 1.236 BTC into 46.88 ETH (around $966), also sending that to the 0x969 address.[13]

At 4:24 p.m., Dephisicru@mailinator.com sent in a third request that, despite its brevity, showed fluency in both English and crypto lingo shorthand: "dao tokens still missing. should be this tx. please send refund tx hash or dao token. thank you."

Megan Mempool said the transaction had failed and sent the BTC funds back.

At 6:13 p.m., the attacker, seeming to have gotten the hang of ShapeShift and no longer needing customer service, converted 0.667 BTC into 25 ETH (about $519), exchanged another small amount of bitcoin to obtain 15 ETH ($308), and then got another 1,284 DAO tokens worth about $231—and had all of it in the 0x969 address.[14] It was 6:43 p.m. Berlin time on Thursday, June 16.

In the 0x969 address, the attacker, who had spent 10 BTC, had amassed 25,805.61 DAO tokens (about $4,650) and 139 ETH ($2,724). All of that was worth $7,377.

Since the ratio of DAO tokens to ETH had been 100:1 during the sale, the contract would currently trade the 25,806 DAO tokens for 258.06 ETH. And because of the flaw in the program for updating balances, the attacker could pull that much out of the DAO each time he or she withdrew. And one lifeboat—child DAO 59—was in the water, ready and waiting.

At 5:34:48 a.m. Berlin time the next morning, the attack began.[15]

THAT FRIDAY, BY 1 p.m. Berlin time (7 p.m. in Shanghai), as 258 ETH was leaving the main DAO dozens of times a minute, Vitalik published a blog post explaining that a "recursive calling vulnerability" was shoveling ETH from the DAO into a child DAO.[16] However, he wrote, "**even if no action is taken, the attacker will not be able to withdraw any ether at least for another ~27 days (the creation window for the child DAO).** This is an issue that affects the DAO specifically; **Ethereum itself is perfectly safe.**"

He said the developers would pursue first what is called "a soft fork," a way of not changing the history of the blockchain but changing the rules going forward such that the attacker would no longer be able to perform such a function on the DAO and any of its child DAOs. That would stop the attacker (but also everyone else who invested in the DAO) from withdrawing any money even after twenty-seven days had passed.

Vitalik proposed instituting this starting at block number 1760000, which would likely occur within the twenty-seven-day window in which the funds were locked. Finally, he cautioned smart contract authors to write code that was not vulnerable to recursive calls and not to create contracts with more than $10 million (read: no more uncapped token sales). He didn't mention that a hard fork was in the works, just in case.

When he hit publish, his post got so many hits, it went offline, and people had to post the text to Reddit so that others could read it.[17]

Surprisingly, at 1:00 p.m. Berlin time, shortly after Vitalik's blog post, the DAO attack stopped.[18] By that point, the attacker had amassed 3,641,694 ETH—$78 million at ETH's high that day or $49 million at its low.[19] The attacker had taken 31 percent of all ETH in the DAO. No one knew why he or she had stopped, but the Slock.it team and other developers speculated that Vitalik's threatening a soft fork made the attacker think that might be avoided if he or she took just a fraction of the ETH in the DAO. (Years later, Griff would also speculate that the attacker's contract just stopped working.)

The day of the exploit was pandemonium for ETH and DAO token holders. In the highest day of ETH trading volume ever—with just over $199 million in ETH changing hands—the price of Ethereum dropped from $21 before the attack to as low as $14 after it.[20] Between the 31 percent of siphoned ETH and the drop in price, the DAO, which that morning had been worth about $250 million, was, at its lowest point on June 17, worth $109 million. As people scrambled to sell their DAO tokens, the value had plunged from $0.19 the day before to as low as $0.06; it slumped further the next day to $0.05. People who panic-sold DAO tokens lost about two-thirds of their investment.[21] A couple dozen created split DAOs to withdraw on their own, but when they did so, they were splitting with 69 percent of the ETH they rightfully owned.

DESPITE THE DRAMA, a philosophical question lurked: Was the DAO attack actually a hack? Or, for that matter, a theft? This might be an abstract question about something that seemed obviously unethical. But Vitalik, ever the researcher, published a blog post addressing this question, which the community was debating hotly.[22] Since the code had permitted the siphoning of ether into the child DAO, and since the DAO's tagline had been "code is law," the recursive call could be seen as a legitimate way of using the contract. He concluded that, because smart contract theft or loss was "fundamentally about differences between implementation and intent," the solution was to shore up security practices so as to reduce the likelihood of such gaps.

A PERSON CLAIMING to be the attacker wrote a less philosophically inclined version of this blog post by publishing a letter that began,

> To the DAO and the Ethereum community,

> I have carefully examined the code of The DAO and decided to participate after finding the feature where splitting is rewarded with additional ether. I have made use of this feature and have rightfully claimed 3,641,694 ether, and would like to thank the DAO for this reward . . .

> I am disappointed by those who are characterizing the use of this intentional feature as "theft". I am making use of this explicitly coded feature as per the smart contract terms and my law firm has advised me that my action is fully compliant with United States criminal and tort law. For reference please review the terms of the DAO:

> "The terms of The DAO Creation are set forth in the smart contract code existing on the Ethereum blockchain at 0xbb9bc244d798123fde783fcc1c72d3bb8c189413. Nothing in this explanation of terms or in any other document or communication may modify or add any additional obligations or guarantees beyond those set forth in The DAO's code. Any and all explanatory terms or descriptions are merely offered for educational purposes and do not supercede or modify the express terms of The DAO's code set forth on the blockchain; to the extent you believe there to be any conflict or discrepancy between the descriptions offered here and the functionality of The DAO's code at 0xbb9bc244d798123fde783fcc1c72d3bb8c189413, The DAO's code controls and sets forth all terms of The DAO Creation."[23]

He or she also claimed, "a soft or hard fork would amount to seizure of my legitimate and rightful ether, claimed legally through the terms of a smart contract," and said that a hard fork would "permanently and irrevocably ruin all confidence in not only Ethereum but also the in the field of smart contracts and blockchain technology."

Similarly, Redditors, responding to Vitalik's blog post announcing the attack and soft fork proposal, wrote things like "I made a bad contract in the first days ETH was online and lost 2k ETH with it, can I also get it back?" IAMnotA_Cylon responded, "I know this is a joke, but it's one of the more poignant comments here. Ethereum worked exactly as intended. I don't believe software should be updated when it works exactly as intended. You assume the risks of your investment."[24] But another Redditor wrote snarkily, "The guy who stole my car just knew more about wiring than me. So no crime committed."[25]

One summed up the dilemma this way: "Ethereum must decide whether to give the 'hacker' the money he rightfully now owns under the smart contract, or decide that 'smart contracts' are meaningless."[26]

WHILE THE COMMUNITY was having this cerebral discussion, another DAO token holder was about to take a very different approach to the situation. In early 2016, Andrey Ternovskiy, the founder and CEO of social webcam phenomenon Chatroulette, moved to Switzerland, specifically to Zug, for tax reasons and also because there was a university nearby. Years before, when he had put ads from Google AdSense on his site, he says Google had closed his account because he was seventeen. Later, the tech giant sent him a check in Russia. He thought checks only existed in movies. He thought, *Why is Google using checks? What am I going to do with this US bank check?* On top of that, Google wanted him to answer all kinds of questions and fill out paperwork for compliance reasons. Even PayPal, which was supposed to be for online payments, was terrible. Then he heard about Bitcoin. It would enable transactions between just him and his users. Nobody would ask questions. He immediately realized it was superior.

When he arrived in Zug, he heard about local crypto darling Ethereum, so he bought some ETH at prices from about $6 to $10. Right around the same time, the DAO crowdsale started, so he participated in that. He had been googling around for good cryptocurrency companies to use in Switzerland and found Bitcoin Suisse, which helped him first buy ETH and then later DAO tokens. His ETH had more than doubled in value—some of it had nearly quadrupled. Based on the price on the morning of June 17, he owned $10 million in DAO tokens. But within a few hours, he, like all other DAO token holders, lost 31 percent of it due to the attack. Plus, the price of his remaining DAO tokens dropped from a high of $0.19 the day before the attack to a low of $0.05 the day after. What had been $10 million was now $1.8 million.

THE DEVELOPERS FELT that the soft fork would only buy time, not be a permanent solution, since it crudely kept not only the attacker from withdrawing but also everyone else who'd put money into the DAO as well. That led Vitalik, the Slock.it team, and other DAO community members to conclude that the best fix, which they believed was the only way for people to get money out of the DAO, would be to implement a hard fork. (Vitalik had said so in one of the group calls during those first hours.) If there was no hard fork, then not only would the DAO contract be attackable by any copycats but so would every child DAO, meaning that *anyone* who hoped to withdraw their ETH from the DAO via a child DAO ran the risk of an attacker entering their child DAO and preventing them from withdrawing money.

To execute a hard fork, they came up with what they would later call an "irregular state change." This meant that at the moment of the hard fork, they would simply move all the funds in the

DAO and the child DAOs to a new contract that sent ETH back to addresses in proportion to the number of DAO tokens sent in, according to the 1:100 ratio of ETH to DAO tokens by which they had been sold. (They would later figure out a plan for people who'd paid at ratios of 1.05:100, 1.10:100, etc.)

But Slock.it and Vitalik could not decide upon this option themselves. That was not the decentralized way (plus, doing so would trip the four prongs of the Howey test and show that the EF or Slock.it controlled the DAO and that therefore DAO tokens were securities.) In a blog post that Saturday outlining the soft and hard fork options, Christoph ended by saying, "**For these reasons, we think hard forking is the way to go forward.**"[27] But, he went on, "it is part of the ethereum protocol that a majority of the miners/community can do an upgrade/split if they think something isn't working as intended. This does not take anything away from decentralization, since no one can decide about the fork except of the miners and the community themselves—and *no one else*. We as software developers can only suggest forks by providing code listings." It was the crypto equivalent of a doctor laying out treatment options, saying which he or she thought was best, then finishing with "The decision is yours."

WHEN GRIFF HAD sent those first panicked messages in the DAOhub forum and Slack, he, Christoph, Lefteris, and other DAO community members proficient in the DAO smart contract were looking at how to hack the rest of the ether in the DAO so as to keep the attacker from getting it. Griff's course for DAO ninjas had created developers perfect to execute these kinds of attacks.

Their idea was to find some open child DAOs, get the private keys to them (which would enable them to send transactions out), and then execute the same recursive call attack on the DAO. They would essentially be siphoning the remaining 69 percent of the ETH in the DAO out to a child DAO, just as the attacker had done, not to take it from the token holders but to prevent the attacker from obtaining anymore him- or herself. They would figure out how to return those funds to the DAO token holders later.

To pull the attack off, the main trick would be to have a lot of DAO tokens. The more they had, the more ETH they could extract with each recursive call. So the first part of their strategy required getting DAO tokens from whales.

Friday night, they planned to use Avsa's DAO tokens, but when Avsa went to start the attack, his internet went down. Saturday evening, several DAO curators and community members regrouped on a call—Lefteris and Fabian in Berlin, Stephan in the United Kingdom, Avsa in Rio, and a private Irishman named Colm (last name unknown) in an unannounced location. They went over some of the rules of the contract to figure out counterattacks, but they worried that if they performed the same attack from a child DAO, other malicious actors would follow them into it and steal the rescued ether. Still, they decided even if, say, four people joined them in a child DAO, that would reduce the number of potential malicious actors from twenty thousand to four.

But attempting a rescue could put them at risk another way. Fabian said, "From a legal perspective, it can be really hard, because suddenly like we are also technically attacking, right?"

Lefteris responded, using the term for an ethical hacker, "Yeah, but we would essentially go out and say immediately after that fact that this was a white hat attack and say we did it for this or this reason, which is exactly what we just described—that the exploit is out there, it's known. Everyone could use it. It's better that we use it and we diminish the attack vectors to four."

For a while, they questioned whether, if they were able to obtain large amounts of DAO tokens from any whales, those whales would have to kiss that money good-bye. But since the DAO contract would transfer money without updating balances, most likely the tokens would be recoverable.

The situation was pressing. Avsa, Fabian, and Lefteris together had about one hundred thousand tokens—enough to empty the remaining DAO, and thereby protect its money from other attackers, in about fifteen hundred transactions. If they recruited more people to donate their tokens, they could get that number up much higher. In fact, if they were able to get the DAO holdings of one whale they knew, they could have enough to empty the DAO in just over twenty-one transactions. But that meant contacting major investors and asking them to hand over large numbers of tokens to protect their own and other people's money. Still, with the DAO weakness exposed, more recursive calls could start at any moment. So they had to decide quickly.

That night on the phone, the mood was tense, and the debate went on for a while. Toward the end of the conversation, they noticed someone doing recursive calls in smaller amounts right then. Lefteris sighed. "Yeah—this is why I said the DAO would be empty by next week."

They made plans to attempt the rescue the following day.

ON SUNDAY, JUNE 19, they reconvened. For legal reasons, several in the group were hesitant to just attack the DAO. They preferred to wait and see if Ethereum would hard-fork, obviating the need to rescue the ETH from the main DAO. Avsa argued that attacking would avert a hard fork, but he was outnumbered. Instead, they laid the groundwork to rescue the remaining ETH if anyone else tried to steal it. Since they weren't sure which child DAO (lifeboat) they would use, they tried to enter as many child DAOs as possible with both a normal Ethereum account and a malicious contract that could perform the recursive call. Griff found the creators and got the private keys to those child DAOs so that the Robin Hood Group, or RHG, a nickname Avsa had given them, could control the DAO tokens and ETH in them. He then checked an ID, such as a driver's license, and had a phone call with each creator. The RHG needed to trust that, if they put the rescued ETH in that person's child DAO, he or she wouldn't abscond with the funds.

On the Ethereum test net, the RHG members perfected their contracts to perform the re-entrancy attack. They also ended up with 6,028,947 DAO tokens—about 94 percent of it all from one whale.[28] Additionally, Ryan Zurrer, a Canadian crypto investor living in Rio, lent five hundred thousand tokens, Avsa, one hundred thousand, and the group got a few more tokens from Griff, Lefteris, and Jordi Baylina, a Barcelona-based developer who had taken Griff's DAO ninja course.[29] The RHG now had an amount that would allow them to drain the contract faster than any other attacker. But should they start rescuing the funds immediately?

Hacking tends to be illegal more often than not. Most definitions say that it is legal only when the hacker has explicit permission to hack from the company or organization running the network being hacked. But in the case of the DAO, which didn't have an entity that could give or deny permission or, depending on how you looked at it, had fifteen thousand to twenty thousand mostly anonymous owners, was hacking the contract to rescue the funds legal or not? Intent aside, they were performing the same action that the DAO hacker had taken: creating a smart contract that would move ETH that other people had given to the DAO to a child DAO without the express permission of the owners. Lefteris remembers that Christoph was adamant that Slock.it *not* do anything in its official capacity, because it was covered legally. Slock.it had not deployed the DAO, so the DAO was not Slock.it's responsibility. (Christoph says it was because the company was focused on coding a hard fork.) Griff argued that the Robin Hood Group should wait until "exigent circumstances" (a legal term used to indicate when prompt action is justified to prevent harm to others) required them to perform the re-entrancy attack on the DAO to rescue the remaining 69 percent of ETH. Even cautious Lefteris agreed. Although they could get in trouble with the law for hacking, there could also be legal consequences for doing nothing. If they attacked the contract when it looked like user funds were again at risk, they could justify it by saying they did it so people would not lose more money.

Finally, on Tuesday, June 21, their opportunity arrived. At 7 p.m. Berlin time, an unknown DAO token holder started attacking the main DAO contract, scooping up funds into a child DAO. Even though it was only a few ETH per round, the attacker had already amassed a few thousand dollars.[30] Thinking perhaps this person was testing the waters for a bigger drain, the Robin Hood Group—Griff and Lefteris in Berlin and Avsa in Rio—jumped in to rescue the remaining ETH in the DAO using child DAO 78.[31] The first attacker from that night picked up the pace, and six others joined in, with some able to do thirty recursions, moving a few hundred ETH with each call. But the RHG had the most tokens, which enabled them to move the most money with each hit. At 7:44 p.m. Berlin time, they started on their contract, collecting 816 ETH ($9,792) twelve times, for a total of about 9,800 ETH (roughly $117,000). After seeing how their contracts performed, they made some tweaks. Their second attack at 7:51 p.m. transferred a little over 816 ETH thirty-one times, for a total of 25,307 ETH (more than $325,000).[32] They debugged further. The third attack, at 8:00 p.m., moved 4,174 ETH ($50,088) thirty-one times, for a total of 129,390 ETH ($1.55 million).[33] They were just getting started. At 8:43 p.m. Berlin time, another attacker also started draining the DAO, doing recursive calls in amounts varying from less than 1 ETH ($11) to nearly 430 ETH (about $5,519).[34] But by 9:02 p.m., the Robin Hood Group, with 6 million DAO tokens, was transferring 41,187 ETH ($494,244) thirty-one times a block, swooping up 1,276,797 ETH per block.[35] At that amount of ETH, with the price that day at $12, they were moving $15.3 million with one hit of the contract. Another DAO attacker joined in at 9:36 p.m., moving 53 ETH ($636) with each recursive call, but gave up quickly.[36] After the Robin Hood hackers had fully debugged their contracts, they could stop manually pressing buttons and just let them run. The DAO Wars had begun.

They spent the next few hours operating their recursive call contracts. Each Robin Hood Group member would run his own until it stopped working. Since the attack they were performing wasn't using the DAO the way it was supposed to work, each contract would break down the way a maltreated car would, maybe after they'd removed 70 to 80 percent of the ETH. Then another person with a contract would take a turn and get another 70 to 80 percent of what remained. In between, they would refine their contracts.

In the Slack, DAO community members were watching: "This is basically like watching a SF [science fiction] novel play out in real time," one said. "10 years from now having DAO tokens will be like having a peace of the Titanic. Cool," said another. But not everyone was impressed by the DAO Wars: "This is an absolute cluster fuck."

Then the Robin Hood Group's contracts ran into a snag. Of the roughly $100 million in the main contract, their contracts could not scrape the last $4 million or so. This was where their next secret weapon came in.

Jordi Baylina was a quiet, bespectacled, rumpled developer with a full head of hair graying at the temples working as the chief technology officer at a small family-owned company in Barcelona. A coder since the age of twelve, he had also gotten an MBA and founded two companies. Now, he directed a team of half a dozen coders creating management software, such as a reservations system for a hotel booking site. Back in 2013, he'd read the Bitcoin white paper and had tried writing some Bitcoin programs, but he felt Bitcoin was limited to being a system for digital money. Plus, the meetups in Barcelona weren't very technical—the attendees were more interested in talking about things like money laundering. Two years later, he discovered Ethereum and realized he could create a smart contract in two minutes. He became absolutely obsessed, spending all his free time studying smart contracts and contemplating decentralization. When the DAO came out, he got caught up in the global movement of dreamers trying to create something new. He took Griff's DAO ninja course and was amazed that, for finishing the exercises, Griff sent him $5 in ETH. He had even had an idea to try to implement "liquid democracy" on the DAO and wrote up a program that would allow people to delegate their DAO tokens to others to vote on their behalf, but it was too late to include before launch. The experience, however, taught him a lot about the DAO.

Discovering crypto changed his life. Before then, he'd just been following the boss's orders. With crypto, he felt he was working on something that the next generation would use. It gave him a level of satisfaction he felt would be impossible to find in what he now considered "the old system."

But he was still new, so when the first calls occurred about the DAO, Jordi just listened. He was amazed at how the whales, who didn't necessarily know the Robin Hood Group, handed millions of dollars' worth of DAO tokens to them.

But seeing that stranded $4 million, Jordi said, "Hey, I have my smart contract. Maybe I can try it." The other RHG members sent him the money he would need to perform the attacks, and sure enough, he got that last $4 million. He was amazed: $4 million was not an amount of money he could have imagined earning across his lifetime through his previous work.

When they began their attacks, Avsa tweeted, "DAO IS BEING SECURELY DRAINED. DO NOT PANIC."[37] (Someone responded, "NOTHING SAYS DO NOT PANIC LIKE ALL CAPS.")

Three and a half hours later, Avsa tweeted, "DAO is now mostly empty. 7.2M ether have been secured so far."[38]

On Reddit, he explained that two other people had entered the Robin Hood Group's DAO, but as he put it, "the risk has been reduced from 20 thousand attackers down to only 2."[39]

He made a call for these two people, as well as other people who had created child DAOs, to come forward to help recover more of the ether in the DAO. Then he said, "If you are the hacker, then all I can say is we are coming for you."

But with 7.2 million ether more secure, the Robin Hood Group slept well that night.

7

June 21, 2016, to July 24, 2016

DESPITE THE RELIEF brought by Avsa's post about the majority of the ETH being rescued, many Reddit comments homed in on one part: "There are very valid points for a limited, voluntary, temporary software upgrade in which miners will be able to prevent other attacks like this from happening, and they may be used to prevent further attacks on these child DAOs."

The top comment said, "With a temporary Soft Fork all this ethers can be send to a refund contract and the nightmare is over!"[1] Stephan Tual, however, replied, "a hard fork still stays (IMHO) the simplest, fastest, safest way forward."[2] The next commenter wrote, "I was a hardforker but now no need to split the community. 30% haircut is perfectly acceptable...Hard forks are the nuclear option."[3]

This debate had been raging since the early hours of the attack: to hard-fork or soft-fork? After Christoph's short blog post on Saturday, June 18, in which he'd told the community the decision was theirs, Lefteris wrote a much longer post on Sunday, detailing all the options.[4] The first was to do neither a soft nor a hard fork and instead to coordinate attacks by a large number of token holders. If executed perfectly, they would prevent the attacker from ever withdrawing ether. The drawback: they would have to make these moves forever, and most likely no one would ever get their money back.

Then he walked through the soft fork. It was a complicated, five-bullet-point process with different deadlines that, as he noted in the first bullet point, would take twenty-five days during which "many things have to go right." On top of that, people wouldn't be able to get the stolen ETH for another seventy-three days. Even then, at the end, the DAO attacker could prevent that from happening by simply draining the DAO into any other random child DAO, even one from which he or she could not benefit financially; the attack would simply render the soft fork useless. Lefteris concluded, "What we described above is a very lengthy process with too many points of failure... In the end the hard fork is the simple solution that will be guaranteed to solve the problem."

The hard fork was indeed less complicated, especially compared to a similar process on Bitcoin. Because Bitcoin was "a peer-to-peer electronic cash system," as Satoshi Nakamoto described it in the Bitcoin white paper, it had a chain of custody that could be followed all the way from the creation of a bitcoin to the one (or fraction of one) that someone owned. It made possible the digital equivalent of being able to trace a dollar bill from the time it gets minted to the time it gets used to tip a cab driver, who then uses it to buy flowers from a florist, who then pays bus fare with it. In order to unwind something like the DAO on Bitcoin, to undo the cabbie's tip, one would also have to rescind the bus ticket and return the flowers.

As Griff put it, the day after the attack in a video interview from Christoph's parents' house, "In Ethereum it's *very* different. In Ethereum, there are *balances*. [In] a token contract, there's none of this chasing coins as they get transferred... It's just a database, like an Excel spreadsheet. You see an address and a balance, and every time a token is transferred, it just changes this number in this Excel spreadsheet... It gives the decentralized autonomous organization that is Ethereum the chance to make a change that doesn't affect everyone."[5]

He explained that Gavin, Vitalik, and Christoph had worked out a solution that would be like instantaneously swapping a CD player for a Bluetooth stereo in a car while it was auto-cruising down the highway. The Eadweard Muybridge–like blocks of the blockchain would make this possible through the creation of a clean break from the DAO debacle to a refund contract at a single point in time without interrupting anything else on Ethereum.

Griff made clear his support for a hard fork and said, "If we can roll…back the whole existence of the DAO…that would make attacking other smart contracts, especially big ones like this, a lot less profitable. It would disincentivize it."

ANDREY OF CHATROULETTE felt he would be happy with a soft fork. It would return 69 percent of the funds—not too bad given everything that had happened. But reading the DAO Slack, he became convinced the community would opt for a hard fork. This was yet another reason cryptocurrencies were so fascinating. Because everything was open-source, he only had to read. It wasn't like stocks, where you needed to be an insider. He could peruse the GitHub repository, check out the Slack, and look at what people were saying. He knew what the developers were thinking, and he could see where the community was going. The hard fork was going to happen. DAO tokens were trading at between 5.4 and 12 cents—or 0.005 and 0.009 ETH. He made his calculation.

ON WEDNESDAY, JUNE 22, the day after the Robin Hood Group rescued 7.3 million ETH, Lefteris wrote up another long blog post explaining the hard fork option.[6] While some details remained to be worked out, such as the exact ratio at which to refund people (since some had paid more than one ETH for one hundred DAO tokens), he said that the solution would probably take three weeks tops: "…everyone would get 100% of their ETH back in a **guaranteed** fashion," he wrote.

Then he walked through the soft fork, which required going after money that had splintered into at least four different universes. (1) For the money in the main DAO, the soft fork would get miners to reject any transactions that transferred value from it, with the exception of those initiated by the curator multisig and the RHG's siphoning contract. Once miners were selectively censoring the blockchain, the RHG would then attack the Dark DAO (#59, the one controlled by the original attacker), putting the ETH in a child DAO. The attacker would not be able to follow because his or her transactions would be blocked. After going through the rest of the steps with the associated child DAO creation and voting periods, "assuming everything works out perfectly," they could access the attacker's 3.64 million ETH—after seventy-one days. (2) As for the 7.6 million rescued ETH in the various White Hat DAOs undergoing the complicated DAO exiting process, those would take thirty-eight days to retrieve. (3) Then there was the Extra Balance of 344,907 ETH. The overage paid by the people who had contributed to the DAO at prices between 1.05 and 1.5 ETH for one hundred DAO tokens, rather than 1 ETH, was called the Extra Balance. That money could be made available only after fourteen days. (4) Finally, as for all the mini Dark DAOs created by copycat attackers who tried to pull the re-entrancy exploit on the main DAO, "there is no need to let them go unpunished," he wrote. They would get the same treatment as the Dark DAO. Calling the soft fork "complicated," Lefteris said executing it would be "a large distraction for the Ethereum Community" but conceded it could "return a considerable amount of the ETH to the Token Holders."

The last option he offered was not really an option: no fork. "I will be frank with you, this is a nightmare scenario," he wrote. At the time he was writing, someone new was donating ETH to the DAO, "likely with a malicious intent," he said. Without any fork, he could foresee the DAO Wars continuing forever.

Again, as all the blog posts thus far had concluded, he recommended going with the hard fork but said, "I trust that the community will make the right choice."

As he was writing, the Robin Hood Group had figured out that their "rescue" was not a clean one. Seven other entities had entered the White Hat DAO, and the RHG could identify every one of them except two—an account and a contract, the basic ingredients necessary to pull off a re-entrancy attack. The contract's code was not visible to them. And that pair—the single account and contract—had entered all the other splits as well. Someone would only do that if he or she was also planning to attack (or rescue). That's when they came to think the new entity in the White Hat DAO with them was the attacker. They could move their funds again, but presumably the attacker would simply join them in the next split. It would be Groundhog Day forever. Lefteris included in his blog post the address of what he called the "suspected malicious actor": 0xe1e278e5e6bbe00b2a41d49b60853bf6791ab614.[7]

THE NEXT DAY, "the suspected malicious actor" posted a letter to Reddit via Bitcoin Suisse, the exchange headed up by the pirate look-alike Niklas Nikolajsen that had helped the Ethereum Foundation get set up in Zug. He explained that the holder of address 0xe1e278e5e6bbe00b2a41d49b60853bf6791ab614 was in contact with Bitcoin Suisse, publishing strings of numbers and letters serving as cryptographic proof the sender was in control of the 0xe1e account. Bitcoin Suisse wrote,

> We received the following message from the above mentioned address-holder:
>
> Hi—So, I have chosen to come forward.
> I have the following message for you all. I do not feel it is in anyone's best interest to allow the white-hat DAO funds to go anywhere at the moment, so I will prevent this.
> I am currently considering my options. You will hear from me soon.[8]

Fabian wrote, "I can verify its him," and then posted a bunch of hashes proving that the message was from what the post said was "the so-called 'malicious white hat DAO "attacker"'"—the 0xe1e account.[9]

The community wasn't sure what to make of this communication. Some thought that the attacker was trying to divide the community so it would not be able to decide about the fork—running down the clock, essentially. Another Redditor wrote, "Anything like that would backfire and increase support for the fork."

SINCE HE'D REALIZED Ethereum was likely going to hard-fork, Chatroulette's Andrey had been scooping up DAO tokens like a whale feeding on plankton. They were trading at 5.4 to 12 cents, 35 to 60 percent lower than the price at which they'd been trading before the attack. If his instinct about the hard fork was right, one hundred DAO tokens would soon again be worth their original price of one ETH, and he would end up with a lot more ETH than he'd put into the DAO.

He was enjoying playing around with the DAO script, calling functions, seeing what he could do with smart contracts. He tried making ones similar to what the DAO attacker had used to perform the re-entrancy attack. When he saw the RHG rescuing the funds, he decided to follow them into each child DAO with his contracts. No one else did, meaning even the original attacker had forsaken the DAO Wars. When Lefteris and Avsa asked the owner of the address 0xe1e278e5e6bbe00b2a41d49b60853b-f6791ab614 to come forward, Andrey remained silent. He wanted to keep buying DAO tokens cheaply.

He decided to write a message to the community and asked his exchange, Bitcoin Suisse, to post it to Reddit. Seeing a member of the RHG "verify" it belonged to the attacker, he laughed, thinking that if the real DAO attacker were watching this, he or she was probably thinking, *What the shit! Who is this guy?*

With his threat to launch more attacks hanging in the air, the price of DAO tokens remained low; Andrey could keep buying them at a steep discount.

EVER SINCE THE attack, different community members had come up with various proposals and petitions to try to either sway the outcome or gauge sentiment for or against a hard fork. One change .org petition to hard-fork Ethereum gathered more than 1,000 signatures. There, the top-rated comment, in favor, downplayed the inviolability of smart contracts: "The only sacred contract in crypto is the social contract. Without that, we're nothing but savage animals... It's time we draw the line between what Ethereum stands for and what anarcho-fundamentalists stand for."[10]

A poll on Consider.it showed many more in favor of the hard fork than against.[11] One popular comment on the pro side, said, "We show that we can police and protect ourselves and that the community will stand up to thieves. It's still decentralized because it takes a majority of miners." On the con side: "This proposal can save our Dao but kills the Ethereum."

That was the more high-minded bickering. Stephan Tual of Slock.it and Emin Gün Sirer, the boyish Cornell professor whose paper had called for a moratorium on the DAO before the hack and who went by his middle name, Gün, were getting into spats all over Twitter, *CoinDesk*, and Reddit. Back on June 20, Stephan tweeted a slide of a talk Gün had given in which he'd showed a screenshot of an email exchange he'd had six days before the attack. It read,

On Sat, 11 Jun 2016 17:42:37 0400 Emin G Sirer <> wrote
Hi guys,
I'm pretty sure I know how to empty out The DAO.
On Sun, 12 Jun 2016 13:34:09 -0400 Emin Gün Sirer
<< wrote
...I still think that splitDAO may have a vulnerability. It violates the withdraw pattern by not zeroing the balances[] field until after the call. So I think it may be possible to have it move rewardTokens to a splitting DAO multiple times. This is happening on lines 640 to 666 (hah!) of DAO.sol. Am I wrong?

Stephan tweeted, ".@el33th4xor [Gün] was aware of exploit but didn't inform the DAO security group he joined on 5/31 #theDAO."[12]

Gün was blocked and so could not see the tweet but wrote, "These guys [Slock.it] will do anything except admit failure and take responsibility."[13] He suggested "[placing] a social wall around Slockit."[14]

On Reddit, MyEtherWallet's Taylor Van Orden, posting under her insomniasexx Reddit handle, wrote, "Stop acting like bickering 5 year olds and grow the fuck up. I expect this type of behavior in the trollbox. But you are a professor with people looking up to you."[15]

Gün shot back that after he'd published the paper calling for a moratorium on the DAO, in a private channel Stephan and Griff alleged he knew about but didn't disclose the bug and then accused him of being the DAO hacker. **"I worked hard to help them and the community, and they responded by accusing me of a felony"** (emphasis his).[16]

Many people, such as Griff, Fabian, and Lefteris, were annoyed with both Gün and Stephan over this. Some felt that, to the media, Gün acted like the guy who had it all figured out but that he wasn't that helpful in the DAO Security Skype channel. (Gün says that he didn't share it because he and another researcher concluded it was a nonproblem and that this is "an effort to deflect the blame by pointing the finger at other parties.") In contrast, Fabian thought, Christoph, the Slock.it CTO who thought his world was ending because he had put other people's money at risk, had been working in the trenches on Ethereum and the DAO and was an actual coder. They were especially incensed that Gün had publicized the vulnerabilities in the *New York Times* for every criminal out there to see instead of just alerting the group so they could fork the DAO to safer code.

But an even greater number of people, such as many in the crypto community, were fed up with Stephan, who was the public face of the DAO. The day of the hack, he posted a photo of a fork whose head and tines had been bent to look like an arm and hand with its middle finger sticking up with the words, "HEY THIEF! FORK YOU!"[17]

Someone responded, "Posting memes after you've caused your investors to lose millions…only in crypto."[18] Others tweeted at him, "don't worry man, if things don't work out this time we can just fork again, then fork after that if the last fork doesn't work," and "yeah it's super frustrating when people represent things like how safe & secure their robo investment program is to the public."[19] One Reddit post asked, "Will Stephan Tual apologize?"[20] It inspired 315 comments.

The other Slock.it members begged Stephan to stop: "Put your phone down. Walk away. Take a couple days off." Taylor says she messaged him, "Get off Twitter. Turn off your notifications." He responded, "Why? This is fun." One time, Griff says, Stephan told him, "Every time I tweet, I get 100 new followers and that has real value." Griff found it gross.

ON JUNE 24, Péter Szilágyi posted on the Ethereum blog links to new versions of the Geth and Parity clients that would institute the soft fork if enough miners used them.[21] On June 28, support for the soft fork was still above the threshold that would cause it to be implemented at block 1800000, which, based on the average block production time of thirteen to fourteen seconds in Ethereum, would most likely be mined on June 30.

But that day, the plan all changed. Gün, as a Cornell professor, received an email from a high school senior and future Cornell freshman, Tjaden Hess, who said he thought the soft fork was unsafe because it could expose the Ethereum blockchain to what were known as "denial-of-service" (DoS) attacks. Since the soft fork would require miners to censor any transactions that reduced the balance of the DAO, except for ones initiated by the curator multisig and the RHG's contract, people could send a ton of complex transactions to the Ethereum blockchain and then, with the very last one, lower the value in the DAO. After wasting all that energy, the miners would have to throw those transactions out, earning nothing for their effort. (Normally, the more computation miners perform, the more money they make.) Even more alarming, the attack wouldn't cost a thing. Tjaden, an undergraduate named River Keefer, and Gün published a blog post about the possible attack vector on June 28, and the ether price, which in the days since the hack had been hovering at around $13 to $14, suddenly dropped to below $12. As usual, Gün ruffled feathers, with Lefteris commenting in Slack, "I would have hoped Prof sirer would have refrained from making a post about this before we have reached a final conclusion." (Gün says he did the right thing by notifying a decentralized community about the dangers of this remedy and added, "The Slock.it team has been playing the decentralization card whenever it is convenient for them," while otherwise demanding that "decisions and power be centralized in their hands.")

Fabian tweeted, "With the soft fork being vulnerable there are two options left: a hardfork only affecting TheDAOs, or doing nothing."[22]

One Slack member commented, "another shameful day in the history of eth/dao."

DURING ALL THIS drama over whether to soft- or hard-fork, the Robin Hood Group still needed to conduct its DAO Wars, to collect all the DAO tokens from the mini Dark DAOs, just in case no fork ever happened. This was one of the more problematic of the four main universes into which all the ETH in the DAO had splintered, partially because this one universe was actually six different ones, all with their own start and end times. After the initial rescue, when Avsa asked in his Reddit post for other child DAO curators to come forward, he was referring to the fact that, in addition to the original attacker's DAO, which they called the Dark DAO, there were now six mini Dark DAOs—child DAOs in which someone had copied the original DAO attacker's maneuver to drain money from the DAO. After the Dark DAO, which had 3.6 million ETH, the second-biggest one had 268,000 ETH, and the third-biggest had 29,000 ETH—worth north of $300,000 at the time.

In order to get the money out of the copycat mini Dark DAOs, over the next couple weeks, the RHG first had to contend with the curators, who were in disarray. Several curators, including those who had talked to lawyers, scattered quickly, so the RHG changed the rules to require the signatures of three out of six curators. They also had the curators change the minimum quorum requirement from 20 to 10 percent.

In early to mid-July, with the lowered minimum quorum and the whales' tokens, they were able to pass three proposals. One was to move the Extra Balance over to the main DAO, which they eked out with a 10.39 percent quorum, 100 percent of the 140 token holders in favor.[23] Now the RHG could use that money to rescue the rest of the funds.

For the second proposal, since the Ethereum community was still debating whether to hard-fork, and it was uncertain what would happen, the Robin Hood Group decided to plan for the worst-case scenario: no fork. If the DAO continued as is, they would have to stay on top of the attacker forever to prevent him or her from cashing out. So they created a proposal to buy one thousand Dark DAO tokens, which would enable the Robin Hood Group to execute a "split attack": whenever the attacker created a split proposal, the RHG could always access that same split and establish a controlling majority in it, thus preventing him or her from ever cashing out.[24] (Of course, this was a till-death-do-you-part move, since it would only work if the Robin Hood Group always kept tabs on the attacker and always followed him or her into each split.)

A third set of proposals for attacking the mini Dark DAOs was to put ETH in all the mini Dark DAOs to perpetrate "a 51% attack," in which they would have the majority of the voting power and could force that DAO to send money to the Robin Hood Group's main DAO, known as the Whitehat DAO.[25]

During these DAO Wars, Griff kept a spreadsheet spelling out what measures had to be taken each day in order to stay on top of the ETH in the various mini Dark DAOs. By this time, they had gotten nearly 25.4 million additional DAO tokens, which enabled them to really jam every time they had to attack other DAOs.[26] For instance, on July 6, the RHG spent all day lowering the minimum quorum down to 10 percent, getting whales to vote, and transferring ownership of the other child DAOs to the Robin Hood Group. It noted the exact times, down to the second, of when the Robin Hood Group needed to buy tokens in the various mini Dark DAOs and also the exact moment that certain DAOs closed so they could take action right away, to keep any adversaries from stealing/rescuing the money before they did. "Thu July 14 3:34:48 [UTC] DarkDAO59 Closes ATTACK THIS DAO!!!" On Monday, July 18, it was a full day of attacking DAOs since Dark DAO 85 closed at 13:11:36, DarkDAO 94 closed at 14:42:41, DarkDAO 98 closed at 15:25:12, WhiteDAO 78 closed at 17:44:21, DarkDAO 101 closed at 18:46:28, and WhiteDAO 99 closed at 22:11:37. (Although they couldn't know it then, their vigilance ended up being for naught, as no one challenged them.)

In order to accomplish these steps, on July 4, Lefteris posted on Reddit asking DAO token holders (and whales) to help them out by voting in the various DAOs to enable the Robin Hood attacks.[27] Because these were technical moves, he put up video tutorials and explained that if they did vote, they would not be able to trade their tokens during the voting period.

Although most comments seemed supportive, one Redditor took issue with the fact that Lefteris kept repeating that these moves needed to be made in case a hard fork didn't go through:

"Come on /u/LefterisJP, you leave us hanging with a statement like 'in case it doesn't happen' and don't follow up with responses? What is the likelihood that we will need to rely on these proposals instead of [a hard fork]?"[28]

THE SIMPLE ANSWER to the Redditor's question was that the RHG had no idea. They were in regular contact with someone at Poloniex who was pulling on some threads he thought might lead to the DAO attacker's identity. Either the attacker was affiliated with a Polo account holder who had given the exchange a photo ID and made a selfie of himself holding it to verify his identity— or quite possibly, the attacker *was* that person. Basically, when the attacker had turned BTC into ETH on ShapeShift, he or she had had to give ShapeShift a return address in BTC in case anything went wrong and his or her funds were returned. The address given was one to which a Polo account holder could be linked (over a few hops) via a small amount of BTC. As Griff noted to the Polo investigator, "one way or another, the attacker knows the guy that is smiling for your verifications...it might be the attacker, or it might be their friend or at least someone that has given them their btc address for some reason."

In fact, just days before Lefteris's Reddit post, the Polo employee had enough information to file a suspicious activity report with the Financial Crimes Enforcement Network. Because the Polo staffer was pretty confident, he even messaged Griff, Lefteris, Stephan, and Colm by Skype back on July 1, saying, "Guys, new evidence has emerged now. Please hold off on the hard fork if you can. I think there is a good chance I have found the attacker...So you know, personally I have no motive in the hard fork or otherwise—I think, if there is time, a physical apprehension of this person could happen and the funds secured." On July 2, he wrote, "99.9% sure I have our guy now. I also have a lead on an accomplice or some sort of insider. Blockchain, IP, behavior, physical location and anecdotal evidence is all very strong. It is not

100% smoking gun—but it is a strong suspect. The attack came from Switzerland." On July 4, the day of Lefteris's Reddit post, he wrote, "This was a conspiracy—a group... I am certain of this. There is a blockchain [company] in Switzerland, this is where it was planned and executed. Those involved are all prominent in the ETH community." He posted some links to those he thought were involved but mentioned that he would not be able to share most of his evidence without a subpoena.

So, even as the RHG was conducting these DAO Wars, they were doing so knowing there was a real possibility that the attacker could be apprehended, which could obviate the need for a hard fork. But because they didn't know whether that effort would pay off, they decided to try a second strategy. On July 9, Stephan Tual published a blog post titled "Why the DAO robber could very well return the ETH on July 14"—with purely speculative supporting evidence. It invoked Bastille Day and said the day is "known for its fireworks."[29] A Redditor commented, "This cocky son of a bitch is playing you all you know."[30]

However, there was a rationale behind his seemingly nonsensical, almost taunting post: the RHG was trying to get the DAO attacker's attention to propose that he or she simply return the funds, which would be possible only from July 14 onward. On Monday, July 11, 2016, they used the Dark DAO's curator key to whitelist the DAO's curator multisig address in the Dark DAO, making it possible for the DAO attacker to send the 31 percent of the ETH drained from the DAO to the curators for distribution.[31] The day before, in the Skype chat discussing this move, Stephan wrote, "The attacker will see the transaction (and the hoopla it creates on reddit) and will know he's been given a choice." But the attacker either didn't get the message or chose to keep the siphoned funds.

WITH THE CLOCK ticking toward the deadline for when the DAO attacker would be able to start moving money out of the Dark DAO, the developers were working on coding up a potential hard fork, just in case the community went for the nuclear option. But leaving aside the fact that it was controversial, it wasn't a simple solution either because of how messy the DAO had become.

On July 7, Christoph published a blog post that laid out three main issues regarding a potential hard fork, the trickiest one of which was how they should handle the Extra Balance, since some of the DAO participants had paid more than one ETH per one hundred DAO tokens. The problem was that, due to the deadline, they did not have the time to perfectly reimburse everyone based on how much they had paid. For all three issues, he outlined options and recommended one. As usual, he ended this post with "Ultimately, it is not up to me, Slock.it or to anyone else to make this decision [whether to hard-fork] for the Ethereum community."[32]

The community coalesced around two of Christoph's recommendations quickly, kept debating the issue of the Extra Balance, and got to work, trying to figure out whether the community was for or against a hard fork. Ethereum enthusiasts in China created a site called carbonvote.com which would tally up votes on whether to hard-fork. However, coins, not people, counted, so whales could strongly influence the vote. The way it worked was that a voter could send zero ETH to the yes address or zero ETH to the no address. Each ETH in the address from which the vote came would be considered a ballot either in favor of or opposed to the hard fork.[33]

On July 15, Jeff Wilcke, the Go Ethereum lead, published a blog post, "To fork or not to fork," in which he wrote, "As this is not a decision that can be made by the foundation or any other single entity, we again turn towards the community to assess its wishes in order to provide the most appropriate protocol change."[34] He explained that, if they chose to hard-fork at block 1920000, all ETH in the DAO, the Extra Balance, and the child DAOs would be moved to a Withdraw DAO. DAO token holders would be able to submit their DAO tokens to the Withdraw Contract and receive back one ETH for every one hundred DAO. (Eight days prior, Christoph had published a post asking the community how it wanted to handle the Extra Balance money. One option was for it to be put in a multisig, from which DAO curators would distribute it.[35]) Now that they had coded up the clients to carry out the hard fork, the big question was whether or not the community wanted to go through with it. This would determine a crucial decision by the developers: whether, when downloading and restarting the new version of the software, it would default to forking or not.

On the opposition side, people were pointing out how, in early 2014, when Mt. Gox had been hacked and nearly half a billion dollars' worth of bitcoin had been stolen, Bitcoin didn't hard-fork. But others felt that wasn't an analogous situation since no one knew where the pilfered bitcoin had gone. With the DAO, on the other hand, everyone could see the stolen loot on any Ethereum block explorer (a website that gives data about a blockchain) and knew that it would be stuck there until July 21. Within the EF, Jeff, who had not been involved with the DAO, recognized that even though the DAO wasn't technically the EF's problem, Reddit comments (and eventually the carbonvote.com results) showed that sentiment was generally in favor of forking. Plus, since so many people had lost their money and Ethereum was so small, he felt it was worth doing while Ethereum was less than a year old.

In his blog post, Jeff announced that the votes on CarbonVote would be tallied at block number 1894000, and that would determine whether the default option on the Geth client would be "to fork" or "not to fork." By July 16, the carbonvote was clear: 87 percent in favor of the hard fork. Despite the fact that only 5 percent of all ETH had voted, at block 1920000, which was set to happen in four days, they were going to hard-fork.

THE CRYPTO EXCHANGES felt unheard by the Ethereum community. Some operators and staff voiced their opinion that there was a huge risk of a chain split, which would result not in the kind of hard fork everyone agreed on but in a contentious hard fork, resulting in a competing ether currency. However, many Ethereum developers seemed concerned that if they didn't try to fight the thief, which they considered the right thing to do, they could get into trouble. This was an extremely different attitude from the one most Bitcoiners would take, as the rules of the protocol would take precedent. To some exchange operators, the Ethereum Foundation developers seemed blind to what was obvious to them: the hard fork was going to cause a chain split.

To some exchanges, the Ethereum Foundation and Slock.it were ideologically minded developers who didn't understand crypto traders. The exchanges, who dealt with all the crypto communities, knew that many Bitcoin "maximalists"—a term Vitalik may have coined referring to purists who felt that Bitcoin would and should be the one and only blockchain—would take any opportunity to hobble the second-biggest crypto network after Bitcoin.[36] Another issue was that, since the Ethereum developers did not think the original Ethereum chain would survive, and since the amount of time in which to implement the hard fork was so short, they didn't institute something known as "replay protection." This referred to a problem that came up when one chain forked into two. Up to a certain moment, the two shared the same exact transaction history. Unless there were actions taken to "split" the ledgers after the fork (called replay protection), any time both ETH and the competing version of ETH (ETHoriginal) ended up in addresses identified by the same hashes on both chains, someone wanting to initiate a transaction with one set of coins would also cause a transaction with the other—for instance, selling not just, say, ETHoriginal but also the ETH they meant to keep.

With the DAO hard fork, since the EF developers didn't think replay protection was necessary, the exchanges that wanted to be safe had to institute it themselves. To the exchanges, failure to account for such an obvious risk was a stunning oversight on the foundation's part. Part of the reason for it may have been that the EF wasn't jeopardizing its capital in the same way. With two chains, the EF might feel the pain if the price of the coin went down, but the exchanges would actually lose the tokens themselves once their customers began depositing and withdrawing unless replay protection was built in.

On top of that, since the final decision to hard-fork came just four days before the scheduled date, the exchanges didn't have much time to implement replay protection. When, by Skype chat, Jeff Wilcke told Bitfinex's Phil Potter (who had said, "fuck this coin" in the Skype group chat shortly after the DAO attack), Phil wrote back, "I wish I never listed this piece of shit coin."

Some of the Ethereum developers' seeming fear of regulators coming after them because of the DAO was not fantastical. Before the hard fork, Vitalik says, Luka of MME, the Ethereum Foundation's Swiss law firm, told Ming and Vitalik that the Swiss regulator, FINMA, wanted to talk to them about the DAO. On July 13, Vitalik flew into Zurich from Shanghai. Luka had given Ming and Vitalik the impression this was a serious meeting, but the regulators accepted their explanation that the DAO was an application unrelated to the Ethereum Foundation and protocol.

DURING THIS TIME, Slock.it's Christoph felt like a disaster was unfolding in his life. He had worked for Ethereum for almost two years, and he loved it. He had ditched his PhD for it. His very first job in Ethereum had been to find bugs that accidentally caused chain splits. Since it looked like he might now become the cause of one, he felt like he had personally disappointed his friends. He also felt responsibility to all the people who had invested in the DAO. It would be especially terrible for the newbies among what he estimated to be fifteen thousand to twenty thousand DAO token holders if their first experience with Ethereum was to lose money.

His focus became fixing the mess. Since others were working on coding up the soft fork implementations in the Geth and

Parity clients (until the DoS attack potential was discovered), he did nothing else but code up the hard fork. Although he had five children—one five months old—he gave them no time. He went dark on social media. He stayed at his parents'. He, Griff, and Simon met there while his mother delivered her one-pot beef stew with potatoes and carrots or store-bought Asian noodles without disturbing them. Griff, who had been a massage therapist, seeing how stressed Christoph was, would sometimes rub his shoulders. Trying not to think about potential lawsuits, Christoph felt that with God and his wife and his family's support, the worst that could happen to him was losing all his money forever. He took hour-long walks every day and prayed more than ever before, coming closer to God than at any point in his life.

The hardest part was that in order to fix the situation, he needed to orchestrate huge changes by people over whom he had zero authority. The solution required a modification in the clients running the Ethereum protocol, and he no longer worked at the EF. He'd actually patched hard forks in the early days of Ethereum.[37] People hadn't even noticed back then. Now, he was reduced to writing blog posts, commenting on Reddit, talking to developers at the foundation, and having calls with Ming and Vitalik. However, the foundation did not want to make the decision. They wanted the community to choose. But because Ethereum had no formal governance process, people basically just talked to each other on the internet.

And the internet was chaos. Everyone was playing philosopher of the day, opining on whether code is law. Watching the debates, Christoph thought, *This is a free market—if they wanted to stay with this chain with the DAO and its siphoned funds forever, let them do so. They decide.* He kept coding up the hard fork even though he had no idea what the outcome would be. And frankly, none of the options were perfect. If the hard fork went through, the DAO problem would be solved, but Ethereum would be hurt. The soft fork seemed promising until it became unviable—and abandoning it stung even more because, due to the arcane seven- versus fourteen-day windows for various processes in the DAO, losing that option shortened the amount of time they had to find a solution.

But after he had written the code for the hard fork and seen the carbonvote results, and after forums and petitions showed 80 to 90 percent support for a hard fork, Christoph went to a Skype chat group with 150 Ethereum developers, the DAO curators, big investors, and other influential people in Ethereum and said the community seemed to have chosen the hard fork. He shared his hard fork specification. The various people from Slock.it and the EF handled the decision to hard-fork like a game of hot potato. No one wanted to be the person to which any regulator could point and say, "You were responsible." The EF did not want to be officially involved with the DAO, so that left Christoph to try to find someone within Ethereum who would implement it for him. Gavin implemented it right away on Parity, but since Parity accounted for a small fraction of the nodes on the network, Christoph really needed Go. Jeff was taking time off before his first child was born, but Christoph got Péter Szilágyi, a head developer on Jeff's team, to implement it as an option.

Eventually, the exact details of handling the Extra Balance and other anomalous cases were worked out. A group of people, including original DAO curators Vitalik and Vlad, agreed to manage a multisig that would be used to disburse those funds to their rightful owners.

ON JULY 17, Vitalik wrote a Reddit post to explain to the community what would happen: "At block 1920000, the HF [hard fork] will take place, and there will effectively be two chains: one chain that executes the irregular state change implemented in the geth 1.4.10 code, and one that does not. After this point, it is broadly expected that one branch will come to be perceived as dominant, while the other branch may either fade into irrelevance or it may continue its existence and even maintain a market price."[38]

Vitalik, who would later say that, at this point, he fully expected the original chain would survive, recommended that people who wanted to stay on the dominant chain "refrain from undertaking any economically meaningful actions between block 1920000 and the time that the hard fork is 'settled' and it is clear which branch is dominant (note that some exchanges are following this advice already, with deposit functionality remaining offline for 1 hour)."

He offered a replay protection contract that people could use to only send the coins on one chain and not the other, but as one Reddit user pointed out, it was far beyond the technical capabilities of most users.[39] Those who didn't know how to use it ran the risk of trying to sell coins they wanted to dispose of—say, ETHoriginal—and in the process also accidentally losing the ETH they meant to keep.

PÉTER SZILÁGYI, JEFF'S deputy, went to implement a portion of the hard fork code. The way it was coded, the client could add a flag—to stay on the original chain or to be on the fork. The carbonvote and other polls made it seem that the majority would choose the new chain; if so, it would end up being longer, since there would be more computers keeping it alive, which would result in production of more blocks. Péter realized that the way it was structured, the original chain would not survive if the new chain did become longer, because nodes would end up syncing onto the longer ledger, and it would simply be impossible to get onto the old chain—even if you set your flag to prefer it. Péter changed this so that if some miners did really want to keep the initial chain alive, it would be possible to do so, even once the forked one became longer.

Now the EF could honestly say people were choosing which chain to support and that the foundation had not forced the decision.

THE ONLY THING left was to code up the Withdraw Contract, which an ex-Googler-turned-Geth-developer named Nick

Johnson volunteered to do. It took a mere twenty-one lines of code to create a contract that, for anyone who sent DAO tokens to it, would shoot back a proportional amount of ETH.[40]

ON WEDNESDAY, JULY 20, in Ithaca, New York, the morning was a summer-perfect cool heading to a high of eighty-one that afternoon.[41] The Initiative for CryptoCurrencies and Contracts (IC3) at Cornell was starting its summer Ethereum Crypto Boot Camp and Workshop that day—but first, Ethereum was going to fork.[42]

Shortly after 9:15 a.m. Eastern Daylight Time, Vitalik, Ming's boyfriend, Casey Detrio, Avsa, and a few other devs, including an Indiana-based coder named Martin Becze, were sitting at some tables outside a cafe in Bill & Melinda Gates Hall, near a Plexiglas railing overlooking an atrium and a baseball diamond outside. Casey wore a red "Sriracha HOT Chili Sauce" T-shirt, and Vitalik sported a purple sublimation shirt covered with a large picture of a cat's face and front paws in fists. A laptop cover showing a black cat face with violet eyes lay on the table between their laptops, one of which sported a decal with the motto "It's not a bug, it's a feature."

Hunched over their laptops, they tracked the effort on fork .ethstats.net. Avsa was watching with Vitalik on the latter's Lenovo laptop. Slowly, the blockchain ticked forward as people mined new ether.

At 9:20:40 a.m., block 1920000 appeared:

1920000   0x498515ca   0x94365e3a

On Vitalik's screen, a vertical line that had previously connected blocks 1919996, 1919997, 1919998, and 1919999 now split into two, with a new line veering over to the 0x94354e3a hash, indicating that two chains now existed.

Avsa said, "O-*kay*!"

Vitalik began giggling and rocking forward and back, emanating nervousness and relief. "Yay," he managed to get out through his laugh.

"We are on," said Avsa.

"Is the fork happening?" Avsa asked while taking a video with his phone. He then smiled into the camera, selfie-style, and behind him, Vitalik, in profile, was still grinning wildly at the computer screen. His long fingers circled the top of his disposable coffee cup and lid.

By block 1920005 on the new Ethereum, the old chain had stalled at 1920001.

Later on in the IC3 bootcamp, Gün got bottles of champagne on which he'd stuck printed labels reading, "Congratulations on a successful hard fork!" and featuring computer clip art of a fork.

To celebrate, Gün's colleague, Elaine Shi, held up a plastic cup holding all the plastic forks, while Gün and Vitalik each grabbed a champagne bottle. Gün advised Vitalik to just rotate the cork. "Ready?" he called. "One, two, three!" Gün's cork popped. Vitalik's took a second longer, and he scrunched his face. *Pop!* Fog floated out of the bottle. Vitalik laughed.

IN THE FAR north of Germany, near Copenhagen, on the Baltic Sea, under a full expanse of sky, long grasses bent in the breeze at the beach in Baabe, where on the white sand lay Christoph, scrolling through his phone.

It was 3:20 p.m. on July 20, and he was monitoring the fork. When he saw it succeed, he could finally relax. That day, he published a Medium post titled "What an accomplishment!"[43]

"Separate from the discussion of whether a hard fork because of the DAO is a good or a bad idea, the very fact, that the Ethereum community (devs, miners, exchanges, researchers,...) has come together, often setting personal opinions aside, and successfully managed a hard fork in this situation is truly remarkable," he wrote. After thanking numerous people for helping out with the DAO funds rescue and hard fork—almost like he was sub-consciously sending the message *See SEC, ETH is not a security since we are not centralized!*—he concluded with "Although some do question the analogy 'code is law'. I do not. We just found out that we have a supreme court, the community!"

The community was not impressed. One sample reaction on Reddit: "These guys have some nerve I have to say. Your 'accom-plishment' was to nearly destroy the whole of Ethereum."[44]

At the time of the fork, the Withdraw Contract had 12 mil-lion ETH in it (about $148 million). Eight hours later, it had 6.4 million ETH ($79 million), and a couple days after that, it had 4.6 million ETH worth $66 million.[45] The DAO, which had been one-third drained of ETH only a month before, was now almost two-thirds filled back up with DAO tokens. The price of Ethe-reum also ticked up, closing above $12 for the first time since July 2. Now, the $140 million crowdsale and ingenious exploit looked like a digital mirage, one that Christoph could forget about as he lay on the beach.

THREE DAYS LATER, at 7:19 a.m. Central European Sum-mer Time, after the DAO tokens that had been in the attacker's 0x969 wallet had been moved four hops away to a new wallet, someone, mostly likely the DAO attacker, transferred them one more hop to a new wallet, 0x26D.[46] At 7:25 a.m., he or she sent 25,805.6141470999999999 DAO tokens to the Withdraw DAO and received back 258.056141470999999999 ETH.[47]

NOW THAT THE value of DAO was once again 0.01 ETH—having risen from 0.005 to 0.009 ETH—Andrey Ternovskiy cashed in his piles of massively discounted DAO tokens, ending up with roughly double the number of ETH he had put in.

WHILE THE ETHEREUM community was consumed with the hard fork, another movement was afoot. Back on July 10, even before the fork had been decided on, someone had created a GitHub page for something called Ethereum Classic (ETHC). Also before the fork, one Redditor, jps_, walked through the incentives different ecosystem players would have to maintain the original chain, noting, "Exchanges have demonstrated that they will trade extremely small fractions of Ethereum, or even marginal less-popular currencies." jps_ also observed that miners had a financial incentive to keep the chain going. If a blockchain is like a Google spreadsheet in the cloud that keeps regular saved snapshots of the state of the ledger, the hard fork was like making a duplicate copy (with duplicate coins) in which a bunch of cells having to do with the DAO got changed and the Withdraw DAO got created. But since blockchains are like timestamped Google spreadsheets without a centralized company like Google at the center that maintains them, that original Google spreadsheet/blockchain could still be kept alive if some group of miners agreed to maintain it. If that happened, then it would still be possible to transact with those original coins. Even if only a small group of miners, or a single miner, mined the original chain, they would get all the new coins being minted and the transaction fees, whereas on the more popular chain, there would be so much competition that they might have a hard time earning fees at all. And as long as miners were keeping the original chain alive, the coins there would also exist—and potentially be tradeable, as long as an exchange listed them. Wallets would also be incentivized to let users exchange their old coins. jps_ concluded, "the end game is two live streams of Ethereum."[48]

On the day of the fork, *Bitcoin Magazine*, Vitalik's old publication, wrote an article about "the launch of a spin-off project: Ethereum Classic."[49] While the author, Aaron van Wirdum, noted that Ethereum Classic "seems to be a bit of a joke, intended to make a point," he wrote,

the project has been gaining some traction, with a small-but-growing user-base on Reddit and Slack, and with the decentralized exchange Bitsquare offering its token—classic ether—as a trading option. Additionally, some 0.5 percent of hash power joined a special Ethereum Classic mining pool even before the split, and seems determined to mine on the Ethereum Classic chain, ensuring blocks are mined and the project is kept alive.

Van Wirdum interviewed the creator of Ethereum Classic, who went by the pseudonym arvicco and was the founder of BitNovosti, a Russian crypto media outlet. "Many of us are supporters of a radical crypto-decentralist stance," arvicco said. "In short, we believe blockchain-systems should always adhere to three characteristics: openness, neutrality, and immutability. Without these characteristics, a blockchain is nothing but a glorified database… Bailing out the DAO undermines two of the three key long-term value propositions of the Ethereum platform."

Still, a few hours after the fork, the chain seemed effectively dead. The hash rate (a proxy for computer power) on the network on July 19, the day before the fork, had been 4.51 terahashes (or a trillion hashes[50]) per second (TH/s).[51] After the fork, the hash rate on the old chain collapsed 99.3 percent to 0.03 TH/s.[52]

But, as jps_ had predicted, many people were interested in Ethereum Classic. The day after the fork, on BitcoinTalk, a user named Seccour, self-described as "Bitcoiner, Crypto-anarchist and Cypherpunk," posted a thread titled "[ETHC] Ethereum Classic Speculation," which featured a new logo for something called Ethereum Classic, with a similar double tetrahedron logo but in green against a black backdrop. The thread included links to an Ethereum Classic block explorer, the Ethereum Classic Reddit, the Ethereum Classic Slack, and the Ethereum Classic Wiki. "This topic can be used to speculate on the price of Ethereum Classic token," Seccour wrote.[53]

The bids began coming in.

Bitsquare's order book for Ethereum Classic/Bitcoin trades showed the top three ask offers at prices ranging from 6,800 ETHC/BTC ($0.10 per ETHC) to 10,000 ETHC/BTC ($0.07 per ETHC).[54]

On the Ethereum subreddit, Mentor77 posted a thread under the subject "Sell us your eTHC/ETH Classic!" "There are people interested in buying your [worthless?] ETHC. If you don't plan on transacting with Ethereum Classic, please consider selling your stake." The thread also included a link to instructions about how to prevent one's transfer from causing a replay attack.

Because this was posted on the Ethereum subreddit and many Ethereans worried about the bad PR and other negative consequences of having two versions of Ethereum, the reception to this post was not warm. Only 42 percent upvoted, and one commenter wrote, "I see your true colors shining through."[55]

Christoph and Vitalik also got a glimpse of the demand for the seemingly defunct tokens. Back on June 17, just hours after the DAO attack, famed Bitcoin core developer Gregory Maxwell had sent Vitalik an email with the subject line "Don't be a greedy idiot." In it, he wrote,

If you rewrite the ethereum consensus rules to recover the coins you and other lost to the as-written execution of that smart contract, you show that the system is really controlled by political whim, in particular via you.

Beyond the personal risk you might take on by demonstrating control of the system, it would risk bringing more uncertainty on the cryptocurrency ecosystem. Other developers might be pushed to try to do the same things by authorities. It's a bad road.

Now that Ethereum *had* actually hard-forked, Gregory wrote Vitalik again, the day after the fork. "An offer to purchase ETHC" was the subject line. "Greetings. Ethereum Classic chain looks like a fun test network," he wrote. "I'll pay you 0.2 BTC [$133] for 500,000 ethc [$0.00027/ETHC]. If that isn't enough, please make a counter offer."

Vitalik ignored the email.

Meanwhile, on July 21, while he was still at Baabe Beach, Christoph received an email from a trader at Kraken:

> Congrats on the smooth hard fork that just happened. I'm glad the DAO holders are going to be made whole. The reason I'm reaching out to you right now is because there has been a large buyer for ETHC that came through our OTC [over-the-counter] desk recently. I was wondering if you guys or anyone you know would be willing to sell me your ETHC so I can fill this order. Obviously ETHC is on the losing chain and isn't worth much so I'm not looking to pay very much for it but if you would like to sell me your ETHC at a cheap enough price, I'd be interested in buying it off you guys.

(OTC desks were used to make manual orders for trades so large they could not be put through on a regular exchange without moving the price and thus cutting into profits.) The Kraken trader made an offer for one million ETHC at $0.01 per and invited Christoph to reach out on Skype. Christoph was soon headed to Japan and so could not access his old ether. But he had nowhere near one million ETH—or, by extension, ETHC—and didn't want to worry about a replay that would make him lose his ETH, so he declined.

BEFORE THE HARD fork, some exchanges, like ShapeShift and Poloniex, prepared for what they expected would be two Ethereum chains after the fork by installing replay protection against the recommendation of the foundation. (As one exchange operator later put it, "They were like, '90+ percent of the coins voted [for]'—and it was like, 'You mean of the 5 percent of the coins that voted?' It was the dumbest straw poll. So 90 percent of 5 percent means consensus. It's a joke, right?") They could see that, in the community at large, Bitcoiners in particular felt that Ethereum's hard fork would illustrate one of Bitcoin's core features: its immutability. And they believed many Bitcoiners would become fans of Ethereum Classic simply because they had always hated the second-biggest crypto network; keeping the original chain alive would remind the world that Ethereum was not immutable. Plus, after the fork, many of their wallet partners—companies who had hired, say, ShapeShift to perform crypto-to-crypto exchanges on the backend for their customers—were coming to ShapeShift saying their users wanted to trade it. Knowing that those Ethereum Classic coins were in their wallets was irresistible to users. It was free money.

The exchanges were also feeling this heat, with customers wanting their free coins. Exchanges make money on trades whether the market is going up or down, whether their users are trading quality coins or what were commonly called shit-coins or, more euphemistically, alt-coins. The king of the alt-coin exchanges was a scrappy outfit called Poloniex founded by a savant named Tristan D'Agosta, a quiet, brilliant (some speculated on-the-spectrum) film/concert/opera composer and coder. His claim to fame before cryptocurrency was founding a sheet music publishing house known for its spiral-bound scores, solving the problem of books of piano sonatas or opera scores that wouldn't stay open or whose pages would fall out due to creased-to-death bindings.[56]

"Polo," as many in the industry called it, had been one of the first three exchanges to list Ethereum when the network launched.[57] In general, Polo was known not just for listing many alt-coins but for doing so quickly—a feat given that each blockchain worked differently and buys and sells needed to be secure. Tristan did all the integrations, not only writing all the code for the site but also keeping all the quirks of the codebase in his head. He was especially intrigued by challenging coins. Partially because it was the center of the alt-coin world, but also possibly because it had, in spring 2015, launched margin trading for alt-coins, Polo became the go-to place to buy ether the moment Ethereum launched.[58] In the winter/spring of 2016, when the ETH price was coming out of its doldrums, giving the foundation more breathing room, Polo, which had previously languished in the teens on a ranking of the highest-volume exchanges, reached the top—hitting number one across all exchanges in the world on the cryptocurrency data site CoinMarketCap.[59]

As the dominant exchange for trading ETH, it had a number of traders, particularly ETH whales, who now had ETHC, the coins on the old chain that became defunct when it had appeared to stall.[60] Whales are an exchange's most prized customers. To a whale with $10 million in ETH, as long as he or she could persuade Polo to add ETHC, he or she could instantly have another $1 million in ETHC or, depending on how the price went, even more. Polo knew that if it didn't, another exchange would list ETHC. (And that competitor would make the fees.) The customer demand to trade this free money was too much to resist. Plus, according to a Polo employee, Tristan himself was quite open to seeing how Ethereum Classic played out. He coded up a replay-safe split smart contract. In the wee hours of Sunday, July 24, three and a half days after the fork, at 12:23 a.m. Eastern Time, Poloniex tweeted, choosing the ticker ETC, "ETC/BTC and ETC/ETH #Ethereum Classic markets added."[61] At 12:25 a.m., it tweeted again: "All users who had an #Ethereum balance at the moment of the fork now have a matching balance of $ETC."[62]

Ethereum Classic had risen from the dead.

8

July 24, 2016, to October 26, 2016

THE REACTION TO Poloniex's announcement about ETC trading was a mix of condemnation, praise, and greed: "wow what a lack of morals...closing my account...prepare to be sued by helping criminal action (dao hacker)."[1] Another said, "the original and the best! This is great news for unadulterated Ethereum!"[2] One miner in China announced his plans to turn his computer hashing power onto ETC to execute a 51% attack, which was a way of using brute-force computer power to take control of a blockchain and either undo recent transactions or rewrite the blockchain's history—a move that supporters of ETC called hypocritical, given that the whole reason Ethereum had forked was because of an attack.[3]

But the miners who had been struggling to keep the original chain, ETC, alive suddenly got rewarded for their efforts. The hash rate was still about 0.03 to 0.04 TH/s, but the day that Polo listed ETC, it jumped to 0.19. The next day, it was at 0.24. The day after, 0.48; the day after that, 0.68.[4] With miners now able to sell the ETC they were mining, it became clear the chain would survive.

The Ethereum crew was caught off guard. Lefteris says he and Christian Reitwießner were in Brandenburg, the lake-filled countryside around Berlin, and thought ETC (or what Lefteris and

Griff called "dead ETH") was a mistake. He recalls they were sure it would disappear in a few days. (In the run-up to the fork, Griff, a dabbler in alt-coins, had been certain the chain would die based on his experience with other forks.) Since the hard fork, the ETH price had rebounded to above $14 from around $11. Lefteris said they decided to sell their ETC.

When Christoph heard, he accepted it: he now knew the DAO would never die. The emergence of ETC would forever be the result of his creation. Even though they'd been able to clean up the DAO on one chain, this shadow would forever exist, to remind everyone of what had happened. Partly because of his spiritual path, he knew there was nothing he could do about it; nor was there any point in worrying about it.

Vitalik was at an Airbnb north of the North Gorge in Ithaca when he found out Ethereum Classic had revived. For the last few days, at the IC3 boot camp, he'd felt pretty calm and relieved the whole drama was over, but now it turned out it wasn't. On the day Polo listed ETC, the ETH price dropped back into the $12 range again, and ETC, which opened the day at $0.75, closed at $0.93.

In a Skype group called "Ethereum foundation [internal only]," the EF devs bashed ETC. Fabian bragged about selling his ETC and getting "nice free money." He joked that Jeff, being a co-founder, could sell a bunch of his ETC and bring the price to zero. Jeff responded, "Hehe I could sell them at 0.01." The group also made fun of ETC, with Fabian asking what the point was of having a chain with no developers and "a hacker with 12% [of all ETC]." Others mock-summarized the argument from a pro-ETC Reddit post as ETC "will make better decisions," so "trust us." (A long-standing philosophy of the cryptocurrency community was "trustlessness," meaning blockchain technology could be used in transactions that normally require people to trust others but would instead operate like a financial vending machine, which one doesn't have to trust.)

Suddenly, they realized someone was posting screenshots of the conversation to Reddit. "Who is that?" wrote Fabian. "He has none as friends but is in this channel?? One of the new ones?" Ian Meikle, the designer from the Spaceship, responded, "Jeez what is this BS."

Jeff asked, "Vitalik could you cull all non-ethereum people? This channel is for employees and contractors."

Fabian added, "yeah I feel also not so internal here anymore.."

Shortly thereafter, Ming, aka Bumper Chan, weighed in:

[Announcement]: This bears repeating. The internal channel is meant for foundation matters ONLY. PERIOD"

After warning that the channel was not for "matters that have nothing to do with our business or supporting R&D of Ethereum platform and the education surrounding it," she wrote,

[Reminder]: We are a non-profit foundation supporting open source decentralized software innovation, specifically, of the Ethereum platform and tech. As a NON-PROFIT foundation we are certainly NOT EVER and NEVER HAVE BEEN involved in the business of:
• Securities
• Market making
• Promoting/Marketing for any for-profit company or their products & services

Later on, she added no channel was safe from leaks. "If you practice being immaculate with your words, you will eliminate 99% of the problems of perception related to *your words*," she wrote. "I practice this myself and it requires a kind of diligence."[5]

The following day, one of the most influential Bitcoin industry players, Barry Silbert, a strawberry blond, baby-faced Wall Street

wunderkind who had been successful in the traditional financial markets and by now had founded Digital Currency Group
(DCG), which had been investing in all kinds of Bitcoin companies, tweeted,

> Bought my first non-bitcoin digital currency...Ethereum
> Classic (ETC)

> At $0.50, risk/return felt right. And I'm philosophically on
> board[6]

Vitalik was stunned. He had met with Barry at the DCG offices
in March, and at that time Barry had offered to help him and be
his advisor. Now he was finding out that despite the friendly over-
ture, Barry had never bought ether and now instead had bought
ether classic.

Several hours later, Barry tweeted again: "For those inquiring, @GenesisTrading is facilitating OTC block trading of Ethereum Classic (ETC). Min block size of $25,000."[7] Genesis was
DCG's institutional trading firm, so it only worked with large
orders. When someone responded asking what that meant, another Twitter account wrote, "It means if you have $25k you had
been planning on lighting on fire, this may be more amusing."[8]
ETC dropped as low as $0.45 that day but closed at $0.60. Vitalik
thought, *Okay, maybe it will be 2 to 3 percent as big as ETH and gain
a cult following.*

But the next day, perhaps now that ETC whales knew they
could trade ETC through Genesis without the price slipping too
much, it closed at $2.55. It also didn't hurt that Kraken and an-
other exchange called Bittrex began offering ETC trading.[9] The
rising price and greater number of exchanges on which to sell had
also attracted miners. The ETC:ETH hashing power ratio went
from 6:94 that morning in New York to 17.5:82.5 by late afternoon.[10] At 6:33 p.m., Barry tweeted,

What a day[11]

Vitalik realized that Barry had probably already made a pile of money off ETC. What Barry had done felt to him like a George Soros–style financial attack on Ethereum.

Avsa tweeted, "Classic feels like a troubled teenager son: you love them, created them, helped them grow, yet all they talk is murdering you on your sleep."[12] Someone wrote back, "teenager son denied to be taken care of by absent alcoholic parents that want to kill him [51% attack him lulz."

Barry wasn't the only one being adversarial to Ethereum. Charles Hoskinson, still unhappy about his treatment by the Ethereum community since being booted two years prior, tweeted, "I never thought I'd tweet this…I'm rejoining Ethereum to start making contributions to Classic. Will report more later."[13]

Vitalik thought, *Okay, whatever, of course he'd do that sort of thing.*

Vitalik received one more email from Bitcoin core developer Gregory Maxwell:

I've received confirmation from others that you received my message and shared its content with others. But I didn't get a response from you.

Do you believe that ETC is much more valuable than my offer? I did invite a counter offer! In any case, my offer still stands.

Vitalik ignored the email from "One-Meg Greg," as he called him—a reference to how, during a Bitcoin civil war over a technical issue with philosophical implications, Greg had aligned with those who wanted to keep the Bitcoin "block size" at one megabyte.

POLO MADE OUT big from its bet. Because it *had* instituted replay protection, it would never send out ETC when someone was withdrawing ETH, and vice versa. However, other exchanges that had *not* implemented replay protection were susceptible to replay attacks. Indeed, three days after Polo had listed ETC, another exchange, BTC-e, published a blog post declaring ETC a "scam." This was perhaps less a factual statement than the exchange pouting over having had all its ETC pilfered. The BTC-e blog post stated, "On the second day after the start of ETC trading BTC-e received a notification from Poloniex, saying that we need to secure the ETCs in our ETH wallet. At the time of notification, most of these coins have already been sent to Poloniex by our users. So there were almost none of these coins in our wallet."[14] What had happened was that people were depositing ETH on BTC-e (or already had ETH there), then withdrawing that ETH, plus getting ETC back, which they could then sell on Polo, perhaps turning it into more ETH, which they could then deposit back onto BTC-e in order to perform the trick all over again. Three days later, BTC-e was still getting requests from customers wanting their ETC, but BTC-e had none left, given that, in the previous twenty-four hours, from its known ETC wallets, at least five hundred thousand ETC ($1.4 million at ETC's high) had flowed to Poloniex.

OVER THE NEXT few days, ETC's price dipped from $2.55, trading in the $1 to $2 range. Vitalik got a ride home to Toronto from IC3 with Ming, Casey, and Martin Becze and kept his eyes on the ETC price while at his parents' place.

Barry gloated again over his trades:

> Given number of people calling me an idiot for buying ETC, I'm feeling real good right no. Reminds me of '12 when I started buying BTC <$10[15]

The next day, August 1, ETC had risen again to the $2 range. Meanwhile, the price of ETH kept dropping.

Someone tweeted at Vitalik,

@VitalikButerin Vitaliy is it true that you left ETH and now working with ETC team? Can you kill this rumor once and for all please![16]

Vitalik wrote back,

I am working 100% on ETH.[17]

Mihai, Joe, Fabian, Stephan Tual, and more than one hundred others retweeted him.[18] It became clear that most of the Ethereum community was still with him.

And yet, on August 2, ETH tumbled to a low of $8.20, while ETC hit a high of $3.53. It wasn't 2 to 3 percent of ETH's market cap as Vitalik had thought it might be. Now it was as high as 43 percent.

Many Ethereum developers couldn't understand why this was happening. They did not see any point to the existence of ETC. They thought it should have died by now. Vitalik prepared himself mentally for the possibility that Ethereum would collapse. He realized that Barry and/or other immutability-revering whale traders could use momentum to push the ETC price above that of ETH, creating a feeling that Ethereum Classic was the real Ethereum. At that point, those who were indifferent would feel the need to switch back so as to be part of "Ethereum," leaving behind the forked version that was currently named Ethereum. While on a train to the Toronto airport to meet his dad and stepmom, he thought, *If ETC actually wins, then what will I do?* He decided if that happened, he would quit Ethereum, stay in the shadows for a bit, work on some of the technical upgrades he had in mind for Ethereum, and then start a new blockchain.

Someone tweeted at Vitalik, "What will you do if ETC price overtakes ETH?"[19]

Vitalik wrote back, "I still won't support ETC."[20]

Meanwhile, elsewhere in the crypto world, the exchange Bitfinex (whose executive Phil Potter had said "fuck this coin" about ETH after the DAO attack) got hacked for about 120,000 BTC, then worth around $66 million.[21] It was the second-largest exchange hack in cryptocurrency history, after Mt. Gox's. That news caused other gyrations, with Bitcoin slumping from above $600 to below $550 and the entire crypto market sinking from around $12.2 billion to a bit more than $10.6 billion. With traders spooked, few were willing to put money into a speculative asset like ETC.

For the next week, ETC held at about $2, then slid below that threshold. The price of ETH rebounded to $10, then $11, then $12. Vitalik felt relieved. As time went on, he realized he needn't have worried. Despite the concerning price swings, nothing had changed about the fundamentals of ETH and ETC. By mid-October, the price of ETC would dwindle to below $1.

AROUND THIS TIME, several people—including Griff, Lefteris, Jordi Baylina (the DAO community member from Barcelona whose smart contract had rescued the last $4 million in the counterattack), and others—organized to return to its owners the ETC created from the rescued 69 percent of the ETH. Dubbed the White Hat Group (WHG), they would bear the legal risks of taking money that belonged to other people without their permission, holding it for them without a banking license, and finding and distributing it to the people to whom it was rightfully owed.

Right after the fork, the White Hat Group found itself going through a sort of "Groundhog-DAO." During the crowdsale, a whale named Chris Harborne had put 38,383 ETH in the DAO. Harborne was a salt-and-pepper-haired British executive who owned an aviation fuel business, lived around the globe so as to avoid paying taxes in any particular country, and had been Vlad Zamfir's longtime benefactor, having funded an apartment for him in London so Vlad could work on something called a proof-of-stake algorithm, which would be a more environmentally friendly way to run and secure Ethereum. On the day of the hard fork, he went to get his ETH from the Withdraw Contract. As he would later tell Griff and Lefteris, he opened Mist, which was his Ethereum wallet, and made the transaction, and a pop-up appeared. He clicked OK. Another pop-up asked him to confirm that he wanted to turn his DAO tokens to ETH. He was surprised that two pop-ups asked him that, but he clicked OK again. However, a few hours later, when he checked Etherscan, instead of showing he'd sent his DAO tokens to the Withdraw Contract and gotten ETH, it said he had sent 38,383 ETH to the DAO.[22] Based on that day's exchange rate, he'd just sent half a million dollars into the DAO, the contract where any funds could be siphoned and because of which Ethereum itself had had to undergo the first-of-its-kind, large-scale, controversial hard fork of a popular blockchain in order to rescue all the funds inside. It was as if a person had been teleported to Komodo island and left alone with Komodo dragons after all the humans on the island had been airlifted out in a onetime helicopter rescue mission. Only he had done that not with himself but with almost half a million dollars.

Because of his large holdings, Harborne already knew the White Hat Group. When he told them what happened, they nicknamed him Fat Finger since they thought he'd mistakenly sent ETH to the DAO rather than DAO tokens to the Withdraw Contract. But when they figured out what had actually taken place, that moniker didn't make sense: back during the crowdsale, he *hadn't* put in 38,383 ETH as he'd thought. For some reason, the transaction hadn't completed, so on the day of the hard fork, when he'd fired up his browser and clicked OK on the first pop-up, he'd confirmed the transaction, all these months later. So, *after* the hard fork, he had sent to the DAO 38,383 ETH, which due to ETH's rising price, soon became $600,000.

So now, again, there was around $600,000 sitting in this contract, which anyone could drain with a re-entrancy attack. The

White Hat Group did not publicize what had happened, but the funds were in plain view for anyone who cared to look. (Since the information was public, Griff later surmised that anyone else who noticed kept mum as well, so as to increase their odds of being the first to siphon the money.)

They got busy, executing DAO Wars Redux. They created a split DAO vote and, luckily, were the first ones to do so. That meant that seven days later, when it matured, all potential attackers would use the White Hat Group's split DAO, where the White Hat Group was the curator. By this point, they had a whopping 33.4 million DAO tokens to use for their recursive calls, up from the 25 million they'd had for the DAO Wars before the hard fork.[23] When the seven-day voting period ended, Griff says, they employed a number of tactics. First, they ran some re-entrancy attack contracts, as they had for the Robin Hood rescue four nights after the original attack. But on top of that, they spammed the Ethereum network at a certain gas price, which was the fee paid to miners to process their transactions. Then they sent their attack transactions with a *higher* gas price so the miners would be incentivized to include those transactions first, and the re-entrancy transactions by other attackers, who joined from watching the drama unfold in Reddit, would be delayed. It was the equivalent of creating a traffic jam in the regular lanes to slow down their competitors and then sending their own transactions through empty HOV lanes.

Then there were the "doped" tokens. Not every DAO token was the same since each had a different associated reward. (The reward was the cut of profits that investors would keep receiving even when they exited the DAO.) The White Hat Group took advantage of a little mathematical calculation each DAO contract would make when sending ETH to someone withdrawing: the equation ended by subtracting the amount in the reward. So the WHG would adjust the payout from a small number of DAO tokens to a number in the billions, and then send these doped tokens with high rewards to the attack contracts trying to get Harborne's coins. That would severely reduce the amount their adversaries could get from their first attack transactions. It was like slashing the tires of their competitors' cars. Finally, they were also able to lock their child DAO so that no one else could buy into it.

But having to do this while, for a week, the 38,383 ETH was visible on Etherscan wasn't ideal. (Etherscan was an Ethereum "block explorer," or site that gives data on a specific blockchain or blockchains.) Indeed, a vocal critic of the hard fork and White Hat Group mentioned it on Reddit; he had found their doped token contracts and was trying to figure out how they worked and what they did. Lefteris messaged him, "Hey man, Can you please delete your comment explaining what the default function of the contract we are using does? I can explain all of it to you next week, but the zero hour to attack the DAO and save that guy's money is really close and [we] don't want to whiff any part of our strategy to other people." Griff also sent a message.[24] (Later both of these would be screenshot and used against them.)

Despite all the challenges, on July 28, they put all their strategies to use the moment their child DAO's voting period closed. By now, they were true DAO ninjas. The smallest unit in Ethereum is a Wei, worth 0.000000000000000001 ETH, or one to the eighteenth decimal place. They got 100 percent of Fat Finger's money, down to the last Wei.

AFTER ALL THIS work, the White Hat Group was *done*. They had spent more than a month working fourteen- to sixteen-hour days, they'd disappeared from their normal lives, they had practically given up their families—and they were ready to enter the real world again. Of course, they would help refund people who had money in the Extra Balance and child DAOs to complete the hard fork plan.[25] But beyond that, they were ready to pack it in.

The thing was, the money that had originally splintered into those four video game universes all had value now. It was just called Ethereum Classic. And just as the whales, whose ETC could be worth millions, had influenced the resurrection of the original chain on exchanges, they now began pestering the White Hat Group to go rescue the money in the DAO on Ethereum Classic. One whale in particular made a lot of noise: Chatroulette's Andrey Ternovskiy.

The White Hat Group had initially connected with Andrey back when Griff had made a mass call for whales to get in touch so they could pass votes and make the counterattacks necessary to rescue all the money they could from the DAO. (Working with whales was efficient since it meant Griff only had to coordinate a handful of people for each vote, not thousands.) Andrey, whose Slack name was AZ, reached out, proud to be a whale. Although Griff didn't know his real identity at first and wouldn't see an image of him until years later, Andrey had an impish face with a rounded, childlike nose, and his eyebrows were arched into a permanent joker's laugh. He was extremely active—when Griff would ping him on Skype, needing to pass a vote, *boom, boom, boom*, Andrey would do his part. Considering how most of the whales were too busy to talk, Griff loved how quick Andrey was to help. Plus, he was funny as hell—a shit talker and troll who made Griff laugh and who broke into giggles at the end of almost every sentence, as if he were still giddy at having hit the jackpot with Chatroulette in his teens. At its peak the site had one million daily users, only a bit more than the number of times Andrey typically said "fuck" in a day.

All that didn't mean Griff trusted or respected him, though. Griff saw that Andrey's main objective was to make a killing—even if he screwed over others. Andrey told him about how he was snapping up DAO tokens, some at 0.005 ETH—half price. When Griff realized how ravenously Andrey had been buying DAO tokens, he wondered how low the DAO price would have dropped otherwise. (A peripheral figure in Ethereum circles, watching the price, speculated erroneously that the tokens were being bought up by a Chinese investment firm friendly with Vitalik, Joe Lubin, and the Ethereum Foundation.) Despite all that, the White Hat had to give Andrey credit for being 100 percent authentic and appreciated his helping to pass votes they needed with his huge number of tokens. By the end of Andrey's shopping spree, he had 52.5 million DAO, approximately 4.55 percent of the total supply.

After the hard fork, once Andrey realized that, at ETC's high, his original coins were worth more than $1.2 million, he began hounding the WHG to go through the motions of gathering the money in the DAO, the Dark DAO, the mini Dark DAOs, and so forth—all the work they'd been trying to avoid by doing the hard fork—only he was asking them to do it on Ethereum *Classic*.

The WHG said to him and the other whales who began badgering them, "You want us to work? Fucking pay us." They were done giving away free labor.

Griff, who was the main point of contact between the WHG and the whales, says they arranged a deal with Andrey. He sent them one thousand ETH, and they began tracking their hours. The thing was, before the hard fork, the DAO attacker had made a proposal to split from the Dark DAO. At that time, before they were certain there would be a hard fork, the White Hat Group had gotten one thousand ETH from the Extra Balance, which they could use to continually create DAO tokens in any split DAO the attacker created in order to prevent this person from cashing out. But this strategy would have required them to follow the attacker into every split DAO every thirty-five days for the rest of their lives. When the hard fork had seemed successful and they thought the original chain was dead, and with it the sin of the DAO, Griff says, at least one member of the White Hat Group had thought they didn't need to stay on top of the attacker any longer and did not continue.

But when the original chain revived, it became clear that they *did* need to. (Andrey had been pressuring them to do so—again, he'd had foresight most other people involved in the DAO did not—but because he was the kind of guy the WHG found hard to take seriously, they hadn't.) Because Ethereum Classic was a "new" chain (actually, technically, it was the original chain, but because the majority of the community went with the new chain, the original one now had to take a new name), there were no block explorers such as Etherscan showing what was happening on the chain. Unable to easily confirm the state of the network, the WHG tried to send votes in the Dark DAO on Ethereum Classic. They had no effect, so voting must have ended. The attacker was able to move all the ETC in the Dark DAO to his or her new child DAO, or a grandchild DAO, as it were.[26] So the attacker got away with 31 percent of the ETC in the DAO. Andrey had been right.

Though they'd missed rescuing that 31 percent of the ETC, they still had control of the other 69 percent—all the then-ETH/now-ETC they'd rescued plus the ETC in the six other attack DAOs, of which they'd gained control, as well as the Extra Balance. Thankfully, because of the lack of block explorers, the other copycat mini DAO attackers were fairly impotent.

While that was good news, it presented a new conundrum: How should they return the money they had rescued, which was supposed to have been erased but had instead revived on Ethereum Classic? Since the tools for dealing with ETC were extremely limited, it was practically unusable. And because there was no replay protection, people could easily lose their coins. So should they return them as ETH instead? Some people argued they should return ETH since people had originally invested ETH.

Although they weren't sure what to do, they knew that, despite their good intentions, hacking, be it white hat or black hat, was illegal, so some of the WHG hackers were nervous about any course of action.

In order to protect themselves, the White Hat Group turned to Bity, the company that had helped Slock.it come up with the DAO.link entity that had the VAT number for the German tax documents. Gian and Alexis, two of the cofounders, invited them to Neuchatel to work it out. On August 5, Griff and Jordi arrived at the Geneva airport, where they met for the first time. (Jordi's greeting to Griff, "Wow, you're tall!") Lefteris came the next day and spent the trip eating one meal a day in the late afternoon because he used lunchtime to run and didn't like running after having eaten breakfast. Gian got the rail-thin Greek to break the rule only once—to eat a slice of pizza.

They slept at Bity headquarters, a thirty-five-hundred-square-foot loft in a former chocolate factory that had floor-to-ceiling windows and gorgeous wood flooring that Bity had outfitted with long tables, cushy leather office chairs, and large monitors. There was a kitchen where a resident would make meals, giving the office a homier feel.

The WHG decided to use the umbrella of a legal entity, similar to an LLC, for protection. With that, they could say certain Ethereum addresses were owned by this legal entity, and any transactions using those addresses they made as agents of that entity. They got it notarized. Voilà, they were protected—but soon that cover would feel flimsy.

ON AUGUST 6, the Saturday Lefteris flew in, the group, plus Gian of Bity, had a call with Bitcoin Suisse, the crypto exchange and trading outfit that had helped Ethereum in the early days, in Zug. But Lefteris was unaware of that fact. He knew nothing about Bitcoin Suisse except that it had posted the Reddit message from the person who had followed the WHG into all their mini DAOs.

The phone call ended up being quite different from what the group expected. The WHG and Gian were at Bity's lawyer's offices in an old, Beaux-Arts-style building.[27] They had the call out in the slate-paved garden. The temperature was in the low seventies, not too hot for an August evening. It was just past 8:30 p.m., the golden hour. They sat in a circle in white wire garden chairs, Griff with his hair in a man bun, a cloth patchwork bag at his feet with one square displaying a peace sign. Lefteris had on an army-style jacket and black-and-fluorescent-yellow sneakers. Jordi wore a turquoise polo shirt with a navy collar and rib knit sleeve hems. Griff put the call on speakerphone and placed his device in a frisbee to amplify the sound. The ponytailed pirate look-alike Niklas Nikolajsen of Bitcoin Suisse did the talking.

According to a recording of the call, Niklas opened by stating that he spoke on behalf of a number of investors, including his client, "AT," and that he would propose a way that Bitcoin Suisse and the White Hat Group could work together and "all stand to profit quite a bit." After a few formalities, he cleared his throat and began outlining the scheme he and his investors had devised.

After the hack, he explained, the White Hat Group ended up with roughly eight million ETC. "And that's not a question for us, but a question for you, what to do with those eight million ether classic. That, of course, I leave completely to you to decide," he said in a deep baritone with his Danish-accented English. "From our perspective, you're not in a position to be actually prosecuted in any way if you stuck it in your pocket. Or you could return it to the various DAO investors, or you could do whatever you want. But, before making any decision, and no matter what decision you will make, we are, combined—you and us—in a position to make a significant, if not historic, market manipulation."

At this point, Griff laughed loudly—twice. In the United States, market manipulation can be a felony punishable with a fine of up to $1 million and up to ten years in prison.

Niklas went on, saying that Bitcoin Suisse had quite a lot of ETH, and the WHG controlled even more ETC, so they could "make some gigantic long positions on ether and some gigantic short positions of ether classic." He then suggested they get together at a "trading boot camp" in which all the stakeholders would come with their computers to execute the plan, step by step, to make a controlled crash of ETC. He recommended they target the primary markets—the USD, BTC, ETH, and EUR markets for ETC on Kraken and the ETH and BTC markets for ETC on Poloniex.

> First, you sell a significant portion on all the markets at the same time. And then as the market then bounces back, you do it again. This should trigger an investor panic on the ether classic side and allow you to recover the ether classic sold at a much lower price, because then you will be buying it from a panicking market. That is, if you at all want it back, in order to give it back to the DAO investors. If you do *not* want it back, then the strategy is a little bit different. Then first, all should be a controlled selloff of a large position of ether classic to secure as many dollars and BTC as possible and the remainder should be used to crash it.

He then explained that Bitcoin Suisse could play a crucial role because some of its clients were the biggest holders of ETH and ETC, and so "we have access to a very large amount of capital with which to do the longs and shorts," as well as the so-called institutional trading accounts (for large businesses) on exchanges as well as the banking connections. "But I think since that you hold the commanding position in ether classic, and we hold the commanding position in ether, it would make absolute sense for us to work on this together," he said, adding that his group had projected that this strategy could cause ETC to lose 90 percent, ETH to gain 15 percent, and BTC to increase 5 percent. "If that's the case, then as we deploy these funds in value of seven to eight million dollars, or maybe even more than that, then you can calculate, that will be a million-dollar profit, or many million dollars, actually—or a few million dollars anyways," he said.

He reassured them that, in Switzerland, there was very little by way of regulation against manipulating cryptocurrency markets. He did, however, note that if people found out, "then primarily Slock.it will be subject of much hate, but a legal process is not possible, because there are no rules...But for sure there will be much hate against the organization. But, I mean, who would mind being hated for $20 million? I wouldn't."

Griff interrupted, "I don't know—I would not like to be hated, to be honest."

Later on, Lefteris corrected Niklas: "You mentioned Slock.it many times, but I just wanted you to understand—the Robin Hood Group has nothing to do with Slock.it." (He had, by this point, officially left Slock.it.)

Niklas pointed out that the names of some of the people in the Robin Hood Group were already known. "This is a decision especially Lefteris has to make up with himself: Do you want to be a millionaire and have some rumors crawling around on the Internet that you are maybe not the nicest guy in the world? Or do you want to rather not get millions of dollars and not have this issue?"

Then, reminding them that Bitcoin Suisse's lawyer believed they could not be sued for any of this, Niklas said, "It's not my decision to make. I am not involved, but I would have seriously thought about whether it should be returned or not. Quote-unquote: Code is law, right?" And then he laughed.

By now, the sun had set. The golden hour had given way to dusk. Throughout the conversation, silent in the background, except for a brief hello at the end, was the client: Andrey Ternovskiy.

DURING THE CONVERSATION, Griff was stunned. In the United States, if this discussion had involved stocks, for which specific regulations prohibit market manipulation, executing the scheme Niklas outlined would have been illegal. He imagined Satan coming out of the phone, a demon talking with Niklas's deep voice. He and the other White Hats thought, *We came all this way to give everyone back all this money, and now you think we're going to fuck everybody?* They felt Niklas and Andrey had no idea where they were coming from.

But before they gave their final decision on this proposal, they had to address a piece of business with Andrey. By this point, the

WHG—Griff in particular—thought they knew Andrey well. Not only had he been instrumental in carrying out all the rescues, but he'd also been much more communicative than all the other whales.

However, during the call, Gian asked Niklas about the DAO attacker, mentioning that he thought Bitcoin Suisse was in contact with this person since Bitcoin Suisse had posted a message from him or her on Reddit. Lefteris corrected Gian, "No, that was a different person. That's not the DAO attacker." After Bitcoin Suisse had posted the message on Reddit from the person who had entered all the White Hat Group's mini rescue DAOs, even though Fabian had verified that the message had come from that person's account, that did not prove that he or she was also the original attacker. After a while, Lefteris and Griff just assumed they were two different people, because there was no motivation for the attacker to do any more than he or she had already done, and there was no evidence they were the same person.

But now they got confirmation, because Niklas then said to Gian, "That is a different person. Our client, AT, was the joiner of the White Hat."

This was news to Griff, who was the only WHG member on the call who knew AT/AZ's real identity.

Lefteris connected with Andrey on Skype, learning that he was the founder of Chatroulette. Then, as Lefteris paced around the second floor of the Bity office, Andrey confessed everything—that he'd joined all the mini DAOs to keep pushing things in the direction of a hard fork, so that he could keep buying DAO tokens cheaply and then cash in on all his 30- to 60-percent-off DAO tokens and make back scads of ETH.

The punchline was that the "attack contract" didn't actually work—it was just Andrey's best attempt to make it *look* like it could drain the DAOs. He hadn't actually known how to code it to siphon money.

Lefteris was in shock. He'd sold his $500 worth of DAO tokens at 70 percent or less of their value. Meanwhile, Andrey had turned what Lef had deemed a floundering investment into a massive payday. (Andrey may also have nudged Ethereum to hard-fork in the process.)

Griff was furious when he found out. Andrey had always made him laugh, but this time Andrey had pissed him off. While he and the other White Hats had been sweating through all the maneuvers to pull off these rescues, Andrey had been trolling them for millions of dollars. The Russian entrepreneur had completely wasted their time.

THE AFTERNOON AFTER Bitcoin Suisse's offer, Griff and Lefteris called—this time just Andrey was on the phone. As politely as he could, Griff said they were declining Niklas's offer. Upon hearing their decision, Andrey stammered, trying to convince Griff that he had not been in favor of the market-manipulation scheme.

Griff cut him off: "Yeah, it was only about Niklas's proposition."

"Okay, so again, I'm not desperate for cash," Andrey said. "I have my own job. Whatever you're going to decide, I will accept it. Because I believe in creating value for people and not just expecting a quick buck." He audibly blew air out of his mouth.

After asking who else was on the call and learning it was only White Hats, Andrey said, "Please don't tell this to Gian, but… okay, well, how much do you trust Gian?" Griff said they trusted him a lot.

Andrey wanted them to understand that Gian's Bity was a competitor to Bitcoin Suisse. "[Bitcoin Suisse] basically said [Gian] went to their office and posed as a client and tried to get information about their business and then started his own," he said, and so "if your opinion is in any way influenced by Gian, treat that with a grain of salt." (Later Gian, who does not view the companies as competitors, would say he had only ever met Niklas when Niklas asked him if he wanted to invest in Bitcoin Suisse, but at that time Gian was already working on Bity, which he'd first registered as a corporation in December 2013.)

Griff and Lefteris said they weren't influenced by him because of how "fucking crazy" the proposal Niklas made was.

"Also, Andrey," chimed in Lefteris, in his softly Greek-accented English, "from my side, it was extremely aggressive. What [Niklas] asked, at some point, if I wanted to be hated by the world but still have $20 million? It's like…you know, it was a bit…you know… *heavy*."

Almost as if feeling bad about having pinned the scheme on Niklas, Andrey then mentioned that, the day before, after hanging up, Niklas had said that he thought the WHG should return the money.

Later, as if to see if he could get them to reconsider, Andrey reminded them that there were many whales who were also capable of dumping the price and that Bitcoin Suisse and its investors were not the only people who had had this idea.

Griff still rejected the offer to "be slightly hated by the community and have millions of dollars." Shortly afterward, they hung up.

AT THIS POINT, the White Hat Group made a decision that at least some of them would later regret. First, they could tell from the queries they were getting—as well as the call from Bitcoin Suisse—that a lot of whales and perhaps the DAO attacker might attempt to crash the market for ETC or at least make a larger profit by trying to get their ETC before the smaller DAO token holders. (Andrey began calling Lef every hour to request, as Lefteris put it, "*really, really intently*" that his funds be sent directly to him rather than included in the mass distribution. He begged so intently, "at certain points, he sounded like a kid." Lef got a little worried: *This shady Russian dude can have us beat up or something!* Eventually, Griff told Lef to stop answering Andrey's calls.) This made them realize that if they did give people back ETC, assuming there would be a mass dump of coins, then that would create the dilemma of what time to begin the withdrawal, since certain time zones would be advantaged over others. Also, a Withdraw

Contract on Ethereum Classic designed like the one on Ethereum wouldn't work because not all exchanges allowed people to withdraw their DAO Classic (DAO-C) tokens, so not everyone who deserved money could access them.

ETH, on the other hand, was more usable, it carried less risk of loss due to replay issues, and the price was not as easy to crash, which would keep whales from exploiting smaller holders. If the WHG themselves converted the ETC to ETH first, they could average out the value for DAO token holders, and since DAO token holders would be less likely to sell ETH than they would ETC, the possibility of a decreasing price would be less of an issue.

So the WHG decided to take the ETC in their possession, convert it to ETH, and return *that* to users. (ETC supporters, Bitcoin maximalists, and proponents of immutability would probably view the rationale above as a thinly veiled excuse to disadvantage ETC and use 10 percent of the ETC supply to tip the scales in favor of ETH.)

The decision to return ETH, not ETC, prompted at least one whale to send multiple legal threats to Vitalik and various Ethereum devs, White Hat Group members, and DAO curators. The first was sent on August 8 by a lawyer, Andrew M. Hinkes, then at Berger Singerman, on behalf of his client, Andrey; it began, "In light of the prospect of potential litigation against you," and informed them that they had to retain all documentation about their response to the DAO exploit "for use at trial in this matter."

Despite the letter, the WHG had made up their minds. Bity had decided it would help the WHG sell on all the exchanges where Bity had accounts. The WHG gave full passport scans and other identifying information so that the exchanges would understand they weren't trying to launder the money. Bity helped the WHG create a bot that would make market orders and bring the price to the same level on all the exchanges at the same time, so traders couldn't conduct arbitrage that would effectively shrink the value of the DAO token holders' money. (Lending credence to the theory that this maneuver was an attempt to harm ETC, the creator of the bot to do the trade says he jokingly named it "takea-dump."[28]) For instance, only selling on Polo because it had the most liquidity would lower the price there, enabling bots or other traders to buy on Polo and sell at a higher price on the other exchanges.

They used a function that would obfuscate the source of the funds so people wouldn't realize that 10 percent of all ETC was about to be sold.[29] Then, on Tuesday, August 9, they spread out the ETC among Polo, Kraken, Bittrex, and Yunbi.[30] Their deposits went through everywhere except Polo.

Shit! Polo had taken the money but not credited their account. And they wanted to put the lion's share of the ETC there because Polo had the deepest order books, meaning the price would change the least there, even with a large sell order. (Although they didn't know it, Andrey had sent legal threats to a number of exchanges.)

Bity called Polo and left messages asking why the money wasn't being deposited. They got no response. Several hours later, however, they were notified the account was no longer blocked. Finally they could execute their plan to sell the ETC. They used their bot to sell on all exchanges simultaneously to bring the price to the same level everywhere.[31] And the price decreased on every exchange...except Poloniex. Again, *shit!* Although Polo had let them deposit funds, it had, without notice, blocked their account from trading.

The WHG was trying to return people's money, but instead they'd gotten the majority of it frozen at an exchange. When they asked Polo why it had blocked the trade, Griff and Jordi say the rep asked how Polo was to know the difference between a white hat and a black hat hacker. According to Griff, the rep then said that Polo was going to hold the money because it wasn't the WHG's money.[32] Bity and the White Hat Group told Poloniex that it wasn't theirs either. (Eventually, the WHG would realize that although Kraken was happy to let the Bity account trade, the exchange had blocked its withdrawals.)

Around the same time, someone working in the Bity office, who was then helping the WHG, recalls hearing a rumor from what they believed to be a credible source that the FBI had opened an investigation into the WHG's activities, which scared the shit out of some group members. For the next two days, they spent a lot of time staring up at a big screen, incessantly refreshing the Poloniex account page to see if the money had been unfrozen. During this stretch of time, they slept very little—going to bed at 8 a.m. the night they realized the funds were frozen—and when people passed out, they did so on the sofas around the office. Weed and bottles of whiskey were strewn about, though the White Hat Group didn't partake.

Either the next day or the day after, another whale, Chris Harborne, aka Fat Finger, also put pressure on the White Hat Group, demanding his money be returned to him as ETC, not ETH, and threatening to talk to a lawyer. On a phone call, which members of Bity took outside the back of the top-floor kitchen, where a hillside road passed by, they say Chris argued that if he lost a gold bar in the street, whoever found it couldn't convert it to dollars. Someone familiar with UK and Swiss law who was working in the Bity office argued back that under the definition of "losing," no one lost ETC and that they'd actually parted with ETH.

To respond to Chris's threats, Gian says he stepped in and told the Brit, "Maybe you went with your boat many places with a colonial attitude, but you won't reach me in Switzerland with your boat. If you want to reach me, you have to come to Switzerland." Switzerland, Gian knew, was a much friendlier environment to him legally.

Around the time they fended off Chris, they heard the FBI investigation had promptly been closed. One person remembers the sleepless crew decided among themselves never to speak of it again.

But the pressure they faced wasn't over yet. The next day, they received a legal letter from MME, again on behalf of Andrey. Delivered to each of them, it came from Ethereum's lawyers, Luka

Müller-Studer and Gabriela Hauser-Spühler. Under the heading "Demand for Refund of Ether Classic (ETC) from the 'Robin Hood Group,'" it noted, "Andrey Ternovskiy can document that his complete share of 'The DAO'...was approx. 4.55 % (52'533'041 Dao Tokens)." It then explained what had happened during the Robin Hood counterattacks, with emphasis in bold,

> **Every person, exchange and/or other entity which would accept, transfer, change, administrate and/or otherwise control the ETC transferred from wallets controlled by one or all members of the Robin Hood Group or their affiliates could be held liable for money laundering.**
>
> Consequently, our client claims the immediate (within 48 hours after service of this notice by e-mail) transfer of **346'718.0706 ETC** (Client holds 52'533'041 DAO tokens), held by the Robin Hood Group and/or its affiliated, which previously has had a value of well over USD 3 per ETC which equals to USD 1.2 million (respectively USD 596'355.08 at the current market price of USD 1.72).

Toward the end, it said, "Please note that we are instructed to introduce criminal, civil and administrative proceedings and notifications if we were notified and/or informed of any transfer of ETC other than refund to the DAO Investors."

Since Lefteris and Griff had stopped responding to Andrey's Skype requests to hand him his ETC directly, ahead of the crowd, his lawyers had sent these threats. If the WHG acquiesced to the letter's demands and immediately transferred the ETC to Andrey, he would have an advantage in selling it before the rest of the DAO token holders received theirs.

Lefteris and Colm were freaked out that MME had found their home addresses. After that, Colm all but disappeared, pretty much never to be heard from again—at least not with that name.

IT WAS CLEAR that Polo would not let them execute their plan. Again, because the White Hat Group was a bunch of developers, much as they had been blind to the exchanges' point of view during the hard fork decision process, they didn't understand how the trading community worked. Although the WHG's reasons for not returning ETC to people rested partially on how difficult it was to *use*, the traders weren't interested in "using" ETC the way the developers envisioned. They wanted to trade it as an asset on an exchange that would take care of all the technical aspects for them. Whether or not there was an Ethereum Classic block explorer was irrelevant. They saw ETC as money and wanted the new asset that had cell-divided from their original holdings, not the more user-friendly twin. The exchanges would make it user-friendly for them. They wanted their free money; they wanted the ability to arbitrage price differences across exchanges and/or the chance to "dump" it on a sucker willing to pay a price that would enable them to profit.

Since Polo wasn't going to unfreeze the deposit unless they returned the funds in ETC, they decided to comply. On Friday, August 12, at 2:33 a.m. Neuchatel time, Jordi published a Reddit post summarizing these events and then noted that they would make another announcement about the distribution of the ETC.[33]

One of the top comments said, "So basically you stole 7 million in ETC and tried to dump it and buy ETH with it. Totally legit, bro!"[34] Another Redditor defended the White Hat Group: "You are aware, that without their efforts, you would see nothing of this money. They worked they asses of for free to help get that money secured and you guys piss on them."[35]

NOW THE WHG and Bity faced the question of who qualified to receive ETC. Some people argued that eligibility should be based on who had DAO tokens at the time the DAO launched on May 28. Some thought it should be based on who held DAO tokens when the re-entrancy attack occurred on June 17. Others advocated to distribute the money to current DAO token holders on the ETC chain. Yet others wanted them to go by who had DAO tokens at block 1919999, the block just before the fork, on July 20.

This last option is what major whales—Chris Harborne, aka Fat Finger, Neopets founder Adam Powell, and Andrey—wanted. (Andrey, of course, had oodles more DAO tokens by the time of the hard fork than he'd had at launch or the time of the hack.) And this was the course of action the WHG ultimately decided upon. (Afterward, Andrey dropped his legal threats.)

A FEW DAYS after Alexis of Bity published a blog post on the status of the ETC refund, which explained why the WHG had first wanted to convert everything to ETH, a Bitcoin maximalist who went by the online handle WhalePanda published a blog post titled "Ethereum: Chain of liars & thieves," in which he delineated the trades that the White Hat Group tried to do on the various exchanges and concluded, "TLDR; **We market dumped the illegally obtained ETC to crash/kill ETC but failed and now we want the locked funds back, sorry.**"

He then showed how connected Bity was to Slock.it through DAO.link (whose four officers/advisors were two people from Slock.it and two from Bity) and said, "it's safe to assume they are working together to try to keep themselves out of legal trouble." He called their blog posts "bullshit and lies" and began picking apart how the members of the Robin Hood and White Hat groups were associated with either the Ethereum Foundation or Slock.it, publishing screenshots of private messages they had sent, such as to the Redditor who had been posting about the doped tokens before the rescue of Fat Finger's funds. He included a screenshot of a comment in which Vitalik denied that the EF and RHG were one and the same. WhalePanda commented, "Do you believe that the benevolent dictator who was in the same chat with RHG members wasn't aware of what was happening?"

Beneath that was a Photoshopped Chinese Communist–style poster of a Soviet flag, at the bottom left picturing a distant view of tiny Chinese proletariat figures marching under the Ethereum logo and, above them, a large, looming image of Mao Zedong from the shoulders up. Pasted on Mao's balding head was Vitalik's face.[36]

Most everyone associated with the DAO faced criticism, but after all his promotion of the DAO, Stephan Tual faced arguably the worst. In the end, Christoph told him he should write an apology to the community. Stephan started to tell Christoph to fuck off, but then he paused. He had been to Christoph's house once. During that visit, he realized Christoph had far better relationships with his kids than Stephan did with his own. He really respected Christoph for that. So, two days after WhalePanda's screed, Stephan published a short blog post titled "On a personal note, from Stephan Tual," which said, "I gave my heart and soul to the DAO project. This has, at times, led to an emotional response to critics and situations. I would like to offer an apology for tweets and posts which have not been appropriate considering the circumstances, but also for all the trouble the DAO has caused, directly or indirectly."[37]

Some of the comments were kind: "In my opinion your only mistake was to act too defiant/arrogant on twitter in the aftermath of the hack."[38] Others were not. One person just wrote, "LOL," and linked to his "No DAO funds at risk" blog post. Another said, "You've lost the respect from 90% of the crypto community. Your narcissistic and arrogant attitude quite literally helped stick a fork in the DAO and potentially ruin the reputation of Ethereum." Yet another responder said, "Biggest Tool there is. Fuck you, Tual, your 'apology' might have meant something weeks and weeks ago. Instead you posted your dank memes and acted like a shit bird."[39]

A WEEK AFTER his blog post explaining the debate with the exchanges and the new plan to create an ETC Withdraw Contract,

Alexis of Bity posted on Reddit the source code for the ETC Withdraw Contract, soliciting comments.[40] One Redditor responded, "Let's get that etc to the DAO holders before it goes to zero."[41] (ETC was at ~$1.75.) Another wrote:

"Free Money!" Part II
This time with way less money.[42]

More people took the WHG to task for basing the refunds on who owned DAO tokens at block 1919999, which caused them grief in two ways: people's complaints plus the difficulty of implementing the solution. They had to recount every transfer that happened in DAO tokens from launch in April to the hard fork on July 20, make the list of addresses with such tokens at that time, and use a script to analyze it. With this list of the number of DAO in each address at the time of block 1919999, people could get back roughly 0.7 ETC to the DAO balance in return. At least they made everything easier by getting MyEtherWallet to create a website so that people could obtain the funds owed to them from the Extra Balance, the Withdraw DAO, and the ETC Withdraw Contract all with one click.

On August 26, on the Bity blog, they posted the revised ETC Withdraw Contract, included a way for people to donate to the WHG for their efforts, and announced that they would deploy the contract starting August 30.[43]

PRIVATELY, THE SAME day, Alexis also emailed Poloniex CEO Tristan D'Agosta, the latest communication in a string of correspondences that had gone unanswered. He explained that Bity had no idea why Polo had frozen their accounts and was unresponsive and that they had tried to reach out through a Polo employee who had been in contact with them earlier about his investigation into the identity of the DAO attacker. Then he referenced another surprising tidbit that the Polo investigator had uncovered.

Back on July 5, in his Skype chats with Lefteris, Griff, and Colm, the Polo employee had written, "I just found another BTC address that confirms yet another person with [name of a Swiss company]. It's further confirmed by logins from the same IP within minutes of the others." Then he added, "he's with Bity." The initial suspect, the head of the company, didn't just have an address that had interacted with an address the attacker had used. He was also suspicious to the Polo investigator because on June 14, three days before the attack, an address to which he had withdrawn BTC from Polo had also been using ShapeShift to convert BTC to ETH—the same behavior as the attacker. It seemed especially odd considering Polo was the most liquid market for ETH in the entire world. Why not do the swap right on Polo? As for the Bity connection, according to a source familiar with the situation, the day before the attack, the head of the Swiss company logged into Poloniex from the same IP within minutes of a somewhat recently departed employee at Bity, who sold about $65,000 worth of ETH. Using the same IP meant they were geographically extremely close, if not in the same exact building. However, Bity was based in Neuchatel, and the Swiss company was based two hours away by train or car. Then, the morning of the attack, three and a half hours after it had begun, the former Bity employee, who had sold his ETH before the price had crashed due to the hack, sent 1,054 ETH (about $16,300, according to Etherscan) to the address to which the CEO of the Swiss company had withdrawn from Polo. Assuming that address was owned by the entrepreneur, it looked to the Polo investigator as if the CEO had perhaps given the former Bity staffer a heads up about the attack beforehand and was receiving a tip in return.

At that time, Alexis had been surprised that the Polo staffer said someone who had previously worked at Bity was implicated. He wrote that Bity had conducted its own investigation and was happy to collaborate if Polo wanted. "But I hope this is not simple defamation from one employee of Poloniex against Bity," he wrote.

"This has already hurt our image among individuals of the ethereum community. For now this is not proven facts." He went on to explain that he believed this is why the ETC Bity had deposited was frozen at Polo, but they still did not know why Polo remained silent. He then offered two options: for Polo to keep the ETC Bity had deposited or to transfer it to the ETC Withdraw Contract that Bity was preparing. Then he asked for Polo to choose. Again, no answer.

On August 29, Alexis published another post on the Bity blog saying the ETC Withdraw Contract would be deployed the next day and filled with 4,171,615 ETC out of a total of 11,538,165 that were linked to DAO-C tokens.[44] Not all the ETC was available in part because 2,800,004 ETC remained frozen on Polo and 499,402 ETC on Kraken. "We have tried to contact both exchanges regarding these funds without receiving any answers," Alexis wrote.

At 5 p.m. Central European Summer Time (CEST) on August 30, the WHG deployed the ETC DAO Withdraw Contract but very quickly realized there was a bug.[45] They had to redeploy a couple times before it worked.

Finally, at 1:31 a.m. Eastern Time (7:31 a.m. Switzerland time) on August 31, Polo broke its silence and tweeted, "We're waiting to get clearance from law enforcement before releasing the White-Hat ETC now that the withdrawal contract is ready."[46]

Ah, law enforcement. That shed some light on some cryptic comments Kraken CEO Jesse Powell had made on Reddit on August 29 in response to a user who said, "These exchanges *really are* the worst. The refund contract is awaiting imminent deployment and yet they're still sitting on these funds?" Jesse replied, "We are *really the worst* because we froze some accounts engaged in some sketchy as hell, inexplicable, activity with your money? My apologies. Unfortunately, we're not the only ones who thought the bizarre actions of the 'whitehat' group warranted additional scrutiny. We're presently seeking approval from other *interested* parties to let the funds go out to the withdraw contract."

MyEtherWallet's Taylor Van Orden got into the fray, commenting back to Jesse that they really *were* the worst and accusing Kraken of making "inside deals." Jesse at first seemed offended that she had criticized him since he had private-messaged her the other day about a phishing site targeting MyEtherWallet's users. Then he shot back, "Allegations of 'inside deals' are completely unfounded. We didn't ask to have this disaster imposed upon us. My preference would be to not be a part of it at all. Next time your white knights want to appear to be laundering and liquidating stolen coins, make sure they do it through an exchange with less regulatory/law enforcement exposure."

In another comment, he wrote, "When we can't say what's going on, you can probably guess what's going on. I wish I could say more. It's our goal to get the coins back to their rightful owners. Whitehat's earlier antics drew a lot of attention that has substantially complicated the matter."[47]

At last, at 10:25 p.m. CEST on Friday, August 31, according to a then Polo staffer, the exchange, following approval from the Department of Justice agency that had stopped the trade, tweeted, "We are preparing to release the WhiteHat ETC to the withdrawal contract within the next several hours."[48] Two minutes later, Kraken tweeted, "Within the next few hours, Kraken will release 499,402.88737 ETC to the WHG's withdraw contract."[49]

AT LAST, THE White Hat Group, which had been doing all this work, mostly around the clock, for free (after the "proposal" from Niklas, the WHG had decided to return the one thousand ETH to Andrey), was done. From the moment of the DAO exploit, Lefteris had worked with other people online from dawn till well after dusk. His wife would ask him to spend time with her, and he would say, "You have no idea what's happening," but she could not care less about his computer world. On top of that, he was making no money from his Robin Hood and White Hat work and actually dipping into his savings. As a sour cherry on top, what the White Hat Group had received in donations didn't cover even a month's worth of expenses.

For his part, Griff never even got paid by Slock.it, because he didn't want to accept anything other than crypto, and Slock.it could not pay him in anything other than fiat. But Griff says he didn't mind because he was already a nonprofit/volunteer-type guy. He did, however, keep a bunch of DAO tokens for years afterward—just in case he ever needed to attack the DAO again, for another Fat Finger incident.

ON SEPTEMBER 6, the final ETC meant for the White Hat Withdraw Contract was deposited—the remaining pools of money added were from one of the child DAOs and the funds that the White Hat Group initially converted to ETH, BTC, and euros on Kraken, Bittrex, and Yunbi. In converting back, they were able to earn an extra 186,516.63 ETC ($274,000) for DAO token holders. With this final deposit, DAO token holders could get the remaining ETC owed to them.

That day, the DAO attacker began to exit. Back on July 23, shortly after the hard fork and before ETC had started trading on Polo, the attacker had sent out the ETC in the Dark DAO to the grandchild DAO in ten transactions of 364,240 each, for a total of 3,642,408 ETC in the grandchild DAO.[50] On September 6, at 12:03 a.m. Switzerland time, he or she withdrew all that ETC (around $5.3 million) from the grandchild DAO to another wallet, 0xc362, and then a few minutes later, at 12:06:33 a.m. CEST, moved the money again to 0x5e8f, his or her main account.[51]

The first thing the attacker did with that money, at 12:34:13 a.m. CEST, was donate one thousand ETC (approximately $1,460) to the Ethereum Classic developers' donation address.[52]

That day at 2:33:25 p.m. CEST, the attacker's wallet received 0.6931 ETC (around $1).[53] The money came from what is known as a vanity address, a phenomenon that began with Bitcoin. Since most cryptocurrency addresses are random strings of numbers and letters, such as the 0x5e8f and 0x969 addresses, crypto enthusiasts have tried to brute-force-create vanity addresses, similar to vanity license plates, which seem less random—for instance, an address that begins with several zeros or spells a person's name. In the case of the DAO attacker, this 0.6931 ETC came from an address that began with eleven *A*s: 0xaaaaaaaaaaaf7376faade1dcd50b104e8b70f3f2.

Such an address would have required the user's computer to run, on average, calculations 8.8 trillion times in order to derive such a public key.[54] This indicated that the owner of the address likely had a lot of computer power, or GPUs (graphic processing units), which are more powerful than the chips on normal computers and were often used to mine Ethereum at that time. Perhaps the transaction from that 0xaaaaaaaaaaa address was the attacker him- or herself, making a "haha, suckers!" gesture.

(The attacker seems to have been a connoisseur of vanity addresses. On both the Ethereum Classic and Ethereum chains, on September 6 at 8:03:41 and 8:03:42 a.m. CEST, respectively, the 0xaaaaaaaaaaa address had received money from a vanity address that began 0x222222222222fc20, and that address had, before the hard fork, received money from a vanity address that began 0xdeadbeefb880, which in turn had received money from an address beginning 0x0000000008b4c9, which had received money from four additional vanity addresses in addition to 0xdeadbeef: 0x666666666660bfe3, 0x111111111b41fad, 0x0000000000015b, and 0xffffffff3984f569b4.[55])

After the transaction from the vanity address graced the 0x5e8f account, nothing happened until October 25, when the attacker then began parceling out the money to different wallets in round amounts such as eleven hundred, five thousand, ten thousand, twenty-five thousand, and so forth, with some wallets receiving multiple transactions.[56] For instance, the 0x085acc address received seven such transactions. From there, the hacker was sending out even smaller amounts, all around 2,310 to 2,340 ETC.

At this point, a DAO helper in Sydney, Australia, Bok Khoo, who was known online by the nickname BokkyPooBah, realized there might be a way to prevent the DAO attacker from cashing out. BokkyPooBah was an actuary who had become bored with insurance premiums and managing people's money. When Ethereum and the DAO came along, he learned about the two by answering a lot of questions on Stack Exchange, a sort of Quora for computer programming questions. After the attack, he was writing detailed instructions on how users could get their refunds and even doing withdrawals for them—usually at 11 p.m. Sydney time, after his four kids had gone to bed.

On October 26, a user in the DAO Slack noticed the attacker's booty was moving. When BokkyPooBah checked, he saw all the transactions were for about 2,333 ETC or less—about $2,500 per transfer. He realized these amounts were within the transaction limits of ShapeShift, which didn't take customer-identifying information. He initially guessed the attacker would have tried to convert the ETC into one of the privacy coins, such as Monero, which would help obscure the movement of the funds and make it easier to cash out, but he was surprised to see that actually the attacker appeared to be trying to turn the ETC into Bitcoin, which *was* traceable.

However, at the time, the Bitcoin network was undergoing a congestion period. A civil war had been brewing over how many megabytes of data a block of the Bitcoin blockchain should have. As volume was growing, the number of transactions at any given time was bumping up against the current cap, one megabyte. Since some blocks were full, many transactions were being delayed until they could be included in less full blocks. At the moment the DAO attacker was cashing out, congestion was at a four-month high. The DAO attacker's transactions were being delayed by half a day or more. BokkyPooBah tried to contact ShapeShift to no avail, so he got Griff to reach out, but by the time ShapeShift had worked out what it might do, the Bitcoin network queue had cleared, so across two days, the DAO attacker was able to execute almost 50 transactions ranging from fractions of a coin to a bit over 3.6 BTC at a time, netting almost 146 BTC (about $96,000). (However, that fall ShapeShift blocked ten transactions totaling 14,566 ETC from the attacker's address and related addresses.)

Although the outcome wasn't optimal, because of the hard fork, what the attacker had obtained had about a tenth the value it would have had, had it remained ETH. And while the hard fork created an evil-twin Ethereum, not having one person controlling 5 percent of all coins was important because Ethereum planned to eventually move to a new mining system where how many coins individual entities had would determine who controlled the network.

So, with that, it seemed Ethereum was over the hardest challenge it had faced in its short lifetime. The whole debacle had shaved $700 million (41 percent) off its market cap, but Ethereum hadn't lost the majority of community support to Ethereum Classic. Although Stephan Tual, who remained working at Slock.it, was widely reviled, Christoph was treated nicely, at least by the other developers. The one thing he would have to live with for the rest of his life was that any presentation about smart contract security would mention the DAO. Although Slock.it had no money with which to pay Griff and Lefteris, they parted on good terms. Lefteris was not sure he would continue working with blockchain technology, as he was sure everyone hated or wanted to kill him. As for Vitalik, one Ethereum developer felt that the experience changed him for the better: whereas before he'd been a boy who got lucky and was selling a dream, he had become more realistic and learned not to overpromise, giving his words more weight.

9

September 13, 2016, to fall 2016

ON SEPTEMBER 13, Griff published a blog post saying the Extra Balance Withdraw Contract on Ethereum (not Classic) would finally be funded on September 15.[1] To create it, BokkyPooBah and three other developers had to independently create lists of Extra Balance contributors, cross-check them, and resolve discrepancies. Griff's instructions on how to obtain one's Extra Balance contained step-by-step instructions with twelve screenshots marked with red circles, boxes, and arrows to help the newbs who didn't know what a blockchain was and just bought DAO tokens to get rich. A couple days later, BokkyPooBah published a Reddit post listing all the pots in which people might have ETH or ETC: ETH in the Withdraw Contract, ETH in the Extra Balance, ETH if they manually did an honest split DAO, and the 73.15 percent that remained of the rescued ETC after the DAO attack (up from 69 percent due to the trades the WHG had made when they'd been forced to convert the tokens they'd traded into ETH and BTC back into ETC).[2] Plus, he had to include instructions on how to avoid replay attacks. He bequeathed this resource to Reddit, saying, "In time so you can all enjoy Devcon2 @ Shanghai."

In three days, DevCon 2 was to begin. It was to be held at Shanghai's Hyatt on the Bund, a riverfront area with an incredible view of the Paris of the East's gleaming skyline.

Ming had been preparing for it furiously, relying only on Hudson Jameson; his wife, Laura Penrod, who also had been hired; and a friend from Ming's Ann Arbor days, Jamie Pitts. It was sold out, and one thousand or so people were attending.

Hudson, a reddish-haired, bushy-bearded twenty-four-year-old, had discovered Bitcoin in 2011 at the University of North Texas, where he'd majored in computer science, mined it, got a professor hooked on it, participated in the Ethereum crowdsale, and then gotten hired as a blockchain architect at the bank USAA. He began helping in Solidity chat channels and then, while volunteering for DevCon 1 in the fall of 2015, met all the people he'd been interacting with online. It changed his life.

He was so excited about Ethereum afterward, he wrote Ming an email with feedback on the conference. According to Hudson, impressed, she said the foundation could use someone with his communication skills and developer background and, in a phone call trying to get him to leave USAA, that it had just cut some toxic people (read: Gavin).

He got hired in the middle of the DAO attack craziness. Hudson's initial role was in dev ops (software development and IT operations)—setting up servers, managing the email system—and working on DevCon with his wife, Laura.

He liked and respected his new boss because of how Ming had handled the foundation finances—getting the burn rate down, making sure the Ethereum Foundation had sufficient runway for years. Plus, she seemed to deeply care about Vitalik and the developers. For instance, she interviewed and onboarded new hires herself.

Hudson says Ming seemed to really like him as well. Soon she was calling him a few times a week, for two to four hours at a time. She would tell him about her personal life, confide things she said she'd discovered about the EF's early period—such as that, according to her, Gavin had mismanaged funds and paid himself a lot, and people had stolen money from the EF—and shared other things that made Hudson feel like she trusted him. Hudson recalls that his wife told him it was inappropriate for his boss to be telling him such things and that, at minimum, the way she spoke to him overstepped boundaries, but barely out of college, he thought it was normal. Ming told the foundation staff not to work on weekends, then, Hudson says, she would Skype chat them on Saturday nights asking why they hadn't responded to her messages. Although his wife thought this was manipulative, Hudson thought that if Ming was clocking in on weekends, he would too. He was so wrapped up in Ming and Ethereum that sometimes, due to the long calls with her, he spent more time talking to her than to his wife.

Ming's lengthy phone calls were, by this point, legendary. She would ring pretty much any staffer and talk for hours. One hour, two hours, four. Some developers tolerated it, like Christian Reitwießner, who would be sure to clear minimum one hour for every meeting with Ming. At least he was informed about what was going on in the foundation, whereas he'd been in the dark under Gavin. Another developer felt the calls were friendly but unfocused. She would start by saying, "I have no time for this, I've barely slept in three days, I had to do Christmas with my family, and my dog is dying, and I have to spend the whole Christmas night writing documents." Then she'd talk about the history of China and what her parents had had there, but how the Chinese Cultural Revolution caused her family to end up in Switzerland. He found these conversations interesting, but after a while he'd have to come up with a graceful exit. Others were not as patient. "You could literally put her on mute and unmute her thirty minutes later, and you just had to say, 'yeah, uh-huh, hm' occasionally," one developer would later recall.

The content of the monologues was not exactly professional. She would sometimes bitch about people for an hour or more. She often cried—talking about how stressful and tough everything was, how bad the state of Ethereum and its finances was, freaking out about regulators and how everyone had made a mess of everything. She would say her job was uniquely hard, no one appreciated her, and if her colleagues didn't start valuing her more, she would quit so people would realize she had saved the foundation. Because she was constantly dumping her problems, the staff felt that phone chats with Ming were therapy for her and emotional labor for them. One person observed to Ming's boyfriend, Casey, that she complained about other people a lot. He was surprised when Casey agreed that she got into crazy spin mode and it was hard to get her out. He thought to himself, *Well*, you're *banging her.* (Casey, a developer, worked on Ethereum but was paid nothing or a nominal amount like $1 a year.) In general, she could not separate the personal from the professional, so when employees wanted to tell her something in the latter capacity, she couldn't hear it because she would be so focused on how awful she was feeling or how someone was doing terrible things to her. Because she was their boss, they couldn't tell her that her behavior was inappropriate. One C++ developer described her as "the least professional person I've ever seen."

People who weren't developers but had business/managerial roles requiring them to deal with her had a hard time accomplishing anything. An hour or more on the phone with her would produce nothing. One administrative staffer avoided calls with her and instead put everything in writing. As people at the foundation realized she was having these long conversations with nearly everybody, they began to question her productivity.

Someone who lived with her in Zug said she spent the whole day on the phone, but even when she was ostensibly working (i.e., not on a call), she had a hard time making decisions. For instance, take an easy question, like "Should we go to CES?" (CES was a technology trade show in Las Vegas attended by more than 150,000 people annually.) A quick analysis—it's lots of exposure, but to the wrong people, and even if we get free entry, the booth will be expensive—would be an easy no for most people, but with Ming it became an emotionally charged issue. *Oh, so you don't like this idea that I spent a lot of time on?*

She got hung up on inconsequential things. At one point, Ethereum Redditors decided to create Ethereum subreddits, calling the one for developers ETH Dev, the name of Gav's EF subsidiary in Berlin. Although the Redditors who chose that name had zero inkling another entity had the same name or that it had any charged meaning (in this case, because of Gavin), Ming called one of the facilitators of the subreddit, going on about how the term was harmful.

Other basic facts of the Ethereum ecosystem were triggers. For instance, Joe. Though many developers dealt with ConsenSys or Joe, since his company was one of the main private companies focused on Ethereum, many of the developers and staff realized they could not mention either of them to Ming. Otherwise they would have to calm Ming down—or rope Casey in to do it.

The conflict with Joe extended back to the previous year when Joe offered to pay for DevCon 1 in London. With that reassurance, the foundation began planning the event, putting down deposits, and paying for items. However, someone who perceived that Joe didn't like giving money out says that when it came to actually sending the funds, he delayed. (Joe says he is happy to spend money in exchange for perceived value and generous even in situations where there isn't an exchange.) One of his top people, Andrew Keys, had to use his personal credit card to front $35,000. The payment holdup was especially stressful because the foundation at that time barely had enough funding for a few months. Joe's dawdling caused the EF (basically, Vitalik and Ming) a liquidity crisis.

Another money-related issue caused Ming to distrust Joe: in March 2015, the foundation had donated $1 million in bitcoin to establish an organization called the Cryptographic Currency Research Group (CCRG) to conduct cryptoeconomic research. Joe's son Kieren James-Lubin was to be a director, but it never got off the ground. The foundation decided instead to donate the money to IC3 (the Cornell institute headed by Gün, whose workshop Vitalik had been attending when the hard fork occurred), since it had the same mission.³ But when the EF tried to transfer that money, it turned out Joe had never given the money to the CCRG in the first place. The bitcoins were still in Joe's hands, so, basically, the foundation had given him a $1 million donation, which was crazy, because Joe was funding ConsenSys singlehandedly. Ming thought the fact Joe still had the money was suspicious. (Joe says he missed Vitalik's first request to receive the funds back and acted upon the second.)

(Of his relationship with Ming, Joe says, "She was not a healthy person." At DevCon 1, he said, a little too loudly, that Ming was "batshit crazy," and someone close to her overheard. "I assume that person reported back to her, because soon after she decided I was The Great Satan," he says.)

One person also found Ming "insular" and felt she "repulsed" any collaboration. In the spring of 2016, the Englishman-turned-Canadian Bob Summerwill, who'd been hired on the C++ team in the wake of Gavin's firing, met with Brian Behlendorf, the executive director of Hyperledger, a Linux Foundation effort by dozens of banks, start-ups, and IT firms, including IBM, to create blockchain software tools for large companies.⁴ Bob thought it would be a good idea to get the C++ client relicensed so a version of Ethereum just for enterprises could be made available for Hyperledger. Brian also thought Bob could help out at Hyperledger to see how Ethereum could work with other blockchains. At the time, Bob says he was a contractor for the EF, working sixty hours a week but being paid for forty. He figured he could take his twenty hours of unpaid overtime for the foundation and instead work for Hyperledger. In a call between Bob, Ming, and Brian, Ming addressed Brian suspiciously, asking whether Hyperledger was trying to take over Ethereum. She eventually ripped into Brian, saying, "How dare you steal my people? If you want fifty percent of Bob, you can have a hundred percent of Bob."

A similar, but seemingly more damaging, situation happened with IBM. At DevCon 1 in 2015, Microsoft had announced it would offer a permissioned version of Ethereum.[5] ConsenSys's Andrew Keys was hoping to do a similar deal with IBM, thinking such deals were similar to how, during the early days of the internet, large corporations worked with private intranets before moving to the public internet.[6] While the Fortune 50 firm was interested, there wasn't a version licensed that would allow them to make such a deal.

Andrew says he set up calls three times for Ming with Jerry Cuomo, IBM's vice president of blockchain technologies, and other senior members of the IBM blockchain team.[7] Three times she blew them off. (The same thing happened with a call Bob set up for her with IBM.) Andrew felt he had egg on his face every time. When he asked why she hadn't shown up, she would say she was overwhelmed and had other priorities, like organizing DevCon 2. From Andrew's perspective, having a large enterprise like IBM develop on Ethereum was ten times more important than DevCon 2. He gave up, but afterward believed these incidents were why IBM's main blockchain codebase was a competing technology, not Ethereum.

By DevCon 2, these were the impressions of Ming held by people in Ethereum, but few knew how Vitalik felt.

MING WASN'T THE only one who shot Ethereum in the foot when it came to IBM before DevCon 2. Andrew Keys and Bob Summerwill began looking into getting an Ethereum client into Hyperledger. Andrew even met with IBM's Jerry Cuomo and another top exec there. As he put it in a chat to Bob, they "applauded our presentation of ETH and essentially said they'll THROW OUT THE CODE THEY DONATED to Hyperledger and push for Ethereum to be the core of the Hyperledger fabric." The problem was all Ethereum codebases were licensed such that any entity making modifications would have to contribute them back to the open-source project so others could use them too.[8] Permissive licenses, however, allowed companies to write private versions of the open-source code that didn't have to be shared back.[9] This was popular with corporations happy to use open-source software as long as they didn't have to give away the recipe for their secret sauce.

Andrew thought that getting Ethereum into Hyperledger required a permissively licensed codebase, and Bob nominated the abandoned C++ Ethereum, which, as a high-performance client, was a good option for enterprise. Gavin had actually previously explored that possibility. Bob and Andrew took on the task of getting the ninety-nine contributors to the C++ codebase to sign paperwork to make it permissively licensed. It was a five-month venture involving chasing down developers, taking them on walks, playing pool with them, or treating them to sushi.

In May, when Bob first embarked on the project, Gavin had told him via chat, "i'd certainly be happy to consider supporting a relicencing if there's some inertia behind it." But in August, a month before DevCon 2, Gavin, whose commits alone amounted to 30 percent of the codebase, responded to the latest of Bob's messages about the licensing documents over chat: "is this about the license change? you'd like me to consider it?" He then asked that Bob not get Parity employees involved in EF efforts, "given that the ethereum foundation refuses to endorse or support our efforts with parity," and went on to air grievances and perceived slights. (By this point, he had renamed his company Ethcore to Parity, after its first Ethereum client.)

In the end, Bob didn't even hear the final answer from Gav himself. Brian Behlendorf of Hyperledger had a call with Parity: Gav's firm had decided not to go through with it.[10] Bob felt Gav was acting out of spite. Bob also wondered if Gavin wanted to kill a potential competitor to Parity. Gav said Parity's lawyer, who handled the company's licensing strategy, had decided against it. Parity had partly gotten its VC funding by pitching an enterprise Ethereum implementation, so if the C++ codebase was permissively licensed, it might compete with Parity's future product.

To Ethereum developers, this epitomized how Parity approached work—competitively, not collaboratively. For example, the Ethereum ecosystem talked on one protocol, but Parity created a separate protocol just for Parity nodes.[11] After multiple instances like this, Péter Szilágyi says he reached out to find out why Parity was making technical choices that he felt were antagonistic to Ethereum and/or Geth rather than ones that he felt would collaboratively benefit the whole ecosystem.[12] Péter says the then-Parity CTO, Fredrik Harrysson, responded it was to create a competitive edge to make switching clients hard. To Péter, this turned the vision of a collaborative ecosystem with multiple clients into a cutthroat battle in which each party tried to screw the other over. Fredrik says that Péter never reached out to him and he doesn't know if Péter ever reached out to anyone at Parity. According to Fredrik, Parity had suggested a better syncing strategy, but Péter thought it could be vulnerable to malicious parties, so he refused to install it. Parity implemented the feature, known as "warp sync," and when it was successful, Fredrik says, "This pissed Péter off because it meant our client was better for the average user, and we gained a huge market share with this feature." Fredrik says Parity hoped Geth would adopt this syncing strategy, but the team didn't "as far as I can tell out of pure stubbornness." According to Fredrik, Parity's philosophy is that competition makes the clients better, and Parity's attendance at the core dev calls shows the company has always wanted to collaborate.

Regardless of what happened, the upshot was that even Ethereum devs who had never worked with Gavin got the impression he was willing to do things that were bad for the community as long as they were good for him or Parity. This meant that when Ethereum was looking for a villain at DevCon 2, he came top of mind.

MING'S ISSUES AROUND micromanaging, holding grudges, and being emotionally unstable came into play for DevCon 2, the single event that brought together the various parts of the community every year. That summer Arthur Falls, an Ethereum-focused podcaster and videographer, approached her about doing videos about DevCon 2. He says she responded excitedly—until she found out Arthur was affiliated with ConsenSys. In a follow-up call, he says she was openly hostile. It was the most belligerent anyone had ever been to Arthur in a professional context. She also left him a nasty message saying she didn't want Joe Lubin muscling his way in to control the foundation.

She would get hung up on small things that would cost the foundation nothing. For instance, Jamie Pitts, whose wife was a bilingual Chinese-English speaker, proposed her as an interpreter in Shanghai. His wife told Ming that she would want to be titled "doctor" because of her PhD. Ming was outraged. Jamie introduced them in person to break the impasse, but Ming dug in. Perhaps this was for the best, as Jamie's wife objected to how Ming called him at all hours—and Ming's working hours in Zug were nighttime for Jamie in San Francisco.

For organizing the conference, Ming instituted a rule that she had to preapprove most emails staffers sent. Only, for her, "preapprove" meant she had to write the email herself—even in cases where someone needed a refund. One time, a staffer says another employee sent an email and copied Ming, who called that staff member and started yelling that the email was all wrong. After an earful, the person informed Ming that actually *she* had written the email.

In general, EF staff said, she could not delegate. So, when the time for DevCon came, little logistical things that a staff member should have taken care of were not done or were done poorly because Ming had tried to do everything herself. For instance, she vetted and hired the audio/video (A/V) team, but at the conference Hudson was supposed to run it. When he showed up, he realized the A/V team spoke very little English. Some Chinese-English bilingual Ethereum community members had to interpret for Hudson in the A/V booth. Even the badges were messed up—so badly that Ming apologized about them in the first panel.[13]

Then, there was her emotional instability. She was the emcee for the whole event and was supposed to introduce each speaker from offstage. At one point, Joe Lubin said something to her that set her off, so she took a seat and closed up. When the current speech finished, Ming had so completely shut down that she wouldn't or couldn't introduce the following presenter. Hudson says he had to grab the mic and intro the next few talks until she recovered.

But for all the problems Ming caused at DevCon 2, they were not the main drama.

AT 5:15 A.M. on Monday, September 19, the first day of the conference, Vitalik was sleeping in the Grand Hyatt on the Bund when he was awakened by his hotel room phone. It was Hudson.

"There's a serious problem," he said. "Come down now."

Vitalik grabbed his laptop and ran down. Former Google engineer Nick Johnson, a Kiwi who had written the Withdraw Contract for the hard fork and had also been awoken by Hudson, went to reception with a list of names of people for the hotel to call, with orders not to hang up until they answered, even though they were guests, because it was *really, really* important. Several developers looked for a conference room in which to work, but because of the hour, they were all closed. Instead, they grabbed chairs in the lobby area outside one on the second floor.

The chain was getting DoSed. In a denial-of-service (DoS) attack, an attacker tries to overwhelm a service to render it unusable. The high school student who had emailed Gün, Tjaden Hess, had realized that such an attack would prevent the DAO soft fork from working.

The group sat in armchairs, either hunched over their laptops or leaning forward to work on low coffee tables. The pattern in the carpet looked like blank STOP signs chained together in rows. It was quiet for the first hour or so, as they tried to figure out how the attack worked. Eventually, they realized it exploited the fact that every time the Ethereum virtual machine read or wrote a value, it would store that value in memory so as to be able to reference it quickly in the future. The attack used up a large amount of the in-memory storage of one contract and then called itself repeatedly. One operation would copy an entire set of cache data, which was one thousand values. But the attacker's contract would call itself one thousand times, so those one thousand values would get copied one thousand times, which meant each block was taking more than a minute to process rather than the typical twelve to fifteen seconds.[14] So, the attacker paid N gas to do N operations but basically used up N^2 memory. Any node that didn't have 32 GB of RAM fell off the network—almost 90 percent crashed off, all Geth.

Eventually someone realized it wasn't necessary to keep all that memory. They made a patch, which took a half hour, spent another hour deploying and testing it to make sure it processed the chain properly, and finally, at around 9:30 a.m., released it, dubbing it "From Shanghai, with Love."[15]

At 9:25 a.m., Vitalik hopped onstage basically on time, since registration, due to the problems with the badges, was running even later than he and the other developers were. Avsa tweeted, "Fixed. It seems that the total damage of the vulnerability was that devcon2 presentations are running 30 min late."[16]

Organizational issues aside, the conference went smoothly— and well for those affiliated with the DAO. After a summer of believing everyone wanted to sue or kill him, Lefteris received encouragement from a lot of people, many of whom said they liked the idea of a DAO. He decided to stay in crypto and later, when getting a job offer, said, "Okay—as long as there is no DAO."

He also met one person he would *never* forget. At a conference lunch, he met a tall, thin, super-likable man. As they were talking, Lefteris kept wondering, *How do I know this guy?* Then his lunch buddy started talking about the DAO. Afterward, Lefteris ran back to his hotel room to check a link sent to him by the Polo staffer investigating the identity of the attacker(s). His new acquaintance, who gave him the impression of being a happy student, was one of the suspects.

The next day, at Bar Rouge, a rooftop bar whose bouncers stood near the edge to protect drunk customers, he ran into the suspect again. Lefteris began talking about how the DAO had fucked up his life, and his happy friend said something like, "But now you're good, right? You're past it?" Then he added, "Maybe the hacker's also feeling bad." Lefteris thought, *Oh my God, could he actually be talking from that perspective?!*

The student continued to surmise that the attacker regretted what he had done—that he'd started the exploit but couldn't stop it. Lefteris thought, *Would a random guy really actually try to explain the side of the hacker??*

The suspect kept talking. Lefteris's mind raced: *Could it be???*

Everyone had gotten their ETH and most of their ETC, and Lefteris found the guy extremely likable and nice. He didn't want to accuse him without proof or dox him (make private info about him public) in a way that could affect his career or life, so he didn't confront him. But half a decade later, he would still *really* want to know who had set off what he would eventually call "the worst year of my life."

Coming out of his DAO hole, Christoph gave a talk on smart contract security. "I've worked for Ethereum for over two years now," he began, "and actually, my job was to prevent hard forks." He ended his talk by saying, "I want to say a personal thank-you. The last couple of months—" At this point, the whole audience erupted in applause and cheers that lasted almost half a minute until he cut them off.[17] "It's only because of the people sitting here"—a hint of emotion crept into his voice—"because of the Ethereum community, that I can stand here today and give this talk, and I just want to say thank you very much." Loud whoops and applause carried him offstage.

On the last night of the conference, just when things were winding down and people were in postconference socializing mode, there was another, more serious DoS attack. Again, a function on Ethereum was mispriced—it forced Geth to fetch a lot more data from disk than was paid for. It was asking Ethereum to read information roughly fifty thousand times per block, so each block was taking twenty to sixty seconds to process.[18] Though they could not create a patch immediately, they got the miners to change the gas costs in a way that at least made the chain work. They urged miners to switch to Parity.[19]

Because the first attack caused only the Geth nodes to fail, and because Gavin was not at DevCon 2, some asked, "Is it Gav? Is it Parity?"[20] They theorized he had orchestrated the attack to make Parity look good. In fact, on October 6, Gav would write a blog post saying, "a Parity-only network would...be able to handle a far higher gas limit than the Ethereum network will allow right now."[21]

Over the next month, the attacker(s) kept coming up with new tactics. They were all exploits in which the gas required for a specific computation was too low, making it free or cheap to hobble the blockchain—sort of like running a bakery into the ground by buying thousands or millions of the one muffin that costs less than it takes to make. Ultimately, the Gav theory didn't hold because the attacks also began targeting Parity. But Whac-A-Mole style, the devs made a fix for each onslaught. The Geth wallet updates would get names like "Into the Woods," "What else should we rewrite?," and "Come at me Bro."[22]

Then the attacker discovered a vulnerability in Ethereum itself, not the clients. It was like finding a flaw in http, the set of standards that enable web browsing, rather than in Chrome or Firefox. This attack involved the "suicide" instruction, which is how a contract would delete itself. Suicide would send any of the ETH in the contract to another contract specified, but even when there was no ETH left, it would still create an account. Since the suicide instruction cost nothing, the attacker did suicides over and over again, until storage bloated from seven hundred thousand objects to twenty million. The sheer size of storage would soon make it impossible for the developers to use any countermeasures against the attacker, which would basically kill Ethereum.

During this time, Vitalik was physically in Shanghai and Singapore but constantly online, staying up all night. Eventually Ethereum had to conduct two emergency hard forks. The first, Tangerine Whistle, on October 18, had the fixes necessary to ensure the network could survive.[23] Afterward, the attacker did another DoS, which wouldn't have been a problem if the account tree in Ethereum only had seven hundred thousand objects, but it now had twenty million. Additionally, since Ethereum is essentially a giant list of every account ever, it was designed to access some of the accounts needed more often in the main memory. But the transactions in this attack involved random accounts, making it impossible for Ethereum to use this efficiency strategy.

The second hard fork, Spurious Dragon, on November 22, made it impossible for empty accounts to exist—if one was created, it would get deleted.[24] Also, if a suicide created an account, it would be charged a transaction fee. Spurious Dragon also made it possible to remove empty accounts that got "touched" by another transaction. After Spurious Dragon, Vitalik planned to run a script that poked empty accounts to make them disappear.

During the second hard fork, the Geth and Parity clients both had bugs, which the teams fixed. Two days later, at 10 p.m., when Vitalik went to run his script, it set off another bug that caused the chains to split. He had inadvertently caused Ethereum's first-ever fork prompted by a consensus bug. Working with others, he stayed up all night, pushed a fix at 7 a.m., then slept for two hours.

The tedious poking and deleting operation took Vitalik a week and cost the foundation $400,000 in gas fees needed to run computation on Ethereum. Through these hard forks, the devs also figured out how to structure data so that transactions could call random accounts without bogging the blockchain down. They hadn't noticed the problem before because there weren't that many accounts. This fix would enable Ethereum to grow much bigger.

The DoS attacks were finally over. Though the period was stressful, Vitalik found fighting—and winning—this cyberwar fun in a way. Throughout, the attacker's motivation was unclear. There wasn't an obvious financial gain, although he or she could have shorted ETH. (The price did slide from about $13 to below $10 over the two months of the attacks.) In fact, he or she had spent one thousand ETH (roughly $12,000) on the attacks, plus the time to research and execute them. Many mused that perhaps the only people with such an incentive would be Bitcoin maximalists. Regardless, Ethereum became stronger and more capable of handling a high load of transactions—a beneficial maturation given what lay ahead.

DURING THE MONTHS of the DAO and the hard fork, another private drama was unfolding in Ethereum, out of the spotlight and without the knowledge of Vitalik and other main players. Jeff Wilcke, the head of Geth, was expecting his first child in September. Though he'd always been a hypochondriac, that June, the month of the DAO attack, he started thinking he might die. He began making a list of things he wanted to do before he departed. One item was to make it to September and see his son. But many nights that summer, he went to bed thinking it might have been his last day, that he might pass away from a heart attack or get cancer.

Though he was thirty-two and none of his family members had ever died of these maladies, he could not stop worrying. Sometimes he'd feel irrationally angry—he'd walk into a park, and rage would surge inside him. He would also hyperventilate and get dizzy, then go into a spiral about whether he had a brain tumor. He looked brain tumors up online, saw they can lead to visual impairment, and became convinced he had a mass growing inside his skull. He wondered if he was losing his mind.

He made it through the DAO hard fork to his son's birth and through the DoS attacks, but in early 2017, one night, lying in bed, he could feel his heart pounding in his chest. It wasn't racing, but it was beating more quickly than normal. He said to his girlfriend, "Something's wrong, I can feel my heart all the time." He then wondered aloud, "What if I'm getting a heart attack?" Seeing how fearful he was, she said, "You need to call an ambulance *now*." That confirmed to Jeff that he was actually having a heart attack. He realized he was going to die that day.

His girlfriend's mother took him to the hospital. The doctor noted his blood pressure was higher than normal, put electronic sensors on his body, and took a few blood tests. A few hours later, a nurse came in and told him that his blood tests indicated he may have had a heart attack. Jeff lay there soaking in the knowledge that something really was wrong with him. Fifty minutes later, she reappeared, apologizing profusely. She had confused him with another patient of the same age. Nothing was wrong with him. He went home.

Two weeks later, the same thing happened—his heart rate was at two hundred beats per minute. The hospital had given him spray that would widen his blood vessels to make it easier for his heart to pump, so he sprayed it under his tongue. Warmth flooded his body, but nothing happened, so he used it again and called an ambulance. From their fourth-floor apartment he could see flashing lights and hear blaring sirens. *Something was wrong with him.* He was scared for his life. His girlfriend ran out the door, crying. Jeff walked out but collapsed just beyond the door. One of the paramedics picked him up, carried him inside, and checked him out. His pronouncement: "There's nothing wrong with your heart. You're having panic attacks."

Jeff says he began seeing a therapist. He recalled how, around age ten, on a camping trip with his parents, in the middle of the night, a woman at the campground had a stroke. Even though she hadn't died, he realized such a thing could happen to him. Also, he had lost a two-day-old brother due to heart problems. But most of all, he saw that the pressure of being in a job where a mistake could cost people billions of dollars weighed on him. When combined with his desire to be a good father and boyfriend, the pressure became too much. During his three years with Ethereum, he had woken up with Ethereum and gone to bed with Ethereum. Even on weekends or holidays, there would be drama caused by Gavin or other events in Ethereum. Plus, the work itself was relentless. The launch in July 2015 was just for the first version. They had to continually improve Geth, and there were other projects to tackle. And not only was the team small, but it was difficult to find good people who were willing to quit stable jobs, particularly if they had families, to work on this cryptocurrency no one had heard of, especially since Bitcoin and crypto were still synonymous with criminal money. The low salaries at the foundation didn't help. Nabbing really good hires like Péter Szilágyi amounted to pure luck, since, if Péter hadn't been so passionate about Ethereum, he could have easily landed a much higher-paying job.

But because Péter was there and Jeff *could* rely on him, he told his team about his panic attacks and gave Péter the role of team lead. Since Jeff wasn't getting a salary and the Dutch subsidiary functioned as a contractor, he simply stopped sending invoices. Aside from Vitalik he was the last cofounder to leave the EF.

ON OCTOBER 25, 2016, a week after the first hard fork to counter the DoS attacks, a new Ethereum legal entity, Ethereum Asia Pacific Ltd. (EAPL), was incorporated in Singapore.[25] This was a long time coming. Ming and Vitalik had been close in the beginning, but now, over a year after Ming had started, there was more distance between them. In the beginning she had seemed joyful, even silly, and they had been on the same wavelength about wanting to experiment with the technology for humanity. But after a while, he realized she shouted and got upset a lot and was constantly stressed. This made it hard for him to be happy and productive. Besides, he also noticed that even though she complained of working eighty to one hundred hours a week, her output was in no way commensurate. Nor was it consistent with a statement she had made to him dozens of times: that she was an A+ MIT graduate committed to perfection. In May 2016, when the DAO was en route to becoming the biggest crowdfunding project in history, after one particularly stressful three-hour conversation with her, he thought about replacing her. But at the time, a lot of legal and bureaucratic maneuvers were underway, such as restructuring the legal entities Gavin, Jeff, Stephan, and Vitalik himself had created after the Ethereum crowdsale and trying to get the $1 million for the CCRG back from Joe. Removing her could delay these other moves by months. Plus, since she was so bad at delegating, she really was the only person who knew about any of these tasks. On top of that, he had no idea how to search for an executive director since posting an open call, as he had done before, would tip her off.

But the ways in which she grated on Vitalik began to pile up. After the IC3 boot camp where Vitalik had been for the DAO hard fork, Ming, Casey, Vitalik, and Martin Becze shared a rental car back to their respective homes. Ming, Casey, and Martin were going to drop Vitalik off first, south of Toronto, from where he would catch a bus, and then the three of them would proceed to Michigan and Indiana. During the drive, Ming started going off on how no one appreciated her. Then she began trying to force Vitalik to wear a suit for some event; he refused. According to a source familiar with the situation, when they arrived at Vitalik's stop, he jumped out, and Ming, upset, demanded they stay until Vitalik messaged that he appreciated her. After he sent a text doing so, they left, but then she and Casey got into a fight, during which she threatened to yell at the border guards as they crossed back into the United States.

Vitalik's disillusionment with Ming came later than it had for most other people in Ethereum. From the start, in the fall of 2015, many people had found their relationship strange. Ming told multiple people that she viewed Vitalik as the son she'd never had or as a child she had to protect against evil. She also bought him the kind of psychedelic unicorn-y T-shirts he liked and copied him in certain ways—buying the kind of silly cat bags he carried—even though she usually tried to act like a businesswoman/CEO. People weren't sure if she did these things out of friendship, to try to keep her boss happy, or to manipulate him. (Vitalik says that he felt she was an emotional person and wanted him to be happy but that he never felt she was the scheming type.) Others watching Ming with Vitalik in late 2015 thought it looked like she was fawning over him, being overly friendly to manipulate and guilt him, but because of his social awkwardness, he couldn't detect it. Another person saw Ming playing the martyr in a passive-aggressive way with him: "I'm so sad, how can you stand there and let me be so sad? I thought we had a connection. I'm here, protecting you, giving you a position, listening to you. I'm being a support you didn't have, with all these people manipulating you." The person watching this thought, *Uhhhh...you're manipulating him right now.*

In the wider foundation, many people viewed her as overprotective of him. Numerous people used the word "micromanager" to describe her relationship with him or said she "babysat" him. One called her "a mother hen who sat on top of Vitalik." For instance, when they were at Cornell for IC3, she would make sure that Vitalik had food and followed him around, as if she were part of his entourage or she were a coach and he her athlete.

Many people felt she tried to give Vitalik the impression she was dealing with everything and saving the foundation. In the end, she did pick up operational duties he couldn't care less about. After all, she had cut expenses drastically, removed unproductive freelancers, moved the EF out of the Spaceship, fired Gavin (although some people felt that Vitalik and Gavin's relationship hadn't deteriorated enough to merit that), put a good face forward for regulators, and consolidated power under Vitalik since his three votes on the foundation board were still unchallenged after the objection of the board members the year prior. Lower-level developers in the foundation were impressed with how she had cleaned things up. And some who were suspicious of Gavin felt positively about Ming, finding her nice, motherly, and responsive to emails.

But even her good qualities had downsides. For instance, even after the foundation found itself in a financially comfortable spot, she lowballed potential employees. When Google employees were applying and stated their salary requirements, she would say things like "Nobody gets paid that much" or that she and Vitalik didn't— as if developers' salaries should be benchmarked against her own. (Entry-level Google engineers would typically have incomes higher than Ming's at the time, plus get valuable stock, and senior-level engineers' compensation could be $1 million including stock.) At least one former Googler at the foundation was paid half his previous earnings; plus he was made a contractor, so he had no leave or benefits; another applicant from Google simply didn't join the EF.

Some ways in which Ming got things under control raised eyebrows. For instance, she brought her sister in as legal counsel, raising questions about conflicts of interest. She cut someone whose salary was high despite his only doing things like going to conferences—which was a good move—but then she told other employees about it, naming that person and saying that others in the foundation did not want to work with him. Or she would complain, annoyed that even though she'd gotten rid of Gavin, Jeff didn't trust her. And the DAO had occurred on her watch. While some credited her with making it clear, on internal Skype channels, that the DAO and the EF were separate, others pointed to all the trolling and FUD (fear, uncertainty, and doubt) that tied the two together, plus the basic fact that a huge percentage of the people involved with the DAO were currently or previously connected to the foundation.

Over time, the bad began to outweigh the good. First, there were the basic requirements of the job. Jeff, as the leader of Geth, was one of the most senior people, which meant he should interact regularly with the ED. But because there was no stopping her talking, he did everything he could to avoid her. When he did have calls with her, he felt she would just cry about all her problems, and when he said she needed to delegate, it was clear she had no idea how to do that—that she just didn't have the emotional stability to be an executive director. Plus, she was a control freak, or "mafia boss," as one person put it. In group Skype chats, if someone said something she didn't like, she would immediately start a private chat or call with the person, saying, "Why did you raise this issue? You should have brought this up with me." She seemed paranoid of writing things down. Hence, the phone calls. Because of her micromanaging, the devs nicknamed her Ming Dynasty and Ming the Destroyer.

People noticed she thrived on conflict. She called her sister, Tung, the foundation's general counsel, every day, sometimes multiple times a day, and they often clashed. People who lived in the Zug apartment with Casey and Ming heard the couple argue constantly—about ten times a day, even over things like the spiciness of takeout that Casey had bought for Ming. At night, the shouting from their room was intense.

Ming's pugnacity spilled over into how she treated the staff. Sometimes, in her epic phone calls, she went off on the person to whom she was talking. Years later, one person who was also friends with her would recall it as "kind of abusive," then added, "in a rational sense, it was kind of necessary at the time, because of the way crypto is. Sometimes to move the stone, you need to be completely, insanely energetic to make things happen. I hope that's not psychological and excusing that abusive stuff she was doing." Even this person acknowledged that, over time, her behavior became inappropriate.

Her outbursts, abusive shouting, and explosive nature led people to speculate privately that she must have psychological issues. One surmised she could have bipolar depression. According to another, who thought she clearly had a mental disorder, Ming *would* talk sometimes about being depressed, but it wasn't clear if she had a clinical diagnosis. One staffer described her problem as "daddy issues," while a friend thought she had been through something abusive or at least had grown up under a lot of pressure. Ming had told someone at ETH Dev that she'd been abused by a boyfriend, not her dad, but would also talk about Tung as if her sister were the chosen child. (Tung had been a commissioner of securities for the state of Hawaii.) Someone with a background in psychotherapy said Ming likely had a personality disorder, citing her "complete inability to take in information and give it back as a factual response." Whatever the root cause, people called her view of reality "delusional," "skewed," "not sane." One said, "Some people would say she's a little bit delusional. I wouldn't go as far, but there's definitely something not very objective about her."

Because she seemed so ill-suited to the position, people who could not understand how she had stayed on as ED would speculate or say they'd heard that Vitalik had hired her to learn Chinese from her. This made no sense, because in addition to Vitalik disputing it, he says her Chinese was worse than his. Others chalked up her position as ED to Vitalik's thing for Asian women. Ming herself, they say, would, in fact, tease him about his interest in Asian women. Other people in Ethereum felt Vitalik had feelings for her that weren't 100 percent platonic. Sometimes, watching them interact, one dev would find himself wondering, *Wait—are they friends or are they together?* Although she treated him like a son, he said, "[Vitalik] was interested in her in not a mother-son way...Even though Vitalik knew Casey was her boyfriend, he wanted this familial, romantic relationship." This person speculated Vitalik's past experience with an Asian girlfriend played a role. (Vitalik says he was not interested in Ming in that way.)

Another person, who felt that Vitalik's interest in Asian women was the only logical explanation for how Ming stayed ED, said of this theory, "my spide-y senses are tingling," adding that he knew himself what it was like to be an awkward twenty-one-year-old. He recalled that, when he was that age, he had had a female boss more than twenty years his senior with whom he'd had a really good relationship that served as a substitute for a romantic one.

Imagine if you could choose your own boss, someone you'd spend a lot of time with. It's really safe, because it doesn't have the intensity of any possibility of a sexual interaction. There's a maternal connection and it fills an emotional void, and you can form a deep emotional connection with someone in that context...It's normal. Imagine if you're a [twenty-one]-year-old running a massive foundation and you have no spare time, the only people you spend time with are people you work with, and you have autocratic control. Beyond normal, it's almost inevitable.

Vitalik, who responded to a question about this on a messaging app, wrote, "wat."

But after a while, Ming's original jovial, joking nature with Vitalik became abusive. She frequently subjected him to long episodes of yelling—shouting sometimes in general, other times about other people, but also often at him. After a while, he felt traumatized by her relentless outbursts. Though he recognized she might have felt motherly toward him, she didn't respect his autonomy. To get out from under her control, he came up with the idea of creating a legal entity in Singapore. She didn't even know about it until Dmitry, Vitalik's father, mentioned it at DevCon 2 and casually said the foundation would likely move to Singapore from Switzerland. (Dmitry does not recall this conversation or even knowing what EAPL was.) Ming was in shock. She sensed that what would eventually become Ethereum Asia Pacific Ltd. would take power from her and that Vitalik, who was already spending so much time in Asia, was slipping away. Reluctant to help set it up, she dragged her feet, but eventually, she agreed to allocate some foundation money to help establish it. Vitalik began paying himself out of it, plus recruited his friend Virgil Griffith, a PhD from CalTech to whom he had sent the first draft of the Ethereum white paper, as a research scientist. Having this entity enabled Vitalik to bring people onto the research team without having to ask Ming for each hire. It was a little plot of freedom, and it gave him a taste of what working on Ethereum without Ming would be like.

But Ming had recently obtained her own advantage. After nearly a year in which the former "professional" board members— Lars, Wayne, and Vadim—had, according to the Swiss Register, remained on the board of the Ethereum Foundation despite having resigned, a new slate was finally announced: Vitalik, Zug-based lawyer Patrick Storchenegger, and Ming.[26]

10

Fall 2016 to July 19, 2017

WHILE THE ETHEREUM developers were battling the DAO and DoS attacks, becoming aware of the protocol's weaknesses, the wider cryptocurrency world was having revelations about the potential of cryptocurrency in general, and Ethereum in particular.

Earlier that year, in May 2016, as the DAO was closing in on its historic crowdsale, Fred Ehrsam, cofounder of US crypto exchange Coinbase, published a blog post titled "Ethereum Is the Forefront of Digital Currency."[1] In it, he posed the question of why the only things built on top of Bitcoin until then had been wallets and exchanges. (In contrast, the internet had given rise to applications such as Google, Amazon, Facebook, Netflix, and more.) "My theory has been that the scripting language in Bitcoin—the piece of every Bitcoin transaction that lets you run a little software program along with it—is too restrictive," he wrote. "Enter Ethereum. Ethereum has taken what was a four function calculator of a programming language in Bitcoin and turned it into a full fledged computer." He said Ethereum, at nine months old, was already showing more app (or dapp) development activity than seven-year-old Bitcoin.

In August, in another post, "Blockchain Tokens and the dawn of the Decentralized Business Model," he noted venture capitalists had so far put more than $1 billion into traditional start-ups focused on digital currency, but in the previous four months, blockchain-based decentralized projects (as opposed to start-ups with CEOs) had raised more than $250 million—without a cent coming from VCs.[2] "So what the heck is going on?" he asked. "Blockchain tokens."

Many projects were, like the DAO, fund-raising by creating a token designated for use on that specific network. He said these tokens weren't just being used to line initial coin offering (ICO) issuers' pockets with ETH; they were actually being used in the dapps themselves. The people who offered services to the network could be paid in that token, which could then be exchanged for other money. Setting these projects apart was the fact that each was not a traditional app with a company at the center pushing out updates and making business deals; these were "*decentralized software protocols*" (emphasis added). Historically, such protocols had not been profitable. For instance, the people working on simple mail transfer protocol (smtp) for email did not make money. Outlook, Hotmail, and Gmail, the applications using smtp, had. However, now tokens made it possible for protocol builders to reward themselves since tokens could be created with the network, and they could keep some, like retaining equity in a start-up, and allocate some for continued work on the protocol.

Tokens also solved another business problem: how to grow a network. "Consider the beginning of Twitter," he wrote. "The value of being one of the first few users on the network was low—no one else was using it, so there was no content! Now millions of people are on Twitter so people find a lot of value in it." Tokens solved the chicken-and-egg problem of how to incentivize people to join a network early when it is small: give them partial ownership, much like offering equity in a start-up, whereby the earlier one joins, the greater one's reward. How was that ownership represented? Tokens.

A few days later, when ETH was pulling away in its tussle with ETC and Andrey Ternovskiy was threatening the White Hat Group with legal letters, Joel Monegro, then an analyst at venture capital firm Union Square Ventures, elaborated in a blog post titled "Fat Protocols," which illustrated the concepts Fred had described with simple black-and-white-marker diagrams.[3] As opposed to the internet, where the value at the protocol layer was thin and the value at the application layer was huge, Bitcoin had a $10 billion market cap, "yet the largest companies built on top are worth a few hundred million at best," he wrote. "Similarly, Ethereum has a $1B market cap even before the emergence of a real breakout application on top and only a year after its public release." Perhaps because of the easily grasped visuals, the crypto community labeled this theory the "fat protocols thesis."

Suddenly everyone was on the hunt for the next big protocol tokens. And creating new ones on Ethereum was so easy. The previous fall, Fabian Vogelsteller of the Robin Hood Group had solicited comments on an idea that Vitalik had long discussed: standardizing a smart contract for creating new tokens. Fabian made it issue number twenty on a board designated for discussing protocol improvements called Ethereum Request for Comments. After 362 comments, they settled on a standard called ERC-20 tokens, which became a class of tokens that, because they were in a standardized smart contract, could be added easily by exchanges, wallets, and so forth.[4]

In addition to the fact that creating new tokens was now a breeze, a whole slew of developers had been enthralled by the story of the DAO—not the spectacular blowup but the raising of almost $140 million from the crowd—and by how Ethereum had raised $18 million and was now worth $1 billion. Some who had been working on proposals to work for the DAO now decided to create their own tokens and sell them to the crowd. In August only $1.3 million was raised this way, but September saw $23.2 million brought in via ICOs. The ICO total was $13.4 million in October and $20 million in November.

ICO issuers were selling in an era when the stock market had been mostly shrinking since the late 1990s and in which companies had been staying private longer.[5] When they finally did go public, there was less upside for everyday investors. Yahoo! was founded in 1994 and went public in 1996. In contrast, Uber was founded in 2009 but, as of fall 2016, was still privately held. So Main Street was hungry for investment opportunities. But those who wanted crypto faced a major hurdle: access. Though some exchanges, like Gatecoin and Bittrex, had made it possible to buy into the DAO directly from their platforms, most were not doing this for other ICOs. The only way to buy tokens in an ICO was to use an Ethereum wallet in which users managed their private keys themselves (whereas exchanges promised to keep their coins safe for them).

One of the easiest ways to do this was through MyEtherWallet (MEW), the website cofounded by Taylor Monahan (née Van Orden), the DAO enthusiast who had gotten her then fiancé Kevin to do the coin flip that chose the contract that became *the* DAO. (They got married shortly after the Tangerine Whistle hard fork for the DoS attacks; some of Kevin's trades in ETC had enabled them to upgrade their wedding alcohol package from Bud/Bud Light/Coors/Coors Light to one that included Blue Moon, Sam Adams, and wine.)

MEW's origins dated back to 2014, when cofounders Taylor and Kosala Hemachandra, best friends and longtime coworkers, discovered Bitcoin. Taylor, an Angeleno and onetime New York University film school student, was a petite, toned brunette whose face could go from wise to jokey in an instant. She would often say something funny, then give a silent laugh with her jaw hanging open and a "Can you believe it?" expression. Kosala had grown up in Sri Lanka before moving to the United States at seventeen to get his computing degree. He'd always been obsessed with computers and was introverted. They had met at a company building websites and marketing materials for multinationals like Coca-Cola, Purina, Target, and Microsoft, among others. In 2014 both became Bitcoin enthusiasts. When the Ethereum presale happened, they tossed some bitcoins in—for him, it was a good chunk of his life savings.

In July 2015, when Ethereum launched, users could only deal with their tokens through command-line interfaces—think of a black screen with glowing green letters. Taylor, who was a designer, couldn't do that. She wondered if all presale participants had the same problem or she was the only idiot who couldn't use Terminal, the interface for typing commands. She also asked Kosala whether googling "How do I move my ETH?" would turn up instructions, but Kosala explained that it wouldn't since nobody had asked that question before. That blew her mind. Kosala decided to create a website so people could access their Ethereum wallets. He made it open-source so people could check his code and see he wouldn't phish them or steal their ETH.

He made a digital version of a "paper wallet," a list of one's private keys on actual paper; his version was a website with one input field for a password to encrypt the private key and one button to generate the address.[6] (A cryptocurrency address, or public key, is like a front slot on a mailbox that only allows people to put money in; the private key is needed to send money out.) The site output both encrypted and unencrypted versions of the user's private key, plus QR codes for the address and private key. Since MyEtherWallet did not hold people's coins, it also did not record users' passwords—safekeeping those was up to them. If a user lost a password, his or her money was gone forever. Knowing his limitations, Kosala begged Taylor to help him design the site.

Four days later, while she was celebrating her birthday on a boat near Catalina Island and he was in Los Angeles, they tried domain names on GoDaddy, but some were really expensive, like $200. MyEtherWallet was $11.99. They nabbed it.[7]

RIGHT WHEN THEY launched, the presale for Augur, a decentralized prediction market in which people could make predictions
and bet on the outcome, was happening. When Taylor went to
put money in, she was stymied, again, by challenging technical
instructions. She asked Kosala to make a one-click button for her.
He did, and they added an "Augur Crowdsale" tab to the site.[8]
Late in the sale, which ended October 1, 2015, the Augur newsletter gave a shout-out to MyEtherWallet for the button. Taylor
and Kosala exchanged chats peppered with "omg omg"—thrilled
to have been noticed by others in the community.

The next day, they even received a donation from a satisfied
user.

In February 2016, they made a Chrome extension so that people
could access their ETH without having to go to MyEtherWallet.com.[9]
Then, for the DAO, they made it easy to buy DAO tokens, and after
the hard fork happened, they created a simple button that would obtain people's money from the Extra Balance, the Withdraw DAO,
and the ETC Withdraw Contract.[10] Throughout this period, Taylor
was on Reddit a lot, answering questions under her oldest, highest-
karma Reddit account (karma reflected how much a Redditor had
contributed to the community): u/insomniasexx. She also answered
support ticket emails, which she says numbered two a week before
the DAO and ten to twenty a day during the fund-raise—plus all
the questions she would get on Reddit, Stack Exchange, and the
DAO Slack. Though she had never met these people in real life,
she became a fixture of the DAO/Ethereum community and, as
one of the only women, was nicknamed "the mother of the DAO."
MyEtherWallet was called MEW.

During this time, Taylor was still doing freelance web design
for ten to fifteen hours a week, at $50 to 60 an hour, and spending
the rest of her time on MEW, which made no money. To pay rent,
she and Kevin sold their ETH at prices below $10.

That summer, MEW realized it needed to become a real company, and at the urging of community members, Taylor and Kosala

explored creating a Swiss company with Bity's help. Preparing for their Switzerland trip, Taylor—who had never met anyone from Ethereum in real life, except for Griff, very briefly, before they got to know each other through the DAO—wanted to be professional and so packed blazers and blouses. Her husband, who felt he functioned better a little high, was fretting about getting weed if he couldn't travel with it. She told him, "You're going to have to deal. Don't ask anyone we have a business relationship with about weed." When she, Kosala, and Kevin walked into the courtyard of the Bity offices, they found four people sitting around rolling joints. Taylor, said, "Look, there's weed for you, Kevin." He thought, *Well, that's cool.* Though Taylor didn't smoke pot, it confirmed her hunch that the crypto world was not like the corporate world, in which, on business trips to Coca-Cola headquarters, she'd constantly felt out of place. Crypto had more of a nights-and-weekends culture, in which people were online at 4 a.m., questioned authority, and had a high tolerance for risk—a good fit for her.

That fall, MEW added a way to buy into an upcoming ICO called Golem, scheduled for November 11, 2016. Golem was pitching itself as an "Airbnb for computers"—a blockchain for renting out spare computing cycles on people's sleeping computers with the Golem Network Token.[11] The Poland-based team aimed to raise 820,000 ETH to stay under the $10 million cap Vitalik had recommended after the DAO implosion.

The Golem ICO hit its cap (based on that day's exchange rate, about $8.6 million) in *twenty minutes.*[12] The DAO had received less in both ETH and US dollars in its first *twenty-four hours.* The sale caused MEW's Ethereum nodes to go down—only that was not obvious to users. MEW was simply an interface that allowed the user to interact with the Ethereum blockchain via the nodes MEW ran. The site itself didn't make anything happen for the user. However, during the Golem ICO, users were going through the steps to participate, but after clicking send, the site would just freeze. Because the nodes had never been overwhelmed before, no explanations popped up if nothing happened with the Ethereum node after ten seconds. Users, frustrated at the delay, refreshed, which caused more overloading. For all the grief wannabe Golem ICO buyers gave them, Taylor thought, *Run your own Ethereum nodes if you're that desperate to get into the sale!* Still, Kosala restructured the back end so that a spike in activity would cause new nodes to kick in. Like Ethereum after the DoS fixes, now MEW was prepared for anything.

AT DEVCON 2, Bob and Andrew had not given up on getting enterprise companies to use Ethereum. After realizing the Hyperledger route wasn't going to happen, Joe began talking with people at UBS Innovation Lab, BNY Mellon, Santander, and Deutsche Bank who had become passionate about Ethereum. The bankers felt the community had handled the DAO saga maturely, since the two communities who disagreed separated cleanly. They were amazed the technology itself made that possible. Although interested in Ethereum, the bankers thought it best to have a corporate-like entity—a separate playground from that used by the cryptoanarchists. They planned to found a nonprofit organization to steward an enterprise version of Ethereum.

On January 23, 2017, Andrew Keys wrote an email inviting Ming to "sync" on Enterprise Ethereum. She responded, "It was unexpected for me to learn about this 'Ethereum Enterprise' effort on the Consensys newsletter and see the author state it had the *blessing* of the Foundation when I had no knowledge of most of the undertakings."

The new organization was to be called the Enterprise Ethereum Foundation, but when Ming heard, she flipped. Two sources say she thought they had purposely, maliciously given it a name so similar to the Ethereum Foundation. (Joe says, "This is an absurd accusation assuming malintent.") They switched to Enterprise Ethereum Alliance (EEA). On January 25, the EF (read: Ming) filed to trademark the terms "Enterprise Ethereum" and "Enterprise Ethereum Alliance."[13] Ming forced the EEA to make promises about the exact wording it would use about certain topics and pay to use the now-trademarked terms "Ethereum" and "Enterprise Ethereum."

In mid-February, she was still livid. In a Skype chat, she explained, "We are handling all kinds of tradename infringement issues (not just the ones with Consensys), but lately I've been receiving numerous inquiries from people in our community due to confusion about Consensys' 'enterprise' alliance."

She corrected herself: "I meant 'ENTERPRISE Ethereum' alliance."

She continued, saying that "Joe outright lied to the foundation and broke all promises"; he used "misleading and misrepresentative names he promised not to use until a written, signed agreement was in place," and even then he "further perpetuated the misinformation." Calling his actions "dishonorable," she mentioned the possibility that people could "donate money to Joe's new 'Ethereum' entity." She said she was surprised by how many queries she had fielded from various people and companies complaining, she claimed, they had been misled or confused by ConsenSys or that they had signed up to be part of the enterprise organization because Joe's firm had led them to believe the EF or Vitalik was endorsing it.

A few days later, Ming wrote in the foundation Skype chat,

[INFRINGEMENT ANNOUNCEMENT—INTERNAL]
Joe Lubin/Andrew Keys as the appointed representative of the **enterprise alliance** promised on a scheduled official call with Foundation on January 25, 2017, that included a major enterprise board member (to be), and our legal team, that HE WOULD NOT USE THE TRADENAME "ETHEREUM" in any name for an enterprise group project or entity before a licensing agreement with Foundation was made.

> It's not worth writing a wall of text here
> Please don't troll me right now.
> It is being addressed and hopefully resolved very soon.

Despite some internal protestations from Avsa and Fabian, Ming's opinion ruled the day.

On February 27, 2017, the EEA was announced, with JPMorgan, Microsoft, Wipro, Banco Santander, Accenture, Intel, BNY Mellon, and CME Group as founding members and BP, UBS, Credit Suisse, ING, Thomson Reuters, and others as nonboard founding members.[14]

To use its trademark that first year, the EF charged the EEA $2,500.

MING CONTINUED IN her quest to remove what she considered dead weight from the foundation. Taylor Gerring, the Spaceship IT manager who had created the dossier on Charles, had, after the crowdsale, worked on Jeff's team, but when that ended, he began doing talks about Ethereum around the world that Vitalik didn't want to do. If Ming and Taylor spoke on the phone, he says he would have to go through the standard hour and a half of her complaining, but when he tried to talk about work-related issues, she would turn the conversation back to her personal problems. When he would say, "Please be professional," she'd get angry. By late 2016, he was emailing Ming to ask about his contract, which had lapsed, and whether he could continue educational work. His emails went unanswered.

On the same day as the EEA announcement, he received an email from Ming's brother-in-law (Tung's husband), J. P. Schmidt, sent from the latter's Gmail account:

> I'm writing you on behalf of the Ethereum Foundation. I'm writing to inform you that after the Foundation's careful consideration of its needs with respect to the services

you provide, the Foundation has determined it will not be needing your services and therefore will not be renewing your contract at this time or in the foreseeable future.

It wasn't clear to Taylor whether anything about his employment status could actually be decided via an email from a Gmail account owned by a family member of the executive director (and the husband of the general counsel), but since his contract had lapsed anyway, he didn't pursue it. With Charles, Amir, Gavin, Jeff, Joe, Anthony, Stephan, Mihai, and now Taylor out of the picture, the entire early leadership team of Ethereum was gone, except Vitalik.

IN THE EARLY months of 2017 through the spring, Vitalik was traveling a lot, often within Asia. Ether, meanwhile, was on an upswing. After trading in the $10 to $13 range for much of fall 2016, the price had dipped below $10 by mid-November and was trading at around $7 during the holidays. But come February, the price had jumped back up to $10 and risen steadily until, the day of the EEA announcement, it crossed $15. People began watching a chart on crypto data site CoinMarketCap showing each coin's percentage of the total crypto markets. For pretty much all of cryptocurrency history, Bitcoin's dominance was at 80 percent or above. In March 2017, it began to drop, first dipping below 80 percent, as it had twice previously; then in mid-March, it hit 70 percent for the first time. ETH, meanwhile, went from 8 to 17 percent in a few days, largely due to its skyrocketing price, which exceeded $50 for the first time on March 24—not even a month after it had reached $15. On March 26, Bitcoin's dominance slumped to 67 percent, with its market cap at $15.7 billion, while Ethereum's was just under 20 percent, with a $4.6 billion market cap. People began discussing something they called the "flippening"—the moment Ethereum's market cap would surpass Bitcoin's.[15]

Around this time, total crypto trading worldwide picked up (after having flattened in January after Chinese exchanges installed trading fees), surging from about $1 billion in weekly volume in late January to over $3 billion by March. Along with Ethereum's rising fortunes came a strong demand to trade it—and that greatly benefited one crypto exchange in particular: Poloniex, the top exchange for trading ETH. The exchange, which had been pivotal to the survival of Ethereum Classic, alone accounted for half of global transaction volume in all cryptocurrencies, mainly due to interest in Ethereum and margin trading. Even as it often topped the charts of crypto exchanges worldwide, the company, which was also a little different in that it didn't have any venture capital backing, was a mystery to much of the outside world. While most exchange owners knew each other, little was known about Polo or its owners, such as where they were based. By this point, Poloniex was the child of not only its gentle-faced founder, Tristan, but also two new co-owners, Jules Kim, a pretty, "heavyset" or "on the bigger side" Asian woman with long wavy hair, and Mike Demopoulos, a big, grungy guy with a goatee who wore rock band T-shirts. The unmarried couple had, according to a former Polo staffer, previously owned a marketing and user-experience consulting firm called RDVO that had done work for major institutions in Boston, where they were based. Jules was initially a customer who hung out in the trollbox, Polo's wild chat room full of trash talk and crypto-trading memes. When Tristan expressed interest in marketing for Poloniex, Jules offered to help. Their signing on as co-owners was never announced, so longtime employees found out about it quite a bit later in October 2016, a year or more afterward.

The three were quite the trio. There was Tristan, who everyone thought was a genius, and who, in his thirties, joked online about playing Nintendo games like Pokemon and Zelda and bragged about his scores; in person, however, he was "unbelievably underwhelming" and socially awkward. (Someone who had met both him and Vitalik surmised Tristan was much farther along the spectrum than Vitalik.) On video calls, Tristan would turn his camera off—and then he'd only say things like "Yes, I think so," in a barely audible whisper. When Polo people met him in real life, they say he was practically unable to make eye contact.

Before Jules and Mike joined Poloniex, Tristan tended to prioritize customers. If a customer was hacked and Polo could recover the funds, Tristan would instruct the staff to do so, even if it would take three hours. According to an early employee, in early 2014, when the exchange had no money, Polo was hacked twice and lost 227.6 BTC, about $100,000. Tristan made it his mission to pay all the users back, forgoing all profits from the company to do so. It took a year. Because crypto was 24/7, customer service would work every day of the month, no days off. Tristan and other early employees would brag in the chat about how many hours they logged each month. The employees thought that since they joined early, they'd become rich off Polo though they hadn't been offered equity. (Finally, in winter 2017, early employees were offered options and signed for them in January but were told the first portion would vest a year after the board approved them in April.)

Then there was Mike, an easygoing, nice guy—a web designer, an "everybody's friend" type. Two different people who did not know each other described him as being "along for the ride" and "one for the ride."

Of the three, Jules was the mastermind. Someone who had never worked with her described her and Mike as "so lovely." Those who had worked with her said she had one persona that was friendly and nice and then another that was cunning, secretive, paranoid, ruthless, "scheming," "vicious," "a control freak." (Her Twitter handle was @cointrolfreak.[16]) If she wanted someone fired, she would make other employees do it, under threat of being fired themselves. She seemed to think yelling would make people work faster or better. Afterward, staff members realized she had been abusive. They felt whenever there was an opportunity to screw someone, she did. The customer service team would usually do as much as possible to fix an issue for someone, but she'd say,

"We're not obliged by law to help them. Screw them." In general, when Jules didn't get exactly what she wanted, she was not happy.

Early on, she hired a friend, Lisa, who was put in charge of the office and immediately well-liked by everyone. Lisa made sure the kitchen was stocked with snacks, such as chips, nuts, granola bars, and fruit. After a while, Jules, on a call with an early employee who didn't work in that office, announced Polo was going to be letting Lisa go, saying, "It turns out she's a terrible office manager. I don't know if you heard about the snacks." Jules then had what this staffer called a "complete conniption" about Lisa buying snacks for everyone. After that, everyone had to buy their own snacks, and they had to work for four hours before they were allowed a break.

After Jules and Mike came on as co-owners, there came a point when, suddenly, Tristan disappeared from chat. The only way to reach him would be through Jules and Mike. "They clearly took Tristan away from us," one employee would later say. But in mid- to late 2016, almost in an act of defiance, he made one final gesture, as if this were the last time he could do something without needing anyone else's approval. Jules reached out to Johnny Garcia, the head of customer service, and said, "Hey, I have to give this to you." It was a bonus in Bitcoin—an amount worth about $24,000 at the time. She said it was from Tristan—and her and Mike. Then she said, "Now I have to go do other things. Bye." She clearly hadn't enjoyed giving him the money. Johnny thought Tristan, with whom he had previously been friendly on chat, had wanted to thank him.

In 2016, as volume picked up, the exchange owners started making bank. Although Tristan, Jules, and Mike kept business information as secret as possible, employees would speculate on revenues. Since the trading fee was 0.2 percent per trade, margin was 0.25 percent, and the exchange picked up 15 percent of interest earned from loans on the platform, they estimated the exchange was getting 0.25 percent of volume in revenue a day, which on an average day in 2016 would mean solidly in the five figures.[17] They guessed—correctly, according to two people familiar with Polo's books—that daily revenue even sometimes hit $100,000.

During this time, observers say some of the owners' choices were questionable. For instance, in the latter half of 2016, Jules and Mike were against instituting basic security features that would prevent huge swaths of customers from falling victim to hacks—a measure called two-factor authentication (2FA), which would send a code via text to customers' phones when they tried to log in. Mike would say it was a user-experience issue, but customer service showed how having 2FA as an option would slash the huge amount of time customer service spent dealing with hacked accounts. Since Polo only had five customer service agents and wasn't going to hire more, that one move would have enabled the existing employees to help many more users. It took weeks, but finally they persuaded Jules and Mike.

By the time of that victory, the exchange was facing a new problem. Due to US sanctions, it needed to block Iranians from using Poloniex. However, it could not, because the exchange did not have a robust know-your-customer (KYC) program to verify customers' identities. (The one instituted in 2015 was, according to an early employee, "super basic" and "really, really easy to work around.") It was a three-tiered KYC system that granted users greater trading access in exchange for higher levels of verification, and part of the reason for it was that Jules and Mike wanted to minimize friction for users to sign up and deposit funds. These discussions dragged on from the end of 2016 into the first half of 2017, when Jules and Mike finally relented.

ICOS CONTINUED TO pick up. After raising $11.7 million in December, the haul swelled in January and February to around $67 million and $73 million, respectively. After a March dip to $22 million, in April, thirteen ICOs raked in almost $86 million.

One ICO that blew the lid off even Golem's in November was Gnosis (GNO), which, like Augur, was a decentralized prediction market. The Berlin-based team held the sale out of Gibraltar, a jurisdiction that, like Switzerland and Singapore, had crypto-friendly regulations. Their goal was $12.5 million, and they tried a new mechanism. Instead of a first-come-first-served-style ICO, they held a Dutch auction, which meant the starting price, $30, would be the ceiling. The price would continuously lower so that after two weeks, it would be $5. Theoretically, people would bid at the price they felt was most reasonable instead of buying early and thus overpaying. They set aside ten million tokens for the sale. A month ahead of the ICO, they thought the sale would last one to three weeks. Instead, due to massive FOMO (fear of missing out), on April 24 it raised its max amount within eleven minutes, selling only 4.2 percent of the ten million tokens set aside. The final price was $29.85 per GNO.[18] When GNO hit exchanges eight days later, those ticket scalpers—er, buyers—could fetch $92 per coin. In two months, GNO was going for $361. The project, which hadn't launched and was mostly a white paper with a newly opened GitHub, was now worth $9.5 billion.

According to a ConsenSys developer who created a detailed visual analysis of the ICO, some Gnosis sale participants took advantage of capabilities enabled by smart contracts.[19] A buyer in, say, Shanghai, for whom the crowdsale started at 1 a.m., could, ahead of time, put his or her bid into so-called programmatic bidding rings, which were smart contracts that collected people's ETH and submitted it for them when the sale opened—all while the buyer was asleep—and sent GNO back. Buyers didn't have to put their faith in a company with a CEO under legal obligations—they could just trust the code.

Since so many people were buying ETH to gamble—er, invest—in these crowdsales, its price was rising. By April's end, ETH was trading at $79, but just a few days after, it closed at $97. On the ICO front, May made April look quaint; twenty-two initial coin offerings that month raised $229 million. MyEtherWallet, the tiny side project started by two best friends, saw its traffic jump tenfold in five months alone: it went from one hundred thousand hits in January to one million in May.

That winter, as ICOs had been picking up, Kosala found it impossible to keep up with all the tokens Taylor, who was the liaison to the community, was constantly asking him to add while also tending to MEW's own development goals. They decided to create "custom token support," which made it possible for anyone to add any ERC-20 token to MEW. Kosala and Taylor did this out of laziness, but now random ICOs didn't have to ask MEW to support their token; the issuers could add it themselves. It was akin to the New York Stock Exchange letting companies enable trading in their own stocks on NYSE.

On May 17, Aragon, which aimed to help build "unstoppable organizations," raised $24.8 million in twenty-five minutes—even though 651 transactions totaling more than thirty thousand ETH (approximately $2.7 million) failed due to insufficient gas or transaction fees.[20] On May 19, the ETH price closed just shy of $130. Two days later, it closed a few cents short of $158. On May 22, the first day of the largest blockchain conference in New York City, Consensus, it hit $174.[21] On May 24, the last day of Consensus, it reached a high of just over $228. May 25 was Token Summit, a follow-on conference dedicated solely to tokens. There, for the first time, an existing company not already in crypto called Kik, which had a chat app, announced it was doing an ICO. The same day, two ICOs raised a total of $84 million: MobileGo, "The First Crypto-centric Mobile Gaming Platform," pulled in $53 million, while Storj, a decentralized version of Dropbox, raised $30 million.[22] Token Summit itself was oversold, and dozens who had flown in from around the world were turned away at the doors in the rain. The following Tuesday, on May 30, twenty-four-hour trading volume on Ethereum surpassed that of Bitcoin for the first time, with $1.2 billion worth of ETH changing hands. The price shot up almost 20 percent to a high that day of nearly $234. By this point, Bitcoin dominance had dropped below 50 percent;

Ethereum's had surpassed 20 percent, and its market cap had more than doubled from $16 billion on January 1 to $35.6 billion.

Taylor, who had been surprised when the Golem ICO had caused MEW's Ethereum nodes to go down, saw the public's increasing hunger for tokens. On April 6, there were two ICOs, and for the first time MEW received 2.25 million requests per hour. For the TokenCard ICO on May 2, a Redditor posted that MEW had failed to submit or complete transactions at the ICO's start. The Redditor said MEW seemed to work properly for each failed attempt, but the transaction did not go through on the Ethereum blockchain until the fifth try.[23] Another user pointed out this may have been a problem with the blockchain, which could only handle fifteen transactions a second.[24] Taylor wrote back, "Holy shit. I think you might be right. I've been running tests and trying to figure out what would cause shit to go down with absolutely no record of anything going wrong on our end. We don't have error messages. We didn't have a queue. We didn't drop txs [transactions]. Us sending transactions and then not being mined would fit into this…Holy shit. Fucking token sales."[25] The demand to get into ICOs was so intense, it wasn't overwhelming MEW's nodes—*it was overloading Ethereum itself.* From the MEW account, she tweeted the Reddit thread saying, "Well guys, that's it. We've literally reached the maximum capacity for FOMO. ICOs can go home now."

That was hardly max FOMO. As ICOs continued to grow, Taylor began rating them based on their "tx pool carnage level," as she called it, giving TokenCard a seven, Aragon a six, Storj a zero ("yay! People actually had more than 10 mins to get in!!!!" she wrote on her graph), and a late-May ICO called Mysterium a nine.

Then, on May 31, there was the Basic Attention Token (BAT) ICO, which was scheduled to run for thirty days, or until its cap of 156,250 ETH was met. BAT raised almost $36 million in twenty-four seconds from just 210 buyers—an average of a little over $171,000 per participant. One bought about $4.7 million worth of tokens; another paid around $6,375 in transaction fees to guarantee his or her purchase would be processed.[26] Only 1.89 percent of attempted transactions got in. Would-be participants spent $67,000 in transaction fees trying to enter the sale.[27] ETH hit a new all-time high of nearly $237 that day. Taylor tweeted from the MEW account,

> Blockchain carnage level: FFS, WHY ARE YOU STILL SENDING?!?!?!?! It was over in 24 seconds! 3 BLOCKS!!! #batshitcrazy

In a chat group for exchange operators, someone from Shape-Shift estimated that due to the backlog caused by the BAT ICO, it would be another seven or eight hours before anything could be posted to the blockchain again. Around this time, Taylor began drowning in support tickets and queries from total newbs who couldn't tell a blockchain from a database but wanted in on get-rich-quick schemes: "Hi I generated an account last month at myetherwallet.com and I was using parity…," "What Alt Coin's does your wallet support?" "i was able to withdraw from an exchange in the wallet, however i would like to send…"

She would wake up and answer support tickets, or if she couldn't, she'd send a screenshot of the issue to Kosala. She'd be in contact with Bity, which enabled MEW users to exchange, say, BTC for ETH. She'd hop into various Slacks to answer questions and onto the MEW Twitter account to respond to direct messages. If there was a token sale, she wouldn't go to bed until 3 or 4 a.m.; then she'd sleep till noon. If she thought May, with a million visitors, was hectic, in June, MEW would get 2.7 million.

AS ICOS WERE blowing up, Ming was getting more preoccupied with details. While developers could previously submit an invoice of their hours and get paid, now she was requiring at least some of them to submit reports on their work by the quarter hour. Despite offering all that information, they would sometimes receive notes saying, "This isn't detailed enough." Even though she wasn't a developer, she would try to dictate some of the team leads' priorities. Some would do the bare minimum to satisfy her and then work on their own.

In April, Nick Johnson, the developer who had written the ETH Withdraw Contract and been working on an Ethereum-based domain name system (called Ethereum Name Service, in which the web addresses would end in .eth), got a volunteer to help out during the launch. Ming became concerned this person would represent himself as part of the EF, due to past experience she said she'd had with people claiming they were foundation volunteers to get some advantage. Because the volunteer had called himself the "launch manager," the role Nick had given him, Ming wrote,

> His language and actions are a risk and now we have to do something about it
> My radar for potential problems is particularly fine tuned now as I am wrapping up 2014 and 2015 issues that cost us dearly

When it came time to bid on Ethereum domain names in May, Ming wanted to bid on domain names that the Enterprise Ethereum Alliance might want because the Ethereum Foundation had the trademark for Enterprise Ethereum. Nick asked, "Do we really want to pursue our beef with the EEA in such a public venue?"

> Bumper Chan: It's not a beef
> Bumper Chan: We own that mark
> Nick Johnson: I understand
> Nick Johnson: But I'm thinking about how it looks to people who don't know the background.
> Bumper Chan: They have a limited and restricted licensing agreement
> Bumper Chan: we already own the TM

Bumper Chan: It is in our interest to protect our IP
Bumper Chan: Joe has already made statements to diminish,
with very explicit statements to me and our lawyers
Bumper Chan: He went as far as to say he will pursue use of
'Ethereum' for Consensys.
Nick Johnson: Nobody outside the foundation has that
background though
Bumper Chan: He has proven 1000x he is neither trustworthy
or a person of good character
Nick Johnson: They'd just see us seizing names they entail
associate with EEA

Later on, she referenced his comment that nobody outside the foundation had that context and replied, "This is the irony. I would like nothing more than to tell the world. We are accommodating Joe/Consensys/EEA by not giving that background as they don't want people to know."

She also dropped hints about administrative moves she had made or was about to make. Referencing her arrival in 2015, she wrote, "I inherited many problems, but in the course of about 21 months, approximately 17 or the 20 biggest problems have been eliminated for resolved. Soon it will be 19/20. This is a great day even though there is still months of work ahead on this issue alone." Later, after the conversation about EEA-relevant domain names and Joe being untrustworthy, she wrote, "Now I'm dealing with restructuring matters that are far more important now than third party bad actors." Twenty minutes later, she wrote,

My God!!
I can't talk about it right now, but I have the best worst news
that involves Joe/Consen
In a stunning lack of integrity, two the most expensive and
problematic people in our space have combined! And
they've provided hard proof all by themselves.

Swiss director and legal team should be able to help resolve this matter, which should expect all other organizational improvements I've been working on since fall of last year. Enjoying this moment while it lasts. Of course there is work to do, but all the pain was worth it—overall impact will be positive for the foundation and our devs.
**everything above it true
The truth is the best protection
please don't troll me...
Don't be fooled by my 'intensity.' My ability to solve problems and think logically in spite of my volume (loudness) and volume (walls of text) is why I've achieved and 'succeeded' my entire life at just about everything I've set out to do. I have no insecurities or feeling of lack in this area. This is a good thing for everyone I've worked for/with. Normally, once the challenge is gone, my work is done and I can hand a well-oiled machine to someone else to maintain—most people don't want to do the hard and unpleasant work (and why would they), or they don't have the skillset to do it. There are people like me out there, but they are also typically stressed, oversubscribed and intense.

There was more—about having "one last big corner" of the foundation to clean up and the statement "crypto may keep me around longer than usual because it has yet to lack intellectual stimulation and challenge. But I won't stay without support of the team, It is not logical." Then she said, "I'm still excited that the unpleasant (restructuring) work I must do will be expedited."

AROUND THE SAME time, Ming began working on DevCon 3 and got a new assistant, Toya Budunggud, a volunteer at DevCon 2 in Shanghai who had been working on a Chinese Ethereum community called Ethfans. Although Toya was supposed to help with DevCon 3, she said the job entailed being Ming's personal assistant more than anything else. The two, along with Casey, lived in Ethereum's Zug apartment, which had a living room, a work room, and two bedrooms. Toya, who had degrees in electrical engineering and computer science, also took care of Ming's grocery shopping and cooking.

On Toya's first day, she was tasked with booking Casey's flight to and hotel in Berlin for an Ethereum-related meetup, but she couldn't because the venue had not been decided, and Ming wanted lodging close by. Toya says the only suitable place for the meetup cost €800, which, despite the fact that this was in the ballpark of single-digits ETH, Ming found too expensive, so she and the meetup organizer fought for hours.

Also, on Toya's first day, ConsenSys bought more than one hundred tickets for DevCon 3. Ming Skyped Hudson and Jamie and began crying about it. There was a limit to the number of tickets any single entity could obtain, so she considered the purchase a threat against or attempt to sabotage DevCon 3. Jamie had to cancel all the tickets. Because of ConsenSys's hub-and-spoke model, whereby projects existed under its aegis, with Joe paying their staffs' salaries, rather than their having to go through the rigors of being scrappy start-ups, ConsenSys bought tickets for those developers, but they could apply to the EF for developer discounts. Ming instructed Toya to be more skeptical of the applications from ConsenSys. The "official" reason was that ConsenSys was making DevCon less diverse and that the EF wanted to make tickets available to people outside that company. (Hearing this, Joe says, "We were used to having to work around Ming's irrationality.")

But mostly, according to Toya, Ming's objection stemmed from her complaints about Joe. For instance, Toya said, she disliked that he called himself an Ethereum cofounder. Ming considered him an early investor. She also thought Joe was narcissistic and that his interest in Ethereum was not genuine or pure and instead driven by a desire for money and fame. (Joe says he's never done anything for money in his life and prefers to be private.) Toya felt that since

Ming had decided she disliked Joe, she found more reasons not to like him.

Around this time, the videographer who worked with Joe, Arthur Falls, wrote an email to a few people, including Joe, Andrew, and others at ConsenSys, plus additional people in the Ethereum community, saying he intended to write an open letter to Vitalik calling for Ming's removal. At a time when the ETH price was swinging between $150 and $400 and the EF's runway was now years long, he and developers in the community and the foundation itself were frustrated that so many projects were not getting grants and that foundation salaries were so low when the EF was flush with cash. (Also, with all these new ICOs rolling in ETH, many new token teams were stealing developers with generous salary packages.) Plus, Ming had stonewalled Arthur's attempts to interview her and other EF staff for his Ethereum-friendly podcast, which seemed suspicious. After Arthur's call for the open letter, a number of people admonished him against it, because they planned to write something similar but signed by fifty community members.

Vitalik knew none of this. It had been a year since he had first thought about replacing Ming. Now that he'd felt the freedom and joy of working on Ethereum without her, through Ethereum Asia Pacific Ltd. in Singapore, their relationship had deteriorated further. In Zug, she would tell Toya things like "We're not together anymore." She would get upset and cry about how he was in Singapore and Asia most of the time, rather than in Zug or North America with her. But Toya sensed she was sad not only because she wasn't around him but also because her influence was waning. Having power in the foundation came from Vitalik's endorsement. And because Vitalik was conflict averse and couldn't say no, others got more sway by being near him. Many of her decisions got overturned when people would complain to Vitalik.

On top of that, in 2016, Vitalik had started dating a Chinese Ethereum events entrepreneur named Pandia Jiang, and according to Toya, who knew both of them, by May 2017 Ming and Pandia hated each other. Ming suspected Pandia was interested in Vitalik for reasons beyond love, such as financial gain or her own professional advancement, and would make comments like "Vitalik is surrounded by bad people," which Toya took to mean Pandia. It didn't help that Pandia was an events organizer and DevCon was, at that time, "the foundation's sole demonstrable product," as Toya put it. Ming felt threatened that Pandia's conference might take attention from DevCon. Their relationship had been good enough that Pandia had been a speaker at DevCon 2 in September, but at some point in the event planning process for Pandia's first event, EdCon, in Paris in February, Ming began to feel that EdCon was intentionally misrepresenting itself as an "official event." Ming began to say things like "If the EF doesn't take active steps to protect its name and brand, the EF's Swiss legal status might be compromised" and that she might have to resort to legal action. By the time of the planning process for DevCon 3, the animosity between Ming and Pandia interfered with work. If a potential DevCon 3 sponsor came to Pandia, Pandia would refer them to Toya, who would then have to keep the fact that the party had come through Pandia a secret "because otherwise Ming would not consider signing a contract with them regardless of their qualifications," said Toya. (Pandia's dislike of Ming started after Ming began acting in a hostile manner toward her. Toya says the rift between them grew to the point that, by the time of DevCon 3 in November, when Vitalik, Pandia, and his friends showed up at the Airbnb they had booked, Ming happened to be there, although she had lodging elsewhere. That forced Pandia to wander the streets—at least with a close friend of Vitalik's to keep her company—until Ming left.) Vitalik declined to comment, saying he didn't want to dignify this storyline.

During this time, on their long phone calls, Vitalik says Ming accused him of things like not appreciating her, of being awful to her. She could not keep things professional—it was all personal.

She would cry. She would make him cry. It was a long time before
he came to think her allegations were unjustified.

BEFORE TOYA BEGAN working for Ming, the Berlin office
manager, a middle-aged man with sparse, graying hair and tor-
toiseshell glasses named Christian Vömel, was hearing that Ming
had told some of the devs in the Berlin office not to tell him that
she was closing or relocating it. Kelley Becker, the COO/director,
was still out on maternity leave, so Christian had been given the
power of attorney to sign official documents in consultation with
her. Once Ming stopped communicating with him, running the
German entity became difficult for him.

Although he'd gotten a raise in February, Ming sharply decreased her communication with him in March and did not speak
to him at all in April. Hearing the office was going to be closed
or restructured and seeing he had been removed from the EF's
Skype channel, Christian emailed Ming asking her about his employment status since he had two children. She responded that she
had not heard from him in a year, that he solely worked for ETH
Dev CFO Frithjof Weinert, that she had asked him to help her
at the foundation but he had declined, and that the UG in Berlin
(ETH Dev) was a for-profit company, so the EF needed a clear
separation from it.

The German UG had a contract with the foundation whereby,
every month, the EF would send it the money needed for salaries,
overhead, and the German tax payments. These were due late in
the month, around the 26th or 27th, but in early 2017, the EF began
sending money to the UG later and later. In May, the money still
wasn't in the UG's account two days before payment had to be
made. If the UG did not contribute to the social insurance, then
Kelley, as the UG's director, would be personally liable for it. Plus,
German law states that if a company knows it will have liquidity
problems for the next three months, it has to begin taking the

steps toward insolvency. Failing to do so is a criminal offense for the director.[28]

Also, without discussing it with the UG, the foundation sent the UG less money than it had agreed to. Ming and the foundation had decided to cut the amount that the EF was paying ETH Dev, which comprised the bulk of the coding staff and contractors, without changing the contracts. (EF board member Patrick Storchenegger would later deny this and the delaying of payments.) Two documents from that time show that Frithjof and Kelley reached out to Ming and Patrick to ask what was going on, but they refused to talk. If there was no change, Kelley realized, the UG would have to close.

Kelley was expecting her second child in mid-June, so this was the worst time for her to run the risk of being personally liable for the UG's social insurance and potentially facing a criminal charge. She managed to schedule a meeting with Patrick and the foundation lawyers for three days before she gave birth. The purpose was for her to sign over the directorship to Patrick. When she showed up, she was surprised to also find Ming.

In the meeting, Ming and Patrick accused Kelley of withholding bookkeeping information from the EF. (Patrick denies this.) The contract said if the EF ever requested such information, the UG would give it in a timely manner, but as the documents show, the EF had never done so. Kelley said the UG would have sent it if the EF had asked. In the end, it was agreed that Patrick would take over the directorship.

Although she didn't say so, Ming, scrutinizing the budgets of ETH Dev, had become convinced that Frithjof, the CFO, was embezzling money—up to $100,000—and that Kelley and Christian were involved. Frithjof, an independent contractor because, Kelley says, he had refused to become an employee, though Frithjof says he was offered a contractor agreement, was partially financially responsible for all the Ethereum entities at that time except the Dutch one. He was tasked with cleaning up the long period without proper bookkeeping and administrative and tax management. Vitalik never looked into whether the accusations were true, and Patrick would later say that there was never any proof but that the foundation needed more transparency and for things to be properly filed. When asked if he suspected Frithjof embezzled money, Patrick said he could not say, that he could not make a false accusation. Frithjof says, "We successfully passed couple of external audits: statutory GAAP, taxes, payroll tax social security etc with perfectly clean opinion by auditors." Ming herself never confronted Christian, Kelley, or Frithjof about it; nor had she ever requested from them information that would have helped her conduct such an investigation. Frithjof says, "[Something] like that was never discussed or even remotely raised." Regardless, in the coming months, Ming would tell her assistants and other foundation devs in her long phone calls that the administrative staff had stolen money from the foundation.

Shortly after this meeting between Kelley, Ming, Patrick, and their lawyers, Christian and Kelley quit. (In response to his notice, Christian says, Ming sent a Skype message saying he should stay.) Patrick and Ming had a discussion with Frithjof saying they needed more transparency and didn't feel Frithjof could continue; he agreed to resign. Although Christian had given zero notice, he begged Kelley to sign his papers. That was her last act as director of Ethereum DEV UG.

As Ming, thinking she was messaging someone else back when she'd started at the EF, had accidentally told then board member Lars Klawitter, now she could "choose [her] own advisory board (not Kelley)." And she had "[gained] control together with Vitalik."

IN 2017, POLONIEX'S volume grew fifty to seventy-five times what it had been in December 2016.[29] With more customers, more volume, and now more processes, the company became buried.

About twenty people were managing almost five million accounts, and the owners had not invested in the company at all. Instead of hiring a third-party know-your-customer vendor, as many companies would, to make sure each submitted ID matched the selfie taken and that the address given wasn't for, say, a strip mall in Nevada, Polo employees had to process IDs one by one. Support was still bare-bones: according to a manager at the time, five people handled more than one hundred thousand support tickets. In the first half of the year, Johnny managed to "poach" a few troll box moderators to be new support agents, bringing the total to eight. According to Johnny, Jules made workers put their phones in cubbies upon entering the office, forbade them from listening to music, and, though this might also be for security reasons, blocked their computers from the internet so they could only do one thing on those machines: work. They had to wear headphones so that they wouldn't accidentally overhear any conversations, they were recorded via cameras inside the office, and they were instructed to communicate with each other only on chat. (Later Jules would acknowledge to employees that they were surveilling all staff chats, including direct messages.)

The owners often enjoyed days of $1 billion in trade volume with low overhead. Someone familiar with Polo said its net profit margin was a staggering 90 percent. Polo often made over $1 million a day—for instance, in the week ending June 12, volume was about $5 billion, yielding on average $1.6 million in pure profit each day. One day, the exchange even raked in $3 million. Employees were kept in the dark about the money streaming in, but some gleaned that Mike, who enjoyed racing cars on a track, had a BMW collection. After Jules and Mike had, for months, resisted instituting robust KYC processes to fully comply with financial regulations, suddenly, the staff's main priority was to overhaul Polo's anti-money-laundering program, making sure the company wasn't servicing individuals from sanctioned countries and terrorists. In late August, the owners finally relented and hired a third-party KYC vendor, Jumio, and began integrating it into the platform in September.

By that spring, like Tristan, Jules and Mike had mostly disappeared. They'd hired a new employee, Ruby Hsu. Since she showed up unannounced, some employees asked Jules who the hell was this person demanding all kinds of stuff out of the blue. Jules said Ruby was covering for her because she was tied up dealing with lawyers and regulators. She said to treat Ruby as if she were Tristan, Jules, and Mike combined. The employees thought she was hired specifically to be mean to them so that the owners didn't have to do it anymore.

MEANWHILE, THE ICOS were crescendoing. On June 12, thirteen days after BAT's twenty-four-second, $36 million ICO, the Bancor ICO took place. The Tel Aviv–based team, which was building a decentralized liquidity protocol, announced the morning of its sale that it had received backing from famed Silicon Valley venture capitalist Tim Draper, whose past investments had included Hotmail, Baidu, Skype, and Tesla, among many others. Although initially planning to block Americans so as not to run afoul of US securities laws, in the end the team decided to allow them.[30] (Bancor's worry about the Securities and Exchange Commission was so strong that it dubbed its ICO a "TDE," short for token distribution event. Some teams felt that using the term "initial coin offering" was basically waving a red cape at the SEC. Another popular alternative was "token generation event.") The team also tried to incorporate lessons from the mistakes of previous token sales. If an ICO was supposed to seed a network, certainly BAT's capped sale, which sold to just 210 whales—er, buyers—was not ideal. Bancor, wanting to follow the crypto ethos of democratizing access, decided to require a minimum of one hour, which would help ensure that anyone who wanted to participate could do so. After that hour, the Bancor team would institute a hidden cap (250,000 ETH) that would be revealed only if the ETH collected hit 80 percent of that limit. If the sale raised the amount of the cap or more within the first hour, Bancor would close it immediately after that first hour.[31]

Instead, during the sale the Ethereum blockchain became backlogged, so some users experienced hours-long delays in their transactions. At one point, more than three thousand transactions were still pending.[32] When it became clear Bancor was going to hit its cap, the transaction that the team sent to hard-code its 250,000 ETH limit into the smart contract got stuck behind all the other transactions. As a result, Bancor raised 150,000 more ETH ($51 million), which angered investors who now had a smaller percentage of the pie than they'd wanted.[33] However, they did manage to sell to 10,887 addresses—and most of all, they raised nearly $153 million, beating the DAO, and they did it in just three hours instead of a month. The Ethereum price hit a new all-time high—almost $415—and its market cap did too: $37.1 billion.

MEW servers logged a type of activity called "sendRaw trans-actions per hour," which counted how many times people deliberately performed an action, like sending money, per hour. During the BAT ICO, two weeks earlier, MEW's sendRaw transactions per hour had gone from an average of less than one thousand when there was no ICO to nine thousand, which blew Taylor's mind. But the Bancor ICO saw almost thirty thousand. Because of the fix Kosala had made after the Golem ICO, MEW's Ethereum nodes functioned the whole time. It was a technological feat. As Taylor told *Quartz* at the time, "With these ICOs you are essentially asking a service to scale from maybe 10% capacity to 1,000% capacity in the course of less than a minute. Every single person presses the send button at the same time."[34]

THE ICO ACTIVITY was generating a ton of interest in Ethereum. On June 18, with ETH holding strong with a high that day of nearly $391, the flippening seemed within reach. Bitcoin market share had plunged to a stunning 37.84 percent, while Ethereum's was at 31.17 percent.[35] Ethereum's market cap was now about $34.4 billion, compared to Bitcoin's $41.8 billion.

Two days later, another big ICO went up to bat, but this time it was going to try other ideas to democratize the sale. Jarrad Hope, a Perth native and internet marketer who had made money with poker bots, and his longtime business partner Carl Bennetts were building Status, an open-source messaging platform and web 3.0 browser. After getting negged by VCs, Jarrad and Carl turned to the crowd. At first their Slack had more than three thousand fans, but once Status.im announced its ICO, membership ballooned to more than fifteen thousand. Most newcomers were scammers, phishers, and "when-mooners," or people who only cared about when Bitcoin was going to go "to the moon." Basically, sharks were now circling the community, ready to snatch up any carelessly dropped private keys.

One day the week before the ICO, in Singapore, where, being digital nomads, Jarrad and Carl happened to be at the time, Jarrad was writing a message warning people never to give away their private keys (because anyone asking for it was a phisher) when a console popped up on his screen showing "¯_(ツ)_/¯." His firewall app began spouting notifications about incoming connections. He shut his laptop and ran up to Carl's hotel room to bang on the door, yelling that his computer had been compromised. Carl ran down in his pajamas, and the two spent the day securing all their accounts for Status, their businesses, and their personal lives.

On one side, they were targeted by scammers; on the other, they were getting queries from regulators like the SEC. (The SEC declined to comment.) They had studied the Howey test to structure the Status Network Token (SNT) so as not to violate securities law, plus blocked US participants based on IP address.

Jarrad felt like he was pulling an Indiana Jones, swinging through a cave just as a boulder was about to seal the exit shut. In order to optimize his time, he was eating only Joylent, a European Soylent, and working fourteen hours or more a day.

One big problem they were trying to resolve was whales getting a disproportionate amount of tokens. Jordi, the White Hat Group member, who was good friends with Jarrad, had an idea to use dynamic ceilings or hidden hard caps that would lift at various points. For instance, the first hard cap would be public and begin when twelve million Swiss francs was hit; after that, the contribution period would stop within twenty-four hours or sooner if the hidden hard ceiling was reached. Also, additional, successively lower hidden caps would be triggered, each beginning after a certain number of blocks. The scheme, the white paper said, was "an attempt to discourage big money investors, whales, from consuming the entire SNT allocation."[36] If someone sent too much money, some would be accepted, the rest returned.

When the sale started at 4 a.m. Singapore time, Jarrad's heart sank. No money was coming in. He eventually realized people were sending in such large amounts that the contract was rejecting the transactions. Just minutes in, there were almost eleven thousand unconfirmed transactions worth 450,481 ETH ($161.7 million).[37] This clogged up the network with many more transactions than it would have had otherwise, since people whose transactions were rejected then sent new ones.[38] It was nearly impossible for anyone to do anything else on Ethereum. Some bids for Ethereum domain name auctions failed because Ethereum itself was too congested. The Status ICO went on for twenty-four hours, allowing every time zone to participate. By the end, Status had raised more than $100 million. (One community member commented, "Status just raised as much as they could possibly want, for chat stickers and ads."[39]) However, the contract had refunded more than it had accepted, so without the hidden ceilings, it would have garnered over $200 million. Unfortunately, Jarrad says, the design didn't deter whales, who bought tokens under each cap but later complained they had paid a lot in transaction fees.

FOR TAYLOR, THE Status ICO was like a tsunami. She'd been amazed when nine thousand sendRaw transactions per hour on

MEW was reached during the BAT ICO and thirty thousand during Bancor's, but Status's hit one hundred thousand. That wasn't even the only ICO that week—a day after Status's ICO completed, an identity-verification project called Civic pulled in $33 million, and a couple days after that, TenX, a decentralized exchange plus crypto debit card, raised $83 million. The following day, a Friday, OmiseGo, a financial services platform backed by Thai payments company Omise, raised $26.3 million in an ICO that verified every participant's identity through Bitcoin Suisse. On a chart of MEW's web visits, this week would later look like a huge spike.

That Sunday, a post on 4chan—a dark, anonymous, anarchic version of Reddit—proclaimed, "Vitalik Buterin confirmed dead. Insiders unloading ETH." The post said, "Fatal car crash. Now we have our answer. He was the glue." The price of ETH dropped 8.6 percent from $315 to $288, wiping $4 billion off Ethereum's market cap.[40] Vitalik quickly quashed that rumor by tweeting a photo of himself with a piece of paper on which he'd written,

Block 3,930,000

=

0xe2f1fc56da

It was a recent block number from the Ethereum blockchain, along with the hash of that block. He captioned his photo "Another day, another blockchain use case."[41] Despite his proof, Ethereum's market share ticked down to 26.7 percent while Bitcoin's rose to 40.3 percent.[42]

The next day, EOS, which billed itself as a faster (but more centralized) competitor to Ethereum, kicked off its nearly year-long ICO. The month before, it had advertised its sale on a massive billboard in Times Square, during the Consensus conference, which had twenty-seven hundred attendees. The advertisement was ironic given that the EOS ICO blocked US IP addresses. That week, the ETH price again traded with highs in the $330s and lows in the $200s.

Dismayed by the frenzy, Taylor tweeted, from the MEW account, things like "Cmonnnnnnn 😟 Have you learned NOTHING from the last week?! Take your heads out greedy asses (you too, FOMO investors!) & look around" (referring to the EOS ICO) and "Sit down—we've got some news for you. Kickass products can exist without a token & taking all the money," along with a gif of a camera zooming in on the face of shirtless wrestler John Cena, mouth open, a look of shock on his face.[43]

In June, ICOs raised around $620 million—and July 1 was the start of one of the buzziest ICOs, Tezos. The project, which had also received investment from Tim Draper, was seen as a potential competitor to Ethereum, with two features that improved upon it: formal verification, a way to mathematically prove that smart contracts would behave as the developers intended, to prevent DAO attack–like situations, and built-in governance, right on the blockchain, to manage questions like whether to fork after the DAO. It would go on to raise a record $232 million.

Like Jarrad, around this time Taylor began to notice a lot of security issues. For instance, fake clones of the Status website (Status.im) popped up with URLs like statusim.info and statustoken.im, which led to a phishing site that advertised an "airdrop," in which free SNT would be placed into your Ethereum wallet. But because this was not a legitimate airdrop but a phishing scam, it claimed you would only get the airdrop if you entered your private key on the site. (Because the private key is used to send money out of an account, giving it to anyone else would be like revealing the code to your bank vault.)

Phishers turned their sights on Taylor and Kosala's baby as well, with URLs such as myethewallet.net, myetherwillet.com, myelherwallet.com, myeltherwallet.com, and so on. These were part of the so-called Coinhoarder scam in which phishers bought

Google AdWords for myetherwallet.com and related terms so that their misspelled URLs would top the search results. The sites themselves looked like clones of MEW, so when users entered their passwords, the hackers could plunder the victims' wallets.[44]

Even Vitalik fell for a scam. Someone hacked Jeff's Skype account and wrote to Vitalik, "Hey V, we're still waiting on 925 ETH to be sent for our invoices," and specified an address. Vitalik messaged Jeff that he'd sent the money. Jeff informed him that was not his Ethereum address. Vitalik had sent a quarter million dollars into the ether.

If ICOs had pushed Taylor into an unhealthy routine in May, the scams now worsened her schedule. If she woke at 10 p.m., she would stay up till 5 or 6 a.m., nap till 7 or 8 a.m., catch her operations guy up on support tickets, and task him with watching for any hacks or other security issues. She'd pass out, wake up at noon or 1 p.m., and, if nothing was exploding, shove some food in her face, shower, and dress. But when there was a security incident, she'd roll out of bed and work until 6 p.m., at which point she would realize she hadn't started her day.

ON JULY 17 yet another ICO, by CoinDash, took place, but before the sale opened, its website got hacked, and the contribution address was changed. The hacker(s) got 43,500 ETH (nearly $8.5 million by the high that day). Though crypto security people tweeted about it, another $1 million was sent within the hour anyway. This brought Taylor to a breaking point. She tweeted from the MEW account,

1/ Alright Crappy Token Creators listen up. I am 100% out of patience. It's 10am. I haven't slept. . . .

4/ You chase a goldmine of stupid money instead of helping Ethereum become what it should become. You promise lots, but deliver lost funds.

5/ Fake addresses, scambots, phishing, exploits, domain takeovers & phone hijacking have been happening since day one yet you don't prepare....
8/ Don't think you are off the hook investors: You get some blame too.
9/ Throwing money at any address, clicking like theres never been a Nigerian Prince & not demanding more from investments is a problem too
10/ Step up your game. 2000 unique addresses in 2hrs fell for the same scam that's been taking money for years. Time to grow up.[45]

The next morning, upon waking, she heard Kevin and her operations manager talking animatedly. She went downstairs. Kevin, referring to the EF, said, "The Foundation's multisig got hacked." Taylor, still groggy, said, "No it didn't," and turned back up the stairs. If it had been, her phone would have been blowing up. But then she realized her phone was dead.

11

July 19, 2017, to November 4, 2017

BERND LAPP, THE president of Swarm City, a decentralized commerce platform, had posted in a Skype group, "I don't want to panic but I think our multisig got hacked. It's at least empty. 44k Ether [around $10 million] gone."

To suss it out, some on Taylor's team looked at the code for the multisig's smart contract. At the top, it said,

> // This multisignature wallet is based on the wallet contact by Gav Wood.
> ...
> // @authors:
> // Gav Wood <g@ethdev.com>

Maybe it was seeing Gav's name; maybe it was seeing it was a multisig. What is the best-known of all the multisig wallets? The Ethereum Foundation's. So, like in a game of Telephone, Kevin and MEW's operations manager relayed to Taylor that the EF's multisig had been hacked when it had been Swarm City's. While alarming, it was of much less import than a hack of the Ethereum Foundation's multisig.

Even after the facts got sorted, that left a conundrum: How could a multisig be hacked? A multisig wallet, like the Ethereum

Foundation footballs, required multiple signers to make a transaction, so in order for it to have been hacked, several people had either been in cahoots to steal from it or had their devices hacked simultaneously.

In Barcelona, Griff, Jordi, and the team of Griff's new venture were drinking wine on a hacker house porch with a view of La Sagrada Familia when Griff got a WhatsApp call from Swarm City's King Flurkel about the hack. Griff assumed Flurkel was wrong. But when he checked it out, he saw a transaction had moved a lot of money with a single signature, not three out of five.

Seeing Swarm City's wallet had been coded by Parity, Griff, Jordi, and the other White Hats there realized this meant it was possible to hack *any* Parity-brand multisig wallet. They had no idea how many entities used one.

They called Hudson, who was at Cornell's IC3 Ethereum boot camp with Vitalik, Avsa, Ming, Casey, Martin Becze, and others. Somehow, once again, something got lost in translation, and Hudson ran into a room where he, Ming, and Avsa had been judging a competition and shouted, "Emergency! Emergency! The Ethereum Foundation multisig has been hacked!" He then slammed the door and ran down the hall to get Vitalik. After a glance at the foundation multisig, which was fine, everyone calmed down.

However, a total of 153,037 ETH, worth around $36 million at the high price that day ($29.3 million once news of the hack got out), *had* been stolen from Swarm City, Edgeless Casino, and æternity. All three projects' logos featured the infinity symbol.

Meanwhile, on the rocky, lizard- and fern-filled island of Ibiza, the Parity team and friends were at a lovely terra-cotta-tiled, exotic-plant-adorned home rented by Brock Pierce, the former *Mighty Ducks* actor turned crypto VC, wrapping up a weeklong retreat that, for at least some attendees, was at times an alcohol- and drug-fueled blur. The previous Sunday, in the VIP room of the club Amnesia, the group had made merry.

On Wednesday, the last night of the retreat, around happy hour, someone yelled, "Every Parity dev get upstairs right now!" Everyone raced up the steps to the pool area, which had the best Wi-Fi. Once they learned about the hack, the Parity team sat, hunched over their laptops, on chaise longues around the pool and hot tub, the light from their screens glowing blue on their faces. As with the DoS attacks, at least everyone was in the same place. But the money was gone, so there wasn't much Parity could do other than answer people's questions and make an update.

The task of making things right fell to the White Hat Group. They figured out how the hack worked but faced a quandary.[1] They could not publicly announce the vulnerability because then anyone could ransack any Parity multisig wallet. As with the DAO, they had to steal/rescue all the money themselves and return it to the rightful owners. They had IC3 attendees do a blockchain analysis to figure out which token teams used Parity's multisig by looking at the byte code pattern, a sort of fingerprint. However, Gavin goofed. At 8:32 p.m. Ibiza time, he posted in the Parity Gitter,

IMPORTANT: SECURITY ALERT
- Severity: Critical. . . .
- Description: Wallets created with Parity Wallet's "multisig" feature have a critical vulnerability. Funds in them are at immediate risk of theft.
- Remedial action: Please move any funds in them to an alternative wallet immediately.

THIS IS NOT A DRILL.[2]

Eight minutes later, WhalePanda, the Bitcoiner who had written the epic blog posts tying the Ethereum Foundation, Slock.it, and the DAO together, saw it and tweeted a screenshot of it, saying, "Critical security alert for $ETH @ParityTech wallet if you're using it for multisig."[3]

Someone tweeted, "Are you ready for Ethereum Very Classic?"[4] Another said, "So hardfork to get the $32M? Or are those people not well connected to the foundation so fuckem?"[5] (A hard fork, which takes weeks of planning and development, wouldn't do anything in this case since no delays were built into the hacker's movements. Indeed, the thief cashed out nearly fifty ETH, about $11,300, the very next day.[6])

Now that the news had spread (by 8:56 p.m. Ibiza time, Parity had published a blog post and tweeted about it[7]), everyone was racing against the clock, because anyone who figured out how the attack worked could drain the funds from any number of accounts. At 11:14 p.m., Parity pushed an update to the wallet code; in a blog post, it said any multisigs created from that point on were now secure.[8]

The White Hats got a spreadsheet of addresses that seemed to be controlled by a Parity multisig, as well as a script that could send transactions from Jordi's address to each one listed that would give him control of that multisig to take the money.

After running the script, Jordi—or rather his address—ended up with 377,106 ETH, worth around $88.6 million, plus $30 million worth of BAT, $27 million in Iconomi, $17.9 million in Cofoundit, $1.4 million in EOS, and many others, including 169.69 FUCKTokens.[9] It was $208 million worth of crypto in total.[10] Jordi thought, *With $200 million, you can contract a full army and still have $100 million left over.* Worried that having access to such a huge amount of money in his home would endanger him and his family, he and the other White Hats wanted to sleep in another location. Jordi tried to convince his wife to sleep at the offices for Griff's new venture, Giveth, since the address was not publicly known, but she refused, so Griff, another White Hat, and Jordi slept on a mattress blocking the door, a baseball bat handy.

The next day, they worked out of an apartment Jordi had just rented that few people knew about. Having learned their lesson from the DAO/ETC debacle, they decided to return the money quickly and securely, changing as few things as possible. Even though Jordi was more familiar with and preferred the Gnosis multisig to Parity's, he decided against switching the wallets to Gnosis ones and instead created Parity multisigs with the patched code. They then mapped each original account to a new multisig so each team could figure out where its money was now located. Four days later, as they were about to send the money back, the community asked how they could put hundreds of millions of dollars' worth of tokens into new code that had barely been audited.[11] In the end, they created a smart contract that enabled the owners of the multisigs to signal where they wanted to receive their funds, and the WHG called each of those people directly and made the transfers. Then $10 million remained, so they contacted as many developers as possible to check the code. After over a week of testing, with no critical bugs found, they sent the remainder to the multisigs.[12]

In September, someone would publish a fictional story on Medium titled "How I Snatched 153,037 ETH After A Bad Tinder Date," which was about a fictional Parity wallet hacker.[13] It got sixty-seven hundred claps. Top highlight: "Look, here's the thing. If you're holding 30 million dollars in 250 lines of code that you haven't audited, then it's on you."

WITH TEZOS RAISING $232 million, EOS only at the start of its yearlong ICO, and a record number of ICOs—as many as forty— scheduled for July, the month was shaping up to be one of the biggest yet in a global crypto party in which everyone was romping around, not in a ball pit but in magic internet money. While tripping on acid, doing lines, and rolling on molly. And while coins, like gold confetti, dropped from the air. And while sober people on the sidelines looked at their watches, tapped their toes, and wondered where the cops were.

A lot of lawyers, Bitcoiners, and others in crypto with a legal or business background were specifically looking at the Securities and

Exchange Commission. While the SEC had performed a handful of enforcement actions involving cryptocurrency, in 2016 there was only one and in 2017 only one regarding a Bitcoin fraud.[14] The agency had, however, dropped hints. At the Consensus conference in May, the head of the SEC's Distributed Ledger Technology Working Group, Valerie Szczepanik, stating that her views were her own, said, "Whether or not you are regulated by the SEC, you still have fiduciary duties to your investors. If you want this industry to flourish, protection of investors should be at the forefront."[15]

While some players in the space initially said regulators were aiming for a light touch so as to not hamper innovation, by this point, things were getting out of hand. Although in 2016 and early 2017 most ICOs tended to be held by crypto builders with legitimate blockchain-based ideas, now many more groups with little to no background in crypto were raising money from everyday people who themselves barely understood blockchain technology.

For instance, on May 26, the day after Token Summit, there was an ICO for something called Veritaseum that hadn't opensourced its code, hadn't published a white paper, and, based on its jumbled marketing, appeared to be a centralized company that could have easily accepted US dollars for payment—not a decentralized network. It did not even take the basic step of having a secure website, despite the hacks rampaging throughout crypto. It raised $11 million. Early on, VERI tokens ranked tenth among crypto assets by market cap. On July 22, the market cap based on circulating supply was $458 million. But accounting for the fact that Veritaseum had only released 2 percent of its tokens, its market cap by the total float was $22.9 billion. By that measure, the one-month-old company was almost twice as valuable as Nasdaq. Its market cap was more than that of Ethereum's, which on that day closed at $21.5 billion. And who controlled 98 percent of VERI? The founder.

Then, on July 23, in a BitcoinTalk post, its founder claimed to have been hacked.[16] From an address controlled by Veritaseum itself, the hacker stole almost thirty-seven thousand VERI tokens.[17] Immediately, Redditors responded. "Sure... 'hacked' fishy af," said one. Another said, "Veri is a scam anyway, this is a scam within a scam." The strangest part of the hack was that the "hacker" had access to an account with 100 million VERI but only took 36,686.9, or 0.037 percent—less than a tenth of a percent—leaving what was at that time $24.7 billion worth of tokens in the wallet.

May, June, and July of 2017 comprised a season of some serious entrepreneurs holding what to some looked like unregistered securities offerings and an avalanche of amateur copycats and tech-savvy scammers engaging in blockchain-based get-rich-quick schemes. (In July, someone with a wry sense of humor advertised an ICO for Useless Ethereum Token, whose tagline was "The world's first 100% honest Ethereum ICO... Let's be honest—everyone's tired of ICOs. They get hyped up for weeks, and then they launch and clog up the Ethereum network for days, Coinbase goes down for a while, and then 'investors' see the new tokens lose most of their 'value'. This ICO is going to be different. The UET ICO *transparently* offers investors no value, so there will be no expectation of gains."[18]) In this environment the SEC finally dropped its first salvo in what would become the regulators versus "blockchain is alegal" battle.

On July 25, the SEC published a report of investigation into DAO tokens, stating they were securities. It said, "Issuers of distributed ledger or blockchain technology-based securities must register offers and sales of such securities unless a valid exemption applies." (Translation: ICOs were securities offerings, which, according to the SEC, "requires the company to file a registration statement containing information about itself, the securities it is offering, and the offering," unless the ICO could claim an exemption.) It continued, "Those participating in unregistered offerings also may be liable for violations of the securities laws." (Meaning: buyers could also be violating securities laws.) And finally: "Additionally, securities exchanges providing for trading in these securities must register unless they are exempt." (This meant crypto exchanges listing these tokens must register with the SEC unless they also were exempt.)

As for the DAO in particular, the SEC said the DAO described itself as a "crowdfunding contract" but did not qualify for a similarly named exemption called Regulation Crowdfunding. Still, Slock.it, its cofounders, and the DAO curators could breathe easy because the report's second sentence said, "The Commission had determined not to pursue an enforcement action in this matter based on the conduct and activities known to the Commission at this time." But then it walked through an eighteen-page recap of the DAO saga, emphasizing the influence of the curators:

> According to the White Paper, the Curators of a DAO Entity had "considerable power." The Curators performed crucial security functions and maintained ultimate control over which proposals could be submitted to, voted on, and funded by The DAO... Curators of The DAO had ultimate discretion as to whether or not to submit a proposal for voting by DAO Token holders. Curators also determined the order and frequency of proposals, and could impose subjective criteria for whether the proposal should be whitelisted. One member of the group...stated publicly that the Curator had "complete control over the whitelist...the order in which things get whitelisted, the duration for which [proposals] get whitelisted, when things get unwhitelisted...[and] clear ability to control the order and frequency of proposals," noting that "curators have tremendous power." Another Curator publicly announced his subjective criteria for determining whether to whitelist a proposal, which included his personal ethics.

Then, in a section subtitled "DAO Tokens Are Securities," it walked through the four prongs of the Howey test. The most damning finding was the fourth—that DAO tokens were (1) an investment of money (2) in a common enterprise (3) with a reasonable expectation of profits (4) *dependent on the efforts of others*. Here the SEC pointedly wrote, "Specifically Slock.it and its co-founders, and The DAO's Curators." It delineated how Slock.it created the DAO website, maintained its online forums, and planned on submitting the first proposal. "Through their conduct and marketing materials, Slock.it and its co-founders led investors to believe that they could be relied on to provide the significant managerial efforts required to make The DAO a success," the SEC report said. It talked about how Slock.it chose the curators, and how the curators had to vet contractors, "determine whether and when to submit proposals for votes," and perform other functions around proposals. That section finished, "When the Attacker exploited a weakness in the code and removed investor funds, Slock.it and its co-founders stepped in to help resolve the situation."[19] (Although cofounders Christoph and Simon hadn't, employees Griff and Lefteris had.)

While the document was incriminating and put the crypto industry on notice, it wasn't entirely accurate. (The SEC, which declined to comment on this matter, had not interviewed Slock.it and reached out only to at least one American curator. An October 2020 FOIA request turned up no documents on any discussion around who deployed the DAO.) Slock.it hadn't set up the DAO-hub forums (though it had set up the Slack), it hadn't deployed the DAO smart contract (unknown DAO community members had created eight of them and Taylor's then fiancé Kevin had tossed the coin that had chosen which DAO to use), and the Robin Hood and White Hat groups, which included some Slock.it employees on their own time, helped resolve the attack. Regardless, the SEC had meant the document to be foundational, to show how the SEC was looking at the space. Lawyers surmised the agency had chosen a "21a report"—giving others notice that going forward the commission would likely follow up with enforcement actions for similar behavior—because the DAO no longer existed and people had not lost money.[20]

The question now was what this meant for Ethereum itself, which *had* conducted an ICO—albeit before the term existed—*and* sold its tokens in the United States. In the Ethereum presale, people *had* invested money in a common enterprise with an expectation of profits dependent on the efforts of others. Would the SEC pursue an enforcement action against Vitalik, the cofounders, and the Ethereum Foundation?

THOUGH THE PARITY hack got resolved, the crypto community was in the throes of a scamming/hacking/phishing onslaught. Monday was CoinDash, Wednesday was Parity, and eight days later was Ziber, which might best be called an "initial coin *taking.*" The team started its ICO, but then its contract was "suicided," or deleted. On its website, the contribution address was changed to a non–smart contract address—meaning, a regular Ethereum address. For twenty-four hours, buyers sent ETH right into the pockets of whoever held the keys to the new address, getting nothing back.[21]

The phishing scams were picking up, creating a leaking-sieve effect for crypto absent any major hacks. On Twitter, MEW constantly posted screenshots of phishing scams targeting its users, such as one from the day after the Parity hack, in which the phishers pretending to be MEW sent emails saying, "We announce to have been hacked. It is possible that the security of your account have been compromised." The email urged recipients to check their ETH balance on the now secured site "to know if your wallet has been compromised." MEW tweeted a screenshot of the email and wrote,

1. We have NOT been hacked
2. We do NOT have your email address!
3. We do NOT have your private keys to hack.[22]

The attacks were especially bad on Slack, the platform du jour for crypto communities. Phishers would hijack a tool called the

Slackbot, which had enabled the DAO Slack to give a preprogrammed answer anytime someone typed the word "presale." Only now, phishers were using the Slackbot to make people panic, forget security protocols, and give away their private keys. For instance, a phisher in the Aragon Slack wrote,

> **Important Notification from the ICO Security team**
> Please be advised that we have some problems with the
> Ethereum based Token smart contracts.
> We decided that the best way to solve the problem is to fork
> the Smart Contracts…
> Please visit https://myetherwallet.co.uk/#view-wallet-info
> to unlock your wallet and follow the instructions on their
> website.
> Failure to do so may result in loss of your tokens.

Of course, following the instructions on that site, which had, among other things, an intentional error in the URL, was exactly what would result in the loss of one's tokens. Other phishers would say that, due to the increasing number of phishing attacks, security on the site was being upgraded, and so people had to log in to take advantage of the higher security features. Others would proclaim the team had decided to open its token sale early: "**Official Announcement form the Santiment team** Santiment Token Last-Sale is OPEN NOW!" Of course, the tokens were offered at "special prices." They would advertise fake notices about airdrops—essentially free tokens—to lure people into clicking on phishing links. Legions of crypto newbies gullibly clicked, hoping to make more money or protect their holdings. Instead, they gave away the keys to their crypto. It didn't help that Slack allowed people to choose any display name. Now even the sketchiest new member of a community could take the name of a coin's creator.[23]

In Etherscan, an Ethereum blockchain explorer, some phishers' addresses would have comments on them like

please return my 14 eth [the commenter's Ethereum address]
please have some humanity.
We are here to get away from Thieves (bankers). You are
stealing from the wrong people...i have nothing left.

Because they were spamming so many crypto Slack groups, the
Mailinator accounts of spammers would be filled with registration
emails from the Slacks for various ICOs: "Welcome to AI Coin!,"
"LAToken on Slack: New Account Details," "Your account on
Cindicator_community," and so forth.[24] By mid-September, according to one crypto security company, just under seventeen
thousand victims had fallen for such scams. Token teams were
targeted, with scammers hacking the Enigma ICO website right
before the sale started and announcing a "special presale"—which
directed all incoming funds to the hackers' wallet, netting them an
easy half million dollars in ETH.[25]

The hackers especially homed in on MEW. Users who kept
coins on exchanges enjoyed greater protection since exchanges had
at least some scam countermeasures. (Still, phishers pilfered coins
from exchange customers.) But with MEW, because the password
entered there unlocked a user's wallet directly and MEW had no
way of seeing into customers' wallets or emailing them about suspicious activity, and because a lot of newbies had been opening accounts in order to participate in ICOs, hackers could easily swipe
tokens from naive crypto users. This was the season for it. MEW
started 2017 with 100,000 monthly visitors but had 3.5 million in
August.

That fall, hackers obtained Taylor's cell phone number—part
of a phenomenon targeting cryptocurrency users since early to
mid-2016.[26] Hackers would call up, say, T-Mobile, pretend to be
the victim (say, Taylor), and claim she wanted to move her phone
number from, say, Sprint to T-Mobile. The hacker would then
have all of Taylor's phone calls and text messages going to his or
her phone on T-Mobile and would attempt to log into Taylor's

various accounts, click "forgot password," and have a code sent to her phone number, which was now attached to the hacker's device. From there, the hacker would then change all Taylor's passwords, locking her out of all her accounts. (Actually, the perpetrators were likely *teams* of hackers since often the victim would be shut out of dozens of accounts within several minutes.) The hackers targeted crypto people specifically because crypto transactions were irreversible, so even after the victim got his or her number back, it was finders keepers for the coins. Hackers had netted millions through these phone hijackings—sometimes from a single victim. In Taylor's case, once the hackers got her phone number, they started hacking the company providing MEW's support system, which then dropped MEW. There was only one Taylor, but there were multiple ways to attack her and MEW— through each account and customer and all of Taylor's and Kosala's accounts. Multiply that by the millions of new people transacting with crypto. For scammers, it was a digital pickpocketing bonanza.

ON AUGUST 10, 2017, a day when ETH closed at $296, Vitalik, Ming, and the early Ethereum crew's Zug liaison Herbert Sterchi, who had helped the Zug crew settle in and find the Spaceship, received a letter from a Swiss lawyer. It began, "Dear Directors, I have been retained by Mr. Anthony Di Iorio and write to demand the 525'000 ether that is owed to him." It continued, "As you know, Mr. Di Iorio purchased 525'000 ether [around $155 million based on that day's price] from Ethereum Switzerland GmbH on March 14th, 2014." It then said he never received the ether. The lawyer noted that he had reviewed correspondence with J. P. Schmidt (Ming's brother-in-law who had declined to renew Taylor Gerring's contract from his Gmail) stating that Anthony had been repaid but that all the fiat payments to Anthony corresponded to loans and other services he provided to Ethereum entities. The lawyer added, "It is simply not credible to suggest that a sophisticated investor like Mr. Di Iorio...would ever accept fiat currency instead of the 525'000 ether that he purchased."

The letter went on to explain that, when Anthony was reviewing his files about the disputed 525,000 ETH, "he was reminded of and uncovered certain questionable actions taken by you as directors of Ethereum Switzerland GmbH and Stiftung Ethereum. I have reviewed the impugned conduct and have concluded that it is serious enough that it may warrant a criminal investigation in Switzerland." It said that Anthony was "considering his options" while awaiting their response to the letter, was "reluctant" to do anything prompting a criminal investigation, and was "obviously conflicted" as he did "not want to harm Ethereum."

The lawyer listed the actions Anthony had found questionable. The first concerned the time "he and other original founders were invited to a meeting in Switzerland under false pretenses"—when they thought they were signing the GmbH documents but instead Ethereum had its Game of Thrones Day. The lawyer wrote that, during that meeting, certain individuals "threatened to fork the source code and hijack the project." The second concern was "the suspicious circumstances surrounding the movement of monies raised from the Ethereum crowd-sale into entities in other countries (Germany, UK and Netherlands), which appears to have benefited certain individuals." (This was the tussle over moving money to the for-profit entities like ETH Dev in Berlin.) It then stated that this "mismanagement of money was contrary to Swiss law." The last two were "accounting irregularities engaged in by some of the directors, some of which may have been fraudulent" and "certain Ethereum staff working in Switzerland in non-compliance with Swiss immigration law."

The letter said Anthony had grounds to bring a civil claim and launch a criminal investigation in Switzerland against each of them and Ethereum and cited the applicable provisions in the Swiss Criminal Code (one of which carried a penalty of up to ten years' prison time).[27] It then said if Anthony needed to sue to obtain the 525,000 ETH, he would "necessarily have to publicly disclose the concerns noted above and other concerns, along with documents, emails, chats, audio and other recordings." It gave a deadline of five days to send the 525,000 ETH, plus an ether address.[28]

At this time, during the ICO craze, Anthony had made a name for himself—not necessarily in a good way. He was slapping his name on ICOs as an advisor in exchange for tokens: Civic, Blockmason, Etherparty, Enjin Coin, Worldwide Asset eXchange, Skrumble Network, Cindicator, Polymath, AION, PayPie, Storm, Unikrn, WAX, Po.et, and Veriblock.[29] Although Civic, Polymath, WAX, and Unikrn were somewhat well-known, the others were no-name projects. He'd also invested in two Chinese projects, Vechain and Qtum. To uninformed cryptocurrency investors, having an Ethereum cofounder on an ICO advisory board gave it an imprimatur of legitimacy, but other crypto community members felt Anthony was mostly just letting them use his name. (Years later, Anthony would say he had been giving them guidance on strategy, the structure of their ICOs, and the economics of their coins but that he stopped advising coins because he felt some projects were just using his name.) He was running Decentral, where he had picked up an entourage who would drink with him after meetups. But a person close to him said these people weren't his friends. He was also running Jaxx, where he had bought Double Robotics robots, remotely controlled videoconferencing robots that roll on a Segway. From outside the office, he'd turn on a robot, roll up behind employees, catch them doing something not work related, and give them a talking-to. In 2016, he'd been chief digital officer at the Toronto Stock Exchange though he left to focus on Decentral after just eight months.

Although Anthony says he has a document signed by Charles and Mihai stating he would receive 3,000 ETH for every Bitcoin he loaned, he declined to share it. Vitalik says that "there were clear decisions that all the BTC would be paid back as BTC." The foundation had proof that it had paid Anthony, in Bitcoin, everything he was owed, so after some contention, Anthony backed down.

He and Vitalik had little contact after that.

ANTHONY WASN'T THE only Ethereum cofounder whose business judgment was thought questionable. Earlier that year, in February, Joe had received a sobering report from several of his ConsenSys employees.

It began by stating that although the company had had a few small successes, "Costs have ballooned, employee infighting is on the rise, and time-to-market for ventures is underwhelming." Calling ConsenSys "effectively a VC fund," it recommended the firm "*model out* ROIs [returns on investment], KPIs [key performance indicators], and any other subsequent framing documents in order to *monitor* and *control* the operational model of the Venture Production Studio [ConsenSys's description of itself]." But it said the company had to face a stark reality stemming from "*the fact that salary burn is so high*":

> The challenge of a high salary burn is that it makes the ConsenSys AG fund an unattractive vehicle to invest in... With no real financial forecasting, no P&L [profit and loss] modeling, nor any understanding of average rate of return, the ConsenSys AG fund would be hard pressed to find any **smart money** investors like A16Z [famed venture capital firm Andreessen Horowitz] in the 2017 calendar year.

Because Joe was giving salaries to what were effectively start-ups that had yet to build traction, these "spokes" were surviving longer than they should: "The release of ventures into the market will produce a 'survive or die' mentality that will force the ventures to make difficult decisions that had been postponed to this point (*here's a thought experiment—how many proto-founders at*

ConsenSys have gone months eating Ramen noodles in order to save on costs?)."

The report, of which Joe says he was never aware, continued, "Early hiring process did not emphasize a strong hiring bar." Further, it said,

> The existing C suite of the company has over represented their capabilities as Chief Officers. From Finance to Strategy, those with the C-level title in this organization have simply underperformed in their duties and in their executions…ConsenSys needs a real advisory committee and a board that can provide critical, unfiltered feedback and advice…We have too many individuals in this organization who over-represent themselves to the detriment of the morale of the highest performers and who tarnish our brand by their falsified skill sets.

(Joe says he heard sentiments like this from a "small, vocal contingent.")

Many current and ex-employees could be far harsher. Some of them raised basic red flags, like the fact that for more than a year, at the start, ConsenSys had paid many staff in freshly minted bitcoin and issued no tax forms to employees, most of whom were contractors and so should have received 1099s, even for as recent as the tax year 2016, though Joe says that "where applicable, some people did receive 1099s for 2016." (An early Ethereum employee who liked to select quotes by people that encapsulated them chose this one by Joe to sum him up: "I only pay as much tax as I want to pay." Joe says, "I would never say something stupid like that.") Those who elected to be paid in US dollars weren't paid via an official payroll. Joe or certain designated staff would make arrangements with LocalBitcoins sellers, who, upon receiving Bitcoin from Joe's address, would then go into physical bank branches and deposit cash into employees' bank accounts. An early employee who elected to be paid in US dollars says such payments never exceeded $3,000; that would have required the LocalBitcoins seller to keep a record of the transaction, according to Bank Secrecy Act requirements. Joe says ConsenSys made many payments in excess of $3,000.

Others felt that Joe protected an executive whom multiple female employees had found abusive. One candidate for a job backed out once he heard this person worked at the company; he had known the exec at a previous firm. One employee called this person "Joe's biggest downfall." Even though, in town hall meetings, staff members often brought up this exec's abusive behavior or pointed to the lack of revenue in that person's department despite its size, Joe would dodge the questions or get irritated. (Joe says he never protected anyone above anyone else and that the company always investigated sensitive matters thoroughly and acted appropriately.)

A chorus of employees practically sang about the lack of performance metrics, goals, and accountability. Some of that stemmed from the fact that people were not given specific job titles, tasks, or job descriptions; they christened themselves with titles. (Then there was Yalila Espinoza, whom multiple people referred to as "the company shaman" and who came to the company retreat in Bali and conducted sound baths at ConsenSys conferences like Ethereal. She was a friend of then chief strategy officer Sam Cassatt. Sam denies there was a company shaman, though in 2018 she signed up for a developer technology event in New York with ConsenSys as her affiliation. In June 2019, she was diagnosed with stage 4 cancer and died in March 2020.) Joe and the senior managers had eschewed a hierarchy, instead promoting a decentralized holacracy (dubbed within ConsenSys as a "meshocracy"), in which people would "self-organize" efficiently.[30] One staffer concluded this was a euphemism for anarchy. Another team lead recalled how Human Resources would ask him to review people on his team, and half of them would be people who had left ConsenSys two years prior. The loosey-goosey MO combined with easy money meant that a huge percentage of employees just hung out. Even some who started as strong performers would see others, say, working from Bali and realize they could get away with working at 25 percent. One former employee said, "There was no reward for good work." Another said, "A lot of people would just smoke weed and chill and that was a normal day at the office."

The anything-goes, gravy-train culture fed into an extravagant attitude toward conferences. By 2017, a constant stream of crypto conferences spanned the globe, and often dozens of people from ConsenSys would attend, do no work, and party every night, with a budget day after day of $10,000 to $15,000 for dinner for everyone. Even employees familiar with the culture at companies like Google, Facebook, and Twitter had never seen anything like it. (Joe says, "The dinner comment is ridiculous," suspecting it came from someone who worked at the company in the first two years; it did not.)

The unusual culture manifested in other ways. The company would hold staff retreats in locations like Bali, and at least after the Bali retreat, "the company shaman" performed a private ayahuasca ceremony with Joe, Sam, chief marketing officer Amanda Gutterman, and several others. (Joe and Sam deny this. Sam says she led meditations at the Bali retreat, and Joe says the company watched a Balinese water ceremony.) Some of the behavior by male employees led to a women's council at the Bali retreat, in which, according to an attendee, female employees were crying about sexual harassment they had experienced. Multiple people said that once ETH hit a certain price, Sam stopped coming into the office. (Sam says it was because he could work remotely and conducted "months of business development in Dubai," led an "IPO readiness process" for the company, and spent time on planes consulting "when seemingly every company in the world needed a blockchain strategy.") One employee who started at ConsenSys at a time when Joe was off the grid at Burning Man recalled paychecks were delayed two weeks because the company needed to convert ETH for payroll. (Joe says he doesn't remember this and says he wouldn't be incommunicado for long or leave the finance department in a bad situation. He says he would typically arrive at Burning Man on Wednesday or Thursday and return to New York on Sunday or Monday.) One former employee described it thus: "The whole situation at ConsenSys was weird honestly, it was 'executives' who seemed more interested in partying and hiring their unqualified friends than building a real company. It seemed they all saw the potential of ethereum and blockchain however had no concept of the work it actually takes to become a real, profitable company." An executive at another firm who had attended ConsenSys's Davos events told this former staffer that ConsenSys seemed like a "smoke-and-mirrors company" that talked about decentralization but couldn't point to anything concrete it was doing. (Joe called these statements "generally wrong" and, though he didn't know the source of these comments, said they must be from people who were unsuccessful at ConsenSys or didn't understand it from their distance.) A different former employee said, "The whole of ConsenSys felt like a Potemkin village where there were facades being put up to make it look like there was something going on. It's super hard to prove something like that. Either something's really being done incompetently or it's being done on purpose." ConsenSys lawyer Matt Corva responded, "We publish the most widely used tools, infrastructure, and wallet for the most widely used blockchain on earth, with millions of users and exponentially successful investments. It really speaks for itself."

Employees with track records at other companies, particularly from Silicon Valley, were embarrassed by ConsenSys's naiveté and ignorance about the basics of entrepreneurship. ConsenSys grouped employees into those working on decentralized projects/spokes; those working on hub operations, such as marketing, enterprise, legal, and so forth, who could be used by any of the dapp teams; and then "floaters," who were so unclearly defined that four different employees gave four different definitions of the term, but Joe says they were people between projects. ConsenSys had a Resource Allocation Committee (RAC), which floaters could join, to which projects would pitch their needs for the next quarter. One employee with VC experience called the RAC "an unorganized and dumbed-down version of 'Shark Tank.'" The projects had no deliverables and lacked traction, and the people doing the evaluations for the RAC also had no VC experience. And anyway, the RAC didn't matter. All that counted was whether the project had a good connection to Joe; if it did, it would get what it wanted. If it didn't, it wouldn't. (Joe says this is "100% wrong.")

Staff members unhappiest with Joe said he'd promised them something verbally but then delayed putting it in writing, and when things were finally documented, the deal was changed in Joe's favor. (Joe says, "Not worth commenting on this silly general statement. Generally deals involve multiple parties and mutual agreement, otherwise there is no deal.") One person who felt he or she had been screwed by Joe said the main story of ConsenSys was how Joe masked his old-school, power-hungry, dominate-and-crush ways with "a love and light story of decentralization and mutual empowerment" to which he only paid lip service, a sentiment echoed by a former employee who said he or she had never before experienced "this type of coldness while talking about this vision." (Matt says this view is "an extreme outlier" and that the company "has always been rooted in decentralization, mutual empowerment, and respect.") Many people worked on a Consen-Sys spoke with the understanding that it would be spun out and they would become cofounders with equity, but Joe would later decide to keep that unit internal, so they were stuck as employees. (This uncertainty around equity was yet another disincentive to put in effort.) For these reasons, ConsenSys grew a culture of upper-level staff muscling in on new token projects, trying, Anthony Di Iorio–style, to become "advisors" who got a cut of tokens but delivered little beyond their name. (Joe says, "All personnel were and are required to register their potential conflicts with our legal department so we can make sure there is no bias in internal decision making.")

According to multiple employees, Joe's tendency to judge people mainly based on how he liked them, plus ConsenSys's lack of hierarchy and metrics, turned the company culture into a popularity contest where accomplishments and promotions were tied to currying favor with Joe. This led to endless internal power struggles. Because Joe seemed blind to the political battles around him and his role in stoking them, one fan of his concluded he must be on the spectrum. (Joe says he's never heard anyone say this about him.) This rule by favoritism led to numerous staff members having titles wildly beyond their experience—they had simply claimed them, and Joe had given his blessing. There was an uproar when Amanda, who was three years out of college, christened herself chief marketing officer. But Joe said titles didn't matter at ConsenSys, so her position stuck. (Joe says, "I was not and am not blind to interpersonal interactions and relationships around me.") Another said, to get things done, one just had to email a colleague and copy Joe: "Some days, I feel like I'm at my dad's company and I'm just copying my dad so you'll do what I need [you] to do." (Joe said this would not be an effective strategy.) By this point, Frithjof, the former CFO at ETH Dev (whom Ming had accused in gossip, without evidence, of embezzling funds from the EF), was the CFO at ConsenSys. Employees joked that anyone could email Frithjof to transfer $5 million to his or her account—and Frithjof would do it, as long as Joe had been cc'ed. (Frithjof says, "ConsenSys has extensive measures like segregation of duties, four-eye-principle, internal controls, risk management etc. in place to ensure full compliance and governance.")

Joe had ardent fans—many of whom called him things like visionary, revolutionary, idealistic, altruistic, brilliant, and generous and talked about their love for him. (But even some who loved him acknowledged he should not be a businessperson, let alone a chief executive.) For instance, one person enjoyed the unstructured atmosphere and said Joe wanted people to be happy, empowered, and autonomous. This employee felt Joe wanted more to inspire people, foster cross-pollination, and make sure everyone was learning. That was why, if representatives from a company came for a meeting with Joe, he would sometimes call out, "Anyone want to join?"

But Joe's relaxed attitude made room for antics. Since employees could give themselves titles, one called himself the "chief anarchy officer" and wrote a "demand letter," asking people to disclose their salaries in a Google doc, saying it would help everyone in salary negotiations.[31] Matt adds that this person "provided several links both for and *against* the case for pay transparency." (The background to this was that there had been a salary cap, so many employees took a salary cut to work at ConsenSys, thinking everyone would be in the same boat. Since that wasn't ultimately what happened, this employee's thinking was to help people get paid more.) He says he was informed that he would be fired if he didn't take his post down. Human Resources' rationale was that due to employee privacy issues, especially in light of Europe's General Data Protection Regulation (GDPR) rules, ConsenSys did not want to host this sensitive employee information on its own systems. The employee forwarded what he called the "threat" he'd received to the entire company. Despite Joe's utopian talk about decentralization, ConsenSys was quite greedy with tokens, with multiple employees saying a standard split for spokes featuring tokens was fifty-fifty and the firm sometimes took 70 percent. (Matt says there was no standard split for tokens.) By this point, though, ConsenSys had also developed a reputation for copying other projects. Even as early as 2016, but again in 2017, West Coast decentralized projects would gossip about how after a token team pitched to ConsenSys, the venture studio would decline to invest but later announce a similar project. It had happened to decentralized prediction marketplace Augur (ConsenSys had Gnosis) as well as decentralized exchange protocol 0x (ConsenSys later announced a dex called AirSwap). (A ConsenSys exec denied that any ConsenSys project came about by copying something that had been presented to them, and Joe said ConsenSys "certainly never got a

chance to invest" in 0x, but documents show Joe reached out to 0x
first, that he and members of ConsenSys, including the founder of
AirSwap, had two meetings with the 0x team, and that it was clear
ConsenSys was being invited to participate in "this pre-crowdfund
round." After the AirSwap announcement, a 0x investor sent the
team an email with the subject line "ConsenSys == Rocket Internet
of Ethereum." A *New York Times* article on Rocket said its business
model was to "mimic already successful Internet companies.") But
ConsenSys had an even worse reputation problem at this point. It
was the middle of ICO madness, Ethereum had finally made it,
and although ConsenSys had built a few good Ethereum infrastructure tools, none of the decentralized apps about which serious
crypto people were excited was a ConsenSys project. (Gnosis had
spun out from ConsenSys before its ICO.) Even at the height of
the ICO craze, there were only a couple, or maybe three, Consen-
Sys tokens in the top one hundred. As one former employee put it,
"There are no good token projects out of that whole situation."

A non-ConsenSys Ethereum dev surmised it was because the
terms the company offered were so bad that savvy developers
wouldn't agree to them, though Joe says if a deal doesn't work out
in any domain, it's because terms are not acceptable to both parties.

Many ConsenSys employees felt Joe, at the very least, was not
focused on the firm's success. (He says of course he would have
been happy if it had been profitable, but that is rare for a start-up.)
They thought he did not seem to know its annual conference,
Ethereal, had never made money—though crypto conferences can
be quite lucrative. (Joe says they did not read his mind accurately.)
One time, a few months after Ethereal 2017, an employee says, Joe
was surprised to learn that Microsoft had not given a cash spon-
sorship even though the conference's T-shirt bore its logo. (Joe
says early Ethereals were not expected to be profitable and does
not remember this incident.)

His lack of interest in profitability puzzled them so much they
came up with a theory about it based on the fact that Joe funded

ConsenSys by loaning it ETH and BTC. Since a loan would not require him to convert his massively appreciated ETH into fiat, no taxation event would be triggered for Joe—and since, by this point, he was likely a crypto billionaire, that amounted to a considerable sum he didn't have to send to the government. ConsenSys itself paid little to no tax since the company spent a lot more than it made; in fact, Joe could have gotten a tax break as an individual foreign investor in the company, in which case Joe would have made more if ConsenSys wasn't profitable. As one equity shareholder put it, "It was strategically advantageous to Joe from the beginning." Joe says, "Wrong. What taxes would I offset with the tax losses?" One early employee theorized that Joe may have dragged his feet on documenting equity, which first occurred in October 2016, two years after the company was founded, so as not to have to disclose that the bitcoin and ether he was using to fund ConsenSys had been given as a loan. The sooner he gave the equity, the earlier shareholders would have had a say about the arrangement. But by the time anyone received equity, he'd been funding ConsenSys with crypto loans for two years. (Joe disputes that he delayed documenting equity.)

However, that also would have meant that as the price of ether increased, the amount ConsenSys owed back to Joe in dollar terms was astronomically higher than it had been when Joe had lent the BTC and ETH, which could be a problem if there were ever a liquidation event (potentially a problem down the line for shareholders). As the former shareholding employee put it, "Joe is paying all salaries in ETH at prices like $20, so whatever the burn rate was at that point, for every month, we would have to pay *at least* 10x that. Say it was even $200 ETH at the time, and the burn rate was $10 million that month, so now that month alone"—at the time of this conversation, ETH was a little over $2,000—"the company would have to pay $200 million for that month alone." Matt says, "Categorically untrue and not how the funding arrangement worked."

In addition to seeming not to care whether ConsenSys was profitable, Joe was blasé about professional norms. For instance, he began dating a decades-younger user experience (UX) designer at ConsenSys named Yunyun Chen.[32] (She had been one of the select few at the private ayahuasca ceremony after the Bali retreat that Joe and Sam deny happened.) At Davos, he brought her to a number of meetings. He did the same on business trips to India and France for meetings with high-level ministers and government officials. Employees felt he seemed oblivious that it was inappropriate for him to date an employee, that he should keep it private, and that bringing her to meetings might be awkward for the staff. It could also be funny. There might be a high-level meeting involving contracts with only a few ConsenSys employees, one being Yunyun, which was so random as to be absurd: *Why is the UX designer here when people directly involved in the project are not?* Joe would even bring Yunyun to some of his one-on-ones with employees. One of them, now a former ConsenSys employee, was resigned: "My job is to use my forty minutes as best as I can. I'm not going to say anything. It's his girlfriend, his company, his problem. Is it professional? No. But would he do this? Yes." (Joe says there was nothing inappropriate about the relationship, that they kept their personal and professional lives separate, and that significant others were invited to dinners, although staff say Yunyun was in the actual meetings with high-level government ministers, not just at the dinners.)

If there seemed to be any rhyme or reason at ConsenSys, employees thought it was that anything could be justified on the theory that it would push up the price of ETH. That fixation on Ethereum and the price of ETH was a point of criticism in the February 2017 report, which said that whether Joe's goal was to make ConsenSys or Ethereum a success wasn't clear. It also called out ConsenSys for "hyping" the price of ether, which raised conflict-of-interest issues when it came to consulting clients who couldn't risk endorsing a particular cryptocurrency. (Joe, who says he was unaware of the report, did not follow any of its recommendations.)

This was the other explanation high-level ConsenSys execs gave for why Joe wasn't focused on ConsenSys's profitability: it was a vehicle for pumping the price of ETH. If he had, say, five million ETH, then he was willing to spend one million of it to make the other 80 percent worth more. In Joe's case, assuming he bought BTC on the day the ETH crowdsale started—a conservative estimate, as he likely acquired it much earlier, when it was at least an order of magnitude cheaper, or mined it, in which case his costs would have been even lower—the value could be, at minimum, one thousand times greater than what he'd spent on it. And since ConsenSys had provided infrastructure tools that Ethereum developers were using, even if they weren't ConsenSys spoke projects, they were at least helping applications that were generating demand for ETH. So if that was Joe's strategy, it paid off. (Joe says boosting the price of ETH was "never remotely a strategy" during this time and that the company was disciplined about not talking about the ETH price, let alone hyping it publicly.)

Whatever Joe's motivations were for building ConsenSys but seeming disinterested in its profitability, most employees at least felt their jobs were safe as long as the price of ETH rose. They surmised that if Joe wasn't *the* largest holder of ETH in the world, he was at least one of the largest.[33] And in fall 2017, ETH was definitely up—after starting the year around $8, it was between $300 and $800.

But though he had financial capital, Joe did not have social capital with the person in Ethereum who mattered most: Vitalik. Vitalik was basically not speaking to him and in fact told at least one new employee at ConsenSys to put any understanding with Joe in writing because Joe himself would never honor it. And because he was on the outs with Vitalik, Joe had no leverage for dealing with Ming.

THAT FALL, POLONIEX'S dominance began to slip. If in June it had sometimes seen trading volume of $5 billion per week, early that fall the peaks were more like $4 billion. Still, even with the dip, the exchange was making a killing. One reason for the drop was

that competitors were investing in upgrades, but Polo was doing
the bare minimum. Seeing competitor Kraken boast about a slew
of new features, Polo employees asked, "Why are we not doing
this? Why are we just letting them take our business?" One example: Kraken launched an efficient, self-service feature for two-
factor authentication allowing users themselves to disable it. Even
though customer service said launching a similar feature would
cut a third of all open support tickets, Jules and Mike wouldn't
let Tristan work on it. (As far as most people could tell, Tristan
controlled nearly every aspect of Poloniex's code—a grasp of its
intricacies wasn't spread out among a team of people, as would be
expected of an exchange transacting in billions of dollars' worth of
crypto every week.) By this point, according to someone familiar
with the matter, the exchange had almost half a million open support tickets. Johnny managed to poach more trollbox moderators
to act as customer service agents, reaching twelve total by year's
end. He would feel really good the few times in the fall of 2017
that they got the number of open support tickets down to one hundred thousand. Jules and Mike did let them hire a few freelancers,
who Johnny, the head of customer support, trained to help out with
the backlog on KYC verification. They were good, so he suggested
hiring them all immediately. He recalls Jules and Mike said, essentially, *No, we're not going to hire anyone. Work with what you've got.*

Around that time, Polo did make a couple new hires, although
not in customer support: both hailed from traditional financial
services. One was a senior vice president from Santander, and the
other was a young trader named Tyler Frederick from Fidelity,
the only traditional financial services firm public about its interest
in cryptocurrency, lending legitimacy to the space.[34] Tyler started
on the foreboding date of September 11, 2017. His interview process, done by phone and email, had been a little strange. When
he'd asked to see the office, Jules and Mike asked what concerns
he had. He said he wanted to see the work environment, so they
promised to get back to him and eventually met him at an office

in the greater Boston area. It was nice, but empty. They told him Poloniex would be there by the time he started.

But on his first day, he says, they told him to show up at a different office, and when he walked in, a bunch of temp workers were sitting at folding tables—not even cubicles—with cables running everywhere as Wi-Fi wasn't considered sufficiently secure. (Eventually, Polo did move into the other office.) Within four months, he started looking for another job, because the owners were obviously not investing in the exchange. With volumes skyrocketing, it didn't seem sustainable.

Although he reported to Jules, after he started he barely ever saw her or Mike. They were never in the office, but both of them had come when he requested to see the office. That confused him—why was he so important? When he'd asked for equity, they'd told him that was off the table. Although he had worked at the blue-chip financial services firm Fidelity, he was too inexperienced to know that was unusual for a start-up.

Some employees began to suspect that Jules, Tristan, and Mike were going to sell Polo. The hints were the owners' complete disinterest in investing in any improvements; the fact that, after initially resisting implementing KYC, they suddenly made it a priority; and this new Ruby intermediary.

Ruby would forbid certain employees, such as the head of compliance and Johnny, the head of customer support, from meeting with each other, even when they needed to collaborate, though some of the rationale may have been they didn't want to pay for lodging for both of them at once. This even happened when Johnny, who lived in Brazil, traveled to Boston and so could meet the compliance chief in person. Then they switched his hotel booking and made him sleep on the couch in Ruby's hotel room. When he complained, Jules told him if he didn't like it, he could book his own ticket and go home. Also, while on that trip, even though he was actually physically in the office and so could talk to his staff and some freelancers face-to-face, Ruby prohibited them from doing so and said they had to talk on chat so she could monitor their conversations.

Some of Johnny's reports did manage to ask him if the owners were selling Polo. The support staff was barely getting any help on the massive backlog of tickets. To them, it seemed like Jules, Mike, and Tristan no longer cared about the company—as if the employees were working just for show. That gave him the courage, when Ruby approached him during a smoke break, to lock his eyes with her and, dead serious, ask, "Are we selling?"

She looked down and turned, but before she finished her first step away from him, she rotated her head slightly, looked him in the eye, and said, "Of course not."

But from the look on her face, he had a gut feeling she was lying.

IN THE LEADUP to DevCon 3 in Cancun, Mexico, on November 1, 2017, Ming was becoming increasingly erratic and emotional. Even mundane Skype chats could suddenly veer into the personal. Someone expressing disappointment that they could have booked premium economy to DevCon 3 instead of economy elicited a "Please don't troll me today" from her, along with "It's very difficult and my dog of 16 years is gone." She acknowledged her instability, posting, "For people who are new in this channel, I'm not supposed to post in internal channel when I haven't slept for 30, 40 or 50 hours. You'll know when I'm sleep deprived because there will be 'removed' posts (when I can't stop myself from posting)."

Meanwhile, unrest in the Ethereum ranks was growing as more people wanted her gone. Vitalik himself was feeling more confident in actually making that a reality. With the price of ETH so high, the foundation had a pile of money, but projects were horribly underfunded because of Ming. Vitalik, on the other hand, wanted the foundation to splash all worthy entities with money. If she remained the bottleneck, the trickle could last forever—and they didn't have forever, because competing smart contract blockchains were preparing to launch.[35] By now, Vitalik realized the foundation would likely not blow up without her. That summer at IC3, when the Parity multisig wallets had been hacked, Vitalik verbalized for the first time to Hudson that he wanted to remove Ming. Hudson, not knowing any better, said she was doing a good job. Still, Vitalik got the impression support for her wasn't overwhelming.

Vitalik didn't know that many people in the EF felt she was far too controlling. They no longer could say what they wanted and felt Ming acted as if it were the fall of 2015 and ETH was below $1 rather than around $300. She made everything too complicated, even just hiring a developer, let alone giving grants to different projects. People also thought the foundation was massively disorganized.

By this point, some developers got stressed out even at the thought of having a phone call with Ming, because they never knew whether the call would be businesslike (with her digressions of course) or full-on acrimonious. Some, even if they had an issue best handled by the executive director, would try to resolve it another way. A few left the EF rather than fight with Ming.

Even a new friend of Vitalik's noticed tension regarding Ming. When he'd been more on the outside, he'd thought of Ethereum as a unified entity, but once he became more involved, he realized there were three groups: the researchers, the development teams, and the foundation—the last of which was basically Ming. Newcomers who got introduced to Ethereum by Vitalik got a casual feel for this decentralized project, whereas Ming gave a spiel befitting an executive director of a traditional foundation. She no longer seemed to fit with Ethereum itself. Someone who worked closely with her felt she didn't even seem that interested in blockchain technology, even though she claimed to be. People found it odd that Vitalik was in Singapore and had created an entity separate from the EF there; they seemed to fear a split.

The tension around Ming contrasted with the crypto euphoria raging as DevCon 3 in Cancun began on Wednesday, November 1.

After starting the year at around $8 with a $715 million market cap, ETH was now at $300, and the Ethereum market cap was $28 billion. Bitcoin had also been on a tear, having begun January just shy of $1,000 with a $16 billion market cap; by then it was over $6,400 with a $113 billion market cap. The total crypto markets, having commenced 2017 around $18 billion, closed that day above $184 billion. Bitcoin was making regular appearances on CNBC—"If it's 5% of gold, in five years, it's $25,000 per unit, and it's $3,300 today," said one pundit—and even Ethereum, ConsenSys, and related token projects were getting airtime.[36] With a crypto mania well underway, his personal wealth in the hundreds of millions of dollars, and Mexico undergoing a spate of crime, Vitalik booked lodging at a hotel separate from the conference under a friend's name. DevCon itself went from eight hundred attendees the year before to almost two thousand.

Organizations holding such large events would typically hire a production company; the EF, aside from an A/V company and the default support the venue provided, had Ming. As she had for DevCon 2, she micromanaged everything, but this time, because she had not delegated and the event was bigger, she had been working nonstop without sleeping and was burned out mentally and physically. The night before, Hudson and Laura stumbled upon a group of volunteers who were supposed to help with the incorrectly sorted badges and defective lanyards. They didn't know what to do; Ming had been there previously giving orders, but she'd disappeared, and she would get mad if people did things without her permission. Hudson eventually found her in her room, oddly nonchalant, preoccupied with a printer. With the cranky volunteers texting him, Hudson had to ask Ming a few times to get permission to direct them so the lanyards and badges could be sorted by the next morning.

Like the year before, insignificant details turned into problems because they hadn't been delegated. Hudson had to put out fires involving the T-shirts and the livestream (which required overnighting equipment); then, the morning of, he had to spend most of the conference in the A/V booth, plus jump onstage occasionally to emcee. After running from one fire to the next for a few days, the first moment Hudson could breathe, he ended up in tears.

Some outsiders were underwhelmed. Attendees noticed registration was a mess—huge packed lines of almost all young men looking impatiently at the registration tables—and wondered why even water had not been provided. Executives from enterprises were unimpressed by such disorganization and wondered what they had stumbled into. A bank doing a $25,000 sponsorship spent almost six weeks negotiating it, which cost them more in legal fees than the sponsorship itself—a joke both for the bank and for the EF, which had hundreds of millions of dollars' worth of ETH at this point. A potential sponsor for DevCon 3 called up Ming for his first-ever conversation with her; he was taken aback when she ranted about how ConsenSys was trying to dominate the EF.

Although some attendees say there were multiple guards at each door, Vitalik himself was appalled by how poor security was. Because there were many newly minted ETH millionaires, because the wider world was clueing in that money was sloshing around in cryptocurrency—the first day of DevCon 3, a coin for dentists called Dentacoin raised almost $2 million, wrapping up its monthlong ICO—and because Mexico was undergoing a wave of violence that would eventually earn 2017 the title of Mexico's deadliest year ever, security needed to be airtight.[37] But Vitalik and a friend, who were "trying to avoid people" but also test security, were able to sneak in through the back door without tickets.[38] Similarly, although Ming had blocked ConsenSys from sponsoring the event, many individual developers from the company came.

In general, Vitalik did not think the conference went well. The food was terrible, and the only other refreshments were tea and coffee in the morning. That meant everyone dispersed for lunch, which killed the community feel. Plus, he noticed how crazed people like Hudson were. Ming spent most of her time on DevCon, the main staff who worked for her felt she had treated them badly, the product was second-rate, and to Vitalik the process seemed inefficient. Plus, in the months since his first chat with Hudson at IC3 about firing Ming, he'd come to realize that she was getting in the way of the EF staff's ability to work.

Foundation staff, normally spread across the world, were finally in one place where they could talk in person. And through these conversations, they began to realize just how unhappy they all were with Ming. About a dozen of them strategized in a chat group about how to remove her—a dicey proposition since she was the boss. Though they appreciated what she had done for the organization, they felt that the EF had different needs now than ones Ming could fulfill. Toya remembers that in the group, people expressed concern that none of them really knew what Ming did. She often mentioned accounting troubles and legal issues, in a way that implied the entire foundation would collapse if she left. Although people were skeptical about her claim, since they didn't understand Swiss compliance or Swiss accounting rules, the biggest fear they had about removing her was that the foundation *would* implode.

Since Toya worked with Ming daily, she was included in the group almost like "the spy." Toya knew who Ming was talking to and what she was doing every day, so they relied on her to explain whether or not Ming really was doing critical work. But Toya's sense was that Ming exaggerated the state of affairs so as to strike fear in people so they wouldn't get rid of her.

In fact, this had also been the topic of a private conversation between Toya and Vitalik a few days before DevCon started. Toya was originally going to stay with Casey and Ming, but they ended up staying elsewhere. This gave Vitalik and Toya an opportunity to talk for at least two hours, during which he asked Toya whether she thought Ming should stay.

At the same time, a seemingly unrelated shift had begun. That fall, Vitalik's social life was gelling in a way it never had before. He had a small group of friends who traveled together, staying in low-key Airbnbs or hotels where they would spend hours on the internet, writing on forums, watching videos, posting on Twitter, and doing research and writing code. Their main nonscreen interests were drinking pu-erh tea and taking long walks. Many were researchers largely separate from the foundation and the development teams, and at least some in this inner group spoke privately about how to remove Ming. (Some were paid by Ethereum Asia Pacific Ltd. and knew little of the tensions with Ming since they did not have to work with her.)

At DevCon, a number of these confidants told Vitalik Ming had to go. One of them had even suggested a new ED with whom Vitalik was somewhat familiar: Aya Miyaguchi, the then departing managing director of Kraken in Japan, who happened to be at DevCon. Although they had met when Vitalik was writing the Ethereum white paper at the office used by some Kraken employees in 2013 and had recently hung out in Korea, they had their first serious conversation at DevCon. By this point, Vitalik was clueing in that Ming's "very frequent, very long episodes of yelling" at him and her accusations that he didn't appreciate her were abusive. Knowing a lot of other people were unhappy with her made him realize *he* wasn't the crazy one. At some point, he took Hudson aside and said, "I want you to help me get rid of Ming." But with Hudson being twenty-six and Vitalik only twenty-three, neither of them knew how—especially since Ming wouldn't go easily. On the second day of DevCon, Vitalik sent Toya a WeChat message, asking her if she could serve as interim executive director while they looked for a replacement; she said yes.

Despite all these machinations, because crypto was finally sweeping the globe, taking off not just in the United States but also in Asia and becoming a full-fledged obsession in Korea, where the price of ETH could be 30 to 50 percent higher than elsewhere in the world (a phenomenon known as "the kimchee premium"), everyone still enjoyed their newfound wealth on the beaches of Cancun.[39] Among these crypto millionaires, whose previous net worths were negligible, there was talk about how to diversify: Are you cashing out? Getting into real estate? Gold? There were soirees at bungalows on the beach. ShapeShift held a cruise on which neon-colored strobe lights flashed as people danced around in onesies and Captain America costumes; someone wore a full-head mask of the ShapeShift fox logo. A one-year-old but well-known crypto hedge fund, Polychain Capital, whose founder had graced the cover of *Forbes* (probably the only person with a mullet ever to do so), had a pool party at a villa with a large backyard that bordered the beach. Alcohol was unlimited, people sauntered around taking tequila shots, and fire dancers roamed on stilts twirling blazing rings.

But on the last day of the conference, the focus veered back to the most urgent task at hand. On Saturday, November 4, a ConsenSys employee sent a short group email:

Ming *must* go

12

November 4, 2017, to January 20, 2018

ANDREW KEYS OF ConsenSys wrote back, "I would love nothing more than that, but I don't think V will ever do that [fire Ming]. I think we just need to add more people to EF that are adults to dilute her." Joe, perhaps the person most beleaguered by Ming, responded, "This sounds like a potentially hellish pathway for all involved. We would need highly evolved enlightenment warriors with near infinite patience to take on such roles." In response to the suggestion that they could create a new research-and-development (R&D) entity, and seemingly unaware of Ethereum Asia Pacific Ltd. in Singapore, he said that could work but "would be viewed as redundant with EF/Vitalik if focussing on Ethereum research and subversive and cooptive if it drove Ethereum development." Then, showing that the Joe-Gav wars were alive and well late into 2017, Joe said ConsenSys was building its own Ethereum client in case "Parity decides to try to kill Ethereum in favor of PolkaDot+." In November 2016, Gavin had published the white paper for a new network called Polkadot (the actual paper was pink with white polka dots), which, while not directly competitive with Ethereum, could pose a threat; on October 27, it had completed its ICO, raising more than $145 million.

To the suggestion that they slowly drain resources into this new R&D entity to take power from Ming, Joe wrote, "Not sure this

would go unnoticed or be acceptable. This would be a direct attack on the Ming Dynasty." Someone else chimed in, "If there is
a strong candidate to replace her, I think it would sway Vitaliks
decision in the right direction." Someone floated Brian Behlendorf
of Hyperledger as a possible replacement for Ming. Joe wrote back,
"This would be killer but would probably not be a good look for
him jumping ship. Would need to position it as some soft merge/
collaboration move." His chief of staff, Jeremy Millar, replied, in a
comment straight out of Ming's nightmares, "If he did, we could
seriously consider merging the EEA into the EF. Two for one—he
could manage both." An Ethereum whale named Angel Mehta
said they needed to deal with the core issues: "1. Persuading Vitalik
to make changes that Ming will object to (to put it lightly) 2. Understanding who else in the foundation is hostile/Ming-loyalist."
He added, referring to the letter that Ethereum and ConsenSys insiders had planned to write to Vitalik after Arthur Falls had floated
the idea of publishing an open letter to Vitalik pushing for Ming's
ouster, "If we're doing the essay...we need to start a document
listing incidents/events and reasons that Ming should go."

Joe added Bob Summerwill to the conversation. Bob wrote, "So
much to tell you guys, but the most important is this. Multiple
sources are saying Vitalik is ready to act on Ming. The only blocker
is presenting him with viable candidates." Bob then explained the
candidate did not need to be the ambassador for the foundation.
"V is the figurehead and the traveller and the speaker," Bob wrote.
"In terms of skills the ED just needs to be somebody who can
build an appropriate organization around themselves such that it
can succeed...[W]hat this really needs more than anything is to
be somebody who Vitalik trusts." Then he asked whether Vitalik
trusted Joe. "Or has Ming weaseled away at that? She obviously
has the ability to poison his mind against her perceived enemies
to some degree...I want Ming gone. That would super-charge
what we achieve in the next year, and take that last anchor off
which is resisting our inevitable victory." He also floated potential

candidates like himself, Hudson, Jamie Pitts (who also helped with DevCons), and Taylor Gerring, ending with "Who else?"

Finally, in the wee hours of Monday, November 6, Vitalik's dad weighed in: "So guys, keep it hush for now but expect big changes soon and please provide all the support you can to Vitalik."

ON THAT SUNDAY, in Tulum, where Parity, the Web3 Foundation (which was shepherding the development of Parity's Polkadot), Polychain Capital, and some other Polychain portfolio companies had gone after DevCon, Gavin and some others were planning on doing a ceremony with the psychedelic San Pedro (a type of mescaline derived from a cactus). Everyone had been told that if they wanted to participate, they could not drink, do drugs, or eat meat for at least forty-eight hours beforehand—the longer the better. People typically have a good experience with San Pedro, and most everyone enjoyed it—except Gavin, who was in the corner sweating, having a terrible time. Someone took him upstairs, arm in arm, to put him in bed. He had a runny nose.

As bad as that was, things were about to get a lot worse for him. At 4:54 p.m. Central European Time (CET), on Monday, November 6, while most of the Parity crew was still asleep after the previous day's San Pedro ceremony, a developer going by the handle "ghost" created a post on GitHub titled "anyone can kill your contract #6995."[1] The text said, "I accidentally killed it." Ghost then posted a link to an Etherscan address. At 5:33 p.m. CET, devops199 posted on Parity's Gitter a link to issue #6995 with a question: "Is this serious issue?"[2] No one responded until the next morning at 7:27 a.m. CET, when someone wrote,

Hey guys
Do you know your multisig was hacked?
Why no one react on this?
Millions of dollars are frozen on the multisig wallets which refers to a killed libraries

So the multisig contracts doesnt work and the ETH can not
be withdrawn[3]

Although people were slow on the uptake, half a million ETH
(then worth $150 million) in 587 wallets had been trapped—locked
away forever—and the culprit, ghost/devops199, claimed to have
done it accidentally. The faulty code was actually the new multisig
wallet code that the Parity team had hastily written up the last
night of their week of debauchery in Ibiza to patch the first Parity
hack. And this code contained not one but *two* fatal flaws. Essentially, Parity had built a bank and told people it was safe to store
their money in its vaults, and people had safeguarded hundreds of
millions of dollars' worth of ETH inside. But it turned out that
the bank had no owner, so devops199 made him- or herself the
owner—and then locked the doors to the bank and obliterated the
key, sealing away the money inside forever. Some suspected this
was a malicious act, but others interpreted it as a blunder: "The
person who killed the library made an understandable mistake.
I can easily see myself doing something similar. I would never
imagine that I could kill a contract I didn't create."[4] Those people
believed that when devops199 had "killed" the contract, he or she
had been trying to undo having taken ownership of the bank.

At 2:29 p.m. CET, devops199 joined the chat, initially just
posting,

:([5]

Then a bit later, he or she wrote, "will I get arrested for this?:("[6]
Tienus, using a shorthand for "transaction," responded, "you
are the one that called the kill tx?"
devops199 wrote,

yes
i'm eth newbie..just learning

qx133 wrote, "you are famous now haha."

Gavin himself didn't find out until he'd gotten off a flight from Mexico in Zurich. At this point, he had a heavy fever.

Parity's two mistakes were, first, making it possible to designate an owner for a piece of public infrastructure and then, on top of that, allowing that owner to kill or suicide a contract, which is what devops199 did to a whole slew of Parity wallets. Of the 587 wallets affected, a few ICO issuers, whose wallets were stuffed with crowdfunded ETH, were affected, including Iconomi, which had $34 million locked up, as well as a smaller ICO, Musiconomi, which had $4.8 million frozen.[7]

But far and away the vast majority of the stuck funds belonged to Parity itself. Its wallet, containing 306,276 ETH (around $92 million), accounted for 60 percent of all the locked ETH; 586 wallets comprised the other 40 percent.[8] It was as if Parity had built the bank to safekeep its own money, but someone stumbling by had locked the door and thrown away the key.

On Reddit, there was disbelief that Parity's multisig wallet had been hacked—*again*—and that the buggy code was actually the "fixed" code from the previous hack. One Redditor said, "How could parity have been so reckless with the multisig wallets?...I will not support a full refund to Parity in this situation."[9]

Even more galling was the fact that Parity had been alerted to the issue in August, when a GitHub contributor recommended that Parity "initialize" the wallet (the equivalent of naming the owner of the bank). In its postmortem, Parity cited this recommendation, but said, "at the time [it] was considered a convenience enhancement...and was to be deployed in a regular update at a future point in time."[10] But a Reddit user pointed out that doing so only solved the first problem, not the second: "Even with initialization, *someone* would have the ability to kill the library. If some disgruntled employee decided to burn everything on his way out, we would have a very similar scenario."[11] Developers inspecting the code were shocked to find the functions to make oneself the owner and to kill the contract were one right after the other.

Immediately, discussion turned to what could be done to access the ETH inside—and of course, a hard fork was on the list. On Wednesday morning Berlin time, Vitalik obliquely tweeted, "I am deliberately refraining from comment on wallet issues, except to express strong support for those working hard on writing simpler, safer wallet contracts or auditing and formally verifying security of existing ones."[12]

However, the year before, he had written an Ethereum Improvement Proposal (EIP) numbered 156 and titled "Reclaiming of ether in common classes of stuck accounts." The proposal "allows for users with ether or other assets in common classes of 'stuck' accounts to withdraw their assets," he wrote. The EIP covered cases in which contracts were accidentally created with no code, cases caused by replay attacks involving ETC, and losses due to a defective Ethereum JavaScript library. He said, "Note, in all these cases, the rightful owner is obvious and mathematically provable, and no user is being deprived of any assets." He acknowledged this proposal could be viewed as "a 'rescue' rather than a 'technical improvement'" and said he was proposing it to have a debate—not to endorse. Even though Vitalik had published EIP 156 on October 14, 2016, discussion about it was still ongoing as of August 17, 2017.[13]

The comments revived again on November 7, as news of the Parity hack spread. However, a user pointed out that, as written, the proposal would not unlock the frozen Parity wallets because they *did* have code at their addresses.[14]

Though Vitalik wasn't stating an opinion, he was getting pressure from Gavin to stay neutral and not actively fight Parity getting its funds back. (Gavin says he doesn't pressure people.) Vitalik didn't take a stand, but he *was* opposed—he felt the community needed a counterprecedent to the DAO, to show that the forking after the DAO did not mean it was open season for anyone to get a fork. When he'd proposed EIP 156, things had been different: the stuck funds amounted to nowhere near $150 million, and they'd been lost at an earlier stage in Ethereum's history. Anyway, he had zero sympathy for Parity. This was the *second time its wallet had been hacked*. And of the $150 million frozen, the majority was Parity's. In fact, just a handful of ICOs accounted for nearly all the money; Parity, Iconomi, and Musiconomi represented 85 percent.[15] Many of the rest of the multisig wallets contained small amounts of ETH, from several hundred down to fractions of a single ETH. Plus, Parity had this history of positioning itself as so much more professional than the Geth team. Vitalik didn't feel the need to air his personal views; he predicted the community would reject a bailout.

He was right: the community, by this point, felt differently than at the time of the DAO. Back then, it seemed like the DAO *was* Ethereum. Now, with the ICO boom creating everything from Golem to BAT to Bancor to Status (as well as much less legitimate ventures such as Veritaseum and Dentacoin) and the number of coins on CoinMarketCap totaling 1,205 versus the 614 at the time of the DAO attack, just a few companies seemed to be losing money among a whole ecosystem of coins.[16] Plus, while the *dollar* amount was greater than at the time of the DAO, that was mainly due to appreciation in the price of ETH; the number of coins frozen, 513,774, was only half a percent of the circulating supply of ETH, not 4.5 percent, and was also smaller in absolute numbers than the DAO attacker had siphoned: 3.64 million ETH.

But most of all, things had been different during the DAO drama. Back then, Ethereum had done so many forks before, the community thought forking was without consequences. At that time, *not* forking was the threat. However, after the DAO, they knew that a hard fork could create yet another Ethereum. And *that* became the threat. Another factor was that, unlike with the DAO, there was no time pressure. The funds were frozen, and absent any decisions, they would be frozen forever. With the DAO, the time for a rescue was limited, and that had prompted people to act. Additionally, with so many new tokens having been built on Ethereum, a contentious hard fork created the risk of producing all kinds of duplicate assets on another chain—Gnosis Very Classic, BAT Very Classic, Status Very Classic, and so forth.

It probably did not help that Gavin had burned so many bridges in the Ethereum community, though this was not stated explicitly. After blog posts using manipulated metrics to diss Geth, after thanking Vitalik for the "kernel" of the yellow paper, after sabotaging the months-long effort to get permissive licensing for the C++ codebase, after making changes to Parity that would benefit only its users, he had few, if any, people to go to bat for him, outside the people he himself employed at Parity. Even in August, Vitalik had tweeted a screenshot of Gavin's first email to him and thanked him for his contributions to Ethereum. Gavin responded,

> Thanks to @VitalikButerin for the same—I could never have built #Ethereum without you:-)[17]

Péter Szilágyi tweeted back,

> Ah yes, thank you @gavofyork for single handedly building #Ethereum! We—the other 30+ programmers—really enjoyed watching you work![18]

And now, at least some of them would, even just a little bit, enjoy watching Polkadot burn.

AFTER THE INITIAL hubbub about the frozen Parity funds died down, the email thread about Ming between ConsenSys, Bob, and others picked up again. Some people advocated for "a legitimate executive search led by a top-tier relevant executive search firm and [evaluating] candidates appropriately," but others agreed with one person who cautioned, "I hope we can avoid the mistake that was made the first time, which was 'Alright, Ming looks great on paper. That should work.'"

In the interim, Ming had crashed post-DevCon. Some Ethereum Foundation staff had booked a few extra days in Mexico to hang out on the beach, and they invited Ming down. Citing work, she stayed in her room. She booked a spa day but missed it.

On November 7, Hudson created a Skype group, at Vitalik's behest, that included the two of them, plus Jamie Pitts, Toya, Avsa, Fabian, Christian Reitwießner, Péter Szilágyi, and other foundation staff, to discuss "changes in EF leadership," as Hudson put it. In opening the channel, Hudson said he and Vitalik would be flying to Zug to tell Ming the decision. The group strategized about how to break the news to her. Vitalik, meanwhile, flew back to Singapore. From the conversations about Ming at DevCon, he was feeling that Aya was the kind of calm presence the EF needed. He called some of the foundation's team leads, informing them he intended to fire Ming.

On November 14, from Singapore, he called Ming in Michigan. (He'd realized scheduling a trip to Zug would put her on notice something was up.) Like all conversations with Ming, this one lasted two hours. He broke it to her: she had to go. He cited "personality issues"—she was too intense, too stressed; she made problems out of nothing and got in the way of people doing their jobs. Basically, he told her she was too difficult to work with. He also explained why DevCon 3 had been a bust, but because she perceived the conference as her crowning achievement, she insisted her performance was an "A+."

Although upset, she ultimately agreed to resign. Even though she loved Ethereum and Vitalik, if he wanted her gone, staying would hold no meaning for her.

Around the same time, I was a senior editor at *Forbes* covering cryptocurrency and got a tip that Ming had been fired. I emailed Bob Summerwill with the subject line "URGENT: Forbes: Ming fired from Ethereum Foundation?"

He forwarded the email to Joe with one comment: "Ding dong."

Later, after I'd communicated with Vitalik, Bob emailed Joe again:

> Vitalik emailed me it is not true. But I still found my goose chase useful—Laura.
> Though I suspect that V lied to Laura and it has happened.
> Nick Johnson says that Casey had told him that this was about to go down.

Joe wrote, "Interesting. I have no insight into whether true or not." Bob wrote another update:

> Looks like it has happened, but has not been announced.
> I will offer my counsel to V in the interim. I reached out to him offering my help in any way, and he has welcomed my advice/input.
> Nick Johnson confirmed to me (off the record) that the hammer did fall, and that V did lie to Laura Shin (presumably to make some space for internal scrambling). V implicitly confirmed that to me with his reply to me.

(After talking to multiple sources, I was not able to get any corroboration and so did not publish a story.)

The day after my email asking whether Ming had been fired, Ming posted in the Ethereum Foundation's internal Skype chat: "**Important:** I'm not going anywhere in the short term so **please disavow the rumors.** They do the foundation and everyone here a disservice on a number of levels. I'm still active ED and will still be hiring, on boarding, attending conferences, working with university programs and working with Vitalik and all our teams to ensure we move in the right direction for 2018...I'm going to miss my plane if I don't leave in 9 minutes." (She had a habit of missing planes.)

Though Ming had initially agreed with Vitalik to resign, she had now begun a campaign to persuade him to agree to a yearlong handoff to her successor.

Her Skype message, of course, set off chatter within the foundation, as many were puzzled as to why Ming would even say these things. Most of the dozens of people in the chat room had not heard any rumors prior to her message, but now many began flying around. The few who knew about my query and one from *CoinDesk*, a crypto-dedicated publication, saw Ming's post and thought she had screwed herself.

Ming continued doing her executive director duties, but around this time, Toya says, Ming either heard about the chat group from DevCon or deduced that people had been discussing her departure. She began calling various EF staff to dissuade them from being part of any plan to remove her. She opened her call to Toya saying something like "Toya, you read a lot. You know tragedy happens because of miscommunication." Then she said—and Toya says these were Ming's exact words—"It's been conveyed to me that you have actively plotted against me." What ensued was, according to Toya, a three-hour phone conversation. Toya says Ming said something like "I'm not going anywhere. I know there are people who don't belong to this organization, but I'm not one of them." She seemed to be implying that anyone who was against her didn't belong at the EF.

Ming also became convinced that Hudson was plotting a coup to take over her position—and she told EF staff, who then told Hudson. Experiencing what he would later call a sort of Stockholm syndrome, he apologized to her. She offered him a promotion to the head of communications, as part of her effort to delegate more, since she'd been warned for a while that her inability to do so was a problem. At first Hudson agreed, and Ming told him she had a plan for keeping her job. Realizing this new position was part of that plan, he then decided against it. Whether Ming was in or out was so up in the air that, in late November, Toya flew to Taipei to attend a meetup featuring Vitalik in order to find out whether Ming would be staying.

There she saw Vitalik surrounded by people eyeing the potential vacancy at the top of the EF. Because Vitalik relies on people he trusts, those confidants act almost like his agents. She says that anyone wanting to invite him to an event would find little success in asking him directly but have better odds by going through Pandia or someone else close to Vitalik. Seeing how many different people were nominating candidates for the executive director position—someone she knew had tasked her with putting someone forward as well—she felt they knew succeeding would "increase their grab," as Toya put it.

When Vitalik was in China that December, Ming requested that he meet her in Hong Kong. He said yes out of basic respect. Vitalik says that in Mongkok, a crowded shopping area of flashing lights and neon signs, he, Ming, and Casey met in a tiny hotel room with space for little more than two beds and a toilet.[19] Ming was upset Vitalik had first talked with various foundation people about his plan to fire her rather than going to her directly. While crying an inordinate amount, she railed at Vitalik for how he'd dismissed her, but also said she was burned out and so had wanted to do a handoff anyway. She just needed time to do it properly. DevCon came up again, and she refused to believe her performance had been less than excellent. Casey acted as Ming's emotional support. Although they talked most of the day, Vitalik didn't try to force her to accept a transition. What he needed was a board meeting.

THE BACKDROP TO this drama was the biggest crypto bubble since 2013, when bitcoin had risen in value by a factor of more than a hundred within one year. In 2017, Bitcoin started at less than $1,000 and gradually rose. From the end of May until early August, it stayed in the $2,000s. On August 2, CBOE, which oversees the largest US options exchange, and Gemini, a cryptocurrency exchange launched by the Winklevoss twins, announced a collaboration on Bitcoin futures, a type of financial derivative, on CBOE.[20] A few days later the BTC price moved firmly into the $3,000 to $4,000 territory. That persisted until mid-October, when it climbed above the $5,000 range.

On October 31, CME, the commodities exchange that handled $1 quadrillion annually in notional value and whose roots extended to 1848, announced it was launching Bitcoin futures.[21] Two days before CME's Bitcoin futures announcement, the price jumped into the $6,000s, and two days after the news, it hit the $7,000s. Unfortunately, right around this time, Bitcoin was undergoing a civil war. Even as Wall Street was taking its first serious interest in Bitcoin, the community, which had always been a weird mix of libertarians, Silicon Valley entrepreneurs, cryptoanarchists, venture capitalists, cypherpunks, get-rich-quick schemers, and tiny-in-number-but-huge-in-holdings Wall Street whales, was on the verge of implosion. As I wrote in *Forbes*, "Bitcoin Twitter has been a toxic stew of name-calling, trolling, bullying, blocking and threats, with some altercations spanning months with replies numbering in the hundreds. No tweet or Bitcoin Talk comment made by anyone is too old to dredge up and hold against them, no quote from Satoshi Nakamoto too out of context (or fictional) to be used to bolster one's argument."[22] It very much looked like Bitcoin was on the verge of a contentious chain split. Then, just eight days in advance of a proposed hard fork, one side backed down. Disaster averted, Bitcoin's upward march continued apace. On November 17, CBOE announced the details of its Bitcoin futures product.[23] On November 19, the BTC price shot up past $8,000. On November 28, it hit $10,000 for the first time and, the next day, briefly surpassed $11,000. On December 1, CME declared its futures would launch on December 18.[24] For the next few days, BTC closed above $11,000. On December 4, CBOE preempted CME by stating its futures would start trading on December 10. On December 6, the

BTC price skyrocketed to $14,000 and the very next day closed at nearly $17,900. On December 15, it reached a high of $18,154. On December 17, it smashed through another ceiling, touching $20,089.

While ETH and ICOs may have been the catalyst for the crypto boom, the price of ETH didn't rally again from its mid-June, Bancor-ICO-fueled high of more than $414 until November 23, Thanksgiving, when it hit a new high of almost $426. That day also saw the soft launch of a game on Ethereum called Crypto-Kitties, which featured adorable, one-of-a-kind digital cartoon cats with bugged-out eyes that could be bred to cultivate certain features.[25] For the first time, everyday people—not just get-rich-quick types, although there were those too—were interested in something on Ethereum. Six days later, ETH busted through $500 to flirt with a new all-time high of over $522. Meanwhile, a CryptoKitty named Genesis sold for $117,712, and trades of Cryp-toKitties began clogging up the Ethereum network, accounting for 20 percent of all transactions.[26] Two days after CBOE's Bitcoin futures launched on December 10, ETH hit an all-time high of more than $657 and, the day after, broke a new record at just shy of $748. Meanwhile, CryptoKitties was reaching so many normies that even Vitalik's noncrypto friends and family, like aunts, uncles, and the parents of close friends, who had never expressed interest in Ethereum, started asking him about the feline collectibles. The blockchain was so congested that every morning, he'd wake up and check how many transactions had occurred. Although he was encouraged that something on Ethereum had mainstream appeal, he'd feel deflated every time he saw more than a million transac-tions in the previous twenty-four hours. (The CryptoKitties team felt the same way for opposite reasons; they estimated that because of difficulties using Ethereum, they lost out on almost 99 percent of the actual interest in their game.[27]) Still, all this fed more ETH demand. Starting when CME's futures launched on December 18, ETH broke or traded near all-time highs in the $800s for several days. (Parity's frozen ETH, initially worth $92 million, was now worth around $250 million.)

CNBC was breathless. Headlines read, "Winklevoss twin predicts multitrillion-dollar value for bitcoin," "Analyst who predicted bitcoin's rise now sees it hitting $300,000–$400,000," and "Trader who called bitcoin rally says cryptocurrency will surge above $100,000 in 2018."[28] News about Bitcoin and Ethereum proliferated: about teens who'd become millionaires off Bitcoin, ETH traders who turned $8,500 into $7.5 million in six months with leveraged crypto trades, and WikiLeaks' founder Julian Assange thanking the US government, because the site was now enjoying 50,000 percent returns since it had been forced to use Bitcoin after being blocked by credit cards and PayPal.[29] Now that Bitcoin had gone "to the moon," a company named Moonlambos made it possible for anyone wanting to buy a Lamborghini to do so with BTC or ETH.[30] It also planned an ILO—initial Lambo offering.[31] On December 13, PineappleFund, an anonymous early Bitcoiner, posted on Reddit, announcing that he or she had "far more money than I can ever spend" and so was going to give away 5,057 Bitcoins—$86 million—to what he or she had christened The Pineapple Fund.[32] (A software engineer who, by email, helped "Pine" distribute the money got a strong sense, from Pine's mannerisms and use of emojis, that Pine was a woman and, from Pine's references to things like *Hacker News*, perhaps an engineer familiar with Silicon Valley.)

MEW, which in the late summer/early fall had been seeing about 3.5 million visitors a month, in November got 4.6 million. In December that reached 7.7 million. In twelve months, the tiny website started by two best friends as a side project had grown to seventy-seven times its original size.

DURING THIS TIME Vitalik was in Asia, doing events in Taiwan and then going on a Christmas vacation/company retreat in Phuket, Thailand, with Virgil, Aya, researchers, and other friends at the sublime, oceanfront Samira Villa, partly owned by another friend in attendance: a bitcoin, litecoin, and ether mining pool operator named Chun Wang of F2pool. The "hillside estate," as the website described it, was one of the sumptuous, sun-filled, high-ceilinged gems on Millionaires' Mile, replete with an infinity pool, a Jacuzzi, rain showers, a fire pit, a game room, and a multitude of views of the cerulean and turquoise ocean, with water so transparent that, from the house, one could see underwater reefs.

Aya Miyaguchi was a quiet, gentle, pretty Japanese woman who had started her career as a high school teacher. Having often told her students that they should see the world, she realized it was hypocritical for her to not do the same. She moved to San Francisco for business school and, in 2011, became interested in using Bitcoin for microfinance for women in developing countries. Soon after, she got a job working for Kraken, the cryptocurrency exchange that had given Vitalik office space when he had written the Ethereum white paper four years prior. She eventually became managing director of Kraken in Japan.

By the end of 2017, Ethereum had a roughly $70 billion market cap, and Vitalik himself was a centimillionaire; he'd been named to the Fortune 40 Under 40 list alongside the likes of Emmanuel Macron, Marie Kondo, Lin-Manuel Miranda, and Tim Ferriss, and he'd even beaten Mark Zuckerberg (among others) for the World Technology Award.[33] He could have done a proper executive search and attracted someone with experience stewarding an open-source technology. In fact, in these last months of 2017, Bob Summerwill was giving Vitalik recommendations around the transition from Ming, advocating that the EF have things like an elected community board, full transparency, defined governance, and the like—typical professional structural features appropriate for an organization shepherding the development of a decentralized technology.

But Vitalik did not seem to care if the next ED was the kind of experienced leader most other foundations in a similar position would seek. Some community members wanted clear, transparent, expert governance. (Vitalik felt that the EF had tried that in 2015 and it had been a disaster.) Those who wanted more professional business leadership saw his approach as part and parcel of his poor judgment when it came to his friends and business associates. (He didn't distinguish between his work and personal lives; it all melded into one.) This may have stemmed from his social awkwardness or his inability to read people. Others felt he disdained the world of business, investors, and management. Vitalik himself admitted he found VCs to be a bunch of "snakes." A crypto investor wished Vitalik would give feedback to Ethereum team leads and other staffers on their management skills, even as he knew Vitalik never would. Vitalik's takeaway from the attempt to bring in a professional board was "alignment is more important than competence" and that "expert" can be harmful "if by 'expert' you mean 'bring in hotshots from the outside without caring too much about values-alignment.'" It was like the biz-guys-versus-devs debates of early Ethereum. Again, the dev prevailed.

The frustration of Ethereum community members with how Vitalik shunned traditional business norms and hierarchy and was suspicious of executive types came to a head around how Ming's successor was chosen. For years, the Ethereum website had lacked information on the basic workings of the foundation. After the announcements about the board members who had joined when Ming did, back in 2015, the website never acknowledged their hasty departure.[34] They simply disappeared from the site in early 2016, replaced by a new governing board and set of advisors.[35]

A person who did have Vitalik's ear in late 2017 was the Zen-like Thomas Greco, an influential, behind-the-scenes figure at the Ethereum Foundation who had previously been named a special advisor to Ethereum in March 2016 and now was a special advisor for an ICO project called OmiseGo.[36] Thomas, who looked half Asian—most people believed he was, with one source saying he or she thought he was half Thai, half Italian—wore his long brown hair in a fold-over ponytail and had a tendency to bow, like someone who had grown up in Asia.[37] (The same person believed he had mostly grown up in Thailand.) He did not have a technical background but was into meditation and, with a soft, hesitant voice, liked to speak in "the old wise man speech pattern of giving out philosophical tidbits," as an employee at OmiseGo put it. He was one of several people "in" the Ethereum Foundation who had no official position but a lot of sway. One person said of Thomas, "He never had a formal role, but he probably was *the* most influential person to Vitalik," adding that he ran Vitalik's schedule for a long time (which Vitalik later denied), setting up a lot of meetings for him, so that, in a sense, Thomas vetted a lot of what Vitalik did or whom he met. When the close group around Vitalik hung out, Thomas decided where they went and when and directed the conversation. (Thomas was the friend of Vitalik's with whom Pandia walked around in Mexico so she would not be on the same premises as Ming.)

Thomas and his other half, the thick-haired Wendell Davis (both were hardcore libertarians and, prior to Ethereum, diehard Bitcoiners), as well as unofficial, powerful people in Ethereum, acted like advisors, but no one knew if they had titles. People in the EF had taken to calling Thomas, Wendell, and others like them the foundation's "shadow government." Someone else who worked with Thomas and Wendell thought their playbook was precisely not to have titles so their actions would have less clear impact and therefore be easier to get away with, since their names wouldn't be on them. Some people seemed afraid of them. Knowing they preferred to work secretively, people were nervous about mentioning their names, that they were connected to any specific event, or that they'd just been at a specific place and time observing something momentous; people were reluctant to even describe their personalities. One said, "The fact that Thomas has some kind of influence [in the foundation] is openly discussed. It's almost like a thing that needs to be worked around...[Thomas and Wendell] are the only people who genuinely make me uncomfortable within the crypto space. If anybody's going to make me worried, it's that duo." Sometimes people would ponder whether Thomas Greco was his real name. Another, when asked why Thomas had so much power in the foundation, given that he didn't have an official role, said, "That sounds like such an obvious question, but the atmosphere in the room was such that that would not be a good question to ask...It was just like, if it was Trump and Jared Kushner, he's around, there's no positive or negative, it's a package deal. He was just always there. Thomas was probably *the* single closest person to Vitalik at that time." This person said they had spent a lot of time with Thomas but repeatedly called him "a mystery" and said, "I just don't fully understand his role or who he is." When asked about Thomas, Vitalik whistled, as if amazed and a twinge uneasy that a reporter had mentioned the name. He said Thomas was an informal advisor whose advice he found valuable.

Some people speculated this shadow government had grown because the foundation was worried about the Securities and Exchange Commission. If Ethereum didn't have a central point of failure, it would succeed even if the SEC came after the foundation. But others felt the EF conflated centralization with having its shit together. One said, "For a while, they thought if they had their shit together, they'd be too productive, too central, they'd have too much decision-making power in the community."

But another reason for the opacity of the foundation could come down to the fact that this whole time, even if he didn't control Ethereum itself, at least at the foundation, Vitalik had the majority vote on the board. Even when Lars, Wayne, and Vadim were around, he'd had three votes, plus the tiebreaker. After they were gone, there were only ever two other votes—Ming's and Patrick Storchenegger's. People in the community felt it was hypocritical for Ethereum to be building a technology for open, transparent, and fair organization but then be opaque itself. And the fact that

Vitalik controlled the foundation board might be seen as the ultimate hypocrisy.

Despite all this, the shadow government finally got done what
many in the foundation and wider Ethereum community had
wanted for so long: it came up with a plan to axe Ming with which
Vitalik was comfortable. At DevCon 3, the person who had introduced Aya to Vitalik was Thomas. Even as he'd left Cancun,
Vitalik had settled on Aya as the next executive director. Although
he hadn't conducted a proper search, he wanted Ming out quickly,
and he felt it was more important to get her out than to quibble
over who replaced her. Plus, he felt, Aya's imperfection was not
being good enough rather than that she would actively do bad
things—a flaw for which it would be easier to compensate.

In fact, although Aya's resume was a better fit than Ming's had
been, many felt she was not at all the candidate a formal recruit-
ment process would have chosen. Aya herself would later admit she
hadn't really been clear on what the Ethereum Foundation even
was.[38] Some observers, many of whom liked Aya, could not help
but point out that she did have a qualification that one wouldn't
necessarily find on a resume: she was an Asian woman. As one
put it, "Young men are driven by hormones, and a professional
relationship can be close but without the intimidation of a physical
relationship as well." (Vitalik wrote via a messaging app that he
chose her for her personality: "Calm and not glory-oriented"; he
then added, "I guess that's an Asian culture thing?")

Over the holidays, Vitalik, Ming, and the developers were in a
limbo where Ming had agreed to resign but then gotten Vitalik to
acquiesce to a yearlong handoff. For Christmas and New Year's, Vitalik and his friends went first to Phuket, where they mostly swam
and ate, and then to Bangkok, where they stayed at some different
whales' homes, for a retreat. Amid all this activity, they worked
on grants and technical upgrades so that Ethereum could handle
more transactions, as well as the next year's budget and plans with

ETH in the $700s; plus they launched an important test net. One attendee recalls that Thomas, who, this person says, "likes to have a lot of girlfriends," joked a few times that Vitalik's girlfriend could have a second boyfriend. But unbeknownst to Vitalik, his friends also had an agenda they dubbed "the Bangkok Plan."

Two days before the end of the retreat, on New Year's Day, during an afternoon walk along a narrow river in a Bangkok park, they came upon a tree with a low branch. One of them clambered up; the others followed. There, Vitalik, Thomas, Aya, and others sat while looking out over the water. Whether it was the peaceful setting, the view of the water, or the novel experience of being nestled in a tree, they opened up. Vitalik's friends told him that the switchover from Ming to Aya needed to be accelerated. It could *not* last a year. As he would later recall it, they all "piled on" Vitalik and told him he had to be mean. The decision wasn't just about him. There were all these other people suffering for every minute the transition was delayed. They told him he needed to give Ming a deadline of the end of the month. He understood one of his mistakes had been letting her set the timetable. He also realized if he didn't do this, he would be letting them all down.

He would later describe this as the moment his friends "staged an intervention," seemingly unaware that, actually, they'd been trying to have this conversation with him for months. Even though Vitalik had been fairly open for a while about the fact that he didn't like working with Ming, he also did not like hurting other people's feelings, so even if Thomas would say that Ming should be fired, that doing so would be good for the foundation, one friend who watched these interactions felt Vitalik would not say no—he'd just nod and walk away, avoiding the bigger conflict of having to fire Ming, plus the smaller conflict of telling Thomas he didn't want to have that conversation with her.

But on the tree branch, comprehending that postponing her leaving was hurting his friends, Vitalik was finally persuaded.

IN LATE DECEMBER, a friend mentioned to Johnny, the customer support manager at Polo, that his friend who was a whale had asked him if Polo was selling to Circle. This was the first time Johnny had heard anyone put a name on the buyer.

Circle was a Boston-based blockchain payments company with backing by Goldman Sachs, whose CEO was a successful serial entrepreneur, though Circle's consumer app itself had never found much traction. Even in 2017, when crypto finally hit the mainstream, Circle had not enjoyed the same rush in users some of its competitors had. However, it did have one extremely active client, Polo, which was using Circle's OTC desk—the largest in crypto at that time—to cash out its crypto into fiat. Hence, Circle had an inside view of Polo's jaw-dropping books.

In late January, Tyler Frederick, Polo's newly hired compliance staffer from Fidelity, was planning to take a long weekend. However, he was told a staff conference call was scheduled for that Saturday. Because Polo was hyperconcerned about security, he would not be able to access his work email or computer at all, and because he was going to be out of state, he would not be allowed to participate in the conference call. So, the night before he left, because, he later surmised, Jules didn't want him to find out in a bad way, she gave him some news: Polo was going to be acquired by Circle. Because Tyler had felt things at Polo were unsustainable, he was happy.

Around the same time, the compliance manager, one of Poloniex's first five employees, who had worked there for four years, was called for an in-person meeting. When he arrived, attorneys from a law firm active in crypto greeted him. Although he'd signed for his options more than a year earlier, in January, he was told that Circle was acquiring Polo *before* his options were supposed to vest in April 2018, a year after the board had approved them. He could sign a waiver agreeing to a single payment of $2,000, or he would get nothing.

He was stunned—he'd been friends with Tristan. A source who was at one such meeting says the lawyers wouldn't tell him what the acquisition price was or what the shares would have been worth. They also told him he could not have a lawyer review the document—he had to sign right then and there, not later. Having been a crafts-person prior to joining Polo, knowing nothing about mergers and ac-quisitions, and believing he would otherwise get nothing, he signed for the $2,000. Part of the agreement was that he had to delete or destroy all his texts, messages, and other documents regarding Polo.

Johnny was in Portugal on his first vacation from Polo. Jules, Ruby, and a lawyer told him about the acquisition via video con-ference. Jules was on one side, Ruby off camera, and the lawyer in the middle. He was all "smiley" and told Johnny that this was a huge opportunity to work for Circle but that his options were worthless—even if they vested. However, now, he would not be able to exercise his options anyway. Johnny refused, saying, "No, I won't work for Circle. I want my options." Jules stood up. Johnny says she told him he wasn't entitled to anything and that if he didn't want to work for Poloniex, he could quit right then. At that point, Johnny said he would start recording unless he was allowed legal counsel. Johnny says the attorney for Polo said it was not possible to do anything productive at that moment, so they should schedule with Johnny's lawyer. They hung up.

Johnny worked for a few more days, but his lawyer was taking too long, so he quit.

When Tyler returned the following Tuesday, he was told that, upon hearing the news, some employees had quit because they were crypto ideologues and thought Polo was selling its soul be-cause Circle was backed by Goldman Sachs. He also thought per-haps they had made a lot of money in ETH and so didn't need to work. However, suddenly the strange interview process he had gone through made sense—looking back, he could see the rosy picture Jules and Mike had painted of what Polo would become was actually a description of Circle.

IN LATE DECEMBER 2017, with ETH trading in the $700s, Vi-talik saw a tweet from his old friend "anarchist Amir," who had invited him to the Macao squat in Milan back in 2013 and then lived with Mihai in a London squat, where he'd showed Gavin around and helped get him into Bitcoin. Amir tweeted, "Bitcoin is turning into a failed project. The seeds of its destruction among the debris of a community blinded by numerical price increases, and imminent divine reclamation. One day you will all understand my words but it will be too late, the ship would have sailed."[39] Vitalik quoted his tweet and wrote, "*All* crypto communities, ethereum included, should heed these words of warning. Need to differentiate between getting hundreds of billions of dollars of digital paper wealth sloshing around and actually achieving something meaningful for society."[40] He followed that up with another tweet that referred to sharding, a way to enable more transactions per second on the blockchain:

> If all that we accomplish is lambo memes and immature puns about "sharting", then I WILL leave.
> Though I still have a lot of hope that the community can steer in the right direction.[41]

On January 4, 2018, for the first time, ETH broke $1,000, reaching a new all-time high of around $1,045. For the next few days, it traded in the $1,000s, inching higher until, on January 7, it hit a new record of a little over $1,153. The next day, it broke yet another ceiling, cresting at nearly $1,267. The day after that, it was just shy of $1,321. The day after that, $1,417 and change. (The same day *Quartz* reported Japan had an all-girl pop group called Kasotsuka Shojo, aka Virtual Currency Girls, in which each of the eight members represented a different cryptocurrency.[42]) On January 13, ETH hit an all-time high of just over $1,432. The same day, the *New York Times* published an article headlined "Everyone Is Getting Hilariously Rich and You're Not." The photo featured two attendees at the San Francisco Bitcoin Meetup Holiday Party, one of whom was wearing a blue Ethereum Christmas sweater replete with black horizontal stripes featuring white geometric snowflakes and the Ethereum double tetrahedron logos; the other wore a yellow Bitcoin version, featuring the slanted *B* logo. The reporter spent some time with a Forrest Gump–like character in crypto, who, wearing a pink button-down and pink pants, told her, "I do I.C.O.s. It's my thing…It's me, a couple V.C.s and a lot of charlatans." He showed her around his home, aka "the Crypto Castle," and its stripper pole. While talking to the reporter about how he wasn't so sure about an invitation he'd received for a reality TV show, he said, "I literally have a date with Bella Hadid not having a reality show."[43]

Around this time, Vitalik, observing the bubble, feeling scared about the skyrocketing price, and wondering if Ethereum really deserved this, had an instinct. He sold seventy thousand of the foundation's ETH for about $1,300—over $90 million.

He was feeling particularly emboldened. When his friends had given him a hard deadline for removing Ming, because he was so fearful of confronting her, they had urged him to do things he wasn't comfortable with, like pick a grain of rice out of a trash can and eat it. (He doesn't remember if he actually ate anything; he didn't like his friends suggesting that.) They also tried to help him learn stress-reduction practices like meditation. One common technique is to repeat a phrase or mantra over and over again, such as "Hamsa" or "Soham." Vitalik tried it, but put his own spin on it, counting perfect squares: 1, 4, 9, 16, 25, 36, 49, and so on.

About a week after the "intervention" in the park, he'd emailed Ming and told her he needed her resignation by month's end. The process entailed signing documents to officially remove Ming and induct Aya. Because both Vitalik and Aya were in San Francisco, a board meeting was scheduled there for January 20.

A few days before, while Vitalik, Thomas, another OmiseGo developer named Joseph Poon, and others were hanging out at Joseph's parents' house in San Francisco, Ming had called Vitalik. For more than an hour, she vented at him. But Vitalik was no longer the same person he'd been in 2015 when he'd had his first phone conversation with Ming and they'd bonded over being geeks and surviving school. In hindsight, he could see that, back then, he'd been surrounded by people who'd acted like his friends but weren't really, and he'd actually found relating to them hard—they'd made his life more difficult rather than more enjoyable. He thought of Anthony, Charles, maybe Gavin. Now he knew that someone's treating him nicely didn't mean that person genuinely liked him. At that time, since he'd never had the experience of people being actively mean to him but had always struggled with loneliness, he'd been happy just to have anyone paying attention to him. He never thought about why he or she was taking an interest. Now he could spot red flags: people being nice to him but not others, those motivated by money. Back then, as one witness recalls, Joe Lubin had jokingly wondered if he had a girlfriend who was a computer. Similarly, now internet memes referred to him as an alien, robot, or "money skeleton"—but his friends didn't.[44] For the first time in his life, the people he hung out with weren't ladder climbers or interested in social status at all; they were just interested in harmoniously enjoying their lives together. Talking to Ming now, he felt less of the angst he'd previously felt; in fact, he was happy, knowing this was one of their last conversations.

Then, she delivered a surprise: Vitalik no longer had three board votes. He had one, just like Ming and Patrick. He assumed Patrick had made this change without informing him. Years later Vitalik still wouldn't be sure exactly why, assuming it was due to some bureaucratic change, such as an adjustment of the articles of the foundation, which had in turn removed his supervotes.

Although Patrick had recently told Vitalik he would support removing Ming as director, Vitalik was spooked. His friends were too. Knowing how unpredictable Ming could be and realizing Vitalik no longer had his trump card, they were on tenterhooks for the next few days. One would later recall, "It was such a tense moment in time." Another would later say he wasn't completely confident the transition would happen: "Logistically, it was a shit show."

THE MORNING OF January 20 dawned unusually sunny in San Francisco. Although it was in the low fifties, Vitalik's friends were feeling a sweat—as if they were early employees, their CEO was off to raise funding, and they couldn't wait to hear whether the pitch had gone well.[45] Because Ming was a wild card and had a lot more power than they had thought until a few days earlier, one question consumed them: *Will Ming sign?*

A block away from Union Square, 140 Geary St. was flanked by a Bottega Veneta and YSL on one side and a John Varvatos and Chanel on the other. The meeting was on the tenth floor. Patrick, Aya, Vitalik, and Ming's sister Tung, the Ethereum Foundation's general counsel, greeted each other. Vitalik got himself some tea. Aya was nervous because she had heard Vitalik had thought he had three votes and just found out he only had one. Although she didn't know the backstory, that fact alone sounded dramatic. Patrick's assistant connected via Skype. Ming had been scheduled to come to San Francisco, but at the last minute she told them she couldn't for health reasons, so she also patched in by Skype. Her face appeared on a large screen on the wall.

The meeting began, and other than the awkwardness of Tung being Ming's sister and everyone knowing that the meeting's purpose was to remove Ming as executive director, things started as normally as could be expected. But as time went on, Ming, as was her wont, became emotional. She requested that Aya step out of the room. Aya stood in the hall for a half hour.

Inside, the discussion with Ming continued. Vitalik felt stressed, just as he did in any conversation with her. The talk was innocuous on the surface—about severance and other mundane details about the transition like the date and the announcement—but every question and issue raised ratcheted up Vitalik's anxiety. He tried to quell his worry that Ming or Patrick or Tung or someone would come up with some kind of trick to delay the transfer of power. He reminded himself that despite the loss of his supervotes, if Patrick kept his word, everything should go as planned. Finally, after a few procedural moves and signatures, he got his wish of almost two years: Ming was no longer the executive director of the Ethereum Foundation.

It had been five years since Vitalik left college with $10,000 worth of bitcoin and a gig writing about the cryptocurrency. He now had hundreds of millions of dollars' worth of ether. A smart sale of about $700 ETH helped him maintain his lifestyle of constant travel, which had been upgraded to mostly business class flights and comfortable Airbnbs. Having reached financial independence, he never needed to worry about money again. Otherwise his lifestyle hadn't changed. He traveled with a small backpack, which held his laptop, seven days' worth of clothing, a jacket, a sweater, a toothbrush, toothpaste, random cables, USB keys, a pouch of the currencies of numerous countries, subway cards from more than a dozen cities, and a universal power adapter. And now, the biggest burden he'd been carrying was gone.

They ended the meeting. Aya, Patrick, Tung, and Vitalik went to Chipotle for lunch, then he and Aya headed back to Joseph's parents' place. In 2013, Vitalik had written the Ethereum white paper in the same neighborhood. He'd picked up Gavin, Jeff, Mihai, Anthony, Charles, Amir, and Joe as cofounders, and now he was once again alone. But not quite. Years later, he would look back and mark January 2018 as a watershed moment in his life: the time when, finally, the people he spent time with were real friends. Less than five miles away, where the roaring blue Pacific met San Francisco's green northwest tip, was the Presidio. It was the perfect spot for one of their rambling walks.

Epilogue

IF 2017 WAS the year the crypto bubble inflated, 2018 began a long deflation. In January, ETH remained above $1,000 for much of the month, though toward the end, it began dipping toward the hundreds. In February, it ranged from the upper $500s to the high $900s. But by the end of March, it was closing below $400. It rallied again in early May up to $750, but then, as regulators came closing in and it became clear that the speculation party was over, the price began a slow decline to the $100 to $300 range (at one point dipping to as low as below $83) by December 2018. Over the same period, the global crypto market cap plummeted 87 percent. During this period, few of the dapps promised by ICOs came to fruition, and those that launched saw modest uptake, so there wasn't a lot of demand for ETH.

But there was one bright spot. As 2018 rolled on, it became clear the Securities and Exchange Commission considered the vast majority of ICOs to have been unregistered securities offerings. The crypto industry parsed the speeches of SEC directors as intently as initial coin offering investors counted down to the start of a token sale. The Ethereum Foundation eventually reached out to the SEC, and on June 1, Aya, Vitalik, some Enterprise Ethereum Alliance members, and EF lawyers had a call with SEC officials, who asked them how decisions were made about the Ethereum protocol, whether or not the foundation owned Ethereum, and details about the sale. (The SEC declined to comment on whether there was a meeting or what might have been discussed.) On June 18, a senior SEC official who was said to have been in the meeting said in a speech that "based on [his] understanding of the present state of ether," it was not a security.[1]

Midway through 2017, right when the scams began picking up, Kosala seemed to check out of MEW. He wasn't doing any work visible in GitHub, though he would later say he was doing back-end stuff like monitoring security, auditing the code, and maintaining infrastructure. His GitHub contributions to the MEW codebase were greater than Taylor's in 2017 up until the last week of June. But right after Status's network-clogging ICO, after EOS began its yearlong sale, and just as Tezos's record-setting crowd-funding was starting, he peaced out. From then until the end of the year, he made three GitHub contributions (and bought a house in Malibu). In 2017, his GitHub contributions totaled 465 and Taylor's 2,184.[2]

During this time, the former best friends had a legal battle involving numerous rounds of lawyers, at least one offer to buy the other out, and one failed attempt at mediation. Finally, Taylor's fourth lawyer, a scrappy, young mixed martial arts aficionado eager to make crypto his niche, dissolved the company as a surprise move over the holidays. Since she no longer had any obligations to MyEtherWallet, she became CEO of her own company, My-Crypto, while Kosala became CEO of MEW. (After the news broke, Andrey Ternovskiy emailed Taylor an offer of $10 million to help her buy MEW; she didn't respond.)

Circle's acquisition of Poloniex closed on February 22, 2018. *Fortune* reported the deal was for $400 million, but according to a source familiar with the matter, the actual amount eventually paid out was between $200 million and $300 million.[3] The sale was al-most perfectly timed to when not only the flood of trading volume began to wane at Polo but also the crypto bubble itself began to burst and volumes globally were lower than at their peak in mid-December. Polo had been shopping itself since the spring of 2017, such as to Barry Silbert's Digital Currency Group and Blockchain.com. Circle had been hoping to close the deal in November, but Jules, Mike, and Tristan, citing the crushing amount of work (which the staff and another person who worked with them attributed to their "greedy" refusal to hire additional employees), managed to drag it out while the exchange was still bringing in obscene amounts of revenue—and yet to close before the employees' shares vested. Some early staff calculated they'd been strong-armed out of $5 million to $10 million apiece.

Because they'd previously been so friendly with Tristan, some suspected he didn't know they'd been cheated—that he was too naive to do such a thing. One reached out and heard nothing. Although lawyers told this employee he had a case to make that his options had vested in January, a year after he'd signed, not a year after the board approval in April, he decided he didn't want to spend years of his life battling Jules, after seeing how ruthless she could be in using lawyers to fight her cause. Johnny, the head of customer service, sent Tristan an encrypted email asking, "Are you really screwing us?" Although Tristan wrote back saying there was no nefarious intention, Johnny wondered if he could not speak openly because, say, his encryption key was shared with Jules; if so, she could read the messages. (Jules shared one with Ruby.) He offered Tristan another avenue to send him a cryptographically private message, away from the possible oversight of Jules and Mike, but Tristan never responded.

Jules and Mike vanished. Someone who knows where they are claims to have been sworn to secrecy. A former employee said of Jules, "I wouldn't be surprised if she's changed her name at this point."

The person who knows their location said, "They're retired. Not only did they sell Polo, they also owned a lot of crypto themselves. They're chillin'. Straight chillin'."

(Through intermediaries, Jules, Mike, and Tristan declined to comment and did not respond to fact checking.)

Less than two years later, in the fall of 2019, Circle would sell Polo, which never recovered the market share it once had.

Charles Hoskinson had founded a network called Cardano, which had held an ICO the year before, selling mostly to investors in Japan.[4] In early January 2018, its market cap peaked at about $29 billion. That fall, on Twitter, when asked about his degree, he claimed, as he had for years, that he'd dropped out of a PhD program.[5] Metropolitan State University of Denver, which doesn't have a graduate math program, said he'd been enrolled part-time as a math major between 2006 and 2008 and again from 2012 to 2014, and the University of Colorado, Boulder, said he was a half-time undergraduate math major for four semesters from spring 2009 to fall 2011. He never earned a degree from either. The Defense Advanced Research Projects Agency confirmed he had never worked directly for the agency.

After an initial interview, Charles did not attend a scheduled follow-up call. The global director of media relations for his company, Charles's assistant, nor anyone on the general press email for his company responded to any of my three emails about the missed interview or the four emails about fact checking, which included questions about the discrepancies between his claims about his education and the schools' statements.

Anthony Di Iorio's ex-girlfriend, Nancy, learned the hard way the expression "Money doesn't change a person, it only amplifies who they really are." In 2017, Anthony had gotten bodyguards and taken to wearing sunglasses inside (since he didn't like the look of regular glasses, he'd decided on prescription sunglasses for his farsightedness); plus he had his entourage. He eventually began a relationship with a young woman whom he had also hired at Decentral, whom someone called "a younger, prettier version of Nancy." He and Nancy are locked in a legal battle because, as two sources put it, Anthony was sharing almost none of the assets they had built together. Anthony scoffs at the phrase "built together," calling her "nothing more than an administrator…In fact, I built what I built in spite of her. So there's no built together. *I* built." (Nancy declined to comment.) Someone who worked closely with Anthony back then said Nancy was "heavily, heavily involved and that Anthony would not be anywhere without her at all. She did all the operations, finances, front desk, admin, making sure staff was happy." This person said Anthony's treatment of Nancy evinces the same pattern that he had with others: "it's still the same story of [her] not having the right contracts in place and then being side-swiped...She definitely does not get enough credit and everyone knew it. She was the first and last face we saw. If anyone had any tension with Anthony, she was the person to mitigate it, and defuse any situation." When hearing the beginning of this quotation, Anthony cut me off before I could finish—"Ridiculous. That's ridiculous. That's crazy...There's absolutely nothing that Nancy did that couldn't have been done by a junior-level administrator, no, there's absolutely nothing—no strategy, no hiring, no legal decisions, nothing involved with accounting, nothing to do with anything. She doesn't have a high school degree."

By early 2018, he'd become "incredibly rich off not a lot of technical experience or necessarily talent," as one Ethereum insider put it. "He's sort of like 'the bling and the bodyguards.'" (Anthony says he's been into computers and tech since he was eight and builds software, though he hires developers to do the developer work.) (The *New York Post* reported that at Consensus 2018, he held a six-hour yacht cruise on the thirty-thousand-square-foot Cornucopia *Majesty* featuring his favorite DJ, Chicane, whom he flew in from London. He also gave away two Aston Martins—at least one emblazoned with the Ethereum logo.[6]) Later that year, he would buy the C$28 million ($21 million), 16,178-square-foot, three-story penthouse in the former Trump International Hotel and Toronto Tower, eventually moving in with his new girlfriend. A *Bloomberg* article announcing the news would photograph him in his sunglasses inside the space, which had been gutted.[7]

A little over a month after my fact checker and I finished the fact checking process with Anthony, part of which involves running by a source everything negative about them in the book, a *Bloomberg* article announced he was "quitting crypto," saying it was due to concerns about his safety.[8]

After Jeff Wilcke left Ethereum, he focused on being a dad. But that gave him time to think about what could go wrong with his health, so he decided he needed a change. He and his brother had always wanted to start their own game company. In March 2018, they began building a massively multiplayer online role-playing game, which improved his mental state. He stopped following what was going on with Ethereum.

That winter, ConsenSys had its first official presence at the World Economic Forum in Davos, spending $1 million that year and the year after; it did not bring in a single client from either event. In February 2018, it also held its company retreat in Portugal. In typical anarchic fashion, some employees published and distributed a zine about how ConsenSys had started for the right reasons but was now working for corporations and governments and asking what the soul of the company was and what its mission was, especially with ETH around its all-time high. Titled "Stateless," it began with an article called "Darq Times," which opened,

> Late night lambasting of broken systems. The smell of burnt Swallow coffee. Chairs for standing, couches for sitting, floors for sleeping. Table Tetris and Tiny Human. Fuze and Catan. Microsoft, Redhat, ubuntu, and tomorrow, Deloitte. In the office by $2, surf and turf at $10, EEA news so just buy the fucking dip. Pizza, polyamory and psychedelic shorts; that spooksexy, freakynaughty, that good meshy love. CC: everyone and invoice Wendycoin. Views from atop a gravitational well, white, yellow, mauve, polkadotted skies and Bogartian sunsets.

(Some of the references were to how there wasn't assigned seating but shared tables, a collaboration ConsenSys's blockchain music project had done with musician Imogen Heap for her song "Tiny

Human," and how, after a while, an employee from China who went by "Wendy" in the United States took over from Joe the handling of payroll via LocalBitcoins payments. Bogart was the name of the street where ConsenSys's office was located.)

It said, "The first two years of ConsenSys was primordial soup, a eukaryotic mélange of crypto-anarchists, computer scientists, quants, perma-culturists, old-time cypherpunks, a rambunctious subset of rebels and rabble-rousers, sprinkled liberally across the globe." It then went on to describe how, slowly, the drive to serve enterprise customers, because ConsenSys Enterprise was "the only revenue generating division," created "cultural tension" in the company, driving people to take traditional titles like "Chief" and "Head." It then mentioned how tension surfaced at the Bali retreat "ranging from internal competition between spokes to isolated cases of inappropriate behavior towards women." It chronicled the changes and organizational issues in the company, noting how an October 2017 presentation said the company had roughly four hundred employees "with 75% joining in the second half of 2017" and making numerous references to how the ETH price was changing along the way and creating a burgeoning class it called the "crypteau-riche." It concluded, "There is still time left to clean up this little Mesh we've made." Although there was a limited number of zines, reserved for people who wrote a letter of reflection to themselves about why they were working at ConsenSys, Joe got ahold of one, had someone make copies, and then handed what one creator of the zine called the "bootlegged" version out. Joe's response: "We generally encouraged open discourse."

The same month, when ETH was still in the $700 to $900 range, Joe, who wouldn't remember this later, told an employee he wanted ConsenSys to have fifteen hundred people on staff by the end of the year. When asked why, he didn't have a particular reason—to the staffer, it seemed the number just sounded good to him. That year, *Forbes* would estimate that ConsenSys's annual burn rate was more than $100 million—and in 2018 it would only bring in $21 million.[9] It would acquire an asteroid-mining company called Planetary Resources. Joe released a statement saying, "Bringing deep space capabilities into the ConsenSys ecosystem reflects our belief in the potential for Ethereum to help humanity craft new societal rule systems through automated trust and guaranteed execution."[10]

Though he wouldn't reach fifteen hundred, ConsenSys would eventually grow, by December, to around twelve hundred people, according to *The Verge*. Early that month, it would announce layoffs of 13 percent of its workforce.[11] A few weeks later, it would spin out most of its start-ups.[12] As eventually reported by *The Information*, by March 2019, only nine hundred employees would remain, and the company would be seeking $200 million in outside investment.[13] By April 2020, it still hadn't found willing investors, though its headcount had shrunk to roughly 550, but it did announce another round of layoffs—14 percent of its staff. In May, it would open-source the intellectual property of its asteroid-mining acquisition and auction off its physical assets.[14] In August 2020, it acquired JPMorgan's enterprise blockchain platform, and *The Block* reported it was set to receive a strategic $20 million investment from the bank but that the deal terms were not finalized and could change.[15] Finally, in April 2021, it announced it had raised $65 million from JPMorgan, Mastercard, UBS, and Protocol Labs, a company that had had one of the biggest ICOs, among others.[16] As a former employee who helped with the zine distributed at the Portugal retreat put it, "The originals, who found out about Ethereum and were committed to decentralization and building a new society that worked differently—those are the people that left [ConsenSys]. The people who stayed are like, 'Let's get JPMorgan better at what they do.'" (Joe disagrees, pointing to several in-house Ethereum infrastructure providers, including the wallet MetaMask, which by spring 2021 had five million monthly active users.)

Some, but not all, early employees eventually got their equity documented. The ones who got their equity seemed to like Joe and be nonchalant about ConsenSys owing him a lot of BTC and ETH. Eventually, during the 2018 shareholders' meeting, which was held in December 2019, he forgave the ETH loans at a fair value totaling 266 million Swiss francs, according to a screenshot from the meeting. (Matt says this overstates the true figure by about 25 percent.) The company was split into two entities—the original one for investment and one for software.[17] According to a Telegram group for ConsenSys shareholders, this deal diluted their shares so that they were now worth one-tenth their previous value—which was after a shareholder meeting to already dilute them by 33 percent, though the new shares had, as of June 2021, not been issued yet. (Referring to the share dilution to one-tenth their previous value, Matt Corva said the company could not comment, and as for the shareholder meeting, he said it had authorized roughly an additional 15 percent of common stock to grant equity to employees who had not yet received equity.) In August 2020, before the JPMorgan deal closed, one chat group member said JPMorgan wanted a clean US entity, as opposed to the original Swiss AG, for which there was little to no clear documentation around what intellectual property it had. "So that's what's been going on; clear out AG and move it all to USA entity while AG shareholders got rekt." Noting that "the AG is a disaster from a due diligence POV for any investor," one member of the group said the new software entity was an attempt to move assets to a clean entity on which it would be easier to conduct due diligence, and then linked to an article about the latest lawsuit against ConsenSys, this one alleging it had copied the code of a company it was investing in and created a competing offering.

Another subset of executives left, many of them having had similar experiences to each other: Joe loved watching them duke things out in front of him, "so he keeps both people in check," said one; another called his style "divide and rule." When those execs departed, they said, he had his team dig up dirt on them and badmouth them. "I can't believe people are still there and don't realize they're just the next to get fucked," said one. (Joe denies this and says they would never dig up dirt on former employees. "We always take the high road," he said.)

At least the removal of Ming helped thaw the ice between Joe and Vitalik. At an Ethereum conference in Toronto in May 2018, Kavita Gupta, a ConsenSys executive who had secured a few meetings with some tech magnates for Vitalik, set up one between him and Joe (and Yunyun). Vitalik was "*just not happy about it*, and was just answering Joe's questions like a machine," she recalled. Kavita then set up a meeting for both of them with former Google CEO Eric Schmidt. Afterward, Joe and Vitalik were so happy with how it went, they hugged and chatted for a half hour to forty-five minutes. When Vitalik left, Kavita says, Joe, who does not remember this, got emotional about having had a good conversation with him again.

Even the EF and ConsenSys finally found themselves on good terms: Aya, the EF's new executive director, and Sam Cassatt, then the ConsenSys chief strategy officer who staff say barely came into the office for a few years before finally moving to Puerto Rico, were friends.

As for Gavin, the Parity team and Web3 Foundation spent the winter of 2018 trying to understand how Ethereum governance worked, to see how they might get an Ethereum Improvement Proposal passed to unfreeze the Polkadot ICO funds. The conclusion was what Ethereum insiders had been complaining about for months: there was no clear decision-making process. At ETH's peak in 2018, Parity's frozen funds were worth around $434 million. A Parity developer still proposed an EIP (999) that would unfreeze the funds in the Parity wallets. A heated debate ensued, with some people worrying the Parity client would run the code on its own, creating a hard fork. In April 2018, a coin vote was taken. Only 639 votes were cast, with nearly 1.6 million ETH for and 2.2 million against; ultimately, no action was taken.[18] Still, although many people in Ethereum had, at best, mixed feelings about Gavin—he could be "mean," "petty," "arrogant," "selfish," and, overall, an "asshole"—they tended to view him as having been a net positive for Ethereum and respected him for his vision, ambition, and dedication. (Gavin says that when faced with the choice of ruffling feathers or seeing a project he's spent countless hours on "disappear down a road of waste, disarray, and eventual failure to everyone's detriment... I'll risk ruffling the feathers.")

Gavin himself was left with a long-lasting paranoia about Joe, attributing a number of bad things that had happened to him—his firing from the Ethereum Foundation, the freezing of the multisigs—to Joe or someone who worked for him. An employee of Parity/Web3 called it "a deep-seated paranoia. It's unhealthy." Gavin responded, "It's not paranoia if they're really after you," then linked to a poster for the 1998 movie *Enemy of the State*, which features that tagline. He also insinuated that Parity lost the coin vote to unfreeze the funds due to "a large Ether holder, perhaps someone with deep-enough pockets to bankroll a 1000+ person organisation, [deciding] that it was not in their interest."

In the case of the frozen funds, some level of paranoia may have been justified. Despite claiming to be an ETH newbie who had "accidentally" killed the multisigs, intriguingly, devops199 had obscured his or her trail beforehand, as if the move had been premeditated. The transaction that froze the Parity multisig wallets came from an account that, on November 1, had received 0.225 ETH from a ShapeShift transaction that had converted from 0.0102 BTC at 18:28 UTC.[19] However, that BTC itself had just come from a ShapeShift transaction that had converted 0.245 ETH into 0.0104 BTC at 18:23 UTC.[20] Why would devops199 take perfectly good ETH, turn it into BTC, and then, five minutes later, swap that right back into ETH before performing the transaction that froze the Parity multisigs?

Even more interesting, the original ETH (that got turned into BTC before being turned back into the ETH used to freeze the multisigs) came from an account that had done 1,215 transactions in the previous six days.[21] One analyst said the characteristics of the transactions were consistent with a technique known as "penetration testing," which looks for exploitable vulnerabilities. Another researcher said they also appeared to be testing this strategy on the test net—and had sent 610 "kill" messages to random contracts—but that it looked to him less like pen testing and more like trying to harvest ETH (basically sending "kill" to contracts to see if they would give devops199 their money). However, he also said this evidence could also be "very good cover." Devops199 also appears to have been involved in an ICO project called PlexCoin, against which the SEC filed a complaint in December 2017 for making "false and misleading statements to potential and actual investors" and whose founders were sentenced to two months in jail in Canada.[22] From the number of Plexcoins to which they had access—forty million, or 0.4% of the total—it appeared devops199 had perhaps been a consultant or advisor, one analyst of such activity said. So, hardly a newbie.

On January 16, 2018, at 5:43 UTC, the person who was presumably devops199 took the remaining 0.09 ETH in the account that had frozen the multisigs and converted it via ShapeShift into 0.256 of the privacy coin Monero (XMR).[23] And although it's not provable, it's reasonable to conjecture that at 7:41 UTC, devops199 also converted 0.23 XMR to 0.073 ETH.[24] Why take perfectly good ETH, convert it to XMR, and then swap that for ETH again, other than to obscure one's tracks?

Gavin's paranoia about Joe *may* also have been justified when it came to a September 2018 *BuzzFeed* article about how, pre-Ethereum, he'd written a blog post about having sex with a certain preteen girl dying of AIDS.[25] (Gavin said it was a work of fiction, and *BuzzFeed* was able to find no evidence of a child of the same name in that location dying at the time mentioned.) The blog post had previously been shopped to me as a tip by an associate of one of Joe's college buddies. (Joe denied having any knowledge of this.)

On January 31, 2018, Ming posted her fifth and final post on the Ethereum blog announcing it was her last day.[26] Right after, another blog post from "Ethereum team" went up about her departure and Aya's appointment.[27] After she was fired/resigned, Ming told at least one friend that she'd left because her doctors told her she needed a long break—that she'd been working too much and sleeping too little for the past few years. Her title on LinkedIn changed to "former executive director at Ethereum Foundation." Under education, her profile said she'd attended MIT from 1984 to 1988 in computer science and architecture and Wellesley for the same years in East Asian philosophy. Although she'd claimed in multiple places that she was an alumna of MIT and often invoked MIT when discussing her philosophy of personal excellence, she'd actually been a Wellesley student who had cross-registered for courses at MIT, which would not have made her an MIT student. Her LinkedIn also stated she attended MIT in media arts and sciences (formerly under the Department of Architecture and Planning) from 1988 to 1991, and she was a member of the MIT Massachusetts Institute of Technology Alumni Group on LinkedIn. However, the MIT Registrar's Office said that she enrolled as a graduate student in architecture in February 1989, dropped out in May of that year, and never earned a degree.

In the course of writing this book, I emailed Ming eleven times for an interview. Once, she responded saying it was not a good time for personal reasons. (I also sent four emails to Casey, asking him if he could persuade Ming to talk with me or if he was open to an interview himself.) Five months later, after sending her more follow-up emails, I made another request to Ming, which was met with this reply:

```
Subject: Delivery Failure
Delivery to the following recipient failed:
[Ming's email address]@gmail.com
```

Closer inspection revealed it was not an actual delivery failure from a system administrator. Although the text of the email said, "Subject: Delivery Failure," the actual subject line of the email had not changed. The email utilized a particular feature of Gmail in which any address can add a suffix attached by a + sign without actually affecting sends and receives to or from that email address. This email came from [her email]+canned.response@gmail.com.

She and Casey did not respond to four additional emails from my fact checker. As of yet, I don't believe anyone has uncovered the identity of Nora.

Finally, I interviewed Patrick Storchenegger *before* hearing the story about how Vitalik had only one vote by the time of Ming's removal. Although Patrick did not respond to eight follow-up emails and two phone calls from me or two emails from my fact checker, I realized that when I had asked him, "How many votes has Vitalik had on the board during this period—this whole period that you've been on the board?" Patrick responded, "He has more votes than anyone else. Three." That leaves open the possibility that Ming's assertion that Vitalik only had one vote at the time of her removal was not true.

Under Aya, the issues with the EF's shadow government continued. Even as employees complained to her about all the unofficial people who exerted power at the foundation—to the point where staffers often felt that these unaccountable figures had more influence than Aya did—she did not or could not do much to make the power structures clearer. The team organizing DevCon 4 set up everything to have the event in Copenhagen. The night before they were about to announce where it would be held—a point at which an organizer said contracts with the venues had been signed and a blog post was all ready to go—Copenhagen as the city was scratched. (The reason was perhaps that "it was too refined and expensive for such a global community," as someone on the planning team put it, and the foundation wanted the event to be accessible to everyone; eventually it was held in Prague.) An event planner, who was in his or her first week on the job, eventually heard the person who had shot down Copenhagen was Thomas. "Oh, it was *Thomas*," the planner would hear people gossip, in a way that gave him an aura of mystery. Since he had had enough sway to stop such a huge decision without even being present or on the team, this person came away with the impression he was the EF's "invisible puppet master." Another person in the shadow government starting in 2018 who people felt directed things behind the scenes was Albert Ni, who had no official foundation role and had visited the group on the Thailand retreat. Others felt that because of him, Aya was not able to make her own decisions, even though she was the executive director and Albert had no title.

Aya said, "It's normal for any organization for leaders to have other people to delegate work." She also noted that the EF is intentionally not structured as a traditional hierarchy. "Do you only listen to smart people because someone has a title?" Albert Ni attributed the story line that Aya was being puppeteered to gender stereotypes and added that, perhaps because English is not her native language, if Albert, an MIT math and computer science alum and former engineer and head of engineering hiring at Dropbox, articulated some of the more technical decisions to people, they may have believed those directives came from him, but decisions were made by her and Vitalik. (Among the sources who discussed the shadow government with me, two were technical; three were nontechnical.) He also said about those criticizing him for wielding so much power without a title, "Didn't we get interested in blockchains in part because we want things to be done when it makes sense for them to be done and not because this person had this title—*therefore* it makes sense for it to be done? If I had known that that would be that much of a sticking point with people, I would have just taken a title." Aya also disputed the notion that the shadow government existed, attributing it to one person making noise on Twitter (Texture). (Texture was not one of my sources expressing concern about the shadow government.) "Honestly, nothing is really shadow government," she said. "We can't hide anything, because people talk about it anyway." As for DevCon 4, she and a spokesperson for the EF said that the city was changed a few times, and as for whether or not Thomas had an influence on the decision against Copenhagen, she said, "He isn't the decision maker. He's a member of the community."

In the spring of 2019, *Coin Jazeera*, a satirical cryptocurrency site, published an article titled "Ethereum Development Halts After Vitalik Discovers Sex." The article asked what had happened to development on Ethereum and said its "special correspondent" Pepe Grenouille traveled to Bangkok to find out. There, Pepe discovered Vitalik's GitHub commits had slowed because he'd been spending time with Thomas Greco, whom the article described as a "shadowy, enigmatic figure who served as special advisor to OmiseGo, the totally not-a-scam billion dollar project which is trying to 'unbank the banked.'...We also learned that Mr. Greco is a highly spiritual man, and Southeast Asia is the perfect place to ~~take advantage of nubile young women~~ practice spirituality to its fullest." Then it quoted someone who said, "Thomas showed Vitalik a...different side of life. The parts of the world that can't be reduced to a line of code or a scalable distributed computing platform. What I'm saying is, he showed Vitalik the power of pussy." There was even a photo of Vitalik, Thomas, and an unidentified Asian woman.

Within a day, all references in the article to Thomas and the photo had been deleted. The reason given for why Vitalik's GitHub commits slowed became "We're not sure what happened to him, he's been a ghost ever since," and the friend is quoted as saying that Vitalik saw a different side of life because of Thailand, not Thomas.[28]

Some of the cofounders' poor judgment when it came to choosing work associates in the early days continued to have ramifications. In September 2019, Steven Nerayoff, the lawyer-turned-technologist who had facilitated the relationship with the US law firm that gave the opinion letter saying ETH was not a security and who had worked closely with Joe on the presale, was arrested for alleged extortion of a company that held an ICO in the fall of 2017.[29] He has pled not guilty and is still awaiting trial.

On October 1, 2019, an email landed in Vitalik's inbox from Chatroulette's Andrey Ternovskiy:

Dear V.
This email is in reference to the post hard-fork White Hat DAO extraBalance legal demand that I have sent in 2016.
 I realize now that all of you had the best possible intentions at heart when you did this. I was extremely wrong to have done these legal threats. I am so sorry. I was very confused and a sad individual. I did have funds locked there, but it is extremely obvious that I had no moral rights whatsoever.

He then said he would like to anonymously donate $200,000 or more to any cause of Vitalik's choosing, adding, "I assume Ethereum Foundation does not need my money."

On October 30, 2019, Andrey called Griff to make sure everything was cool between them. Griff reassured him it was. Looking back now, Andrey says the reason he had the idea to try to crash the price of ETC was that it would be fun, "kind of like playing *Wolf of Wall Street* movie—in the real world," as he put it. He also thought that since ETC was bad, crashing its price "would be like doing service for the community...Ethereum Classic was like a joke. It was like, what is this? But how can there be a copy of the chain worth $100 million or whatever?...Like a Dogecoin." When asked about his legal threats, which he pursued almost as an academic exercise, since these issues were legally unprecedented, he says that, at that time, he was "careless with people," adding, "I was more like a troll," who amused himself trying to make the front page of Reddit. Five years later, having grown up, he thinks his legal letters were "a stupid mistake and bullshit, but back then, I didn't think much of it. I thought it was like fun—like, 'documents.' Before, I was like, 'Cool, lawyers'—like a movie. 'Some mysterious letter.'" Niklas says Bitcoin Suisse cannot talk about its client relationships or even confirm that Andrey is a client. However, he would not refute anything

Andrey said. He also added that if a client wanted to do something with his or her assets on Bitcoin Suisse, the company would be obliged to carry that out as long as it was not illegal.

In November 2019, *The Times* of London reported that Christopher Harborne, who gave £3 million to the Brexit party in 2019, had a Thai "doppelgänger."[30] Chakrit Sakunkrit, whose headshot in the 2014 annual report of a Thai company, Seamico Securities, was the same as Harborne's, also had an identical record of accomplishments as the Brit. He also had the same birth month and year: December 1962. In April 2021, *Protos* reported that Harborne's donations to the Reform UK party, formerly Brexit Party, totaled 13.7 million GBP ($19 million) overall. It noted that Reform UK's total funds raised were 18 million GBP ($25 million), "which means Harborne's donations **made up the bulk** of the party's Brexit funds."[31]

The Poloniex investigation into the DAO attacker was inconclusive. The link between the DAO attacker's return address on ShapeShift and the Swiss businessman turned out to be that they had transacted on ShapeShift at the same time.

However, the Swiss businessperson *had* bought more than one thousand ETH on Bity the night before the attack, knowing the transaction would execute at the ETH price at the time his bank funds arrived—which was the next day, when it dropped to $13.57. (The Ethereum address the Polo investigator attributed to the former Bity employee was actually Bity's "hot wallet" for customer transactions.) But the businessman couldn't have pulled off the attack. Two of his technical associates (including Lefteris's happy friend from DevCon 2) denied they had done it.

That seemed to be the end of the road. As I was wrapping up the book, Avsa reached out, saying Brazilian law enforcement had opened a formal investigation into the DAO—and into him, prompting him to commission a forensics report, discounted by Coinfirm for credit in the book.

Avsa and I began going over the activities of the various addresses associated with the DAO attacker, both from the report and from other data. Hopping back a couple steps from the vanity addresses reveals an address beginning 0xf0e42, which, during the DAO crowdsale, tried to DoS-attack Ethereum.[32]

About two weeks after the crowdsale ended, 0xf0e42 sent 0 ETH to random addresses, increasing blockchain bloat,[33] and entered the DAO 1,001 times, one Wei (0.000000000000000001 ETH) at a time, plus one transaction for 0.000111111111111 ETH.[34] Finally on May 2, 0xf0e42 sent a stream of one-Wei transactions, permanently inconveniencing (as opposed to temporarily clogging) the blockchain.[35] The attacks totaled over fifteen thousand transactions.

After the fork, they moved the Dark DAO ETC to a grandchild DAO.[36] On September 5, they transferred the sum to 0xc362ef, which Avsa called HackerOne,[37] then to 0x5e8f (HackerTwo),[38] from which they donated to the Ethereum Classic developer's fund.[39] (Afterward, the 11-A's vanity address sent HackerTwo 0.693 ETC.)

In late October, the presumed attacker began a digital cat-and-mouse game with ShapeShift, which often froze the ETC they were trying to cash out. At first, the attacker was converting ETC to BTC via ShapeShift, withdrawing to a Bitcoin address beginning 1M2aaN.[40] Their main wallet was HackerTwo, and they cashed out with another that Avsa called HackerThree, periodically topping it up with fifteen thousand to thirty thousand ETC from HackerTwo. On Tuesday, October 25, they made thirty-two conversions from 4:50 a.m. to 10:41 a.m. UTC. Another seventeen trades happened from 11:56 p.m.[41] to 3:15 a.m. UTC on Wednesday.[42] (Eventually ShapeShift blocked 1M2aaN.)

A couple days later, the wallet associated with a Russia-based Ethereum Classic developer named Dexaran sent HackerThree 1.05 ETC.[43] Could Dexaran be the attacker, accidentally transacting between wallets meant to stay separate? Dexaran agreed to be interviewed but did not reply to my last four emails, even when I only asked why he'd sent money to the presumed attacker's wallet. In an interview with an ETC supporter, he denied being the attacker: "If I were [T]heDAO hacker then why do I need an ICO to fund my own team?"[44]

November 14 was a successful day of cashing out. But it ended with a transaction being blocked,[45] as was another two days later.[46] Having lost 5,326 ETC in three days, the attacker changed tactics: move to a fresh ETC account, send to ShapeShift, withdraw to a new BTC address. The ETC hops took between six and nineteen minutes, but each ShapeShift transaction got sent less than a minute later, as if they were trying to catch ShapeShift off guard and prevent their transactions from being blocked. This worked on December 2, 5, 6, and 7.[47] But six attempts on December 9 and 11 were blocked.[48]

After this, the presumed DAO attacker stopped, leaving over 3.36 million ETC ($181 million as of early October 2021) in HackerTwo,[49] plus 47,262 ETC ($2.6 million in early October 2021) in an address beginning 0x1b63b[50] and smaller amounts in others.

They'd turned 235,114 ETC (then $214,000) into almost 282 BTC ($15 million in early October 2021).

The DAO attacker's cash-outs generally spanned from 0:00 to 15:00 UTC, with almost none from 15:00 to 24:00, though a few occurred in the 22:00 and 23:00 hours. Social media activity for the businessman, his associates, and Dexaran all spanned roughly from 5:00 to 22:00/23:00 UTC, which overlapped with the attacker's presumed sleeping hours. All these people were in Europe/Russia, but the cash-outs mapped onto an Asian-morning-through-evening schedule, like 9 a.m. to midnight in Tokyo.

But the attacker's messages to ShapeShift, though written in shorthand, seemed to be the work of a fluent English speaker: "dao tokens still missing. should be this tx. please send refund tx hash or dao token. thank you." Another author, Matthew Leising, had followed a lead from a copycat attacker, who had sent the Robin Hood group a note, which included the sentence "Don't you do it also to see productive future ?" It led Matthew to a Japanese developer.

I had dismissed the message since it came from a copycat attacker and wasn't in fluent English, making it seem like a different person. The cash-out times made me wonder if I'd been mistaken.

Jumping off from the Coinfirm data, two sources saw that the presumed attacker sent fifty BTC to a Wasabi wallet, a private desktop Bitcoin wallet that aims to anonymize transactions by mixing several together[51] in a so-called CoinJoin, which they did multiple times. However, Chainalysis demixed their Wasabi transactions and tracked their output to four exchanges. An employee at one of them confirmed to a source the funds were swapped for privacy coin Grin and withdrawn to a Grin node. The name of the node contained an alias based on a recognizable Western name.

The IP address for that node also hosted Bitcoin Lightning nodes containing that same alias. The IP address for all those nodes was consistent for eighteen months; it was not a VPN.

It was hosted on Amazon Data Services Singapore.

Lightning explorer 1ML showed that a node at that IP had another telling name—this time, the name of a company.

The company was owned by a person with the same Western name as was in the alias used in the Grin node. In fact, he had used that alias on AngelList, Betalist, GitHub, Keybase, LinkedIn, Medium, Pinterest, Reddit, StackOverflow, and Twitter.

The person is based in Singapore. And speaks fluent English.

The cash-out transactions occurred mainly from 8 a.m. until 11 p.m. Singapore time.

And the email address used on that account at the exchange went to a domain name using his alias.

IN SPRING 2016, this person was into the DAO. On May 14, the day Slock.it realized everyone had one more day to get one hundred DAO tokens for one ETH, he posted on social media, laughing at how Slock.it had made an error.

A few days later, in the DAO Slack, he made fifty-two comments, minimum, about the DAO's vulnerabilities. One spurred

him to email Christoph, Lefteris, and Griff. He began by saying he was writing a proposal for the DAO, then said, "For our
due diligence, we went through theDAO code and found a few
things that are worrisome." He outlined scenarios in which an attacker could blackmail account holders, resulting in a target having to exit without any funds, losing their entire deposit, or having
to give the attacker 20 percent of their ETH. Shortly after, he
emailed another attack vector.

Christoph responded, sometimes refuting, sometimes conced-
ing his points. The emails ended with this person writing, "I'll
keep you in the loop if we find anything else."

He found more. On May 28, he wrote three posts about various
vulnerabilities in the DAO. The fourth was a little more alarmist,
calling out Slock.it for not taking his concerns seriously and drawing more attention to the most significant of the vulnerabilities he
had seen. Almost a week later, his last Medium post was about a
venture for blockchain security challenges and invited people to
hack blockchains in various ways.

Two weeks later the DAO attack happened. Afterward, he
tweeted and retweeted posts that were either trolling of Vitalik,
Ethereum, and the DAO or against the hard fork. He seemed
excited when Poloniex listed ETC and by Barry Silbert's "Bought
my first non-bitcoin digital currency... Ethereum Classic (ETC)"
tweet.

Curiously, on July 5, a couple weeks after the attack, he and
Lefteris exchanged Reddit direct messages titled "DarkDAO
counter attack"—though the substance of the messages is unclear
since this person has deleted nearly all his Reddit posts.

He wrote to Lef, "Sorry for not contacting first. I got carried
away from finding it and telling the community that there is a way
to fight back.

"In any case, I don't see any way the attacker can use this."

After Lefteris told him the RHG's plans, this person replied,
"I took down the post." Lefteris responded, "I will keep you up to

date with what we do from now on." The suspect's last message included, "I'm sorry if I messed up the plan."

Upon hearing the name of the suspect, without knowing that evidence indicated he was the DAO attacker, Lefteris immediately said, "He was obnoxious...he was quite insistent on having found a lot of problems," but felt the issues were annoying, not serious. Lefteris, who has never met the suspect, thought his impression came from photos. "He looks a bit full of himself," Lef said, adding that his gut reaction to the name was "Oh god, no, I *hated* that guy."

Hearing that the Dark DAO ETC had been cashed out to a Grin node with the suspect's alias, Lefteris said that if the suspect had instead rescued the funds, the Ethereum community would have given him "huge kudos." Amazed he didn't try to rectify things while the money was frozen, Lefteris thought the attacker was "not a good person...because they would have the choice to actually fix the thing. They had *plenty* of time."

Similarly, Griff felt the DAO attacker's life would have been "way better" if he had informed the community. "He's early Solidity 2016. He would be a hero," said Griff. "He really screwed the pooch...Reputation is way more valuable than money."

In May 2017, the Bitcoin address used by the suspect's company sent 4.6 bitcoins ($10,500) to 1EuUQ (technically an address beginning 1E8Kr clustered with 1EuUQ). That wallet also, from June 2017 to December 2018, sent money to the company's address. 1EuUQ received money from an address beginning 3NNmRt, which interacted with the company's wallet. 3NNmRt also sent money to an address beginning 3N1YdR, which eventually went to an exchange account, which also received the presumed attacker's Wasabi outputs.

A second exchange that had received the attacker's Wasabi outputs told a source that these were converted to Grin on the exchange but not withdrawn.

After reading a fact-checking document with statements showing what would be said about him in the book, the suspect wrote

in an email, "Your statement and conclusion is factually inaccu-
rate"; if I needed, he said, he could give me more details. Despite
three follow-up messages asking for these details, he did not send
them by the time of a deadline I mentioned to him five times.

In a 2016 blog post, he wrote, "I'm a white hat hacker by heart."
But when it came to the DAO, he was a black hat.

With Ming's viselike grip gone, the foundation faced its biggest crisis yet: on Thanksgiving Day, 2019, Vitalik's friend Virgil Griffith, who was one of the five most-powerful people at the
foundation (including members of the shadow government) and
whom people often described as a "chaotic neutral" character, was
arrested at Los Angeles International Airport for allegedly assisting North Korea in evading sanctions.[52] Virgil is awaiting trial and
faces up to twenty years in prison if convicted. Vitalik, who had
known what Virgil had planned to do beforehand, had been neutral on Virgil's choice, deciding that "he is not just an Ethereum
person, but a person, and if he wants to go do things, he can go do
things." So, earlier that year, when Virgil had tweeted his plans to
take a "vacation" in North Korea, Vitalik had replied, "Enjoy!"[53]

In crypto, 2020 felt much like 2016 had—new trends were
popping up that could grow really big, really fast, and new users
were coming in and becoming believers. Billionaire hedge fund
managers admitted to buying bitcoin.[54] Corporations, including
Tesla, one of the world's most valuable companies, and Mass Mutual, the sober insurance giant, socked away money in it. PayPal
added bitcoin, ether, and other cryptos to its offerings.[55] Even
banks were now allowed to store cryptoassets.[56] A new trend in
Ethereum called DeFi flared up—punctuated by frequent attacks,
like mini versions of the DAO.[57] The network also began a momentous transition to a new version called Ethereum 2.0.[58]

As 2021 dawned, bitcoin tripled its 2017 all-time high, breach-
ing $60,000, and ether blew past its previous record from the
ICO bubble, surpassing $2,000 then $3,000, and even $4,000.
By late August, even Charles's blockchain, Cardano, likely buoyed

by the fact that it had a circulating supply of 33 billion coins (as opposed to 117 million for ETH and 18.8 million for Bitcoin), had reached a market cap of around $90 billion, and briefly become the third-largest cryptocurrency. A new CryptoKitties-like game called NBA Top Shot, which sold digital collectibles (aka non-fungible tokens, or NFTs) of basketball highlight clips, generated more than $700 million in sales by late August.[59] Major artists like Kings of Leon and Grimes made millions selling Ethereum-based digital collectibles.[60] Storied auction house Christie's sold an NFT for $69 million, shattering the record for previous online auctions—and, in another first, accepted payment in ether. Someone bought an NFT of a clip art rock called an EtherRock for about $2.9 million.[61] In August, the biggest platform for buying NFTs, OpenSea, closed the month at more than $3 billion in monthly volume,[62] the same as 16-year-old Etsy had done in the previous quarter.[63] Jpegs of cartoon-like "CryptoPunks" and bored apes from the Bored Ape Yacht Club flooded profile pics on Crypto Twitter, where people debated whether NFTs were the ICOs of 2021.[64] It looked like the early stages of a second big cryptocurrency craze.

Timeline

2011

Late winter	Vitalik starts learning about Bitcoin, writing for *Bitcoin Weekly*
June 1	*Gawker* article, "The Underground Website Where You Can Buy Any Drug Imaginable," is published
	Bitcoin price shoots up from less than $9 to almost $32 within a week
August	Vitalik becomes a writer for *Bitcoin Magazine*

2012

May	*Bitcoin Magazine* publishes its inaugural issue
	Vitalik graduates from high school
September	Vitalik begins at University of Waterloo

2013

May	Vitalik decides to take time off from school
August	Vitalik decides to extend his break from school
September	Vitalik spends a week in a squat with Amir Taaki in Milan
September	Vitalik spends four to six weeks in Israel; has revelation about "layer 2" functionalities on Bitcoin

Early October	Bitcoin price in low $100s
Early November	Bitcoin price in the low $200s
November 4–8	Vitalik in Los Angeles
November 8– December 10	Vitalik in San Francisco
Mid-November	Bitcoin price in the $400s, breaks through $800
	Vitalik takes walk in the Presidio, where he has a technical breakthrough on Ethereum's structure
November 27	Vitalik sends Ethereum white paper to friends
	Bitcoin price crosses $1,000 for the first time
December 10–11	Vitalik and Anthony Di Iorio attend the Inside Bitcoins conference
December 19	Gavin Wood writes Vitalik
December 25	Jeff Wilcke and Gavin start writing implementations of the Ethereum white paper

2014

January 1	Anthony's Decentral opens in Toronto
January 20–21	Ethereum group arrives in Miami
January 25–26	BTC Miami conference
Mid- to late February	Jeff, Gavin, and Joe added as cofounders (announced on blog March 5)
March 1	Zug crew moves into Spaceship
March 5	Ethereum GmbH established in Switzerland
Early April	Gavin publishes the Ethereum yellow paper
April 11–13	Bitcoin Expo in Toronto
May 26	Skype call between Stephan Tual and Mathias Grønnebæk in Twickenham and Mihai Alisie, Taylor Gerring, Roxana Sureanu, and Richard Stott in Zug
May 31–June 1	Vitalik and Gavin in Vienna; receive call from Stephan and Mathias
June 3	Ethereum's Game of Thrones Day
July 9	Stiftung Ethereum created
July 22	Crowdsale begins

September 2	Crowdsale ends
November 24–28	DevCon 0 at ETH Dev in Berlin

2015

Late February to early March	Foundation meeting; decision to remove current board members and recruit "professional board"
February–March	Kelley Becker begins as COO of ETH Dev UG
June 12	Anthony Di Iorio accused of holding one of the footballs "hostage"
Mid-June	Wayne Hennessy-Barrett, Lars Klawitter, and Vadim Levitin are brought on as board members
	Ming Chan is hired as executive director
July 30	Ethereum launches
~August 1–2	Ming makes accusation against Vadim
Week of August 9	Stephan tries to get Vitalik to change early contributor allocations
August 10	First version of MyEtherWallet created
August 15	Ethereum Foundation pays early contributors
August 16	Stephan and Vitalik argue on Reddit about early contributor distributions
August 18	MyEtherWallet domain name registered
Mid- to late August	Stephan fired
August 22–23	First Ethereum Foundation board meeting
~September 2–7	Vitalik, Ming, and Casey stay at a cabin in Toronto
September 11	Casey, Ming, Vitalik, Joe Lubin, Andrew Keys, and others meet at ConsenSys about DevCon 1
September 28	Vitalik publishes blog post about how Ethereum is close to running out of money
	Board directors send official resignation letter
November 9–13	DevCon 1 in London
	Christoph Jentzsch demonstrates the Slock; announces the DAO
Late November/ early December	Gavin fired

2016

January 24	ETH closes above $2
February 2	Ethcore publishes a blog post about how Parity is the fastest Ethereum client
February 11	ETH closes above $6 for the first time
March 2	The DAO is added to GitHub
March 13	ETH hits a new high of $15.26; Vitalik feels comfortable about the Ethereum Foundation's multiyear runway
Mid-April	Ming reams Hyperledger's Brian Behlendorf in phone call
April 25	Vitalik, Gavin, and others from the Ethereum Foundation announced as DAO curators
April 26	Announcement about establishment of DAO.link
April 29	Slock.it makes first proposal to the DAO
	Taylor Van Orden's fiancé, Kevin, flips a coin to choose the DAO contract
April 30	The DAO sale ("creation period") launches
May 13	Gavin resigns as curator
May 14	Miscalculation of when DAO token price rises
May 24	"Ethereum is the Forefront of Digital Currency" blog post by Coinbase cofounder
May 25	Slock.it makes first DAO security proposal
May 27	Emin Gün Sirer and paper coauthors call for a moratorium on the DAO
May 28	DAO sale ends/DAO created
June 5	Christian Reitwießner discovers the re-entrancy bug exploit, warns other devs about it
June 9	Peter Vessenes publishes a blog post about the re-entrancy attack vector
June 10	Christian also blogs about it
June 11	Vitalik tweets he has been buying DAO tokens since the security news
June 12	Stephan Tual publishes "No funds at risk" blog post

June 14, 02:52 UTC	Child DAO 59, which becomes the Dark DAO, emptied
June 14, 11:42 UTC	DAO attacker begins turning BTC into DAO tokens and ETH via ShapeShift in multiple transactions (until June 16)
June 15, 4:26 UTC	DAO attacker votes yes for proposal 59
June 17	DAO hits value of $250 million
03:34 UTC	DAO attacker begins re-entrancy attack on the DAO
12:27 UTC	Attacker stops draining funds
	Greg Maxwell emails Vitalik, "Don't be a greedy idiot"
	That evening, developers later called the Robin Hood Group (RHG) consider attacking the DAO; Alex van de Sande's internet goes down
	Highest day of ETH trading ever
June 18, 10:21 UTC	Someone purporting to be the DAO attacker publishes an open letter about how he or she "rightfully claimed 3,641,694 ether"
	Christoph publishes blog post laying out options
	Robin Hood Group has phone call discussing attempting a rescue
June 19	Lefteris Karapetsas publishes a blog post explaining the options
June 21	Copycat attacks begin; Robin Hood Group rescues 7.2 million ETH
June 22	Lefteris writes another blog post walking through how the hard and soft forks would work
	RHG realizes there is a "suspected malicious actor" in the White Hat DAO
June 23	Bitcoin Suisse posts a letter from the suspected malicious actor to Reddit
June 24	Péter Szilágyi posts soft fork versions of Geth and Parity clients
	Denial-of-service (DoS) attack on soft fork discovered
	Soft fork called off

Early to mid-July	RHG conducts "DAO Wars" (re-entrancy attacks/rescues) on various mini Dark DAOs in order to make sure neither the DAO attacker nor the copycats can cash out
	Polo employee investigating identity of DAO attacker thinks he may have good leads on culprits
July 7	Christoph publishes blog post laying out the remaining issues regarding a hard fork, including how to handle the Extra Balance
July 9	Stephan publishes "Why the DAO robber could very well return the ETH on or after July 14" blog post
July 10	GitHub page for Ethereum Classic (ETHC) created
July 11	RHG whitelists the Dark DAO address in the curator multisig, hoping the DAO attacker will send the siphoned funds there
July 16	Carbonvote shows 87 percent of voters in favor of a hard fork
July 17	Vitalik publishes blog post explaining how the hard fork will happen
July 20	Ethereum hard-forks
	Fat Finger accidentally sends 38,383 ETH to the DAO after the hard fork
July 21	On BitcoinTalk, people post bids to buy "ETHC"
	Kraken trader emails Christoph asking to purchase his "ETHC"
	Gregory Maxwell emails Vitalik offering Bitcoin for his "ETHC"
July 23	DAO attacker sends out "ETHC" from the Dark DAO to a grandchild DAO
	Ethereum Foundation devs start bashing Ethereum Classic in internal Skype chat
July 24	Poloniex lists ETC
	Ethereum Foundation devs continue trashing ETC in internal Skype chat; a conversation screenshot is posted to Reddit
July 25	Barry Silbert tweets that he bought ETC

	Genesis begins offering over-the-counter trading of ETC
July 26	Bittrex and Kraken list ETC
	ETC:ETH hashing power ratio goes from 6:94 in the morning to 17.5:82.5 by late afternoon Eastern Daylight Time
July 27	BTC-e publishes a blog saying most of its ETC was sent to Polo by its users
	Greg Maxwell emails Vitalik again about purchasing his ETC
July 28	White Hat Group (WHG) rescues every last Wei of Fat Finger's money from the DAO
August 1	ETC price rising; ETH dropping
	Vitalik's "I am working 100% on ETH" tweet
August 2	ETH falls to $8.20, while ETC jumps to new high of $3.53, 43 percent of ETH's market cap
	Bitfinex is hacked; crypto markets slump 14 percent
August 5	White Hat Group starts flying into Neuchatel to work on returning ETC
August 6	Call with Bitcoin Suisse
August 7–8	The WHG decides to return money as ETH, not ETC
August 8	The WHG receives its first legal threat, from Berger Singerman
	"Fat Protocols" thesis blog post published
August 9	WHG/Bity deposit ETC to exchanges; deposit blocked on Polo, eventually allowed, then trading on Polo blocked
August 10	By phone, second whale demands ETC, not ETH
August 11	The WHG receives a second legal threat, demanding immediate refund of ETC, from MME
August 12	WHG announces decision to distribute the funds as ETC
August 16	WhalePanda publishes blog post "Ethereum: Chain of liars & thieves"
August 18	Stephan publishes an apology

August 26	Bity posts a revised ETC Withdraw Contract and announces it will be deployed
August 30	Bity/WHG deploy the ETC Withdraw Contract
August 31	Polo and Kraken deposit the WHG ETC into the Withdraw Contract
September 6	The final ETC for the White Hat Withdraw Contract is deposited
	The presumed DAO attacker moves money from the grandchild Dark DAO on ETC to his or her main account, 0x5e8f
September 15	The Extra Balance Withdraw Contract on Ethereum is funded
September 19	DevCon 2 begins in Shanghai
	DoS attacks on Ethereum begin
October	Poloniex employees realize that new owners have been added
	Sometime this fall, Jules Kim grudgingly gives bitcoin bonus to Johnny Garcia
	Sometime mid- to late 2016, Jules and Mike Demopoulos allegedly first oppose and then finally acquiesce to adding two-factor authentication to Polo
October 18	Tangerine Whistle hard fork
October 25	Ethereum Asia Pacific Ltd. incorporated in Singapore
	DAO attacker begins moving ETC to ShapeShift
November 10	Golem ICO
November 22	Spurious Dragon hard fork
December	Jules and Mike purportedly oppose adding a know-your-customer program to Poloniex so the exchange can comply with US sanctions against Iran; finally acquiesce in first half of 2017

2017

January	Early Poloniex employees sign contracts for options for equity in the company, though they are not approved by the board until April

January 25	EF files for trademark on "Enterprise Ethereum" and "Enterprise Ethereum Alliance"
January 31	Nine ICOs in January raise almost $67 million
	MEW hits one hundred thousand visitors in January
	Global weekly crypto trade volume hits about $1 billion
January/February	Jeff Wilcke collapses
February 27	Enterprise Ethereum Alliance announced
	ETH price breaks $15 for the first time since the DAO attack
	Taylor Gerring's contract is not renewed by the EF
February 28	Eight ICOs in February raise just over $73 million
	MEW hits 150,000 visits in February
Spring	Poloniex owners begin seeking buyers
March 11	ETH closes above $20 for the first time
March 24	ETH closes above $50 for the first time
March 31	Six ICOs in March raise $22 million
	MEW hits three hundred thousand visits in March
	Global weekly crypto trade volume reaches over $3 billion
April 24	Gnosis ICO ends
April 27	Ming upset about "volunteer" project manager
April 30	Thirteen ICOs in April raise $85.5 million
	MEW hits 386,000 visits in April
May 4	ETH closes just shy of $97
	In Skype chat, Ming expresses wish to buy domain names associated with Enterprise Ethereum Alliance on the Ethereum domain name system
May 22	ETH closes above $174
	Consensus 2017 conference begins
May 23	SEC "crypto czar" Valerie Szczepanik makes her first comments on initial coin offerings
May 25	Token Summit
May 26–27	Ethereum Foundation delays payment to Ethereum DEV UG

May 30	ETH twenty-four-hour volume exceeds that of BTC for the first time
	ETH price closes just shy of $232
May 31	Basic Attention Token raises nearly $36 million in twenty-four seconds from 210 buyers
	Twenty-two ICOs in May raise $229 million
	MEW hits one million visits in May
June	Security issues—scams, phishing attempts, hacks—pick up
	Poloniex sometimes sees trading volume of $5 billion a week
June 10	ETH price closes just under $338
June 12	Bancor raises $153 million
	ETH price closes above $401
June 14	Kelley, Ming, and Patrick Storchenegger meet; Kelley quits
Mid-June to mid-July	Other ETH Dev office staff—CFO Frithjof Weinert and office manager Christian Vömel—also leave
June 20	Status ICO
June 25	4chan post claims Vitalik is dead
	ETH price falls, closes above $303
June 26	EOS launches its yearlong ICO
June 30	Thirty-one ICOs in June raise nearly $619 million
	MEW hits 2.7 million visits in June
July 1–13	Tezos ICO raises $232 million
July 11	ETH falls to close below $198
July 13–19	Vitalik expresses to Hudson Jameson he would like to remove Ming
July 16	ETH price closes above $157
July 18	CoinDash hack
July 19	First Parity multisig hack
July 25	SEC DAO report
	Thirty-five ICOs in July raise more than $555 million
	MEW sees 2.6 million visits in July

Early August	Ethereum transaction count begins to consistently exceed that of Bitcoin
August 10	Anthony Di Iorio sends legal letter to Vitalik, Ming, and Herbert Sterchi
	Gavin tweets to Vitalik that he could have never built Ethereum without Vitalik
August 31	Forty-one ICOs in August raise nearly $438 million
	MEW hits 3.1 million visits in August
September	Weekly trading volume peaks on Polo drop to $4 billion, down from $5 billion
September 11	Trader from Fidelity and senior vice president from Santander hired at Polo
September 30	Sixty-two ICOs in September raise almost $533 million
	MEW hits 3.5 million visits in September
October 27	Polkadot raises over $140 million in ICO
October 27–November 1	Account presumed to be controlled by devops199 appears to conduct penetration testing, as if looking for contract vulnerabilities
October 31	Eighty ICOs in October raise over $3 billion
	MEW sees 3.5 million visits in October
November 1–4	DevCon 3 in Cancun, Mexico
November 4	ConsenSys "Ming must go" email chain begins
November 5	Polychain portfolio company San Pedro ceremony
November 6	Second Parity multisig attack; funds frozen by devops199
November 8	Bitcoin hard fork called off
November 14	Vitalik fires Ming by phone
November 15	My email inquiring whether Ming has been fired
November 16	Ming posts in Skype channel to "disavow the rumors"
November 23	CryptoKitties soft launch
November 30	Eighty-four ICOs in November raise nearly $1 billion
	MEW sees 4.6 million visits
Early December	Ming, Vitalik, and Casey meet in Hong Kong
December 17	Bitcoin hits new all-time high of $20,000

Late December–early January	Vitalik, Aya Miyaguchi, and Vitalik's friends have a retreat in Thailand
December 31	Ninety ICOs in December raise $1.3 billion
	MEW hits 7.7 million visits

2018

January 1	Friends persuade Vitalik to accelerate Ming's departure
January 4	ETH breaks past $1,000 to a little over $1,045
January 7	ETH trades at $1,153
January 8	ETH hits just under $1,267
January 9	ETH nearly hits $1,321
	Around now, Vitalik sells seventy thousand of the EF's ETH
January 10	ETH reaches $1,417
January 13	ETH hits an all-time high over $1,432
	The *New York Times* publishes "Everyone Is Getting Hilariously Rich and You're Not"
January 20	Vitalik and board meet in San Francisco to finalize transition from Ming as executive director to Aya
Late January	Polo employees informed Circle will be acquiring Polo
January 31	Seventy-nine ICOs raise $1.28 billion
	MEW hits ten million visits
	Ming publishes farewell post on Ethereum blog
	Aya introduced as new executive director

Glossary

51% attack   a type of attack on a blockchain in which an entity or multiple collaborative entities try to take over a network by obtaining more than half the mining power

2FA   see two-factor authentication

account (aka address)   an entity that can receive, hold, and send ether; can be owned either by a person with the private keys or by a smart contract

address   see account

alt-coins   any cryptocurrency that is like Bitcoin with just a few parameters tweaked; also used pejoratively to refer to any coin that is not Bitcoin, aka "shitcoin," often by Bitcoin maximalists

asset   anything that produces economic value

Bitcoin (uppercase)   the first blockchain; the peer-to-peer electronic cash network that runs the software enabling the first cryptocurrency, bitcoin (lowercase), to be transferred without an intermediary

bitcoin (lowercase)   the first cryptocurrency, the digital asset native to the Bitcoin network, with a supply of twenty-one million, giving it characteristics of digital gold

Bity   a crypto exchange, based in Neuchatel, Switzerland, that helped Slock.it form a Swiss legal entity so it could take payment from the DAO and helped the White Hat Group in its attempt to return the ETC from the DAO to DAO token holders

block explorer   a website giving data on the transactions in a blockchain

blockchain a time-stamped, distributed, decentralized, historical ledger of all the transactions on a crypto network; copies of the ledger are held on a global network of computers; it acts as a golden copy of time-stamped transactions that can replace intermediaries normally tasked with executing the transactions

BTC the ticker for bitcoin

carbonvote a type of vote by blockchain that does not require the voter to send coins but instead records the number of coins inside the wallet from which the vote was sent; at the end, it tallies the number of coins in the wallets that sent to the yes address versus the number of coins in the wallets that sent to the no address

chain split see hard fork

child DAO a new instance of the DAO created from coins sent from a parent DAO

client, software the piece of software, like a desktop app, that connects a user's computer to a service; in the case of Ethereum, the software that helped individual users run or connect to the Ethereum network

CME an exchange for trading futures and options

coin another word for cryptocurrency or token

CoinMarketCap a popular cryptocurrency data site ranking coins by their market capitalization

cold storage the most secure way of storing one's crypto, with the private keys held offline

consensus (lowercase) the desired state of a blockchain in which all nodes agree on the state of the ledger and on what transactions should be included in what order

Consensus (uppercase) the largest blockchain conference, held annually in New York City by crypto-focused publication *CoinDesk*

ConsenSys the Brooklyn-based Ethereum venture production studio founded by Joe Lubin, which created Ethereum infrastructure tools and tried to foster decentralized applications on Ethereum

cryptocurrency a digital asset produced by a blockchain that is highly fungible, divisible, and transportable and whose movements can be tracked, unless the chain has built-in privacy features

cryptoeconomics (aka tokenomics)   the game theory that gives different actors in a crypto network the incentive to offer services on it that will keep the decentralized network alive without any company in the middle hiring employees and tasking them with specific responsibilities

curator, DAO   the role that would determine whether or not an English-language proposal to the DAO matched the code submitted and, if the proposal were approved, check that the Ethereum address for receiving funds belonged to the contractor

cypherpunk   a person or ethos advocating strong encryption and privacy preserving technologies, often to evade government detection or surveillance or to push for sociopolitical change

DAO   decentralized autonomous organization; an organization managed via votes on a blockchain

DAO, the   the decentralized venture fund built by Slock.it that aimed to have its token holders decide to which projects it would allocate its capital

dapp (decentralized application)   any application built on a blockchain without an intermediary, such as a company in the center hiring for all the roles to provide all the services; it instead has built-in incentives, usually involving its native coin, to entice individuals and entities to offer those services on the network

Dark DAO (also see mini Dark DAOs)   child DAO 59; the child DAO into which the DAO attacker siphoned 3.64 million ETH

Decentral   the blockchain/decentralized application community center and coworking space in Toronto founded by Anthony Di Iorio

DevCon   the annual Ethereum developer conference

difficulty   a way of keeping a cryptocurrency mining algorithm competitive for miners such that miners will find blocks at a targeted average interval, such as ten minutes on bitcoin or twelve to fifteen seconds on Ethereum

DoS attack   denial of service attack; a way of hobbling a company or blockchain by spamming it, or inundating it with more requests than it can handle

early contributors   people who worked on Ethereum before the crowdsale

East Asia Pacific Ltd. a business entity Vitalik Buterin created in Switzerland to have freedom from Ming Chan; it was used to pay the researchers on his team

EEA Enterprise Ethereum Alliance, the industry organization promoting use of Ethereum in companies

EF Ethereum Foundation

EIP Ethereum Improvement Proposal, a technical suggestion for improving things related to the Ethereum network, such as the protocol, clients, or standards for specific types of contracts

ERC-20 token a token created using a standard for new tokens on Ethereum, so called because it was the twentieth issue posted on a discussion board called Ethereum Request for Comments

ETC the ticker for the ether classic price

ETH the ticker for the ether price

ETH Dev the German business entity (UG) created by Gavin Wood in Berlin; after the crowdsale, it hired the bulk of the developers building the protocol and C++ client

Ethcore (also see Parity) the start-up Gavin Wood founded when he left the Ethereum Foundation, now called Parity

Ethereum Foundation (aka EF or Stiftung Ethereum) the Swiss-based nonprofit organization tasked with stewarding the development of the Ethereum protocol

Ethereum GmbH The Swiss business entity first set up for Ethereum; even after the founders decided to go with a nonprofit structure, the entity held the crowdsale and then was liquidated after the network launch

Etherscan a popular "block explorer" or website offering data for the Ethereum blockchain

exchange a business that enables its customers to trade one asset for another, such as BTC for ETH

Extra Balance the extra people paid to the DAO for DAO tokens after the price increased from 1 ETH:100 DAO in the first half of the crowdsale to 1.05 to 1.5 ETH:100 DAO in the second half

fiat currency a type of money issued by a government by decree and not backed by anything such as gold

fiduciary members   the group of Ethereum cofounders who would also be financially responsible

FUD   fear, uncertainty, doubt. A slang term, often used to dismiss criticism of a cryptocurrency as invalid but sometimes used to describe fake criticism about a cryptocurrency stoked by fans of a rival coin

Game of Thrones Day   the day Ethereum leadership removed Charles Hoskinson and Amir Chetrit

gas   the fee paid to have transactions processed or computation executed on the Ethereum decentralized computer

Geth   the Go Ethereum software client

GitHub   a website for software development

GmbH   the German version of an LLC (limited liability company)

GPU   graphics processing unit; a type of computer chip from a gaming computer that is more powerful than a typical computer's central processing unit, or CPU, making it a more efficient and profitable way to mine cryptocurrencies (though not the most efficient and profitable)

hard fork   a non-backward-compatible software upgrade to a crypto network; usually refers to a "contentious" hard fork, in which one portion of the nodes on a crypto network make the upgrade and another portion of the nodes do not. This causes the nodes that upgrade to create a blockchain separate from the nodes running the original software, resulting in two cryptocurrencies with a shared history until the moment of the fork. (If the whole network simultaneously upgrades, which is a noncontentious hard fork, everyone stays on the same blockchain, and the hard fork will not result in a second chain and cryptocurrency.)

hash   a string of numbers and letters of fixed length that results from running an encryption function on a piece of data so that even changing one punctuation mark in the data will result in a wildly different hash; used to uniquely identify things like blockchain transactions or addresses

hashrate   a way to measure the amount of computing power and security on a blockchain, as well as the efficiency of any miner or piece of mining equipment; technically, the rate at which a blockchain miner can create new hashes per second or do the calculations necessary to win the cryptocurrency being minted by the software

holon   a live-work space

hot wallet   a wallet whose private keys are online, making it more vulnerable to hacking, phishing, and theft

Howey test   the test used by the US Securities and Exchange Commission to determine whether an investment contract is a securities offering

Hyperledger   an open-source community for enterprise blockchains hosted by the Linux Foundation

ICO   initial coin offering; a crowdsale of new tokens, usually in exchange for cryptocurrency, to fund the development of a new blockchain and to distribute the tokens to a large population in order to seed the network with users incentivized to bring more people to the network and thereby see the value of their tokens increase

immutability   the principle that blockchains should be immutable or unchangeable

key   see private key

KYC (know-your-customer) process   identity-verification process to comply with financial regulations

Mailinator   a service offering temporary, public, disposable, anonymous email addresses

maximalist   a person who believes only in one cryptocurrency; most commonly used to describe hardcore Bitcoiners (i.e., "Bitcoin maximalists") but also occasionally used to describe diehard fans of other cryptocurrencies (e.g., "Ethereum maximalists")

miner   someone running cryptocurrency software, usually on specialized equipment, so as to win the new coins minted by the software, usually as a by-product of their participation, and simultaneously offering a benefit to the network, such as security

mini Dark DAOs   the child DAOs into which copycats of the original DAO attacker siphoned their funds

mining   attempting to win new cryptocurrency being minted on a blockchain, in a process that also results in the addition of new transactions to the ledger

mint   to create new units of a crypto asset or currency

multisig   a type of crypto wallet requiring some fraction of multiple possible signatures, such as 2/3 or 3/5, in order to execute transactions for enhanced security

MyEtherWallet (aka MEW)   a website that enabled people to directly interact with the Ethereum blockchain with simple buttons but did not require them to turn over control of their coins to a company

Nakamoto, Satoshi   the anonymous creator of Bitcoin

node   a computer that helps run the software for a cryptocurrency or asset and usually maintains a copy of its blockchain

Parity   the Rust-language Ethereum software client; also the company (originally called Ethcore) founded by Gavin Wood after he left the Ethereum Foundation, which created Ethereum-based software and products, such as a multisignature wallet, and later worked on its own blockchain, Polkadot

phish   a type of hack in which the hacker gets the victim to give a password to the hacker

Polkadot   the decentralized network that Gavin Wood/Parity proposed; its ICO raised $145 million, but shortly thereafter, $95 million was frozen

Poloniex (aka Polo)   the popular alt-coin cryptocurrency exchange that for a long time was the top venue for trading ETH

pre-mining   the mining of a new coin before its release to the public so as to allocate some coins to the creators or early investors as a reward

private key   the cryptographic string of numbers and letters that enables one to send cryptocurrency from a specific public address (the other half of the cryptographically connected "public/private key pair")

protocol   an established set of rules for the computers running a particular type of network; in Bitcoin, the rules processing Bitcoin transactions; in Ethereum, the rules for running decentralized applications

public key/address   the cryptographic string of numbers and letters that function as an address where someone can receive funds as long as they have the matching private key (the other half of the cryptographically connected "public/private key pair")

recursive call (aka re-entrancy attack)   the type of attack used in the DAO that exploits a poor sequence of functions in the execution of a transaction, such as a withdrawal in which the attacker is able to start the withdrawal over and over again before the balance has been updated to reflect the previous withdrawal

re-entrancy attack   see recursive call

replay attack   a type of attack possible after a contentious hard fork without replay protection, in which someone unwittingly makes a transaction that causes them to send coins that they did not mean to send

replay protection   a step taken to split two chains with a shared history up until a hard fork; it prevents a user from sending coins on both chains when they mean to send them on one, which occurs if the different assets are in addresses with the same identifiers

Reward Contract/reward   a contract in the DAO that will pay someone leaving the DAO their future revenues from any investments they have made

Robin Hood Group (RHG)   the group of White Hat hackers who rescued the remaining ETH in the DAO after an initial 3.64 million was drained from it

Securities and Exchange Commission   federal agency that enforces securities laws and regulates exchanges

service providers (the DAO)   contractors that the DAO would hire to create and sell products and services so as to return an investment to DAO token holders

ShapeShift   a crypto-to-crypto exchange that did not hold customers' coins and did not require customers to open accounts or identify themselves; for the trades, ShapeShift was always the counterparty, buying the asset the customer wanted to trade and selling back the asset he or she desired

Silk Road   the first online drug marketplace, made possible because of bitcoin, which enabled drug dealers to accept payment online without using the traditional banking system

Slock.it   the start-up founded by Christoph and Simon Jentzsch and Stephan Tual that tried to fund itself by first creating a decentralized venture fund that could then grant it money

smart contract   a software program, rather than a company or other intermediary, that executes the terms of an agreement between two transacting parties

soft fork   a backward-compatible change in a cryptocurrency protocol; it only narrows what is possible, so nodes running the older software will still accept the new blocks as valid

Solidity   a programming language for writing smart contracts

Spaceship   the original Ethereum house in Baar, the town next to Zug

split DAO   see child DAO

spoke (ConsenSys)   a start-up housed under ConsenSys in which the employees are paid a salary by ConsenSys

Stiftung   a foundation with a purpose that ensures its funds are used in accordance with that mission, overseen by a Swiss government agency

token   specifically, a coin issued in ICOs, usually an ERC-20 token; the term can be interchangeable with cryptocurrency

tokenomics   see cryptoeconomics

transaction fees   fees paid to cryptocurrency miners to process transactions; a higher fee results in a higher likelihood of a transaction being mined and also of it being mined quickly

two-factor authentication   a way of securing an online account to a website by requiring two unrelated methods of identity verification, such as a password and a code sent via text message

tx   abbreviation for transaction

UG   a type of German limited liability company with lower capital requirements

wallet   a device or software program that keeps a user's private keys safe, interacts with blockchains, and makes it possible for the user to view his or her balance and send and receive money

whale   someone so wealthy in a particular cryptocurrency that their holdings could enable them to impact the market

Whitehat DAO   the child DAO into which the Robin Hood and White Hat groups siphoned ETH so as to return it to DAO token holders

White Hat Group (WHG)   the group of White Hat hackers who returned the ETH and ETC to DAO token holders after the hard fork

whitelist   to place a person or thing on a list determined to be trustworthy

yellow paper   the Ethereum paper, written by Gavin Wood, outlining how Ethereum would work on a technical level

Acknowledgments

Writing this book has been the most difficult and fun task of my career. I've learned a lot of life lessons through the process, so while this may be an unusual gesture, I want to thank the book itself for bringing so much joy to my life and also for being such a great teacher.

My sources deserve a ton of credit here. Not only did they share with me a great deal of themselves and their time, often to explain technical details, but they also gave me documents, chat group logs, emails, audio recordings, videos, photos, and a ton of other tips and information. This book really would have been a fraction of what it became if not for the hundreds of people and companies who patiently answered my questions and passed on details that helped me tell this story with nuance and granularity. I cannot emphasize enough the depth of my gratitude to them. To my hundreds of sources, who I cannot name: thank you, thank you, thank you.

Extra special gratitude to the four sources at the end of the book who helped solve one of the biggest mysteries in crypto. You know who you are. And especially to the two at the very, very end who were crucial: every night as you sleep, from now until your last breath, may the universe grace you with extra sprinkles of fairy dust.

With great gratitude and affection, I thank my agent, Kirby Kim, who does multiple jobs for me—all with grace and aplomb. Kirby, you're the best therapist/negotiator/advocate a writer could ever dream of. From Day 1, I've felt like my career was in hands I could trust, and I appreciate it both when things feel uncertain and when opportunity strikes. Thanks for believing in me.

To my editor, Ben Adams, I'm so grateful you took a chance on me and on a crypto book during the lows of the last bear market. From the moment I first spoke with you, I knew we would work well together, and I appreciated having your wise and assured perspective guiding this book. Thanks for sticking with me past the first draft and sculpting this decentralized story into a strong narrative.

To my fact checker, Ben Kalin, for you, I have only the highest gratitude and awe for taking on what would turn out to be your toughest gig ever. I'm beholden to you for learning about blockchain technology in a month, helping me wordsmith every last verb and attribution, and staying up late to check the minutest details. I always felt you had my back, and that gave me a lot of peace and comfort during those last stressful months.

To my production editor, Michelle Welsh-Horst, thank you for keeping the trains running and being understanding even when I was delayed. I appreciated your calm and reasonable approach during those last deadlines.

To Jennifer Kelland, my copy editor, kudos to you for being incredibly detail-oriented and so good at what you do. Even when the near final drafts were still messy, I never doubted for a second that all would be perfect by publication time. To my audiobook producer Kathryn Carroll, much appreciation for letting me narrate my own book, as I know not every author gets to do that. To audiobook director Pete Rohan, thank you for being so fun to work with, for putting up with my flubs, and for being willing to re-record whenever I wanted.

Much gratitude to the marketing and publicity teams at Public-Affairs: to Miguel Cervantes III, for the multitude of excellent marketing tips and for your patience in perfecting every last pixel on the gradient; to Pete Garceau, for my gorgeous cover; and to Johanna Dickson, for quickly and happily getting the word out about the book to all the right places and for managing the many press queries that began coming in. I'd also like to extend a round of applause to designer Trish Wilkinson, proofreader Lori Lewis, and indexer Jean deBarbieri.

To my dear friends and draft readers, Michelle, Ruben, Shirley, Matthias, and Tosin, thank you for reading the unpolished work and giving me helpful feedback that enabled me to make the book more accessible to noncrypto people. I love you all forever and cannot wait to see each of you in person.

Many thanks to Janet Novack and Matt Schifrin, my *Forbes* editors, who have been beyond supportive over the years. I have learned so many reporting and writing tips and techniques from you that, whatever merit is in this book, a big dose of it is due to your generosity in passing on your expertise.

To my many other writing teachers, some who know me and others who don't, including David Hochman, Laura Hillenbrand, Elizabeth Gilbert, Jonathan Weiner, Nicholas Lemann, and Evan Cornog, and to some of my life teachers, Deganit, Sonia, Marie, and Catherine, thanks for your guidance and inspiration.

To my tribes scattered across the globe—the Goats (especially Megy, my accountability partner in the last grueling months), the Glowing Pharaohs (with golden suns to my light partner Sarah and sparkly cosmic love to Jenny, Tahira, Becky, and Crystal, who all helped me immensely in those last weeks), various Binders (especially Bourree, who introduced me to Kirby), and my drawmies (with special thanks to Nancy)—much gratitude to all of you for being there. I love it that I can count on you.

Big, warm thanks to everyone who has helped me with my podcasts/videos—Chris Curran, Anthony Yoon, Daniel Nuss, Mark Murdock, Elaine Zelby, Josh Durham, Shashank Venkat, Bossi Baker, Raelene Gullapalli, Cynthia Hellen, and Stephanie

Bleyer—and to my lawyer, John Mason. I'm so lucky to have had you all as a part of my team.

Similarly, much gratitude to everyone who has read my articles and/or listened to my podcasts or watched my videos over the years. Little did I know when I became obsessed with Bitcoin in 2015 where that passion would lead me.

Much gratitude to the many sponsors of my shows over the years. I truly appreciate the support that you've given me, my podcasts and videos, and the audience of *Unchained*.

Shoutout to Focusmate, which was crucial to my writing this book.

Thanks to my close friends who put up with my long periods of being socially distanced—well before the pandemic—due to this book: in addition to my readers, Stacie, Tom, Beckey, Hande, Mariana, Graciela, Gizem, Vanessa, Jessica, Alden, Fiona, Daniel, and Colleen, you all hold a place in my heart.

To my very cool, creative, and brave ancestors: even though we never shared breath together on Earth, your life stories have inspired me for decades, and I hope my work carries on your legacy.

To my sister Melissa, my brother-in-law Spencer, and my nephews, thanks for being so supportive and entertaining and for listening to me during this book's long gestation.

Most of all, thank you to my parents for being such relaxed, nonjudgmental, humble, nice people. I really hit the jackpot to have been born to and raised by you, and I hope that everything I do makes you proud. I love you both very much.

Notes

Preface

1. Andrew Ross Sorkin, "Lehman Files for Bankruptcy; Merrill Is Sold," *New York Times*, September 14, 2008, http://www.nytimes.com/2008/09/15/business/15lehman.html.
2. Gloria McDonough-Taub, "The Collapse of Merrill Lynch Now Told in 'Crash of the Titans,'" *CNBC*, November 12, 2010, http://www.cnbc.com/id/40028933; Reuters staff, "TIMELINE: History of Merrill Lynch," *Reuters*, September 15, 2008, http://www.reuters.com/article/us-merrill-idUSN1546989520080915.
3. Tim Paradis, "Stocks End Worst Week Mixed After Wild Session," Associated Press via Wayback Machine, October 11, 2008, https://web.archive.org/web/20081015170539/http://ap.google.com/article/ALeqM5gHs5OM3gFG_DytQQZFbWfgPT08MAD93NULL80.
4. Satoshi Nakamoto, "Bitcoin P2P e-cash paper," metzdowd.com, October 31, 2008, https://www.metzdowd.com/pipermail/cryptography/2008-October/014810.html.
5. James Chen, "Low Interest Rate Environment Definition," Investopedia, November 29, 2020, http://www.investopedia.com/articles/markets/060816/us-interest-rates-why-rates-have-been-low-long-time-gs-jpm.asp.
6. "The March of Financial Services Giants into Bitcoin and Blockchain Startups in One Chart," *CB Insights*, February 19, 2017, https://www

.cbinsights.com/research/financial-services-corporate-blockchain
-investments.

7. "The State of the Token Market," Fabric Ventures and Token
Market, January 31, 2018, https://static1.squarespace.com/static
/5a19eca6c027d8615635f801/t/5a73697bc8302551711523ca
/1517513088503/The+State+of+the+Token+Market+Final2.pdf;
"2017 Venture Capital Investment in Blockchain," *CoinDesk*, last
modified February 18, 2018, https://docs.google.com/spreadsheets
/d/1lDtzMD3Bb-shQCtkVOareMANjo9E7N2JUmQnhBfpl8E
/edit?usp=sharing, sourced from https://www.coindesk.com
/bitcoin-venture-capital/.

8. "Timeline of CME Achievements," CME Group, accessed March
28, 2021, https://www.cmegroup.com/company/history/timeline
-of-achievements.html; "Company Achievements in 2016," CME
Group, accessed March 28, 2021, https://www.cmegroup.com
/investor-relations/annual-review/2016/financials.html.

9. Jared Podnos (@jpodnos), "Cryptocurrency: The Discussion on
Twitter Keeps Growing," Twitter, November 15, 2017, https://blog
.twitter.com/official/en_us/topics/insights/2017/Cryptocurrency-The
-Discussion-on-Twitter-Keeps-Growing.html.

10. "Presidio Forest," National Park Service, last modified March
31, 2012, https://www.nps.gov/prsf/planyourvisit/presidio-forest
.htm; "History of the Presidio," The Presidio, accessed March 28,
2021, https://www.presidio.gov/visit/history-of-the-presidio; "Fort
Point National Historic Site," The Presidio, accessed March 28,
2021, https://www.presidio.gov/places/fort-point-national-historic-site.

Chapter 1

1. Satoshi Nakamoto, "Bitcoin: A Peer-to-Peer Electronic Cash
System," Bitcoin.org, accessed April 3, 2021, https://bitcoin.org
/bitcoin.pdf.

2. "Quick Facts," The Abelard School, accessed April 3, 2021, https://
www.abelardschool.org/quick-facts.

3. Steven Leckart, "The Stanford Education Experiment Could Change
Higher Learning Forever," *Wired* via Wayback Machine, March 20,
2012, https://web.archive.org/web/20140421091649/https://www
.wired.com/2012/03/ff_aiclass.

4. @kiba, "Bitcoin Weekly Looking For Writers," BitcoinTalk, March 25, 2011, https://bitcointalk.org/index.php?topic=4916.msg71816 #msg71816.

5. @kiba, "[RANSOM] Bitcoin Weekly ransoming experiment," BitcoinTalk, June 20, 2011, https://bitcointalk.org/index.php?topic =20235.msg253364#msg253364.

6. Adrian Chen, "The Underground Website Where You Can Buy Any Drug Imaginable," *Gawker*, June 1, 2011, https://gawker.com /the-underground-website-where-you-can-buy-any-drug-imag -30818160.

7. Vitalik Buterin, "Bitcoin and the Goldbugs," *Bitcoin Weekly* via Wayback Machine, June 12, 2011, https://web.archive.org/web /20110617050611/http://bitcoinweekly.com/articles/bitcoin-and-the -goldbugs.

8. Vitalik Buterin, "Social Democracy Enforced in Currency," *Bitcoin Weekly* via Wayback Machine, August 15, 2011, https://web.archive .org/web/20110828021149/http://bitcoinweekly.com/articles/social -democracy-enforced-in-currency.

9. *Bitcoin Weekly* (@BitcoinWeekly) Twitter page, Twitter, accessed April 3, 2021, https://twitter.com/BitcoinWeekly. *Bitcoin Weekly* homepage via Wayback Machine, static for months after September 2011, https://web.archive.org/web/20110601000000*/http://bitcoinweekly .com.

10. Mihai graduated with a degree in cybernetics and economy informatics.

11. Matthew N. Wright, "Pre-order Bitcoin Magazine—Quality Control, Final Revisions on Proofs," BitcoinTalk, January 25, 2012, https://bitcointalk.org/index.php?topic=61017.msg711286 #msg711286.

12. Vitalik Buterin, "Introduction to Bitcoin Terminology Part II," *Bitcoin Magazine*, March 3, 2012, https://bitcoinmagazine.com /articles/introduction-to-bitcoin-terminology-part-ii-1330796614.

13. Vitalik Buterin, "Common Misconceptions About Bitcoin—a Guide for Journalists," *Bitcoin Magazine*, December 29, 2012, https:// bitcoinmagazine.com/articles/common-misconceptions-about-bitcoin -a-guide-for-journalists-1356758643. Note: This article is from December 29, 2012, which is after this point in the book, but few of his articles from before then still exist.

14. Matthew N. Wright, "September 2012 Bet Resolution," BitcoinTalk, February 2, 2013, https://bitcointalk.org/index.php?topic=140654.

15. Ripple homepage via Wayback Machine, April 8, 2013, https://web .archive.org/web/20130408174039/https://ripple.com.

16. Vitalik Buterin, "Mastercoin Suggestion: Contracts for Difference," November 4, 2013, https://bitcointalk.org/index.php?topic=324830.0.

17. J. R. Willett invented the initial coin offering: Laura Shin, "Here's the Man Who Created ICOs and This Is the New Token He's Backing," *Forbes*, September 21, 2017, https://www.forbes.com/sites /laurashin/2017/09/21/heres-the-man-who-created-icos-and-this-is -the-new-token-hes-backing/?sh=4a22cd0b1183.

18. Vitalik Buterin, "Bitcoin in Canada, Part I: Introducing the Bitcoin Alliance of Canada," *Bitcoin Magazine*, October 11, 2013, https:// bitcoinmagazine.com/articles/exploring-the-bitcoin-alliance-of -canada-part-i-1381547131.

19. Anthony Di Iorio (@Anthony Di I.), "Meet at Pauper's Pub in T.O. for a beer and wings and talk all things Bitcoin," Meetup, November 3, 2012, https://www.meetup.com/decentral_ca/events/87122762.

20. Charles Hoskinson, "Charles Hoskinson of the Bitcoin Education Project," Let's Talk Bitcoin, audio posted to YouTube by The LTB Network, June 9, 2013, 0:24, https://www.youtube.com/watch?v =lBrQ07aPsL0.

21. Inside Bitcoins homepage via Wayback Machine, December 10, 2013, https://web.archive.org/web/20131210091116/https://www .mediabistro.com/insidebitcoins.

22. James Ball, "Silk Road: The Online Drug Marketplace That Officials Seem Powerless to Stop," *The Guardian*, March 22, 2013, https:// www.theguardian.com/world/2013/mar/22/silk-road-online-drug -marketplace.

23. "Past Weather in Toronto, Ontario, Canada—January 2014," TimeandDate.com, https://www.timeanddate.com/weather/canada /toronto/historic?month=1&year=2014.

Chapter 2

1. "Past Weather in Miami, Florida, USA—January 2014," TimeandDate.com, https://www.timeanddate.com/weather/usa /miami/historic?month=1&year=2014.

2. "BTC Miami Program Final Preview 5," Scribd via Wayback Machine, February 8, 2014, http://web.archive.org/web /20140208025634/http://www.scribd.com/doc/201301458/BTC -Miami-Program-Final-Preview-5.

3. "Background on the mechanics of the ether pre-sale," *Ethereum Foundation Blog*, July 9, 2014, https://blog.ethereum.org/2014/07/09 /how-to-make-a-purchase-in-the-ether-presale.

4. Gavin Wood (@gavofyork), "Ethereum contributions until February 22, 2014," GitHub, https://github.com/ethereum/aleth /graphs/contributors?from=2013-12-25&to=2014-02-22&type=c; Jeffrey Wilcke (@obscuren), "Go Ethereum contributions until February 22, 2014," GitHub, https://github.com/ethereum /go-ethereum/graphs/contributors?from=2013-12-29&to=2014-02 -22&type=c.

5. Although Gavin didn't tell anyone at the time, he had previously been propositioned by someone who suggested that Gavin "fork" (or make a copy of) the Ethereum codebase before launch and go off and build it himself, but Gavin had refused.

6. Cryptoeconomics is the game theory that gives different actors in a crypto network the incentive to offer services on it that will keep the decentralized network alive without any company in the middle hiring employees and tasking them with specific responsibilities.

7. "Ethereum Booth at the Bitcoin Expo 2014," video posted to YouTube by Ethereum, April 30, 2014, https://www.youtube.com /watch?v=O4nHKA3EsME.

8. Gavin Wood, "ÐApps: What Web 3.0 Looks Like," gavwood.com, April 17, 2014, https://gavwood.com/dappsweb3.html.

9. Gavin Wood, "Less-techy: What Is Web 3.0?," gavwood.com, April 23, 2014, https://gavwood.com/web3lt.html.

10. Armand Tanzarian, "Recap: Central European Bitcoin Expo 2014," *Cointelegraph*, June 5, 2015, https://cointelegraph.com/news/recap _central_european_bitcoin_expo_2014.

11. When Jeff said he would not remain, perhaps others took it to mean he *and* Gavin would not continue, because years later many would say Gavin, seen as the ringleader of the devs, had said this.

Chapter 3

1. "SEC Charges Bitcoin Entrepreneur with Offering Unregistered Securities," SEC, June 3, 2014, https://www.sec.gov/news/press -release/2014-111.
2. Jake Frankenfield, "Howey Test," Investopedia, updated March 29, 2021, https://www.investopedia.com/terms/h/howey-test.asp.
3. "Foundation Ethereum (Foundation Ethereum), in Baar, CHE-292 .124.800, Grienbachstrasse 55, 6340 Baar, Foundation (new registration). Certificate date: 09.07.2014," Swiss Official Gazette of Commerce, July 17, 2014, https://shab.ch/shabforms/servlet/Search ?EID=7&DOCID=1618923.
4. Vitalik Buterin, "Launching the Ether Sale," *Ethereum Foundation Blog*, July 22, 2014, https://blog.ethereum.org/2014/07/22/launching -the-ether-sale.
5. Out of that second allocation, people who worked on the protocol between the crowdsale and network launch could buy ETH from the foundation at the crowdsale price for up to 20 percent of their salaries.
6. "Terms and Conditions of the Ethereum Genesis Sale," Ethereum.org via Wayback Machine, July 23, 2014, https://web.archive.org/web /20140723212709/https://www.ethereum.org/pdfs/TermsAnd ConditionsOfTheEthereumGenesisSale.pdf.
7. "Dan Larimer and Vitalik Buterin at the North American Bitcoin Conference in Miami," video posted to YouTube by BitShares, April 18, 2014, https://www.youtube.com/watch?v=mP82Xm UNgNM.
8. Daniel, "The Coming Demise of the Altcoins (and What You Can Do to Hasten It)," *The Mises Circle*, March 14, 2014, http:// themisescircle.org/blog/2014/03/14/the-coming-demise-of-the -altcoins.
9. @Spoetnik, "[ETH] Ethereum = Scam," BitcoinTalk, July 23, 2014, https://bitcointalk.org/index.php?topic=707237.0.
10. @GameKyuubi, "I AM HODLING," BitcoinTalk, December 18, 2013, https://bitcointalk.org/index.php?topic=375643.0.
11. Via LocalBitcoins.com.
12. "Mittweida," Wikipedia, accessed March 8, 2021, https://en .wikipedia.org/wiki/Mittweida#cite_note-1.

13. Gavin Wood (@gavofyork), "Initial commit, Ethereum / yellowpaper," GitHub, April 2, 2014, https://github.com/ethereum/yellowpaper /commit/0d0d23301d077bbdab5cafae6ab06001e282fae2.

14. Gavin chose yellow because it "seemed like a reasonable choice after white."

15. Shideneyu, "I am a developer and I don't understand the Yellow Paper," Reddit, March 21, 2016, https://www.reddit.com/r /ethereum/comments/4bbnp4/i_am_a_developer_and_i_dont _understand_the_yellow; Polo46, "If you find the Yellow paper hard to read, this will help you," Reddit, October 5, 2016, https://www .reddit.com/r/ethereum/comments/560h6s/if_you_find_the_yellow _paper_hard_to_read_this.

16. Yoichi Hirai (@pirapira), "Remove the modulo 2^{256} effect in the memory size computation #185," GitHub, September 9, 2016, https://github.com/ethereum/yellowpaper/pull/185, "Fix mistakes in DELEGATECALL semantics #187," September 29, 2016, GitHub, https://github.com/ethereum/yellowpaper/pull/187, and "Nitpicking equation (100) #188," GitHub, September 29, 2016, https://github .com/ethereum/yellowpaper/pull/188.

17. Vitalik Buterin, "Olympic: Frontier Pre-Release," *Ethereum Foundation Blog*, May 9, 2015, https://blog.ethereum.org/2015/05/09 /olympic-frontier-pre-release.

18. Gavin Wood, "Another Ethereum ÐEV Update," *Ethereum Foundation Blog* via Wayback Machine, June 15, 2015, https://web .archive.org/web/20150629033357/https://blog.ethereum.org/2015 /06/15/another-ethereum-dξv-update.

19. "What Is Ether?," Ethereum.org via Wayback Machine, August 7, 2015, https://web.archive.org/web/20150807141640/https:// ethereum.org/ether; "Ethereum Frontier Release," Ethereum.org via Wayback Machine, August 2, 2015, https://web.archive.org/web /20150802035735/https://www.ethereum.org.

20. Stephan Tual, "Announcing the New Foundation Board and Executive Director," *Ethereum Foundation Blog*, July 30, 2015, https:// blog.ethereum.org/2015/07/30/announcing-new-foundation-board -executive-director.

Chapter 4

1. Anthony Di Iorio, "Ethereum Foundation is hiring an Executive Director," *Ethereum Foundation Blog*, April 8, 2015, https://blog .ethereum.org/2015/04/08/ethereum-foundation-is-hiring-an -executive-director.
2. Ming Chan (@mingchan88), "Lived in CO for almost a decade...," Twitter, May 10, 2019, https://twitter.com/mingchan88/status /1126683499757428736?s=20.
3. @cjphi, "Looks like the early contributor distribution was released about 20 hours ago from the Ethereum foundation via the multisig smart contract," Reddit, August 16, 2015, https://www.removeddit .com/r/ethereum/comments/3h7oel/_.
4. Stephan Tual (@Ursium), "No, it's not...," August 16, 2015, comment on "Early Contributor Distribution," Reddit, August 16, 2015, https://www.reddit.com/r/ethereum/comments/3h7oel/early _contributor_distribution/cu59240.
5. Vitalik Buterin (@vbuterin), "Okay, let me elaborate...," August 17, 2015, comment on "Early Contributor Distribution."
6. Stephan Tual (@Ursium), "So for the interest of clarity here...," August 17, 2015, comment on "Early Contributor Distribution."
7. Vitalik Buterin (@vbuterin), "The 'I don't remember...,'" August 17, 2015, comment on "Early Contributor Distribution."
8. Vitalik Buterin (@vbuterin), "Also, it's worth noting that...," August 20, 2015, comment on "Early Contributor Distribution."
9. Stephan Tual, "A message from Stephan Tual," *Ethereum Foundation Blog*, September 3, 2015, https://blog.ethereum.org/2015/09/03/a -message-from-stephan-tual.
10. Vitalik Buterin, "The Evolution of Ethereum," September 28, 2015, *Ethereum Foundation Blog*, https://blog.ethereum.org/2015/09/28/the -evolution-of-ethereum.
11. Shanghai's Wanxiang Blockchain Labs.
12. Jemima Kelly, "Nine of World's Biggest Banks Join to Form Blockchain Partnership," *Reuters*, September 15, 2015, https://www .reuters.com/article/us-banks-blockchain-idUSKCN0RF24M2015 0915; Jemima Kelley, "Thirteen More Top Banks Join R3 Blockchain Consortium," *Reuters*, September 29, 2015, https://www.reuters.com /article/banks-blockchain-idUSL5N11Z2QE20150929.

13. "DevCon 1," YouTube, video playlist, last updated March 1, 2016, https://www.youtube.com/playlist?list=PLJqWcTqh_zKHQUFX4Ia VjWjfT2tbS4NVk.

14. "DECVON1: Slock.it—Christoph Jentzsch," video posted to YouTube by Ethereum, January 7, 2016, https://www.youtube .com/watch?v=uy6P5_WQoUI.

15. "Former Ethereum CCO Stephan Tual Joins Slock.it Team," *Slock.it* (blog), November 6, 2015, https://blog.slock.it/former-ethereum-cco -stephan-tual-joins-slock-it-team-9fd956f2408.

16. Ethcore homepage via Wayback Machine, November 23, 2015, https://web.archive.org/web/20151123010243/https://www.ethcore.io.

Chapter 5

1. Gavin Wood, "The last Blog Post," *Ethereum Foundation Blog*, January 11, 2016, https://blog.ethereum.org/2016/01/11/last-blog-post.

2. Vitalik Buterin, "Ethereum Foundation Internal Update," *Ethereum Foundation Blog*, January 7, 2016, https://blog.ethereum .org/2016/01/07/2394/.

3. Parity Technologies, "Performance Analysis," February 2, 2016, *Parity Technologies Blog*, https://www.parity.io/blog /performance-analysis.

4. Gavin Wood (@gavofyork), "ANNOUNCING PARITY, the World's Fastest and Lightest Ethereum Implementation Written in Rust Language," Reddit, February 9, 2016, https://www.reddit .com/r/ethereum/comments/44y9vv/announcing_parity_the_worlds _fastest_and_lightest/cztzz5p.

5. "CoinScrum & Proof of Work Present: Tools for the Future—Gavin Wood," video uploaded to YouTube by Satoshi Pollen, December 10, 2014, https://www.youtube.com/watch?time_continue=13&v=Wdg QI6CA4-E&feature=emb_logo.

6. DAO contributions from June 21, 2015, to July 26, 2016, GitHub, https://github.com/slockit/DAO/graphs/contributors?from=2015-06 -21&to=2016-07-26&type=c.

7. Other DAOs pushed back on Slock.it for giving its DAO the generic name of all DAOs. In the end, they stuck with the name, deciding that once the DAO was created, the DAO token holders could vote on what to christen it.

8. Stephan Tual, "On Contractors and Curators," *Slock.it* (blog), April 9, 2016, originally at https://blog.slock.it/on-contractors-and -curators-2fb9238b2553#.d3447n7i0, now at https://laurashin.com /cryptopians/05/08-On-DAO-Contractors-and-Curators.

9. After a fourteen-day discussion.

10. The forum was to "cater to the communications needs" of not just *the* DAO but all kinds of DAOs.

11. Stephan Tual, "A Primer to Decentralized Autonomous Organizations (DAOs)," *Slock.it* (blog), March 3, 2016, originally at https://blog.slock.it/a-primer-to-the-decentralized-autonomous -organization- dao-69fb125bd3cd, now at https://laurashin.com /cryptopians/05/11-A-Primer.

12. The forum was moved to forum.daohub.org.

13. Homepage of The DAO at daohub.org via Wayback Machine, April 27, 2016, https://web.archive.org/web/20160427120234/http:// daohub.org.

14. Homepage of The DAO at daohub.org via Wayback Machine, April 30, 2016, https://web.archive.org/web/20160430204625/https:// daohub.org.

15. Stephan Tual, "Daohub.org gets a facelift, full scope of The DAO is revealed," *Slock.it* (blog), April 21, 2016, https://web.archive.org/web /20201108111107if_/https://blog.slock.it/daohub-org-gets-a-facelift -full-scope-of-the-dao-is-revealed-4d4c43eaf7b.

16. "The Curator: World-Class Signatories," daohub.org via Wayback Machine, April 27, 2016, https://web.archive.org/web /20160427071543/http://daohub.org/curator.html.

17. This code was called the open-source "Standard DAO Framework."

18. MyEtherWallet homepage via Wayback Machine, April 28, 2016, https://web.archive.org/web/20160428051624/http://www .myetherwallet.com.

19. Judy Gordon, "11 Questions for Blockchain Community Manager, Auryn Macmillan," Medium, February 1, 2019, https://medium.com /omnisparx/11-questions-for-blockchain-community-manager-auryn -macmillan-c0b7997d44d4.

20. Transaction creating DAO Token contract: "Transaction Details," Etherscan, April 30, 2016, https://etherscan.io/tx/0xe9ebfecc2fa101 00db51a4408d18193b3ac504584b51a4e55bdef1318f0a30f9.

21. Wallet that sent roughly $2 million worth of ETH into the DAO (1 ETH, 50,000, 75,000, 135,000, 5.5555, and 53,000): "Transactions: For 0x198ef1ec325a96cc354c7266a038be8b5c558f67," Etherscan, https://etherscan.io/txs?a=0x198ef1ec325a96cc354c7266 a038be8b5c558f67&p=31.
22. For "#DAO #LMDAO" with "Just DAO it" meme, see The DAO (@The_DAO_Project), Twitter, May 2, 2016, https://twitter.com /The_DAO_Project/status/727221296623435776?s=20.
23. Stephan Tual, "The Inexorable Rise of the DAO," *Slock.it* (blog), May 6, 2016, originally at https://blog.slock.it/the-inexorable-rise-of-the -dao-2b6e739b2615#.ao9c9xi8s, now at https://laurashin.com /cryptopians/05/23-The-Inexorable-Rise.
24. By end of day May 6, it had raised $20,867,694.
25. The DAO (@The_DAO_Project), "The #DAO now has 3% of ALL #ETH in existence!! @DAOhubORG...," Twitter, May 7, 2016, https:// twitter.com/The_DAO_Project/status/728904324521308160?s=20.
26. DAOhub (@DAOhubORG), "This is going to be the most epic crowdfunding project in history...," Twitter, May 8, 2016, https:// twitter.com/DAOhubORG/status/729377184054448129.
27. BTCWagering, "And we're supposed to believe this was an honest mistake?...," Medium, May 14, 2016, https://medium.com/@BTC Wagering/and-were-supposed-to-believe-this-was-an-honest-mistake -ba703a58d50a.
28. @ReaderE, "This is the first evidence...," May 14, 2016, comment on "The DAO Creation Period Price Schedule: There is 24 more hours until the price *actually* rises," Reddit, May 14, 2016, https://www .reddit.com/r/TheDao/comments/4jap6d/the_dao_creation_period _price_schedule_there_is.
29. Gavin Wood, "Why I've Resigned as a Curator of the DAO," Medium, May 13, 2016, https://gavofyork.medium.com/why-ive -resigned-as-a-curator-of-the-dao-238528fbd447.
30. Johann Wolfgang von Goethe, "The Sorcerer's Apprentice," trans. Katrin Gygax, accessed March 28, 2021, http://www.gygatext.ch /english_translations_zurich_sorcerers_apprentice.html.
31. 11,727,772.78, to be exact.
32. Gertrude Chavez-Dreyfuss, "Virtual company may raise $200 million, largest in crowdfunding," Reuters, May 17, 2016, https://www

.reuters.com/article/us-blockchain-crowdfunding-idUKKCN0Y82LI
?edition-redirect=uk.

33. Ethereum address that sent 315,000 ETH into the DAO:
"Transactions: For 0x198ef1ec325a96cc354c7266a038be8b5c558f67,"
Etherscan, accessed March 28, 2021, https://etherscan.io/txs?a=0x19
8ef1ec325a96cc354c7266a038be8b5c558f67&p=31.

34. Elaine Ou (@eiaine), "#theDAO is a risk-free investment because
token prices increase by time: Early buyers can split off after
crowdsale...," Twitter, May 16, 2016, https://twitter.com/eiaine
/status/732260022294454272.

35. Stephan Tual, "DAO.Security, a Proposal to guarantee the integrity
of The DAO," *Slock.it* (blog), May 25, 2016, originally at https://blog
.slock.it/dao-security-a-proposal-to-guarantee-the-integrity-of-the
-dao-3473899ace9d, now at https://laurashin.com/cryptopians/05/35
-DAO.Security.

36. @miadeg600, "Slock is trying to loot the DAO...," May 26, 2016,
comment on "DAO.Security, a Proposal to guarantee the integrity
of The DAO," Reddit, May 25, 2016, https://www.reddit.com/r
/ethereum/comments/4l2d7m/daosecurity_a_proposal_to_guarantee
_the_integrity.

37. Dino Mark, Vlad Zamfir, and Emin Gün Sirer, "A Call for a
Temporary Moratorium on the DAO," *Hacking, Distributed*, May
27, 2016, https://hackingdistributed.com/2016/05/27/dao-call-for
-moratorium.

38. Nathaniel Popper, "Paper Points Up Flaws in Venture Fund
Based on Virtual Money," *New York Times*, May 27, 2016,
https://www.nytimes.com/2016/05/28/business/dealbook/paper
-points-up-flaws-in-venture-fund-based-on-virtual-money.html.

39. Alex van de Sande (@avsa), "The Moratorium and how to move forward,"
Reddit, June 1, 2016, https://www.reddit.com/r/TheDao/comments
/4m1t24/the_moratorium_and_how_to_move_forward/?sort=new.

40. Michael del Castillo, "Will The DAO Become Ethereum's Mt Gox?,"
CoinDesk, June 9, 2016, https://www.coindesk.com/dao-can-keep
-becoming-next-mt-gox.

41. In GitHub, where the open-source code was managed.

42. LefterisJP, "DAO Improvement Request 5—Add Option to
withdraw() from the DAO #148," GitHub, May 17, 2016, https://
github.com/blockchainsllc/DAO/issues/148.

43. CryptoCompare Index ETH All Data (Trading Volume Chart), up to the week of June 20, 2016, https://www.cryptocompare.com/coins /eth/charts/USD?p=ALL&fTs=1457413200&tTs=1485061200.

Chapter 6

1. Vitalik Buterin, "Bitcoin Network Shaken by Blockchain Fork," *Bitcoin Magazine*, March 13, 2013, https://bitcoinmagazine .com/articles/bitcoin-network-shaken-by-blockchain-fork -1363144448.
2. A Guest, "Untitled [Ethereum Foundation/exchanges Skype chat log]," Pastebin, June 17, 2016, https://pastebin.com/aM KwQcHR.
3. Peter Vessenes, "More Ethereum Attacks: Race-to-Empty is the Real Deal," *Vessenes* (blog), June 9, 2016, https://vessenes.com/more -ethereum-attacks-race-to-empty-is-the-real-deal.
4. "About Peter," *Vessenes* (blog), accessed March 29, 2021, https:// vessenes.com/about; Christian Reitwiessner, "Smart Contract Security," *Ethereum Foundation Blog*, June 10, 2016, https://blog .ethereum.org/2016/06/10/smart-contract-security.
5. Stephan Tual, "No DAO funds at risk following the Ethereum smart contract 'recursive call' bug discovery," *Slock.it* (blog) via Wayback Machine, June 12, 2016, https://web.archive.org/web /20160617173409/https://blog.slock.it/no-dao-funds-at-risk -following-the-ethereum-smart-contract-recursive-call-bug-discovery -29f482d348b?gi=2c2267d6aa56.
6. Vitalik Buterin (@VitalikButerin), "I will provide my opinion in the way that @Truthcoin would approve of: I have been buying DAO tokens since the security news," Twitter, June 11, 2016, https://twitter .com/VitalikButerin/status/741832934814949377.
7. Child DAO 59 creation transaction: "Transaction Details," Etherscan, June 8, 2016, https://etherscan.io/tx/0x5798fbc45e3b6383 2abc4984b0f3574a13545f415dd672cd8540cd71f735db56.
8. Child DAO 59 creator moves 305,000 DAO tokens to Kraken: "Transaction Details," Etherscan, June 14, 2016, https://etherscan.io /tx/0x0b5dfbbce4c4dad6eb92c0790fa9903cd7f27e70d9cadcd6aa30a6 3c0c11f7d6; child DAO creator moves 306,914.7019250663811563 DAO tokens to Poloniex: "Transaction Details," Etherscan, June 14,

2016, https://etherscan.io/tx/0xf0daeb80b0635bc78eb724660d878
8c6758ffe7f5ce705c943121c43b388d7f0.

9. DAO attack begins, "Transaction Details," Etherscan, June 17, 2016,
https://etherscan.io/tx/0x0ec3f2488a93839524add10ea229e773f6b
c891b4eb4794c3337d4495263790b.

10. DAO attacker exchanging 2 BTC for 7,910.21 DAO tokens via
ShapeShift: on Bitcoin blockchain, see "Summary," Blockchain
.com, June 14, 2016, https://www.blockchain.com/btc/tx/a04811
d0f721000be7ff090a85a7363040d564071073ba26bb3214eea9ce
7a1e, originally via ShapeShift API, https://shapeshift.io/txstat
/1HLmLSobXDdgKDvVcxFNGHAEYaFzENJgDr, now at
https://laurashin.com/cryptopians/06/10a-1HLmL., on Ethereum
blockchain, see "Transaction Details," Etherscan, June 14, 2016,
https://etherscan.io/tx/0xc017561624884dff6916f1e4e6f450cd1c
cefc0c922727eccb8ed791e224c0e2; DAO attacker exchanging 2
BTC for 8,306.09610816 DAO tokens via ShapeShift: on Bitcoin
blockchain, see "Summary," Blockchain.com, June 14, 2016, https://
www.blockchain.com/btc/tx/7999c3b21a8972422cb5fef03934
2f549e793bf052931a5b2a5325dc7c39a15c, originally via ShapeShift
API, https://shapeshift.io/txstat/1HAiPwQsBqSmFpgyBmbPpLJX
uxXEeqEs6T, now at https://laurashin.com/cryptopians/06/10b
-1HAiP., on Ethereum blockchain, see "Transaction Details,"
Etherscan, June 14, 2016, https://etherscan.io/tx/0x099ef900a2b9
959a191a67a58c81897776c66942aac0a7166760a7896c3c52a2; DAO
attacker exchanging 2BTC for 8,306 DAO tokens via ShapeShift:
on Bitcoin blockchain, see "Address," Blockchain.com, June 14,
2016, https://www.blockchain.com/btc/address/1C4dt6HozjP3Ea9
aCdmy54sq4aNSVMDUBp, originally via ShapeShift API, https://
shapeshift.io/txstat/1C4dt6HozjP3Ea9aCdmy54sq4aNSVMDUBp,
now at https://laurashin.com/cryptopians/06/10c-1C4dt., on
Ethereum blockchain, see "Transaction Details," Etherscan, June 14,
2016, https://etherscan.io/tx/0x11476dd78f9495e4c6abde63f973b8
b441cce7c9889715d7096ad416d7d4272e; DAO attacker exchanging
1.4 BTC for 52.02 ETH via ShapeShift: on Bitcoin blockchain, see
"Summary," Blockchain.com, June 14, 2016, https://www.blockchain
.com/btc/tx/04b06448610397cde63253bd4a8551fbcea2bcd61ba
4fd0552b86384eb0fcd18, originally via ShapeShift API, https://
shapeshift.io/txstat/1BBtWCku9TRYkT9ZTvAJKVsYVTBJbpkZ9s,

now at https://laurashin.com/cryptopians/06/10d-1BBtW., on
Ethereum blockchain, see "Transaction Details," Etherscan, June 14,
2016, https://etherscan.io/tx/0x40b63d8b2d6933e126f2707dee9545ad
c54461d24f464a016dc6b9a71ef159cc; DAO tokens in the DAO
attacker's main Ethereum address: "Token TheDAO," Etherscan,
https://etherscan.io/token/0xbb9bc244d798123fde783fcc1c72d3bb8c
189413?a=0x969837498944ae1dc0dcac2d0c65634c88729b2d.

11. DAO attacker voting yes on child DAO 59 from the 0x969 account
using contract 0xc0ee9: "Transaction Details," Etherscan, June
15, 2016, https://etherscan.io/tx/0x1de9b7db4d55af395518b83a49
dafe0c37cb746e840ce9d4bc367cb050dbe6ac; DAO attacker voting
yes on child DAO 59 from the 0xf35e2 account using contract
0xf835a: "Transaction Details," Etherscan, June 15, 2016, https://
etherscan.io/tx/0xb5ff2d7a165baba4ca8d7bf8223af9dcf956ec6a4f4f8
5dbdd3ebea0111251ed.

12. DAO attacker attempts to exchange 0.67744325 BTC on ShapeShift;
the money is returned to the attacker's return address: ShapeShift
API, June 16, 2016, originally at https://shapeshift.io/txstat/1GYm
oQPGh9S9dj3ADnhwK32TRh8U7pjBVD, now at https://laurashin
.com/cryptopians/06/12-1GYmo., on the Bitcoin blockchain, see
"Summary," Blockchain.com, June 16, 2016, https://www.blockchain
.com/btc/tx/afd6fc9cb2910445b126cbfd8a8dd58b4d535935
6688f416635c12b15fcab7bf.

13. DAO attacker exchanges 1.23628167 BTC for 46.87979279 ETH
via ShapeShift, June 16, 2016: on Bitcoin blockchain, see "Summary,"
Blockchain.com, https://www.blockchain.com/btc/tx/8883a039f
4b5df3e90a0aa15fc485dcbc1efbbef3bee32bfa0e985ae63c1e11a,
originally via ShapeShift API, https://shapeshift.io/txstat/17yqy
Lree8URtSnZbZu6S5EMKjTMnzo8b7, now at https://laurashin
.com/cryptopians/06/13-17yqy., on the Ethereum blockchain, see
"Transaction Details," Etherscan, June 16, 2016, https://etherscan.io
/tx/0x512df37c9702e2cbfd761d4f336e6f01911a84a1b3b91f731e9675e
f79b81d13.

14. DAO attacker converted 0.667 BTC into 25 ETH on ShapeShift, June
16, 2016: on Bitcoin blockchain, see Blockchain.com, https://www
.blockchain.com/btc/tx/009ab0293e8f24c76f1d7fce018dfca1059c1bef
6819670d8f11c6c277531bdc, originally via ShapeShift API, https://
shapeshift.io/txstat/14mMb4xdSW8hZtzboHFHVzAUhnwLf11

sSK, now at https://laurashin.com/cryptopians/06/14a-14mMb., on
Ethereum blockchain, see "Transaction Details," Etherscan, June 16,
2016, https://etherscan.io/tx/0xc6a773490f9e69f4bce6dc1c887c52fb5d5
1917be256bbb873ef2c18014cf1a8; DAO attacker exchanges .4 BTC for
14.9258 ETH on ShapeShift, June 16, 2016: on Bitcoin blockchain, see
"Summary," Blockchain.com, https://www.blockchain.com/btc/tx/3b2
6f606cc9e381b48a1aa87585af3611cee6fcfab325c61a216a783a4866f46,
originally via ShapeShift API, https://shapeshift.io/txstat/1FB1MuuCn
G9ERrKqZAcsKUPgy19WReRAub, now at https://laurashin.com
/cryptopians/06/14b-1FB1M., on Ethereum blockchain, see "Transaction
Details," Etherscan, June 16, 2016, https://etherscan.io/tx/0xd120cfdb
68baa17e519cf1e3d18efb35432a77afe8a080961aff42d07199515b;
DAO attacker converts .31304245 BTC into 1,283.55 DAO tokens via
ShapeShift: on the Bitcoin blockchain, see "Summary," Blockchain.com,
https://www.blockchain.com/btc/tx/e90687a4e7f3593e5dee704b801b
46164509e6e887ecc0ac5a3fc8c44723a285, originally via ShapeShift
API, https://shapeshift.io/txstat/1ERErQFpZUjfqmc4HR9SLovx9Qxh
GiZa1Q, now at https://laurashin.com/cryptopians/06/14c-1ERE.r., on
the Ethereum blockchain, see "Transaction Details," Etherscan, June 16,
2016, https://etherscan.io/tx/0x46de32fec895a13373c523a8e20263faf2ae
5410468b3d9af41127d08dd42688.

15. DAO attacker's first successful recursive call attack on the DAO:
"Transaction Details," Etherscan, June 17, 2016, https://etherscan.io
/tx/0x0ec3f2488a93839524add10ea229e773f6bc891b4eb4794c3337
d4495263790b.

16. Stephan Tual, "DAO Security Advisory: live updates," *Slock.it*
(blog) via Wayback Machine, June 17, 2016, https://web.archive.org
/web/20160622212451/https://blog.slock.it/dao-security-advisory
-live-updates-2a0a42a2d07b?gi=e1baac16ac65; Vitalik Buterin,
"CRITICAL UPDATE Re: DAO Vulnerability," *Ethereum
Foundation Blog*, June 17, 2016, https://blog.ethereum.org/2016/06/17
/critical-update-re-dao-vulnerability.

17. "THE FILTER #88 'Tough Day for The DAO,'" interview with
Griff Green, video posted to YouTube by The Filter, June 18, 2016,
https://www.youtube.com/watch?v=GvgTivwzcuo.

18. Last recursive call by DAO attacker on the DAO: "Transaction
Details," Etherscan, June 17, 2016, https://etherscan.io/tx/0xa348da
60799bff3ca804b3e49c96edebea44c5728a97f64bec3e21056d42f6e3.

19. Amount the DAO attacker siphoned: "Contract 0x304a554a310C7e5 46dfe434669C62820b7D83490," Etherscan, June 17, 2016, https://etherscan.io/address/0x304a554a310c7e546dfe434669c62820b7d83 490#analytics.

20. Volume of ETH traded on June 17, 2016: "Ethereum," CoinMarketCap, accessed April 4, 2021, https://coinmarketcap.com /currencies/ethereum/historical-data.

21. WhalePanda, "The Un-ETH-ical fork," Medium, June 18, 2016, https://medium.com/@WhalePanda/the-un-eth-ical-fork -2d87041c9591.

22. Vitalik Buterin, "Thinking About Smart Contract Security," *Ethereum Foundation Blog*, June 19, 2016, https://blog.ethereum.org /2016/06/19/thinking-smart-contract-security.

23. Guest, "An Open Letter," Pastebin, June 18, 2016, https://pastebin .com/CcGUBgDG.

24. @IAMnotA_Cylon, "I know this is a joke…," June 17, 2016, comment on "Critical update RE: DAO Vulnerability," Reddit, June 17, 2016, https://www.reddit.com/r/ethereum/comments/4oiqj7 /critical_update_re_dao_vulnerability/d4d5ne7?utm_source=share &utm_medium=web2x.

25. [Deleted user], "The guy who stole my car…," June 18, 2016, comment on "Critical update RE: DAO Vulnerability."

26. @lehmakook, "It is. Even DAO's own website…," June 17, 2016, comment on "Critical update RE: DAO Vulnerability."

27. Christoph Jentzsch, "What the 'Fork' Really Means," *Slock.it* (blog), June 18, 2016, https://blog.slock.it/what-the-fork-really-means -6fe573ac31dd.

28. This whale had interviewed Slock.it before investing in the crowdsale to make sure Slock.it was legit.

29. Alex van de Sande (@avsa), "Update on the White Hat attack," Reddit, June 21, 2016, https://www.reddit.com/r/ethereum/comments /4p7mhc/update_on_the_white_hat_attack.

30. Avsa, "Update on White Hat attack."

31. Earliest recursive call from Robin Hood rescue: "Contract Internal Transactions: For Address 0xb136707642a4ea12fb4bae8 20f03d2562ebff487," Etherscan, June 21, 2016, https://etherscan .io/txsInternal?a=0xb136707642a4ea12fb4bae820f03d2562ebff4 87&p=15.

32. Second recursive call from Robin Hood rescue: "Contract Internal Transactions: For Block 1745931," Etherscan, June 21, 2016, https://etherscan.io/txsInternal?block=1745931. (For those examining closely, DAO tokens were sent thirty-two times, but ETH was returned only thirty-one times. The last send of DAO tokens was back to the Robin Hood Group's malicious contract, because otherwise those tokens would be burned, and the Robin Hood Group, or any attacker, would have to source new coins.)

33. Third recursive call from Robin Hood rescue: "Contract Internal Transactions: For Block 1745967," Etherscan, June 21, 2016, https://etherscan.io/txsInternal?block=1745967.

34. Copycat DAO attacker begins attempting to drain the DAO: "Contract Internal Transactions: For Address 0xf4c64518ea10f9 95918a454158c6b61407ea345c," Etherscan, June 21, 2016, https://etherscan.io/txsInternal?a=0xf4c64518ea10f995918a454158c6b6140 7ea345c&p=18.

35. Robin Hood Group begins re-entrancy attack with 6 million DAO tokens: "Transaction Details," Etherscan, June 21, 2016, https://etherscan.io/tx/0xf8bf7170b0b380efe43130c99c399953032b3a074af 44ec92f8ced11cbbb30f7. (They were only getting 41,187 ETH back per hit, because the attacker had drained 31% of the DAO, and others had drained a bit more, so the ratio was no longer 100 DAO to 1 ETH, but 100 DAO to 0.685 ETH.)

36. Copycat attacker tries, immediately gives up attacking the DAO: "Contract Internal Transactions: For Address 0xaeeb8ff27288bd abc0fa5ebb731b6f409507516c," Etherscan, June 21, 2016, https://etherscan.io/txsInternal?a=0xaeeb8ff27288bdabc0fa5ebb731b6f40950 7516c&p=2.

37. Alex van de Sande (@avsa), "DAO IS BEING SECURELY DRAINED. DO NOT PANIC," Twitter, June 21, 2016, https://twitter.com/avsa/status/745313647514226688.

38. Alex van de Sande (@avsa), "DAO is now mostly empty. 7.2M ether have been secured so far...," Twitter, June 21, 2016, https://twitter.com/avsa/status/745364898583056385?s=20.

39. van de Sande (@avsa), "Update on the White Hat attack."

Chapter 7

1. Fabian Vogelsteller (@frozeman), "We know the curator...," June 21, 2016, comment on "Update on the White Hat attack."
2. Stephan Tual (@Ursium), "This is being heavily debated...," June 21, 2016, comment on "Update on the White Hat attack."
3. @C1aranMurray, "I was a hardforker but now no need...," June 22, 2016, comment on "Update on the White Hat attack."
4. Christoph Jentzsch, "What the 'Fork' Really Means," *Slock.it* (blog), June 18, 2016, https://blog.slock.it/what-the-fork-really-means -6fe573ac31dd; Lefteris Karapetsas, "A DAO Counter-Attack," *Slock .it* (blog), June 19, 2016, https://blog.slock.it/a-dao-counter-attack -613548408dd7#.c2nmoe60a.
5. "THE FILTER #88 'Tough Day for The DAO,'" interview with Griff Green, video posted to YouTube by The Filter, June 18, 2016, https://www.youtube.com/watch?v=GvgTivwzcuo.
6. Lefteris Karapetsas, "White Hat Siphoning Has Occurred. What Now?," *Slock.it* (blog), June 22, 2016, https://blog.slock.it/white-hat -siphoning-has-occurred-what-now-f7ba2f8d20ef#.mglcr7m9y.
7. Karapetsas, "White Hat Siphoning."
8. Bitcoin Suisse AG (@BitcoinSuisseAG), "Communique from the White hat DAO joiner," Reddit, June 23, 2016, https://www.reddit .com/r/ethereum/comments/4pij7r/communique_from_the_white _hat_dao_joiner.
9. Fabian Vogelsteller (@frozeman), "I can verify its him...," June 23, 2016, comment on Reddit, "Communique from the White hat DAO joiner."
10. "Hard Fork Ethereum to Revert the Hack of The DAO," Change.org, accessed March 29, 2021, https://www.change.org/p/ethereum-hard -fork-ethereum-to-revert-the-hack-of-the-dao.
11. Jan Kocjan, "Hard fork to revert stolen DAO funds," The DAO, June 18, 2016, https://dao.consider.it/hard-fork-to-revert-stolen-dao-funds.
12. Stephan Tual (@stephantual), ".@el33th4xor was aware of exploit but didn't inform the DAO security group he joined on 5/31 #theDAO," Twitter, June 20, 2016, https://twitter.com/stephantual/status/74501 3737074081792?s=20.
13. Emin Gün Sirer (@el33th4xor), "These guys will do anything except admit failure and take responsibility," Twitter, June 20, 2016, https:// twitter.com/el33th4xor/status/745016651800805376?s=20.

428 Notes to Chapter 7

14. Emin Gün Sirer (@el33th4xor), "If the ETH community bails out the DAO (and I believe they should), we need to put in place a social wall around Slockit to avoid a repeat," Twitter, June 21, 2016, https://twitter.com/el33th4xor/status/745231124583026688?s=20.

15. Taylor Van Orden (@insomniasexx), "And THIS is the hate I am talking about...," June 22, 2016, comment on "Cornell Professor Calls for DAO 2.0 Movement," Reddit, June 22, 2016, https://www .reddit.com/r/ethereum/comments/4pcsq8/cornell_professor_calls_for _dao_20_movement/d4jwbce/?utm_source=reddit&utm_medium =web2x&context=3.

16. Emin Gün Sirer (@el33th4xor), "Hi there, I'm the professor to whom you said, 'grow the fuck up.'...," June 23, 2016, comment on "Cornell Professor Calls for DAO 2.0 Movement."

17. Stephan Tual (@stephantual), "The only acceptable way forward," Twitter, June 17, 2016, https://twitter.com/stephantual/status/743856 574620270592?s=20.

18. @Revofever, "Posting memes after you've caused your investors to lose millions...only in crypto," Twitter, June 17, 2016, https://twitter .com/revofever/status/743929415751573504?s=20 (tweet no longer available).

19. Ryan Radloff (@RyanRadloff), "don't worry man, if things don't work out this time we can just fork again, then fork after that if the last fork doesn't work," Twitter, June 24, 2016, https://twitter .com/RyanRadloff/status/746452955025506304?s=20; Frank F (@Lightrider), "yeah it's super frustrating when people represent things like how safe & secure their robo investment program is to the public," Twitter, June 23, 2016, https://twitter.com/Lightrider/status /746112635549081601?s=20.

20. [deleted user], "Will Stephan Tual Apologize?," Reddit, June 18, 2016, https://www.reddit.com/r/ethereum/comments/4oq6yh/will _stephan_tual_apologize.

21. Péter Szilágyi, "DAO Wars: Your voice on the soft-fork dilemma," *Ethereum Foundation Blog*, June 24, 2016, https://blog.ethereum.org /2016/06/24/dao-wars-youre-voice-soft-fork-dilemma.

22. Fabian Vogelsteller (@feindura), "With the soft fork being vulnerable there are two options left: a hardfork only affecting TheDAOs, or doing nothing...," Twitter, https://twitter.com/feindura/status/7478 36161452875776?s=20.

23. "TheDAO Proposal_ID 242," Etherscan via Wayback Machine, July 8, 2016, https://web.archive.org/web/20160714055313/http://etherscan.io/token/thedao-proposal/242.

24. "TheDAO Proposal_ID 243," Etherscan via Wayback Machine, July 13, 2016, https://web.archive.org/web/20160713002933/http://etherscan.io/token/thedao-proposal/243.

25. "TheDAO Proposal_ID 263," Etherscan via Wayback Machine, July 11, 2016, https://web.archive.org/web/20170722132438/https://etherscan.io/token/thedao-proposal/263; "TheDAO Proposal_ID 265," Etherscan via Wayback Machine, July 10, 2016, https://web.archive.org/web/20160710103342/http://etherscan.io/token/thedao-proposal/265; "TheDAO Proposal_ID 266," Etherscan via Wayback Machine, July 7, 2016, https://web.archive.org/web/20160710103139/http://etherscan.io/token/thedao-proposal/266.

26. White Hat DAO recursive calls with 25.4 million DAO tokens: "Transaction Details," Etherscan, July 11, 2016, https://etherscan.io/tx/0xa08553f20ff46a944e8c3a0a8df8bc56a2c8daea41037ba5b3f212dc07a9b47d.

27. Lefteris Karapetsas (@LefterisJP), "DTH [DAO Token Holders]: Voting request for Counter-Attack Proposals," Reddit, July 4, 2016, https://www.reddit.com/r/ethereum/comments/4r89jq/dth_voting_request_for_counterattack_proposals.

28. [deleted user], "Come on /u/LefterisJP, you leave us hanging…," July 4, 2016, comment on Karapetsas, "DTH: Voting request."

29. Stephan Tual, "Why the DAO robber could very well return the ETH on July 14th," Medium Ursium blog via Wayback Machine, July 9, 2016, https://web.archive.org/web/20160709150904/https://medium.com/ursium-blog/why-the-dao-robber-could-very-well-return-the-eth-on-july-14th-4ecb950c2592.

30. @logical, "Hmmmm. So Stephan Tual thinks…," July 9, 2016, comment on "Why the DAO robber could very well return the ETH on July 14th—Ursium blog," Reddit, July 9, 2016, https://www.reddit.com/r/ethereum/comments/4s0l1k/why_the_dao_robber_could_very_well_return_the_eth.

31. Transaction in which the Robin Hood Group whitelisted the Dark DAO in the multisig: "Transaction Details," Etherscan, July 11, 2016, https://etherscan.io/tx/0x9257c2e0a11de7b7427d4607f5908d6448278070bb73500139387930826fedc0.

32. Christoph Jentzsch, "Options in the Hard Fork," *Slock.it* (blog), July 7, 2016, https://blog.slock.it/options-in-the-hard-fork-90e467483c0.

33. "Vote: TheDAO Hard Fork," Carbonvote.com, accessed March 31, 2021, http://v1.carbonvote.com.

34. Jeffrey Wilcke, "To fork or not to fork," *Ethereum Foundation Blog*, July 15, 2016, https://blog.ethereum.org/2016/07/15/to-fork-or-not-to -fork.

35. Christoph Jentzsch, "Options in the Hard Fork," *Slock.it* (blog), July 7, 2016, https://blog.slock.it/options-in-the-hard-fork-90e467483c0 #.10qltz4hw.

36. Vitalik Buterin (@VButerin), "All monetization schemes fragment...," October 9, 2014, "Comment on 'What's Wrong with Counterparty,'" Reddit, October 9, 2014, https://www.reddit.com/r /Bitcoin/comments/2is4us/whats_wrong_with_counterparty.

37. For instance, two weeks after launch, in the middle of the night, he and others saw that the chain had split due to an error in the Go client, so they fixed it and called all the mining pools to upgrade the client.

38. Vitalik Buterin (@vbuterin), "Quick HF safety tips for users," Reddit, July 17, 2016, https://www.reddit.com/r/ethereum/comments/4t9mzg /quick_hf_safety_tips_for_users.

39. Vitalik Buterin (@vbuterin), "A contract to conditionally send ether to another account post-hF to protect yourself from replay attacks if desired/needed," Reddit, July 17, 2016, https://www.reddit.com /r/ethereum/comments/4t9jv5/a_contract_to_conditionally_send _ether_to_another.

40. WithdrawDAO smart contract: "Contract 0xBf4eD7b27F1d6665 46E30D74d50d173d20bca754," Etherscan, accessed March 31, 2021, https://etherscan.io/address/0xbf4ed7b27f1d666546e30d74d50d173d 20bca754.

41. July 20, 2016, on "Past Weather in City of Ithaca, New York, USA— July 2016," TimeandDate.com, https://www.timeanddate.com /weather/@5122440/historic?month=7&year=2016.

42. "IC3-Ethereum Crypto Boot Camp and Workshop at Cornell University," The Initiative for CryptoCurrencies and Contracts, accessed March 31, 2021, https://www.initc3.org /events/2016-07-20-IC3-Ethereum-Crypto-Boot-Camp-and -Workshop-at-Cornell-University.html.

43. Christoph Jentzsch, "What an accomplishment!," *Slock.it* (blog), July 20, 2016, https://blog.slock.it/what-an-accomplishment -3e7ddea8b91d.

44. @pokerman69, "These guys have some nerve...," July 20, 2016, comment on "What an accomplishment!—Slock.it Blog," Reddit, July 20, 2016, https://www.reddit.com/r/ethtrader/comments/4tr62w /what_an_accomplishment_slockit_blog/d5jmhvm?utm_source=share &utm_medium=web2x.

45. "How do I convert my The DAO tokens into ethers using the withdrawal contract after the hard fork?," StackExchange, Ethereum, July 19, 2016, updated July 20, July 23, https://ethereum.stackexchange .com/questions/7204/how-do-i-convert-my-the-dao-tokens-into -ethers-using-the-withdrawal-contract-aft.

46. The DAO attacker's DAO tokens move one hop: "Token Transfers: For 0xc0ee9db1a9e07ca63e4ff0d5fb6f86bf68d47b89," Etherscan, June 17, 2016, https://etherscan.io/tokentxns?a=0xc0ee9db1a9e07ca63e4f f0d5fb6f86bf68d47b89&p=1; second hop: "Contract 0xca04D26035 6D19f0D7255041542C9Cbc866F2cB3," Etherscan, July 10, 2016, https://etherscan.io/address/0xca04d260356d19f0d7255041542c9cbc8 66f2cb3#tokentxns; third hop: "Contract 0x038DDC33dB89d12C 4B92607F9ED4a5d6D0D84C2e," Etherscan, July 11, 2016, https:// etherscan.io/address/0x038ddc33db89d12c4b92607f9ed4a5d6d0d84 c2e#tokentxns; fourth hop: "Address 0xBe3aE5Cb97c253DdA67181C 6E34E43F5C275E08b," Etherscan, July 11, 2016, https://etherscan.io /address/0xbe3ae5cb97c253dda67181c6e34e43f5c275e08b#tokentxns; Wallet from which DAO tokens used in DAO attack were sent to Withdraw contract: "Address 0x26D2d3c9020926020b06923A38Fa3 D21572cEb5F," Etherscan, July 23, 2016, https://etherscan.io/address /0x26d2d3c9020926020b06923a38fa3d21572ceb5f#tokentxns.

47. Transaction in which DAO tokens used in DAO attack were sent to Withdraw contract: "Transaction Details," Etherscan, July 23, 2016, https://etherscan.io/tx/0x0774db73b879b2fb4821286ced1c1ea6958b 1799ee9d6c25c58e8bbd91c797cf.

48. @jps_, "Two Chains," Reddit, July 15, 2016, https://www.reddit.com /r/ethereum/comments/4sx5kz/two_chains.

49. Aaron van Wirdum, "Rejecting Today's Hard Fork, the Ethereum Classic Project Continues on the Original Chain: Here's Why," *Bitcoin Magazine*, July 20 2016, https://bitcoinmagazine.com/articles

/rejecting-today-s-hard-fork-the-ethereum-classic-project-continues
-on-the-original-chain-here-s-why-1469038808.

50. A hash represents the number of times a certain type of blockchain network can solve a mathematically difficult puzzle every second.

51. "Ethereum Network Hash Rate Chart," Etherscan, accessed March 31, 2021, https://etherscan.io/chart/hashrate.

52. "Daily Average Hashrate (TH/s)," Ethereum Classic Explorer, accessed March 31, 2021, https://etc.tokenview.com/en/chart /dailyHashrate.

53. @Seccour, "[ETHC] Ethereum Classic Speculation," BitcoinTalk, July 21, 2016, https://bitcointalk.org/index.php?topic=1559738.msg1 5659195#msg15659195.

54. Jameson Lopp (@lopp), "Ethereum Classic has < 1% of @ethereumproject's hashing power and while there are plenty of sellers, no one's buying," Twitter, July 21, 2016, https://twitter.com /lopp/status/756261363819905025.

55. @Mentor77, "Please sell us your eTHC / ETH Classic!," Reddit, July 21, 2016, https://www.reddit.com/r/ethereum/comments/4tzf9o /please_sell_us_your_ethc_eth_classic.

56. Celina Guerrero, "Enterprising Young Composer Founds Sheet Music Publishing House," Musical America Worldwide, January 25, 2012, https://www.musicalamerica.com/news/newsstory.cfm ?archived=0&storyID=26629&categoryID=5.

57. The others were Kraken and a Chinese exchange, Yunbi.

58. Tristan D'Agosta, "An Open Letter from Tristan D'Agosta," Poloniex, press release, accessed March 31, 2021, https://poloniexus .circle.com/press-releases/2015.05.19-Open-Letter.

59. "24 Hour Volume Rankings (Exchange) Week of March 11, 2016," CoinMarketCap via Wayback Machine, March 11, 2016, https:// web.archive.org/web/20160311200242/http://coinmarketcap.com /exchanges/volume/24-hour; "24 Hour Volume Rankings (Exchange) Week of February 21, 2016," CoinMarketCap via Wayback Machine, February 21, 2016, https://web.archive.org/web/20160221144920 /http://coinmarketcap.com/exchanges/volume/24-hour.

60. "Responses to Common ETC Questions," Poloniex, press release, July 27, 2016, https://poloniexus.circle.com/press-releases/2016.07.26 -responses-to-common-etc-questions.

61. Poloniex (@Poloniex), "ETC/BTC and ETC/ETH #Ethereum Classic markets added...," Twitter, July 24, 2016, https://twitter.com /Poloniex/status/757068619234803712?s=20.

62. Poloniex (@Poloniex), "All users who had an #Ethereum balance at the moment of the fork now have a matching balance of $ETC," Twitter, July 24, 2016, https://twitter.com/Poloniex/status/7570691 27018315777?s=20.

Chapter 8

1. Heriberto Montalvo (@HMontalvo369), "wow what a lack of morals...," Twitter, July 24, 2016, https://twitter.com/HMontalvo369 /status/757126269951545344?s=20.

2. @Crypto_Bitlord, "the original and the best! This is great news for unadulterated Ethereum!," Twitter, July 24, 2016; tweet since deleted.

3. Chandler Guo (@ChandlerGuo), "I am Chandler Guo, a 51% attack on Ethereum Classic (ETC) is coming with my 98G hashrate http://powtopos.com," Twitter, July 24, 2016, https://twitter.com /chandlerguo/status/757191880740184064?lang=en.

4. "Daily Average Hashrate (TH/s)," Ethereum Classic Explorer, accessed March 31, 2021, https://etc.tokenview.com/en/chart /dailyHashrate.

5. "Ethereum Foundation Skype Chat," Imgur, July 26, 2016, https:// imgur.com/a/DHexx#4I1WrPY.

6. Barry Silbert (@BarrySilbert), "Bought my first non-bitcoin digital currency...Ethereum Classic (ETC)...," Twitter, July 25, 2016, https://twitter.com/barrysilbert/status/757628841938472 961?s=20.

7. Barry Silbert (@BarrySilbert), "For those inquiring, @GenesisTrading is facilitating OTC block trading of Ethereum Classic (ETC). Min block size of $25,000," Twitter, July 25, 2016, https://twitter.com /barrysilbert/status/757705666915995648?s=20.

8. Fellow Traveller (@JZAK07), "It means if you have $25k you had been planning on lighting on fire, this may be more amusing," Twitter, July 26, 2016, https://twitter.com/JZAK07/status /757792669447749643?s=20.

9. "Kraken opens classic ether (ETC) markets and credits ETC to accounts," *Kraken* (blog), July 26, 2016, https://blog.kraken.com /post/227/kraken-opens-classic-ether-etc-markets-and; Barry Silbert (@BarrySilbert), "Ethereum Classic (ETC) added to Bittrex exchange," Twitter, July 26, 2016, https://twitter.com/barrysilbert /status/758010212154507264?s=20.

10. Barry Silbert (@BarrySilbert), "Watch the hash rate. ETC up to 6% http://fork.ethstats.net," Twitter, July 26, 2016, https://twitter .com/barrysilbert/status/757932068261203968; Barry Silbert (@BarrySilbert), "ETH: 3400 GH/s [82.5%] ETC: 720 GH/s [17.5%] http://fork.ethstats.net," Twitter, July 26, 2016, https://twitter .com/barrysilbert/status/758038319322324992.

11. Barry Silbert (@BarrySilbert), "What a day," Twitter, July 26, 2016, https://twitter.com/barrysilbert/status/758067873604665345.

12. Alex van de Sande (@avsa), "Classic feels like a troubled teenager son: you love them, created them, helped them grow, yet all they talk is murdering you on your sleep," Twitter, July 26, 2016, https://twitter .com/avsa/status/757943094293721088.

13. Charles Hoskinson (@IOHK_Charles), "Two words to guarantee downvotes on the ethereum or bitcoin reddit. Put Charles Hoskinson in the title. So glad to be loved:)," Twitter, March 13, 2015, https://twitter.com/IOHK_Charles/status /576497897358823424?s=20; Charles Hoskinson (@IOHK_ Charles), "I never thought I'd tweet this...I'm rejoining Ethereum to start making contributions to Classic. Will report more later," Twitter, July 27, 2016, https://twitter.com/IOHK_Charles/status /758277705766989830?s=20.

14. "Ethereum Classic," BTC-e News via Wayback Machine, July 27, 2016, https://web.archive.org/web/20160729025821/https://btc-e .com/news/230.

15. Barry Silbert (@BarrySilbert), "Given number of people calling me an idiot for buying ETC, I'm feeling real good right now. Reminds me of '12 when I started buying BTC <$10," Twitter, July 30, 2016, https://twitter.com/barrysilbert/status/759384165099896832.

16. Хуёвый Путин (@Banderovetz), "@VitalikButerin Vitaliy is it true that you left ETH and now working with ETC team? Can you kill this rumor once and for all please!," Twitter, August 1, 2016, https:// twitter.com/Banderovetz/status/760200055341056000?s=20.

17. Vitalik Buterin (@VitalikButerin), "I am working 100% on ETH," Twitter, August 1, 2016, https://twitter.com/VitalikButerin/status /760232885483806720?s=20.

18. Mihai Alisie (@MihaiAlisie), "I am working 100% on ETH #ethereum @AkashaProject," Twitter, August 3, 2016, https:// twitter.com/MihaiAlisie/status/760791821287120897?s=20; Joseph Lubin (@ethereumJoseph), "I am working 100% on ETH. @ ethereumproject @ConsenSysLLC," Twitter, August 2, 2016, https:// twitter.com/ethereumJoseph/status/760601142032211968?s=20; Retweets of Vitalik Buterin's "I am working 100% on ETH" tweet: Twitter, accessed March 31, 2021, https://twitter.com/VitalikButerin /status/760232885483806720/retweets.

19. blank (@kristopherives), "What will you do if ETC price overtakes ETH?," Twitter, August 2, 2016, https://twitter.com/kristopherives /status/760597317116305409?s=20.

20. Vitalik Buterin (@VitalikButerin), "I still won't support ETC," Twitter, August 3, 2016, https://twitter.com/VitalikButerin/status/76 0865764236627968?s=20.

21. Stan Higgins, "The Bitfinex Bitcoin Hack: What We Know (and Don't Know)," *CoinDesk*, August 3, 2016, https://www.coindesk.com /bitfinex-bitcoin-hack-know-dont-know.

22. Chris Harborne sends 38,383 ETH into the DAO after the hard fork: "Transaction Details," Etherscan, July 21, 2016, https:// etherscan.io/tx/0xe10c1efa895d2ec1aa343c9d1282acfa3c43183b684 a484023c3f094ab84fb6f.

23. Transaction showing the White Hat hackers had 33.4 million DAO tokens: "Transaction Details," Etherscan, July 28, 2016, https:// etherscan.io/tx/0x3ff544bff23ec89463b247889097300537c1d0690ef 973c93e8bf59990c04983.

24. WhalePanda, "Ethereum: Chain of liars & thieves," Medium, August 16, 2016, https://medium.com/@WhalePanda/ethereum -chain-of-liars-thieves-b04aaa0762cb.

25. Griff Green, "The DAO's Edge Cases Multisig (Post Hard Fork)," Medium, August 2, 2016, https://medium.com/edge-cases-multisig -phf-official-channel/the-daos-edge-cases-multisig-post-hard-fork -2f107380bd61.

26. DAO attacker sends 3.6 million (siphoned) ETC to a grandchild DAO in 10 transactions: "Token Address: 0x10abb5efecdc09581f8b7

cb95791fe2936790b4e," Ethereum Classic Explorer, July 23, 2016, https://etc.tokenview.com/en/address/0x10abb5efecdc09581f8b7cb95 791fe2936790b4e.

27. Gian, by this point, was also a DAO curator.

28. Technically, it was the repository.

29. The function is called "internal transactions."

30. Jordi Baylina (@jbaylina), "Follow Up Statement on the ETC Salvaged from attackDAOs," Reddit, August 12, 2016, https://www.reddit .com/r/EthereumClassic/comments/4xauca/follow_up_statement_on _the_etc_salvaged_from; Alexis Roussel, "The White Hats and DAO Wars: Behind the Scenes," *Bity Blog*, August 13, 2016, https://blog.bity .com/2016/08/14/the-white-hats-and-dao-wars-behind-the-scenes.

31. Griff Green, "$55 Million Shockwave: How the DAO Hack Changed Ethereum," interview by Matt Leising, *CoinDesk*, July 29, 2020, video, 36:35, https://www.coindesk.com/video/55-million -shockwave-how-the-dao-hack-changed-ethereum.

32. A then Polo employee believed that Tristan had not supported the hard fork, thinking it was a bailout to the whales who had put a lot of money into the DAO, and that he also felt token holders should decide whether they wanted ETC or ETH rather than having the WHG decide for them.

33. Baylina, "Follow Up Statement."

34. @openvpn_squid, "So basically you stole 7 million in ETC...," August 12, 2016, comment on "Follow Up Statement."

35. @frozeman, "You are aware, that without their efforts...," August 12, 2016, comment on "Follow Up Statement."

36. WhalePanda, "Ethereum: Chain of liars & thieves."

37. Stephan Tual, "On a personal note, from Stephan Tual," *Slock.it* (blog) via Wayback Machine, August 18, 2016, https://web.archive .org/web/20170623155231if_/https://blog.slock.it/on-a-personal-note -from-stephan-tual-710f32e6eeb.

38. This blog post, formerly at https://medium.com/p/710f32e6eeb /responses/show, has been deleted.

39. The comments formerly at https://www.reddit.com/r/ethereum /comments/4ybe4t/on_a_personal_note_from_stephan_tual_slockit _blog have been deleted.

40. Alexis Roussel (@rachyandco), "ETC withdraw contract to be reviewed," Reddit, August 19, 2016, https://www.reddit.com

/r/ethereum/comments/4yhz8h/etc_withdraw_contract_to_be
_reviewed.

41. [deleted user], "Let's get that etc…," August 19, 2016, comment on Roussel, "ETC withdraw contract to be reviewed."

42. @DaxClassix, "'Free Money!' Part II…," August 19, 2016, comment on Roussel, "ETC withdraw contract to be reviewed."

43. Alexis Roussel, "Whitehat Withdrawal contract—Update and Next Steps," *Bity Blog*, August 26, 2016, https://blog.bity.com/2016/08/26 /whitehat-withdrawal-contract-update-and-next-steps.

44. Alexis Roussel, "Whitehat Withdrawal contract—Last update before deployment," *Bity Blog*, August 29, 2016, https://blog.bity .com/2016/08/29/whitehat-withdrawal-contract-last-update-before -deployment.

45. Roussel, "Whitehat…Last update before deployment," updated August 30, 2016.

46. Poloniex (@Poloniex), "We're waiting to get clearance from law enforcement before releasing the WhiteHat ETC now that the withdrawal contract is ready," Twitter, August 31, 2016, https:// twitter.com/Poloniex/status/770858288783196160?s=20.

47. Jesse Powell (@jewpow) and Taylor Van Orden (@insomniasexx), "We are really the worst…" and "You are the worst because…," comments on "Whitehat Withdrawal contract—Last update before deployment," Reddit, August 30, 2016, https://np.reddit.com/r /ethereum/comments/50781i/whitehat_withdrawal_contract_last _update_before.

48. Poloniex (@Poloniex), "We are preparing to release the WhiteHat ETC to the withdrawal contract within the next several hours," Twitter, August 31, 2016, https://twitter.com/Poloniex/status/7710 81593855307776?s=20.

49. Kraken (@Krakenfx), "Within the next few hours, Kraken will release 499,402.88737 ETC to the WHG's withdraw contract," Twitter, August 31, 2016, https://mobile.twitter.com/krakenfx/status /771081955790065665.

50. DAO attacker sends 3.6 million (siphoned) ETC to a grandchild DAO in 10 transactions: "Token Address: 0x10abb5efecdc09581f8b 7cb95791fe2936790b4e," Ethereum Classic Explorer, July 23, 2016, https://etc.tokenview.com/en/address/0x10abb5efecdc09581f8b7cb 95791fe2936790b4e.

51. 3.6 million siphoned ETC moves from 0x10abb address to 0xc362: "Transaction Info: 0xa4031e961908b82e19911e780ec9836635dc92ce 7444a97f6af8316d55850650," Ethereum Classic Explorer, September 5, 2016, https://etc.tokenview.com/en/tx/2202824/0; 3.6 million siphoned ETC moves from 0xc362 address to 0x5e8f: "Transaction Info: 0x7089794758f739f54fcd17d86f947c1f94dc8ef2d6d9fc16451b3 e5e7eb74cca," Ethereum Classic Explorer, September 5, 2016, https:// etc.tokenview.com/en/tx/2202833/12.

52. Presumed DAO attacker donates 1,000 ETC to Ethereum Classic developers' donation address: "Transaction Info: 0x38d8dda6e d65444762143215ff1c2742b8c16f312766415755661389b1a6198b," Ethereum Classic Explorer, September 5, 2016, https://etc.tokenview .com/en/tx/2202943/1; @bit_novosti, "Call for action: What can I do to help Ethereum Classic project?," Reddit, July 22, 2016, https:// www.reddit.com/r/EthereumClassic/comments/4u4o61/call_for _action_what_can_i_do_to_help_ethereum.

53. DAO attacker's presumed address receives 0.6931 ETC from 11 A's vanity address: "Transaction Info: 0xb0a0cdb4c3991242aefb74a4db d51c377cd4b635613f0d6aebee67047bc32239," Ethereum Classic Explorer, September 6, 2016, https://etc.tokenview.com/en/tx /2206508/1.

54. The average number of calculations it would take to brute-force-derive such a public key is (16^11)/2 times, which is 8.8 trillion. The number sixteen is used in the calculation because such addresses are "hexadecimal," meaning they use 0 to 9 and A to F for a total of sixteen letters and digits. The calculation is to the eleventh power for the eleven As, and then one divides by two to get an average of the number of tries.

55. 0xaaaaaaaaaaa address receives ETH from 0x222222222222fc20 at 8:03:41: "Normal Address: 0xaaaaaaaaaaaaaf7376faade1dcd50b1 04e8b70f3f2," Ethereum Classic Explorer, September 6, 2016, https://etc.tokenview.com/en/address/0xaaaaaaaaaaaaf7376faade 1dcd50b104e8b70f3f2; 0xaaaaaaaaaaaa address receives ETH from 0x222222222222fc20 at 06:03:42 + UTC: "Transaction Details," Etherscan, September 6, 2016, https://etherscan.io/tx /0x9b8f549455673b63145160465f6ed72984e532ea12b850c738e6 7361c7ba6faf; "Transaction Details," Etherscan, September 6, 2016; 0x222222222222fc20 receives ETH from 0xdeadbeefb880:

"Address 0x22222222222fC2025C46a84d8c1fE44265054446,"
Etherscan, June 28, 2016, https://etherscan.io/address/0x2222
2222222fc2025c46a84d8c1fe44265054446; 0xdeadbeefb880
receives from 0x0000000008b4c9: "Address 0xdeAdbEeFb8
80c9C347a173Bb5B69A629389937a9," Etherscan, May 10,
2016, https://etherscan.io/address/0xdeadbeefb880c9c347a173bb
5b69a629389937a9; 0x0000000008b4c9 receives from four other
vanity addresses: "Transactions: For 0x0000000008b4c94610f112
d6bae67a198ca6269d," Etherscan, accessed March 31, 2021, https://
etherscan.io/txs?a=0x0000000008b4c94610f112d6bae67a198ca
6269d&p=3.

56. Presumed DAO attacker sends ETC to other addresses: "Normal
Address: 0x085acc2d9794fc82e88b9b7b561ac3fea56406a9," Ethereum
Classic Explorer, accessed March 31, 2021, https://etc.tokenview.com
/en/address/0x085acc2d9794fc82e88b9b7b561ac3fea56406a9.

Chapter 9

1. Griff Green, "ExtraBalance Withdraw Contract to be Funded on
September 15th," Medium, September 13, 2016, https://medium
.com/curator-multisig-phf-official-channel/extrabalance-withdraw
-contract-to-be-funded-on-september-15th-a800b4d746f0#
.2mbcbpa59.

2. Bok Khoo (@BokkyPooBah), "The DAO ExtraBalWithdraw
Contract Has Now Been Topped Up," Reddit, September 16, 2016,
https://www.reddit.com/r/ethereum/comments/532523/the_dao
_extrabalwithdraw_contract_has_now_been.

3. "Directors," IC3: The Initiative for CryptoCurrencies & Contracts via
Wayback Machine, September 10, 2016, https://web.archive.org/web
/20160910051422/https://www.initc3.org/people.html.

4. "Founder of the Apache Software Foundation Joins Linux
Foundation to Lead Hyperledger Project," Hyperledger, May 19,
2016, https://www.hyperledger.org/announcements/2016/05/19
/founder-of-the-apache-software-foundation-joins-linux-foundation
-to-lead-hyperledger-project.

5. Azure, the first blockchain-as-a-service.

6. IBM was known for building relationships with open-source projects
by contributing code to an open-source foundation and building an

enterprise consulting business around that, as it had done with Red Hat and Linux.

7. "Jerry Cuomo," LinkedIn, accessed April 1, 2021, https://linkedin .com/in/jerry-cuomo-0891902.

8. Specifically, all Ethereum codebases were GPL licensed.

9. An example of such a permissive license would be Apache 2.0.

10. Ian Allison, "Hyperledger Project Reflects on Blockchain Politics," *International Business Times*, January 31, 2017, https://www.ibtimes.co .uk/hyperledger-project-reflects-blockchain-politics-1603381.

11. The Ethereum ecosystem talked on the Light Ethereum Subprotocol (LES); Parity created the Parity Light Protocol (PIP) just for Parity nodes.

12. Some of the complaints were chronicled in Piper Merriam, "An open letter to Gavin and Ethcore," Medium, March 6, 2017, https:// medium.com/@pipermerriam/an-open-letter-to-gavin-and-ethcore -a733714646c5#.5eqmywscm; Piper Merriam (@pipermerriam), "An open letter to Gavin and Ethcore," Reddit, March 6, 2017, https://www.reddit.com/r/ethereum/comments/5xv3yn/an_open _letter_to_gavin_and_ethcore; and Piper Merriam, "An open letter to the Ethereum community," Medium, March 7, 2017, https:// medium.com/@pipermerriam/an-open-letter-to-the-ethereum -community-e03170423e4f.

13. Ming Chan, "Devcon2: Welcome & Introduction Panel," video posted to YouTube by Ethereum Foundation, October 11, 2016, 15:04, https://www.youtube.com/watch?v=1wayaZ1-iBE&list =PLaM7G4Llrb7xqzgOwbvNv63_KM7VH84Rd&index=2&t=0s.

14. For average block time data between July 1 and September 20, 2016, see "Ethereum Average Block Time," YCharts, July 1, 2016, to September 20, 2016, accessed April 1, 2021, https://ycharts.com /indicators/ethereum_average_block_time.

15. Péter Szilágyi (@karalabe), "From Shanghai, with love (1.4.12)," GitHub, September 18, 2016, https://github.com/ethereum /go-ethereum/releases/tag/v1.4.12.

16. Alex van de Sande (@avsa), "Fixed. It seems that the total damage of the vulnerability was that devcon2 presentations are running 30 min late," Twitter, September 19, 2016, https://twitter.com/avsa/status /777738871899422720.

17. Christoph Jentzsch, "Smart Contract Security," video posted to YouTube by Ethereum Foundation, October 25,2016, https://www.youtube.com/watch?v=466bmp6bs9g&list=PLaM7G4Llrb7xqzgOw bvNv63_KM7VH84Rd&index=14&t=0s 11:15-11:35.
18. Jeffrey Wilcke, "The Ethereum network is currently undergoing a DoS attack," *Ethereum Foundation Blog*, September 22, 2016, https://blog.ethereum.org/2016/09/22/ethereum-network-currently -undergoing-dos-attack; Vitalik Buterin, "Transaction spam attack: Next Steps," *Ethereum Foundation Blog*, September 22, 2016, https:// blog.ethereum.org/2016/09/22/transaction-spam-attack-next-steps.
19. Wilcke, "The Ethereum network is currently undergoing a DoS attack."
20. Others did as well: @TommyEconomis, "Why did Gavin leave the Ethereum team?," Reddit, November 12, 2016, https://www.reddit.com/r/ethereum/comments/5clffg/why_did_gavin_leave_the _ethereum_team.
21. Gavin Wood, "Onwards," Parity, October 6, 2016, https://www.parity.io/onwards.
22. Péter Szilágyi (@karalabe), "What else should we rewrite? (1.4.14)," GitHub, September 28, 2016, https://github.com/ethereum /go-ethereum/releases/tag/v1.4.14; @woodaxed, "Into the Woods (1.4.13) not syncing #3049," GitHub, September 27, 2016, https:// github.com/ethereum/go-ethereum/issues/3049; Péter Szilágyi (@karalabe), "Come at me Bro (1.4.15)," GitHub, October 3, 2016, https://github.com/ethereum/go-ethereum/releases/tag/v1.4.15.
23. Hudson Jameson, "FAQ: Upcoming Ethereum Hard Fork," *Ethereum Foundation Blog*, October 18, 2016, https://blog.ethereum.org/2016 /10/18/faq-upcoming-ethereum-hard-fork; Hudson Jameson, "Hard Fork No. 4: Spurious Dragon," *Ethereum Foundation Blog*, November 18, 2016, https://blog.ethereum.org/2016/11/18/hard-fork-no-4 -spurious-dragon.
24. Jameson, "Hard Fork No. 4."
25. "Ethereum Asia Pacific Limited," OpenGovSG, accessed April 1, 2021, https://opengovsg.com/corporate/201629253N.
26. Tagesregister-Nr. 13416 vom 21.10.2016 / CHE-292.124.800 / 03128115, Swiss Official Gazette of Commerce, October 21, 2016, https://shab.ch/shabforms/servlet/Search?EID=7&DOCID =3128115.

Chapter 10

1. Fred Ehrsam, "Ethereum Is the Forefront of Digital Currency," *Coinbase Blog*, May 24, 2016, https://blog.coinbase.com/ethereum-is -the-forefront-of-digital-currency-5300298f6c75.

2. Fred Ehrsam, "Blockchain Tokens and the Dawn of the Decentralized Business Model," *Coinbase Blog*, August 1, 2016, https://blog.coinbase.com/app-coins-and-the-dawn-of-the -decentralized-business-model-8b8c951e734f.

3. Joel Monegro, "Fat Protocols," *USV Blog*, August 8, 2016, https:// www.usv.com/writing/2016/08/fat-protocols.

4. Fabian Vogelsteller (@frozeman), "ERC: Token standard #20," GitHub, November 19, 2015, https://github.com/ethereum/EIPs /issues/20.

5. "Listed Domestic Companies, Total—United States," World Bank, accessed April 2, 2021, http://data.worldbank.org/indicator/CM .MKT.LDOM.NO?locations=US&year_high_desc=false.

6. Kosala Hemachandra (@kvhnuke), "Ether Wallet: Open Source JavaScript Client-Side Ether Wallet," GitHub via Wayback Machine, August 17, 2015, https://web.archive.org/web/20150817002506 /http://kvhnuke.github.io/etherwallet/#.

7. "Whois Record for MyEtherWallet.com," DomainTools, accessed April 2, 2021, https://whois.domaintools.com /myetherwallet.com.

8. MyEtherWallet homepage via Wayback Machine, September 1, 2015, https://web.archive.org/web/20150901202109/http://www .myetherwallet.com.

9. Taylor Monahan (@insomniasexx), "MyEtherWallet Chrome Extension: The Beta Has Arrived," Reddit, February 9, 2016, https:// www.reddit.com/r/ethereum/comments/44vbef/myetherwallet _chrome_extension_the_beta_has.

10. Taylor Monahan (@insomniasexx), "How to participate in 'The DAO' creation via MyEtherWallet (yes…right NOW!)," Reddit, April 30, 2016, https://www.reddit.com/r/ethtrader/comments/4h3xph /how_to_participate_in_the_dao_creation_via; "Withdraw DAO," MyEtherWallet via Wayback Machine, October 3, 2016, https://web .archive.org/web/20161003170011/https://www.myetherwallet.com /#the-dao.

11. Alex Sunnarborg, "Blockchain for CPU? Analyzing Golem's Ethereum Token Sale," *CoinDesk*, November 11, 2016, https://www .coindesk.com/analyzing-golems-blockchain-token-sale.

12. "Golem: Will It Enable the P2P Computing Market?," Smith + Crown via Wayback Machine, November 5, 2017, https://web.archive .org/web/20171105091745/https://www.smithandcrown.com/golem -will-enable-p2p-computing-market.

13. "Enterprise Ethereum," Trademark Electronic Search System (TESS), United States Patent and Trademark Office, accessed April 2, 2021, https://tmsearch.uspto.gov/bin/showfield?f=doc&state=4809: v6zvyt.2.2; "Enterprise Ethereum Alliance," Trademark Electronic Search System (TESS), United States Patent and Trademark Office, accessed April 2, 2021, https://tmsearch.uspto.gov/bin/showfield?f =doc&state=4809:v6zvyt.2.1.

14. Michael del Castillo, "Big Corporates Unite for Launch of Enterprise Ethereum Alliance," *CoinDesk*, February 28, 2017, https://www .coindesk.com/big-corporates-unite-for-launch-of-enterprise -ethereum-alliance.

15. "Week in Ethereum News: February 19, 2017," Week in Ethereum News, February 19, 2017, https://weekinethereumnews.com/week-in -ethereum-news-february-19-2017.

16. Jules Kim's Twitter profile: ScoobyDoo (@CointrolFreak), Twitter, accessed April 2, 2021, https://twitter.com/CointrolFreak.

17. "Margin Trading," Poloniex via Wayback Machine, August 17, 2016, https://web.archive.org/web/20160817225211/https://poloniex.com /support/aboutMarginTrading.

18. Laura Shin, "The Emperor's New Coins: How Initial Coin Offerings Fueled a $100 Billion Crypto Bubble," *Forbes*, July 27, 2017, https:// www.forbes.com/sites/laurashin/2017/07/10/the-emperors-new -coins-how-initial-coin-offerings-fueled-a-100-billion-crypto-bubble /#3f10cbe16ece.

19. Johannes Pfeffer, "The Gnosis Token Auction," ConsenSys, May 2, 2017, https://media.consensys.net/the-gnosis-token-auction-9c2f5 9d2387.

20. "The Aragon Token Sale: The Numbers," Aragon, May 19, 2017, https://blog.aragon.org/the-aragon-token-sale-the-numbers -12d03c8b97d3; Corey Petty, "A Look at the Aragon ICO Investment Distribution," Medium, May 18, 2017, https://medium

.com/blockchannel/a-look-at-the-aragon-ico-investment-distribution
-a78f601229d8.

21. "Consensus 2017: Making Blockchain Real," *CoinDesk* via Wayback
Machine, May 21, 2017, https://www.coindesk.com/events/consensus
-2017.

22. MobileGo homepage via Wayback Machine, May 20, 2017, https://
web.archive.org/web/20170520190735/https://mobilego.io.

23. @aknnig, "Stability of myEtherWallet during hectic ICO," Reddit
via Removeddit, May 3, 2017, https://www.reddit.com/r/ethtrader
/comments/68zgjn/stability_of_myetherwallet_during_hectic_ico.

24. @hiamat, "i had that issue too, my transaction went through for the
3rd try…," May 3, 2017, comment on "Stability of myEtherWallet";
"How Ethereum Mining Works," *CoinDesk*, March 30, 2017, https://
www.coindesk.com/learn/ethereum-101/how-ethereum-works.

25. Taylor Monahan (@insomniasexx), "Holy shit. I think you might be
right…," May 3, 2017, comment on, "Stability of myEtherWallet."

26. Jonathan Keane, "$35 Million in 30 Seconds: Token Sale for Internet
Browser Brave Sells Out," *CoinDesk*, May 31, 2017, https://www
.coindesk.com/35-million-30-seconds-token-sale-internet-browser
-brave-sells.

27. MyEtherWallet (@MyEtherWallet), "WAT #batshitcrazy, 1.89% got
in; $67k in failed fees, largest fee paid: $6,374.51," Twitter, May 31,
2017, https://twitter.com/myetherwallet/status/870029936941162
496?s=20.

28. "Insolvenzverschleppung," Wikipedia, accessed April 2, 2021, https://
de.wikipedia.org/wiki/Insolvenzverschleppung.

29. $525 million in 2017 versus $7.5 million in December 2016:
"CryptoCurrency Market Capitalizations," CoinMarketCap
via Wayback Machine, June 19, 2017, https://web.archive.org
/web/20170619185948/https://coinmarketcap.com/exchanges
/volume/24-hour; "CryptoCurrency Market Capitalizations,"
CoinMarketCap via Wayback Machine, December 19, 2016, https://
web.archive.org/web/20161219192347/https://coinmarketcap.com
/exchanges/volume/24-hour.

30. [deleted user], "IMPORTANT: Bancor's terms state that you can't
participate in the IPO if you're American," Reddit, June 11, 2017,
https://www.reddit.com/r/Bancor/comments/6go169/important
_bancors_terms_state_that_you_cant.

31. "Bancor Network Token (BNT) Contribution & Token Allocation Terms," Medium, June 5, 2017, https://medium.com/@bancor/bancor -network-token-bnt-contribution-token-creation-terms-48cc85a63812.

32. MyEtherWallet (@MyEtherWallet), "We're doing everything we can to keep shit online. CHECK your ACCOUNT—your TX may / may have shows up. 3k+ pending TXs still in pool," Twitter, June 12, 2017, https://twitter.com/myetherwallet/status/874285733707526145.

33. Joon Ian Wong, "Ethereum unleashed the 'initial coin offering' craze, but it can't handle its insane success," Quartz, June 15, 2017, https://qz.com/1004892/the-bancor-ico-just-raised-153-million-on -ethereum-in-three-hours.

34. Wong, "Ethereum Unleashed the 'initial coin offering' craze."

35. "Global Cryptocurrency Charts: Percentage of Total Market Capitalization (Dominance)," CoinMarketCap, accessed April 2, 2021, https://coinmarketcap.com/charts.

36. "The Status Network: A Strategy Towards Mass Adoption of Ethereum," Status, accessed April 2, 2021, https://status.im /whitepaper.pdf.

37. Ryan Shea (@ryanshea), "The Status ICO on Ethereum started just minutes ago and already has over 10,000 unconfirmed TX's worth 450,000 ETH https://slacknation.github.io/medium/018/," Twitter, June 20, 2017, https://twitter.com/ryaneshea/status/8771969583808 10240?s=20.

38. @legosexual, "Can we make a mega thread for people to explain what's happening to ETH today?," Reddit via Removeddit, June 21, 2017, https://www.removeddit.com/r/ethereum/comments/6imd5u /can_we_make_a_mega_thread_for_people_to_explain.

39. Dan Finlay (@danfinlay), "No? Status just raised as much as they could possibly want, for chat stickers and ads," Twitter, June 21, 2017, https://twitter.com/danfinlay/status/877333592346476544?s=20.

40. Joon Ian Wong, "Fake news of a fatal car crash wiped out $4 billion in ethereum's market value yesterday," Quartz, June 26, 2017, https:// qz.com/1014559/vitalik-buterin-dead-a-hoax-on-4chan-crashed -ethereums-price.

41. Vitalik Buterin (@VitalikButerin), "Another day, another blockchain use case," Twitter, June 25, 2017, https://twitter.com/VitalikButerin /status/879127496024772610?s=20.

42. "Global Cryptocurrency Charts," CoinMarketCap.

43. MyEtherWallet (@MyEtherWallet), "Cmonnnnnn 😔 Have you learned NOTHING from the last week?! Take your heads out greedy asses (you too, FOMO investors!) & look around," Twitter, June 26, 2017, https://twitter.com/myetherwallet/status/87927998 7378987008?s=20; MyEtherWallet (@MyEtherWallet), "Sit down—we've got some news for you. Kickass products can exist without a token & taking all the money," Twitter, June 29, 2017, https://twitter .com/myetherwallet/status/880372623225442304?s=20.

44. Jeremiah O'Connor and Dave Maynor, "COINHOARDER: Tracking a Ukrainian Bitcoin Phishing Ring DNS Style," Talos, February 14, 2018, https://blog.talosintelligence.com/2018/02 /coinhoarder.html.

45. MyEtherWallet (@MyEtherWallet), "1/ Alright Crappy Token Creators listen up. I am 100% out of patience. It's 10am. I haven't slept. And you are going to get to hear me rant," Twitter, July 17, 2017, https://twitter.com/myetherwallet/status/886997735911546 880?s=20.

Chapter 11

1. The culprit was a library that Parity was using to deploy the multisig.

2. Blockchain at Berkeley (@CalBlockchain), "WARNING!!," Twitter, July 19, 2017, https://twitter.com/CalBlockchain/status/887742667 928608772?s=20.

3. WhalePanda (@WhalePanda), "Critical security alert for $ETH @ParityTech wallet if you're using it for multisig," Twitter, July 19, 2017, https://twitter.com/WhalePanda/status/88774390105398 0672?s=20.

4. Hirish (@hirishh), "Are you ready for Ethereum Very Classic?," Twitter, July 19, 2017, https://twitter.com/hirishh/status/887769486 606168064?s=20.

5. If I don't Survive, I was BORN FREE! (@Get_Liquid), "So hardfork to get the $32M? Or are those people not well connected to the foundation so fuckem?," Twitter, July 19, 2017, https://twitter.com /Get_Liquid/status/887782487715442689?s=20.

6. Lorenz Breidenbach et al., "An In-Depth Look at the Parity Multisig Bug," *Hacking, Distributed*, July 22, 2017, https://hackingdistributed .com/2017/07/22/deep-dive-parity-bug. On the Parity multisig

attacker cashing out of 50 ETH the day after the attack: "Transaction Details," Etherscan, July 20, 2017, accessed April 2, 2021, https://etherscan.io/tx/0x774fe88a114804eb8484df7b716f381d4b6bae0e7d145d5f820c16c8097bd42b.

7. Parity Technologies (@ParityTech), "IMPORTANT: SECURITY ALERT: https://blog.parity.io/security-alert-high-2/...Move funds in multi-sig wallet created in Parity Wallet 1.5 or higher immediately," Twitter, July 19, 2017, https://twitter.com/ParityTech/status/887747980719206401?s=20.

8. Parity Technologies, "Security Alert," Parity, July 21, 2017, https://www.parity.io/security-alert.

9. Transaction showing WHG member Jordi Baylina received 366 million BAT: "Transaction Details," Etherscan, July 19, 2017, https://etherscan.io/tx/0x9b9ce2bf968aa430e0117627f337ea697b4bb70a450d108f82f13bfadc68c35f; transaction showing WHG member Jordi Baylina received 169.69 FUCKtoken: "Transaction Details," Etherscan, July 19, 2017, https://etherscan.io/tx/0x79251a90595a257399c2bb4421e1f113a1fcf8c80b6c2303adfee32c4ba1da70.

10. Jordan Pearson, "How Coders Hacked Back to 'Rescue' $208 Million in Ethereum," *Vice*, July 24, 2017, https://www.vice.com/en_us/article/qvp5b3/how-ethereum-coders-hacked-back-to-rescue-dollar208-million-in-ethereum.

11. Jordi Baylina (@jbaylina), "Rescued Multisig Owners Can Use a Smart Contract to Request Where the WHG Should Send the Funds," Reddit, July 23, 2017, https://www.reddit.com/r/ethereum/comments/6p4luj/rescued_multisig_owners_can_use_a_smart_contract.

12. Jordi Baylina (@jbaylina), "The WHG has Returned ~95% of the Funds and Now Hold Less Than $10 Million Worth of Rescued Funds," Reddit, July 26, 2017, https://www.reddit.com/r/ethereum/comments/6povrc/the_whg_has_returned_95_of_the_funds_and_now_hold.

13. Mitch Brenner, "How I Snatched 153,037 ETH After a Bad Tinder Date," Medium, September 12, 2017, https://medium.com/@rtaylor30/how-i-snatched-your-153-037-eth-after-a-bad-tinder-date-d1d84422a50b.

14. "Cyber Enforcement Actions: Digital Assets/Initial Coin Offerings," US Securities and Exchange Commission (SEC),

accessed April 2, 2021, https://www.sec.gov/spotlight/cybersecurity
-enforcement-actions; "U.S. SECURITIES AND EXCHANGE
COMMISSION, Litigation Release No. 23870," SEC, June 30,
2017, https://www.sec.gov/litigation/litreleases/2017
/lr23870.htm.

15. Gertrude Chavez-Dreufuss, "U.S. SEC Official Urges Companies
    Issuing Tokens to Protect Investors," Reuters, May 23, 2017,
    https://www.reuters.com/article/us-sec-blockchain-idUSKBN
    18K05Q.

16. @megashira1, "$4.5million USD worth of VERI stolen," BitcoinTalk,
    July 23, 2017, https://bitcointalk.org/index.php?topic=1887061.msg20
    335511#msg20335511.

17. 36,688 exactly (analytics/token transfers): "Address 0x3fff90bF31
    4673194c3A265Ed1c0aA68f59550C4," Etherscan, June 15, 2021,
    https://etherscan.io/address/0x3fff90bF314673194c3A265Ed1c0aA
    68f59550C4#analytics.

18. Homepage of the World's First 100% Honest Ethereum ICO via
    Wayback Machine, June 27, 2017, https://web.archive.org/web
    /20170627123240/https://uetoken.com.

19. "SECURITIES AND EXCHANGE COMMISSION;
    SECURITIES EXCHANGE ACT OF 1934; Release No. 81207
    / July 25, 2017; Report of Investigation Pursuant to Section 21(a) of
    the Securities Exchange Act of 1934: The DAO," SEC, July 25, 2017,
    https://www.sec.gov/litigation/investreport/34-81207.pdf.

20. "A Section 21(a) Report History Lesson: SEC Issues New One
    Cautioning Rating Agencies," TheCorporateCounsel.net, September
    1, 2010, https://www.thecorporatecounsel.net/blog/2010/09/nyse
    -regulation-transfers-its-regulatory.html.

21. Harry Denley (@sniko_), "People need to do their DD. Suicide was
    23 hrs 35 mins ago:/," Twitter, July 28, 2017, https://twitter.com
    /sniko_/status/890935790523600900.

22. MyEtherWallet (@MyEtherWallet), "1. We. Have NOT been
    hacked...," Twitter, July 20, 2017, https://twitter.com/myetherwallet
    /status/888111215448178688?s=20.

23. Muneeb (@Muneeb), "Crypto communities using Slack get targetted
    by phishing attacks and removing unique usernames massively
    adds to that problem," Twitter, October 12, 2017, https://twitter
    .com/muneeb/status/918577964643766272.

24. Harry Denley (@sniko_), "A quick peek into a #phishers mail box. Look at the number of targets (and it's not a full list)—this is for 1 domain," Twitter, August 20, 2017, https://twitter.com/sniko_/status /899342140572131328/photo/1.

25. Lily Hay Newman, "A Very Dumb Mistake Costs Cryptocurrency Investors Big Time," *Wired*, August 21, 2017, https://www.wired.com /story/enigma-ico-ethereum-heist.

26. Laura Shin, "Hackers Have Stolen Millions of Dollars in Bitcoin— Using Only Phone Numbers," *Forbes*, December 20, 2016, https:// www.forbes.com/sites/laurashin/2016/12/20/hackers-have-stolen -millions-of-dollars-in-bitcoin-using-only-phone-numbers.

27. "Swiss Criminal Code, Article 146," Federal Council of the Swiss Confederation, accessed April 2, 2021, https://www.admin.ch/opc/en /classified-compilation/19370083/201903010000/311.0.pdf.

28. Anthony even asked Dmitry, Vitalik's father, who was also in Toronto, to persuade them to talk to him. Dmitry had already intervened in cases when Anthony had split on bitter terms with Decentral employees. Each time, it was like the psychology study showing that if someone were shown a mug to buy and another person were given the same mug to sell, the one selling would believe it could fetch a much higher price. Anthony exhibited an extreme version of the seller's bias. Given his history, when Anthony told Dmitry he believed he was owed what amounted to $155 million, Dmitry was skeptical.

29. "Token Sale," Civic, accessed April 2, 2021, https://tokensale .civic.com; Anthony Di Iorio (@diiorioanthony), "I am an advisor to @skrumblehq," Twitter, April 18, 2018, https://twitter.com /diiorioanthony/status/986604519294291968?s=20; "Anthony Di Iorio," ICO Holder, accessed April 2, 2021, https://icoholder.com/en /ico-advisors/anthony-di-iorio-2618.

30. Simona Pop, "How Blockchain Bounties Helped Our Far-Flung Employees Collaborate," ConsenSys, August 6, 2018, https://media .consensys.net/how-blockchain-bounties-helped-our-far-flung -employees-collaborate-104ddec409ab?gi=23cd544e4291.

31. "Ashoka Finley," LinkedIn, accessed April 2, 2021, https://www .linkedin.com/in/ashoka-finley-813aa223.

32. "Yunyun Chen," LinkedIn, accessed April 2, 2021, https://www .linkedin.com/in/yunyunchen; Sarah Baker Mills, "Blockchain

Designer Profile: Yunyun Chen," *ConsenSys Media*, November 15, 2017, https://media.consensys.net/blockchain-designer-profile -yunyun-chen-7cb6dd2a3386.

33. Some of them reverse-calculated his comments into estimates that, at least at one point, he held 9 percent of all ETH.

34. "Robert Bench," LinkedIn, accessed April 2, 2021, https://www .linkedin.com/in/robert-bench-7a535b11.

35. Cosmos, Dfinity, Polkadot, Tezos, etc.

36. Matthew J. Belvedere, "Unfazed by Wild Swings, Strategist Tom Lee Still Sees Bitcoin Surging Another 600% in 5 Years," *CNBC*, updated September 15, 2017, https://www.cnbc.com/2017/09/15/bitcoin -could-surge-another-600-percent-to-25000-dollars-in-5-years-says -strategist-tom-lee.html; "Tom Lee: Here's Why Bitcoin Will Hit $25,000," *CNBC*, September 15, 2017, video, 2:48, https://www.cnbc .com/video/2017/09/14/tom-lee-heres-why-bitcoin-will-hit-25000 .html.

37. Eli Meixler, "With over 29,000 Homicides, 2017 Was Mexico's Most Violent Year on Record," *Time*, January 21, 2018, https://time.com /5111972/mexico-murder-rate-record-2017.

38. While the EF had thought about security ahead of time, the conference moved from continent to continent; it was North America's turn. The Bitcoin Expo had been in Canada in 2014, and in 2017 the Donald Trump administration had banned citizens of seven countries from entering the United States, leaving Mexico.

39. Elaine Ramirez, "Crazy for Cryptocurrency: Why South Koreans Are Risking It All on Ethereum," *Forbes*, August 2, 2017, https:// www.forbes.com/sites/elaineramirez/2017/08/02/crazy-for -cryptocurrency-why-south-koreans-are-risking-it-all-on-ethereum /#12a3aad46341.

Chapter 12

1. This post, formerly at https://github.com/openethereum /openethereum/issues/6995, has been deleted.

2. devops199 (@devops199), "paritytech/parity#6995 is this serious issue?," Gitter, November 6, 2017, https://gitter.im/paritytech/parity?at =5a008ef75a1758ed0f9610d6.

3. Andrey Degtyaruk (@hlogeon), "Hey guys, Do you know your multisig was hacked? Why no one react on this?," Gitter, November 7, 2017, https://gitter.im/paritytech/parity?at=5a018a7bf7299e8f53808e81.

4. A. F. Dudley (@AFDudley), "The person who killed the library made an understandable mistake," Gitter, November 7, 2017, https://gitter.im/paritytech/parity?at=5a01b297e44c43700ac9eb2b.

5. devops199 (@devops199), ":(," Gitter, November 7, 2017, https://gitter.im/paritytech/parity?at=5a01b552614889d4754e037a.

6. devops199 (@devops199), "will i get arrested for this?:(," Gitter, November 7, 2017, https://gitter.im/paritytech/parity?at=5a01b9d2b20c6424299b0380.

7. Iconomi multisig dollar value: "Contract 0x376c3E5547C68bC26240 d8dcc6729fff665A4448," Etherscan, accessed April 2, 2021, https://etherscan.io/address/0x376c3E5547C68bC26240d8dcc6729fff665A 4448#analytics; Musiconomi multisig dollar value: "Contract 0xc 7CD9d874F93F2409F39A95987b3E3C738313925," Etherscan, accessed April 2, 2021, https://etherscan.io/address/0xc7cd9d874f93f 2409f39a95987b3e3c738313925#analytics.

8. List of many multisig wallets frozen by Parity bug: "Accounts Parity Bug," Etherscan, accessed April 2, 2021, https://etherscan.io/accounts /label/parity-bug/2?ps=100.

9. @latetot, "How could parity have been so reckless with the multisig wallets?...," November 8, 2017, comment on @heliumcraft, "MegaThread: Parity Multi-Signature Library Self-Destruct," Reddit, November 8, 2017, https://www.reddit.com/r/ethereum/comments /7bl6da/megathread_parity_multisignature_library/dpismzz; @latetot, "I will not support...," November 8, 2017, comment on "MegaThread."

10. "A Postmortem on the Parity Multi-Sig Library Self-Destruct," Parity, November 15, 2017, https://www.parity.io/a-postmortem-on -the-parity-multi-sig-library-self-destruct.

11. @BeezLionmane, "Even with initiatizliation...," November 8, 2017, comment on "MegaThread."

12. Vitalik Buterin (@VitalikButerin), "I am deliberately refraining from comment on wallet issues, except to express strong support for those working hard on writing simpler, safer wallet contracts or auditing and formally verifying security of existing ones," Twitter, November

8, 2017, https://twitter.com/VitalikButerin/status/928172344631
115776?=20.

13. Vitalik Buterin (@vbuterin), "Reclaiming of ether in common classes
    of stuck accounts #156," GitHub, https://github.com/ethereum/EIPs
    /issues/156.

14. @sciyoshi, "As noted elsewhere, this EIP as written won't allow
    withdrawing ether from multisig contracts created using the
    recently suicided Parity wallet library, since they *do* have code at
    their address...," GitHub, November 7, 2017, https://github.com
    /ethereum/EIPs/issues/156#issuecomment-342698012.

15. List of accounts affected by the Parity bug: "Accounts Parity Bug,"
    Etherscan.

16. "Historical Snapshot—05 November 2017," CoinMarketCap,
    November 5, 2017, https://coinmarketcap.com/historical/20171105;
    "Historical Snapshot—19 June 2016," CoinMarketCap, June 19,
    2016, https://coinmarketcap.com/historical/20160619.

17. Gavin Wood (@gavofyork), "Thanks to @VitalikButerin for the
    same—I could never have built #ethereum without you:-)," Twitter,
    August 10, 2017, https://twitter.com/gavofyork/status/895536200626
    425856?s=20.

18. Péter Szilágyi (@peter_szilagyi), "Ah yes, thank you @gavofyork
    for single handedly building #Ethereum! We—the other 30+
    programmers—really enjoyed watching you work!," Twitter, August
    10, 2017, https://twitter.com/peter_szilagyi/status/89556035495187
    2512?s=20.

19. Yung Nam Cheah, "The Best Things to Do in Mong Kok, Hong
    Kong," The Culture Trip, June 24, 2019, https://theculturetrip.com
    /asia/china/hong-kong/articles/the-top-10-things-to-do-and-see-in
    -mong-kok-hong-kong.

20. Gunjan Banerji, "CBOE Teams Up with Winklevoss Twins for
    Bitcoin Data," *Wall Street Journal*, August 2, 2017, https://www.wsj
    .com/articles/cboe-teams-up-with-winklevoss-twins-for-bitcoin-data
    -1501675200.

21. "Timeline of CME Achievements," CME Group, accessed April
    2, 2021, https://www.cmegroup.com/company/history/timeline-of
    -achievements.html; "Bitcoin Pricing Product Frequently Asked
    Questions," CME Group, May 14, 2017, https://www.cmegroup.com
    /education/bitcoin/frequently-asked-questions.html; CME Group,

"CME Group Announces Launch of Bitcoin Futures," CME Group, October 30, 2017, https://www.cmegroup.com/media-room/press-releases/2017/10/31/cme_group_announceslaunchofbitcoinfutures.html.

22. Laura Shin, "Will This Battle for the Soul of Bitcoin Destroy It?," *Forbes*, October 23, 2017, https://www.forbes.com/sites/laurashin/2017/10/23/will-this-battle-for-the-soul-of-bitcoin-destroy-it/?sh=46b3512e3d3c.

23. Brady Dale, "CBOE Releases New Details on Bitcoin Futures Contracts," *CoinDesk*, updated November 21, 2017, https://www.coindesk.com/cboe-releases-new-details-on-bitcoin-futures-contracts.

24. CME Group, "CME Group Self-Certifies Bitcoin Futures to Launch Dec. 18," CME Group, December 1, 2017, https://www.cmegroup.com/media-room/press-releases/2017/12/01/cme_group_self-certifiesbitcoinfuturestolaunchdec18.html.

25. Axiom Zen, "CryptoKitties: The World's First Ethereum Game Launches Today," *PR Newswire*, November 28, 2017, https://www.prnewswire.com/news-releases/cryptokitties-the-worlds-first-ethereum-game-launches-today-660494083.html.

26. Joon Ian Wong, "The ethereum network is getting jammed up because people are rushing to buy cartoon cats on its blockchain," *Quartz*, December 4, 2017, https://qz.com/1145833/cryptokitties-is-causing-ethereum-network-congestion; Alyssa Hertig, "Loveable Digital Kittens Are Clogging Ethereum's Blockchain," *CoinDesk*, December 4, 2017, https://www.coindesk.com/loveable-digital-kittens-clogging-ethereums-blockchain.

27. Roham Gharegozlou, "What Makes a CryptoKitty Worth $140,000?—Ep.75," interview by Laura Shin, *Unchained*, August 7, 2018, podcast, 54:39. https://unchainedpodcast.com/what-makes-a-cryptokitty-worth-140000-ep-75.

28. Seema Mody, "Winklevoss Twin Predicts Multitrillion-Dollar Value for Bitcoin," *CNBC*, December 9, 2017, https://www.cnbc.com/2017/12/09/bitcoin-cameron-winklevoss-predicts-multitrillion-dollar-value-for-cryptocurrency.html; Dan Murphy, "Analyst Who Predicted Bitcoin's Rise Now Sees It Hitting $300,000–$400,000," *CNBC*, December 17, 2017, https://www.cnbc.com/2017/12/17/bitcoin-price-ronnie-moas-sees-cryptocurrency-at-300000

-400000.html; Dan Murphy, "Trader Who Called Bitcoin Rally Says Cryptocurrency Will Surge Above $100,000 in 2018," *CNBC*, December 11, 2017, https://www.cnbc.com/2017/12/11/bitcoin-could -exceed-100000-dollars-by-2018-says-trader.html.

29. Michelle Castillo, "This High School Dropout Who Invested in Bitcoin at $12 Is Now a Millionaire at 18," *CNBC*, June 20, 2017, https://www.cnbc.com/2017/06/20/bitcoin-millionaire-erik-finman -says-going-to-college-isnt-worth-it.html; Laura Shin, "Return of the Day Traders," *Forbes*, July 10, 2017, https://www.forbes.com /sites/laurashin/2017/07/10/return-of-the-day-traders; Defend Assange Campaign (@DefendAssange), "My deepest thanks to the US government, Senator McCain and Senator Lieberman for pushing Visa, MasterCard, Payal, AmEx, Mooneybookers, et al, into erecting an illegal banking blockade against @WikiLeaks starting in 2010. It caused us to invest in Bitcoin—with > 50000% return," Twitter, October 14, 2017, https://twitter.com/DefendAssange/status /919247873648283653?s=20.

30. Chris O'Brien, "Moonlambos Sells Lamborghinis for Bitcoin to Help Gilded Cryptocurrency Generation Spend Its Windfall," *VentureBeat*, December 15, 2017, https://venturebeat.com/2017/12 /15/moonlambos-sells-lamborghinis-for-bitcoin-to-help-the-gilded -cryptocurrency-generation-spend-its-windfall.

31. John Saddington, "INITIAL LAMBO OFFERING— MoonLambos.io—Get YOUR Bitcoin Lambo Now!," Medium, January 1, 2018, https://medium.com/@saddington/initial -lambo-offering-moonlambos-io-get-your-bitcoin-lambo-now -cf769d07612a.

32. @PineappleFund, "I'm donating 5057 BTC to charitable causes! Introducing The Pineapple Fund," Reddit, December 13, 2017, https://www.reddit.com/r/Bitcoin/comments/7jj0oa/im_donating _5057_btc_to_charitable_causes.

33. "40 Under 40: 2016," Fortune, accessed April 2, 2021, https://fortune .com/40-under-40/2016.

34. Vitalik Buterin, "Ethereum Foundation Internal Update," *Ethereum Foundation Blog*, January 7, 2016, https://blog.ethereum.org /2016/01/07/2394.

35. "About the Ethereum Foundation," Ethereum.org/foundation via Wayback Machine, September 6, 2015, https://web.archive.org

/web/20150906200827/https://www.ethereum.org/foundation;
"About the Ethereum Foundation," Ethereum.org/foundation via
Wayback Machine, March 4, 2016, https://web.archive.org/web
/20160304212822/https://www.ethereum.org/foundation.

36. June (@JUN_SYNQA), "Omise is now official Special advisor
    (Thomas) for Ethereum. #omise #blockchain #ethereum https://
    ethereum.org/foundation," Twitter, March 8, 2016, https://twitter
    .com/jun_omise/status/707168442449661952.

37. "Thomas Greco—About ECF," video uploaded to YouTube by
    LinkTime, May 17, 2018, https://www.youtube.com/watch?v=R6bl9
    vClE0M&t=216s.

38. "Clarifying the Role of the Ethereum Foundation with Ethereum's
    Aya Miyaguchi | EDCON Toronto 2018," video uploaded to
    YouTube by LinkTime, June 19, 2018, 0:13, https://www.youtube
    .com/watch?v=r3GhsbhsdSg.

39. Amir Taaki (@Narodism), "Bitcoin is turning into a failed project.
    The seeds of its destruction among the debris of a community blinded
    by numerical price increases, and imminent divine reclamation. One
    day you will all understand my words but it will be too late, the ship
    would have sailed," Twitter, December 26, 2017, https://twitter.com
    /Narodism/status/945693434500829184?s=20.

40. Vitalik Buterin (@VitalikButerin), "*All* crypto communities,
    ethereum included, should heed these words of warning. Need to
    differentiate between getting hundreds of billions of dollars of digital
    paper wealth sloshing around and actually achieving something
    meaningful for society," Twitter, December 27, 2017, https://twitter
    .com/VitalikButerin/status/945987507941978112?s=20.

41. Vitalik Buterin (@VitalikButerin), "If all that we accomplish is lambo
    memes and immature puns about 'sharting,' then I WILL leave...,"
    Twitter, December 27, 2017, https://twitter.com/VitalikButerin
    /status/945988644661207040?s=20.

42. Zheping Huang, "The world now has a cryptocurrency pop group,"
    Quartz, January 10, 2018, https://qz.com/1177249/japans-kasotsuka
    -shojo-the-worlds-first-cryptopop-group-sings-about-bitcoin-and
    -cryptofraud.

43. Nellie Bowles, "Everyone Is Getting Hilariously Rich and You're
    Not," *New York Times*, January 13, 2018, https://www.nytimes.com
    /2018/01/13/style/bitcoin-millionaires.html.

44. @CryptoOnly, "Money Skeleton," Reddit, December 25, 2017, https://www.reddit.com/r/ethtrader/comments/7m3uvm/money _skeleton.

45. "Past Weather in San Francisco, California, USA—January 2018," TimeandDate.com, https://www.timeanddate.com/weather/usa/san -francisco/historic?month=1&year=2018.

Epilogue

1. Anna Irrera, "U.S. SEC Official Says Ether Not a Security, Price Surges," *Reuters*, June 15, 2018, https://www.reuters.com/article /us-cryptocurrencies-ether/u-s-sec-official-says-ether-not-a-security -price-surges-idUSKBN1JA30Q.

2. Taylor Monahan, "A New Beginning: MyCrypto.com," Medium, February 8, 2018, https://medium.com/mycrypto/mycrypto-launch -6a066bf41093.

3. Robert Hackett, "This Big Cryptocurrency Acquisition Could Create a Wall Street–Style Financial Giant," *Fortune*, February 26, 2018, https://fortune.com/2018/02/26/circle-cryptocurrency-trade -bitcoin.

4. Charles Hoskinson, "Blockchain Podcast #36—Charles Hoskinson, Founder of Cardano," interview by Finance Magnates, February 15, 2018, audio, 6:55, 7:32 https://soundcloud.com/finance-magnates /blockchain-podcast-36-charles-hoskinson-founder-of-cardano/s-0vn8v.

5. Charles Hoskinson (@IOHK_Charles), "I graduated but did not complete a PhD. I will return and finish it after I retire . . . ," Twitter, September 9, 2018, https://twitter.com/IOHK_Charles/status /1038919675231358976?s=20.

6. Kevin Dugan, "Inside the Crypto Bro Fest That Took Over New York City," *New York Post*, May 17, 2018, https://nypost.com/2018 /05/17/inside-the-extravagant-money-and-parties-that-define -cryptocurrency-craze.

7. Natalie Wong and Gerrit De Vynck, "Crypto Pioneer Buys Penthouse in Former Toronto Trump Tower," *Bloomberg*, June 20, 2018, https://www.bloomberg.com/news/articles/2018-06-20/crypto -pioneer-buys-canada-s-biggest-condo-in-former-trump-tower.

8. Olga Kharif, "Ethereum Co-Founder Says Safety Concern Has Him Quitting Crypto," *Bloomberg*, July 16, 2021, https://www.bloomberg

.com/news/articles/2021-07-16/ethereum-co-founder-says-safety
-concern-has-him-quitting-crypto?sref=m9L277rN.

9. Jeff Kauflin, "Cryptopia In Crisis: Joe Lubin's Ethereum Experiment
Is a Mess. How Long Will He Prop It Up?" *Forbes*, December 5,
2018, https://www.forbes.com/sites/jeffkauflin/2018/12/05/cryptopia
-in-crisis-billionaire-joe-lubins-ethereum-experiment-is-a-mess-how
-long-will-he-prop-it-up/?sh=1bc648dd2f0a.

10. Nikhilesh De, "Ethereum Studio ConsenSys Just Bought an
Asteroid Mining Company," *CoinDesk*, November 1, 2018, https://
www.coindesk.com/blockchain-studio-consensys-acquires-asteroid
-mining-space-startup.

11. David Canellis, "What we know about the ConsenSys layoffs,
as told by a 'fired' employee," *The Next Web*, December 7, 2018,
https://thenextweb.com/hardfork/2018/12/07/consensys-blockchain
-layoffs.

12. Bijan Stephen, "ConsenSys Plans to Spin Out Most of Its Startups,
and It's Going to Mean Layoffs," *The Verge*, December 20, 2018,
https://www.theverge.com/2018/12/20/18150036/consensys-layoffs
-employees-pending-startup-ethereum.

13. Jon Victor, "ConsenSys Seeks $200 Million from Investors After
Bumpy Year," *The Information*, April 15, 2019, https://www
.theinformation.com/articles/consensys-seeks-200-million-from
-investors-after-bumpy-year.

14. "After Buying Planetary Resources, ConsenSys Sets Its Space
Ideas Free—but Will Sell Off the Hardware," *Geekwire*, May 1,
2020, https://www.geekwire.com/2020/buying-planetary-resources
-consensys-gives-away-science-asteroids-will-sell-rest.

15. Ian Allison, "ConsenSys Acquires JPMorgan's Quorum Blockchain,"
CoinDesk, August 25, 2020, https://www.coindesk.com/consensys
-acquires-jp-morgan-quorum-blockchain.

16. "Blockchain Firm ConsenSys Raises $65 Million from J.P. Morgan,
Others," Reuters, April 13, 2021, https://www.reuters.com/technology
/blockchain-firm-consensys-raises-65-million-jp-morgan-others-2021
-04-13.

17. Ian Allison, "ConsenSys Confidential: Ethereum Builder Is Back
in Growth Mode, Document Reveals," *CoinDesk*, March 15,
2021, https://www.coindesk.com/consensys-confidential-ethereum
-builder-is-back-in-growth-mode-document-reveals.

18. "Etherchain coin vote on EIP 999," etherchain.org via Wayback Machine, April 25, 2018, https://web.archive.org/web/20180425010204/https://www.etherchain.org/coinvote/poll/35.

19. Transaction showing devops199's address had received 0.225 ETH from ShapeShift at 18:28 UTC on November 1, 2017: "Transaction Details," Etherscan, November 1, 2017, https://etherscan.io/tx/0x63e2f15fabb98351038961067c37b6015043b53427e6f1ffe8ae2414bd867611; converting 0.01018338 BTC to 0.22458989 ETC on ShapeShift: originally via ShapeShift API, accessed April 3, 2021, https://shapeshift.io/txstat/37b8Emgp2c2KF8GcqUUsSQdq92y5xEnQXP, now at https://laurashin.com/cryptopians/Epilogue/19-37b8E.

20. Transaction converting Bitcoin at 18:23 UTC on November 1, 2017: "Summary," Blockchain.com, November 1, 2017, https://www.blockchain.com/btc/tx/7ab55f84f3138aac405634e006ed766c729c16ff60f330e1e1fb3bb6b88409e8; transaction converting 0.2450965 ETH into 0.01041138 BTC on ShapeShift: originally via ShapeShift API, accessed April 3, 2021, https://shapeshift.io/txstat/0x7214fc28ff65bf775d4b333d7ae7df40734c4084, now at https://laurashin.com/cryptopians/Epilogue/20-0x721.

21. Account that provided original funding for the ETH that, after some conversions, was used to freeze the Parity wallets had done 1,200 transactions in six days: "Address 0x18788EdabBABc203BC7C157518dc4B2d4529F884," Etherscan, accessed April 3, 2021, https://etherscan.io/address/0x18788EdabBABc203BC7C157518dc4B2d4529F884.

22. "SEC v. PlexCorps, Dominic LaCroix, and Sabrina Paradis-Royer Case No, 17-cv-7007 (CBA) (RML) (E.D.N.Y.)," SEC, December 1, 2017, https://www.sec.gov/divisions/enforce/claims/plexcorps.htm; Jordan Pearson, "PlexCoin Scam Founder Sentenced to Jail and Fined $10K," Vice, December 8, 2017, https://www.vice.com/en/article/qvzkx7/plexcoin-scam-founder-sentenced-to-jail-and-fined-10k.

23. Transaction showing conversion of 0.09 ETH into 0.256 XMR on ShapeShift: "Tx Hash: d78721d954fd66c1427a18711b467501db44a86db15bb4f09ea9033b4c564de6," xmrchain.net, January 16, 2018, https://xmrchain.net/tx/d78721d954fd66c1427a18711b467501db44a86db15bb4f09ea9033b4c564de6.

24. Transaction showing conversion of XMR via ShapeShift to 0.07329 ETH on January 15, 2018 at 7:41 UTC: "Transaction Details,"

Etherscan, January 16, 2018, accessed April 3, 2021, https://etherscan
.io/tx/0x683c62528ec178049f29971427c6bbead552dcc1687c20a6
19069be5a9aa0f90; transaction showing conversion of 0.23 XMR
to 0.07329 ETH on ShapeShift: originally via ShapeShift API,
accessed April 3, 2021, https://shapeshift.io/txstat/04d2ab51122411
24b917d131c9e3858b73c1ff15c04f7330dc55d26491beadee, now at
https://laurashin.com/cryptopians/Epilogue/24-04d2a.

25. Ryan Mac, "A Cryptocurrency Pioneer Wrote About Sex with a
Preteen Girl on His Blog. He Says It Was Fiction," *BuzzFeed News*,
September 19, 2018, https://www.buzzfeednews.com/article/ryanmac
/ethereum-cofounder-sex-underage-girl-fiction.

26. Ming Chan, "To Infinity and Beyond!," *Ethereum Foundation Blog*,
January 31, 2018, https://blog.ethereum.org/2018/01/31/to-infinity
-and-beyond. The other four *Ethereum Foundation Blog* posts were
"Devcon3 videos available now!," November 26, 2017, https://blog
.ethereum.org/2017/11/26/devcon3-vids-available-now; "Devcon3!!!,"
November 16, 2017, https://blog.ethereum.org/2017/11/16/devcon3;
"The Devcon2 site is now live!," July 8, 2016, https://blog.ethereum
.org/2016/07/08/devcon2-site-now-live; "Ethereum Foundation and
Wanxiang Blockchain Labs announce a blockbuster event combining
Devcon2 and the 2nd Global Blockchain Summit in Shanghai,
September 19–24, 2016," April 5, 2016, https://blog.ethereum
.org/2016/04/05/devcon2-and-blockchain-summit-shanghai
-september2016.

27. Ethereum Team, "Farewell and Welcome," *Ethereum Foundation Blog*,
January 31, 2018, https://blog.ethereum.org/2018/01/31/farewell-and
-welcome.

28. "Ethereum Development Halts After Vitalik Discovers Sex," *Coin
Jazeera*, accessed April 3, 2021, https://coinjazeera.news/ethereum
-development-halts-after-vitalik-discovers-sex.

29. "Two Arrested for Extortion of Startup Cryptocurrency Company,"
Department of Justice, US Attorney's Office, Eastern District of New
York, September 18, 2019, https://www.justice.gov/usao-edny/pr/two
-arrested-extortion-startup-cryptocurrency-company.

30. Dominic Kennedy and Oliver Wright, "Christopher Harborne: Brexit
Party's Bankroller Has a Thai Doppelganger," *The Times*, November
27, 2019, https://www.thetimes.co.uk/article/christopher-harborne
-brexit-partys-bankroller-has-a-thai-doppelgaenger-jnd0v9qdp.

31. "Brexit's top donor outed as Bitfinex, Tether parent shareholder," *Protos*, April 23, 2021, https://protos.com/bitfinex-tether-digfinex -shareholder-harborne-brexit-bankroller/.

32. 0xf0e42 address (presumed DAO attacker) attempts to spam Ethereum or commit a denial-of-service attack: "Transactions for 0xf0e42abda410cefb5b4dc4de92a3de5b309e02f2," Etherscan, April 17, 2016, https://etherscan.io/txs?a=0xf0e42abda410cefb5 b4dc4de92a3de5b309e02f2&ps=100&p=152.

33. 0xf0e42 address (presumed DAO attacker) sends zero ETH to random Ethereum addresses as if attempting to increase blockchain bloat: "Transactions for 0xf0e42abda410cefb5b4dc4de92a3de5b309e02f2," Etherscan, April 30, 2016, https://etherscan.io/txs?a=0xf0e42abda 410cefb5b4dc4de92a3de5b309e02f2&ps=100&p=60.

34. First transactions of 0xf0e42 address (presumed DAO attacker) enter the DAO one Wei at a time: "Transactions for 0xf0e42abda410cef b5b4dc4de92a3de5b309e02f2," Etherscan, April 30, 2016, https:// etherscan.io/txs?a=0xf0e42abda410cefb5b4dc4de92a3de5b309e 02f2&p=141; last transactions of the presumed DAO attacker entering the DAO one Wei at a time: "Transactions for 0xf0e42abda410cefb5b4 dc4de92a3de5b309e02f2," Etherscan, April 30, 2016, https://etherscan .io/txs?a=0xf0e42abda410cefb5b4dc4de92a3de5b309e02f2&p=121; one transaction for 0.000111111111111 ETH: "Transaction Details," Etherscan, April 30, 2016, https://etherscan.io/tx/0x2a56423a22 c1a11d5552fa29d6909ca6534ab9094e144dc7bd95b9079cbf84ae.

35. 0xf0e42 address (presumed DAO attacker) sends a stream of one-Wei transactions, which can't be deleted as dust: "Transactions for 0xf0e42abda410cefb5b4dc4de92a3de5b309e02f2," Etherscan, May 2, 2016, https://etherscan.io/txs?a=0xf0e42abda410cefb5b4 dc4de92a3de5b309e02f2&ps=100&p=1.

36. Presumed DAO attacker moving almost 364,241 ten times from Dark DAO to child DAO: "Address Info," Ethereum Classic Explorer, July 23, 2016, https://etc.tokenview.com/en/address /0x10abb5efecdc09581f8b7cb95791fe2936790b4e.

37. Presumed DAO attacker moves more than 3.6 million ETC from the Dark DAO from a child DAO to 0xc362ef: "Transaction Info," Ethereum Classic Explorer, September 5, 2016, https://etc.tokenview .com/en/tx/0xa4031e961908b82e19911e780ec9836635dc92ce7444 a97f6af8316d55850650.

38. Presumed DAO attacker moves nearly all the money from HackerOne to HackerTwo: "Transaction Info," Ethereum Classic Explorer, September 5, 2016, https://etc.tokenview.com/en/tx /0x7089794758f739f54fcd17d86f947c1f94dc8ef2d6d9fc16451b3e5e 7eb74cca; presumed DAO attacker moves the last roughly twenty-one ETC from HackerOne to HackerTwo: "Transaction Info," Ethereum Classic Explorer, September 5, 2016, https://etc.tokenview.com/en /tx/0x3f23a60f8055889d37db263f30985bc1bb675331261689c0179 c06d3b8b0d302.

39. Presumed DAO attacker donates to the Ethereum Classic developers' fund: "Transaction Info," Ethereum Classic Explorer, September 5, 2016, https://etc.tokenview.com/en/tx/0x38d8dda6ed6544476 2143215ff1c2742b8c16f312766415755661389b1a6198b?_ga=2.252282177 .99485005.1629491395-1255823513.1608842673.

40. First transactions of BTC into 1M2aaN address: "Transaction Info," Ethereum Classic Explorer, October 25, 2016, https://etc.tokenview .com/en/tx/0x6946cf3cfe9117cc416e6141bbb5061ea06f838e7be753 effcf919430078606e, originally via ShapeShift API, https://shapeshift .io/txstat/0x7bde7ea1eff53b95262c7597050ae9e0bc6315da, now at https://laurashin.com/cryptopians/Epilogue/40-0x7bd, on Bitcoin blockchain, see "Address," Blockchain.com, October 25, 2016, https://www.blockchain.com/btc/address/1M2aaNN3GTw6dy13u ScodHaQ8Egr6xr6Ew?page=12.

41. Presumed DAO attacker resumes another string of cash-outs on October 25–26, 2016: "Address Info," Ethereum Classic Explorer, https://etc.tokenview.com/en/address/0x440afde443c7bcfdb7414 aa9028e20cda74fc5d2, originally via ShapeShift API, https://shapeshift .io/txstat/0x440afde443c7bcfdb7414aa9028e20cda74fc5d2, now at https://laurashin.com/cryptopians/Epilogue/41-0x440, on Bitcoin blockchain, see "Summary," Blockchain.com, October 25, 2016, https://www.blockchain.com/btc/tx/8246fcc1ec4bad0826edd3b1419030 c402b2dd458c490a5eb18828a829da238a.

42. Presumed DAO attacker finishes cash-outs on October 26, 2016: "Transaction Info," Ethereum Classic Explorer, October 26, 2016, https://etc.tokenview.com/en/tx/0xfc079d1d9c991f5e78fddf57e5601b 623bd1c71fa5337bfc96aebc79823110cb, originally via ShapeShift API, https://shapeshift.io/txstat/0x01aedbcbe712ad602a53f2880 c5aeb0b436ae762, now at https://laurashin.com/cryptopians/Epilogue

/42-0x01a, on Bitcoin blockchain, see "Summary," Blockchain.com, October 26, 2016, https://www.blockchain.com/btc/tx/b2a1853 ff1963dd29100a3901064b1eaaf6c20000bf4c85e7f6491f780ad3ff3.

43. Dexaran sends the presumed DAO attacker 1.05 ETC: "Transaction Info," Ethereum Classic Explorer, October 28, 2016, https://etc.tokenview .com/en/address/0xc9bea9379a8fade01240ee583535fac713b71014.

44. Christian Seberino, PhD, "The Dexaran Interview," Medium, December 20, 2017, https://medium.com/@cseberino/conversation -with-the-dao-attacker-dexaran-speaks-11d747a43083.

45. Presumed DAO attacker's attempted cash-out of 2,634.93 ETC blocked by ShapeShift: originally on ShapeShift API, November 14, 2016, https://shapeshift.io/txstat/0x55ba70d07ccd4c56247 ededa3c53531ad797146d, now at https://laurashin.com/cryptopians /Epilogue/45-0x55b.

46. Presumed DAO attacker's attempted cash-out of 100.23 ETC blocked by ShapeShift: originally on ShapeShift API, November 16, 2016, https:// shapeshift.io/txstat/0xaa8b2834b45493f45702a56f33ce750ce41bd867, now at https://laurashin.com/cryptopians/Epilogue/46-0xaa8.

47. First presumed DAO attacker cash-out transaction on December 2, 2016: "Transaction Info," Ethereum Classic Explorer, December 2, 2016, https://etc.tokenview.com/en/tx/0xbcc26b8d6290c6657ef6bc 86361f5cfba9e46603b8fb5c9caf3ab0a9b3ee1187, originally via ShapeShift API, December 2, 2016, https://shapeshift.io/txstat/0xd9e7 681e234136c6871a159c6e0ef0fc6c3240be, now at https://laurashin .com/cryptopians/Epilogue/47a-0xd9e, on Bitcoin blockchain, Blockchain.com, December 2, 2016, https://www.blockchain.com /btc/tx/f66a327f25fe99b39fd977c58f548ce440293ece1d294be1c140 a01e9a5c6a6e; first in a series of the presumed DAO attacker's successful conversions of ETC to BTC on December 5, 2016, on ShapeShift: "Transaction Info," Ethereum Classic Explorer, December 5, 2016, https://etc.tokenview.com/en/tx/0x91bea0f7 f3196ef1cfd20f1f2937152ce166762de24cc8de7f7451b64994abd1, originally via ShapeShift API, https://shapeshift.io/txstat /0xdabd6c8c83e66e67eecec11292af849f5cd74f29, now at https:// laurashin.com/cryptopians/Epilogue/47b-0xdab, on Bitcoin blockchain, see https://www.blockchain.com/btc/tx/7b8a83690 b1f3d104255c801a3da61467fcc10417d51930cbf09d17f285c8016; first in a series of cash-outs from ETC to BTC on December 6:

"Transaction info," Ethereum Classic Explorer, December 6, 2016, https://etc.tokenview.com/en/tx/0xaa984428299993512555000d0617 0863fc09f1a801e8502688eba2cb5fa158e3, originally via ShapeShift API, https://shapeshift.io/txstat/0x6a9f6edf4984ca7da52bc2c9b763 c2f972af4f5b, now at https://laurashin.com/cryptopians/Epilogue /47c-0x6a9, on Bitcoin blockchain, see "Summary," Blockchain.com, https://www.blockchain.com/btc/tx/3669c98967bebe9e2470fffba 5a372a63210e1b34139d388148d171066fdd349; first in a series of thirteen successful cash-outs from ETC to BTC: Ethereum Classic Explorer, December 7, 2016, https://etc.tokenview.com/en/tx/0x7b31bae94a9 e594e5d23f8c72d5804afd859f2174de745f21ded6ffe3e16b8d8, originally via ShapeShift API, https://shapeshift.io/txstat/0x32395d7c89af0be 5a32118340492e9e714fbd9bd, now at https://laurashin.com/cryptopians /Epilogue/47d-0x323, on Bitcoin blockchain, see "Summary," Blockchain.com, https://www.blockchain.com/btc/tx/2a215bbbff 9e534ad0ac60c1051811afdacb80e8d5ef65fe24ac40e1302b46aa.

48. First in series of five attempted cash-outs from ETC to BTC that were all blocked by ShapeShift: originally on ShapeShift API, December 9, 2016, https://shapeshift.io/txstat/0x75ece5ff90 e323459b5cece076e058cdeaf3ee58, now at https://laurashin.com /cryptopians/Epilogue/48a-0x75e; last in a series of five attempted cash-outs from ETC to BTC that were all blocked by ShapeShift: originally on ShapeShift API, December 9, 2016, https://shapeshift .io/txstat/0xe49d037273e03ed8caaf509b70ca7020add550ca, now at https://laurashin.com/cryptopians/Epilogue/48b-0xe49; final attempted cash-out from ETC to BTC on ShapeShift is blocked: originally on ShapeShift API, December 11, 2016, https://shapeshift .io/txstat/0x204719cb08dceca8fd575c576083948d58450d11, now at https://laurashin.com/cryptopians/Epilogue/48c-0x204.

49. Amount remaining in the Dark DAO on Ethereum Classic: "Address Info," Ethereum Classic Explorer, https://etc.tokenview.com/en /address/0x5e8f0e63e7614c47079a41ad4c37be7def06df5a.

50. Amount remaining in one of the presumed DAO attacker's cash-out addresses: "Address Info," Ethereum Classic Explorer, https://etc .tokenview.com/en/address/0x1b63be2d056b4a3befcda120b16ebde0 c3315118.

51. Presumed DAO attacker sends fifty BTC to Wasabi: "Summary," Blockchain.com, September 7, 2019, https://www.blockchain.com

/btc/tx/aa8d7407f88dca9b1779880c3d2e3245e02217f7366972
d617f812c8dd73a96a.

52. "Manhattan U.S. Attorney Announces Arrest of United States Citizen for Assisting North Korea in Evading Sanctions," Department of Justice, US Attorney's Office, Southern District of New York, November 29, 2019, https://www.justice.gov/usao-sdny /pr/manhattan-us-attorney-announces-arrest-united-states-citizen -assisting-north-korea.

53. Kieran Smith, "Ethereum Developer Arrested over North Korea Controversy," Brave New Coin, December 3, 2019, https:// bravenewcoin.com/insights/ethereum-developer-arrested-over-north -korea-controversy; Vitalik Buterin (@VitalikButerin), "Enjoy!," Twitter, January 18, 2019, https://twitter.com/VitalikButerin/status /1086190896515694592?s=20.

54. Erik Schatzker, "Paul Tudor Jones Buys Bitcoin as a Hedge Against Inflation," Bloomberg, May 7, 2020, https://www.bloomberg.com /news/articles/2020-05-07/paul-tudor-jones-buys-bitcoin-says-he -s-reminded-of-gold-in-70s; Billy Bambrough, "A Legendary Hedge Fund Billionaire Just Flipped to Bitcoin—Calling It 'Better' Than Gold," Forbes, November 12, 2020, https://www.forbes.com/sites /billybambrough/2020/11/12/a-legendary-hedge-fund-billionaire -just-flipped-to-bitcoin-calling-it-better-than-gold; Ray Dalio, "What I Think of Bitcoin," Bridgewater, January 28, 2021, https://www .bridgewater.com/research-and-insights/our-thoughts-on-bitcoin.

55. Steve Kovach, "Tesla Buys $1.5 Billion in Bitcoin, Plans to Accept It as Payment," CNBC, February 8, 2021, https://www.cnbc.com /2021/02/08/tesla-buys-1point5-billion-in-bitcoin.html; Paul Vigna, "MassMutual Joins the Bitcoin Club with $100 Million Purchase," Wall Street Journal, December 10, 2020, https://www.wsj.com/articles /massmutual-joins-the-bitcoin-club-with-100-million-purchase -11607626800; Anna Irrera, "Exclusive: PayPal Launches Crypto Checkout Service," Reuters, March 30, 2021, https://www.reuters .com/article/us-crypto-currency-paypal-exclusive/exclusive-paypal -launches-crypto-checkout-service-idUSKBN2BM10N.

56. "Federally Chartered Banks and Thrifts May Provide Custody Services for Crypto Assets," Office of the Comptroller of the Currency, July 22, 2020, https://www.occ.gov/news-issuances/news -releases/2020/nr-occ-2020-98.html.

57. Brady Dale, "With COMP Below $100, a Look Back at the 'DeFi
Summer' It Sparked," *CoinDesk*, October 20, 2020, https://www
.coindesk.com/comp-below-100-defi-summer-over; Laura Shin,
"DeFi Security: With So Many Hacks, Will It Ever Be Safe?,"
Unchained, May 5, 2020, https://unchainedpodcast.com/defi-security
-with-so-many-hacks-will-it-ever-be-safe.

58. William Foxley, "Ethereum 2.0 Beacon Chain Goes Live as 'World
Computer' Begins Long-Awaited Overhaul," *CoinDesk*, December 7,
2020, https://www.coindesk.com/ethereum-2-0-beacon-chain-goes
-live-as-world-computer-begins-long-awaited-overhaul.

59. "NFT Collectible Rankings by Sales Volume (All-time),"
CryptoSlam, accessed April 3, 2021, https://cryptoslam.io.

60. Samantha Hissong, "Kings of Leon Will Be the First Band to
Release an Album as an NFT," *Rolling Stone*, March 3, 2021,
https://www.rollingstone.com/pro/news/kings-of-leon-when-you
-see-yourself-album-nft-crypto-1135192; Sam Moore, "Kings of
Leon Have Generated $2million from NFT Sales of Their New
Album," *NME*, March 12, 2021, https://www.nme.com/news/music
/kings-of-leon-have-generated-2million-from-nft-sales-of-their-new
-album-2899349; Grace Kay, "Grimes Made $5.8 Million in Under
20 Minutes Selling Crypto-based Artwork," *Business Insider*, March
1, 2021, https://www.businessinsider.com/grimes-nft-art-warnymph
-sells-for-millions-20-minutes-2021-3.

61. EtherRock Price (@etherrockprice), "EtherRock 27 purchased for
E888 Ether ($2,872,733.28) 5 hrs 56 mins ago (Aug-28-2021
09:37:29 AM +UTC) Txn: etherscan.io/tx/0x12c646e37...#EtherRock
#EtherRocks," Twitter, August 28, 2021, https://twitter.com/
etherrockprice/status/1431641800431714313.

62. OpenSea monthly volume, DuneAnalytics, accessed August 30, 2021,
https://dune.xyz/queries/3469/6913.

63. Stephani Crets, "Etsy continues to grow sales and find new buyers,"
Digital Commerce 360, August 6, 2021, https://www.digitalcommerce360
.com/2021/08/06/etsy-continues-to-grow-sales-and-find-new-buyers/.

64. Nathaniel Whittemore, "Are NFTs Just This Cycle's ICOs?,"
CoinDesk, March 2, 2021, https://www.coindesk.com/podcasts
/coindesk-podcast-network/nfts-this-cycles-icos.

Index

467

Laura Shin is a writer, crypto journalist, and podcaster. A former senior editor at *Forbes*, she left the magazine in 2018 to commit to her podcast and video show, *Unchained*, which has had fifteen million downloads and views. Her writing can also be found in her Facebook Bulletin newsletter and on Medium. Shin has spoken about and led discussions on cryptocurrency at places such as TEDx San Francisco, the International Monetary Fund, Singularity University, and the Oslo Freedom Forum. She lives in New York City.

PublicAffairs is a publishing house founded in 1997. It is a tribute to the standards, values, and flair of three persons who have served as mentors to countless reporters, writers, editors, and book people of all kinds, including me.

I. F. STONE, proprietor of *I. F. Stone's Weekly*, combined a commitment to the First Amendment with entrepreneurial zeal and reporting skill and became one of the great independent journalists in American history. At the age of eighty, Izzy published *The Trial of Socrates*, which was a national bestseller. He wrote the book after he taught himself ancient Greek.

BENJAMIN C. BRADLEE was for nearly thirty years the charismatic editorial leader of *The Washington Post*. It was Ben who gave the *Post* the range and courage to pursue such historic issues as Watergate. He supported his reporters with a tenacity that made them fearless and it is no accident that so many became authors of influential, best-selling books.

ROBERT L. BERNSTEIN, the chief executive of Random House for more than a quarter century, guided one of the nation's premier publishing houses. Bob was personally responsible for many books of political dissent and argument that challenged tyranny around the globe. He is also the founder and longtime chair of Human Rights Watch, one of the most respected human rights organizations in the world.

•   •   •

For fifty years, the banner of Public Affairs Press was carried by its owner Morris B. Schnapper, who published Gandhi, Nasser, Toynbee, Truman, and about 1,500 other authors. In 1983, Schnapper was described by *The Washington Post* as "a redoubtable gadfly." His legacy will endure in the books to come.

Peter Osnos, *Founder*